ETHICS

ESSENTIAL WORKS OF
FOUCAULT
1954–1984

PAUL RABINOW
SERIES EDITOR

Ethics
Edited by Paul Rabinow

Aesthetics, Method, and Epistemology
Edited by James D. Faubion

Power
Edited by James D. Faubion

MICHEL FOUCAULT

ETHICS

SUBJECTIVITY AND TRUTH

Edited by
PAUL RABINOW

Translated by
ROBERT HURLEY AND OTHERS

ESSENTIAL WORKS OF
FOUCAULT
1954–1984

THE NEW PRESS
NEW YORK

English translations of "Friendship as a Way of Life" and "The Ethic of
the Concern for the Self as a Practice of Freedom" reprinted from
Foucault Live: Interviews 1961-1984, Lotringer, ed. (New York:
Autonomedia, 1989), by permission. English translations of "Sexual
Choice, Sexual Act" and "The Masked Philosopher" reprinted from
Michel Foucault: Politics, Philosophy, Culture, Lawrence D. Katzman,
ed. (1988), by permission of the publisher, Routledge: New York
and London. "Sex, Power and the Politics of Identity" reprinted from
The Advocate no. 400, August 7, 1984, by permission. "Sexuality
and Solitude" reprinted from the *London Review of Books*,
vol. III, no. 9, May 21–June 5, 1981. English translation of "The Battle
for Chastity" reprinted from *Western Sexuality*, Ariès, Bejin, eds.,
with permission from the publisher, Blackwell Publishers.

Library of Congress Cataloging-in-Publication Data

Foucault, Michel.
  [Selections. English. 1997]
  Ethics : subjectivity and truth / by Michel Foucault; edited by Paul
Rabinow; translated by Robert Hurley and others.
    p. cm.—(The essential works of Michel Foucault, 1954–1984 ; v. 1)
  Includes bibliographical references and index.
  ISBN 1-56584-434-3
  1. Ethics. I. Rainbow, Paul. II. Title. III. Series: Foucault, Michel.
Dit et écrits. English. Selections ; v. 1.
B2430.F722E5 1997
194—dc20   96-31819
                                        CIP

Selections from *Dits and Ecrits, 1954–1988*,
ed. Daniel Defert and François Ewald, with the assistance of
Jacques Lagrange, published by Editions Gallimard, Paris
Published in the United States by The New Press, New York
Distributed by Perseus Distribution

The New Press was established in 1990 as a not-for-profit alternative
to the large, commercial publishing houses currently dominating the
book publishing industry. The New Press operates in the public interest
rather than for private gain, and is committed to publishing, in innovative ways, works of educational, cultural, and community value that
might not normally be commercially viable.

The New Press is grateful for support for this publication from the
French Ministry of Culture.

Book design by Paul Carlos

Printed in the United States of America

19 18 17 16 15 14 13 12 11

CONTENTS

Michel Foucault provides a splendid definition of work: "That which is susceptible of introducing a significant difference in the field of knowledge, at the cost of a certain difficulty for the author and the reader, with, however, the eventual recompense of a certain pleasure, that is to say of access to another figure of truth."[1] Diverse factors shape the emergence, articulation, and circulation of a work and its effects. Foucault gave us intellectual tools to understand these phenomena. In Michel Foucault's *Essential Works*, we use these very tools to understand his own work. Though he intended his books to be the core of his intellectual production, he is also well known for having made strategic use of a number of genres—the book and the article to be sure, but also the lecture and the interview. Indeed, few modern thinkers have used such a wide array of forms in so skillful a fashion, making them an integral component in the development and presentation of their work. In this light, our aim in this series is to assemble a compelling and representative collection of Foucault's written and spoken words outside those included in his books.

Foucault died on June 25, 1984, at age fifty-seven, of AIDS, just days after receiving the first reviews of the second and third volumes of *The History of Sexuality*, in the hospital. A year previous to his death, when he was showing no signs of illness, he had written a letter indicating that he wanted no posthumous publications; through the course of complex negotiations between those legally responsible to him, intellectually engaged with him, and emotionally close to him, it was decided that this letter constituted his will. He left behind, as far as we know, no cache of unpublished texts; we must conclude, then, that his papers were "in order." Ten years later, Editions Gallimard published *Dits et Écrits*, well over three thousand pages of texts, organized chronologically. The editors, Daniel Defert and François Ewald, sought to collect all Foucault's published texts (prefaces, introductions, presentations, interviews, articles, interventions, lectures, and so on) not included in his books. We have made a selection, eliminating overlapping or repetition of different versions of similar materials. Likewise, a number of the lectures and courses will in time be published separately in English.

What we have included in this and the following two volumes are the writings that seemed to us central to the evolution of Foucault's thought. We have organized them thematically. Selecting from this corpus was a formidable responsibility that proved to be a challenge and a pleasure. Many of these texts were previously unavailable in English. In broad lines, the organization of the series follows one proposed by Foucault himself when he wrote: "My objective has been to create a history of the different modes by which, in our culture, human beings are made subjects. My work has dealt with three modes of objectification which transform human beings into subjects."[2] In Volume One, following his course summaries from the Collège de France, which provide a powerful synoptic view of his many unfinished projects, the texts address "the way a human being turns him- or herself into a subject."[3] Volume Two is organized around Foucault's analysis of "the modes of inquiry which try to give themselves the status of the sciences."[4] Science, for Foucault, was a domain of practices constitutive of experience as well as of knowledge. Consequently, this volume treats the diverse modes of representations, of signs, and of discourse. Finally, Volume Three contains texts treating "the objectivizing of the subject in dividing pratices,"[5] or, more generally, power relations.

NOTES

1   Foucault, "Des Travaux," in *Dits et écrits* (Paris: Gallimard, 1994), vol. 4, p. 367.

2   Foucault, "The Subject and Power," in *Michel Foucault: Beyond Structuralism and Hermeneutics*, 2d ed., Hubert Dreyfus and Paul Rabinow (Chicago: University of Chicago Press, 1983), p. 208.

3   Idem.

4   Idem.

5   Idem.

ACKNOWLEDGMENTS

Thanks for their detailed reading and comments to João Biehl and James Faubion. The support and/or comments of Judith Butler, Didier Eribon, Claude Imbert, Mike Panisitti, Marc Rabinow, André Schiffrin, Marilyn Seid, and Arpad Szakolczai are much appreciated.

INTRODUCTION

THE HISTORY OF SYSTEMS OF THOUGHT

Michel Foucault delivered his first lecture at the Collège de France, France's most prestigious academic institution, on December 1970, at the age of forty-four.[1] He named his chair at the Collège "The History of Systems of Thought." "*Systems of thought*," he wrote, "are the forms in which, during a given period of time, knowledges [*savoirs*] individualize, achieve an equilibrium, and enter into communication."*

Foucault divided his work on the history of systems of thought into three interrelated parts, the "re-examination of knowledge, the conditions of knowledge, and the knowing subject."[2] Faithful to the broad contours of this program, he moved increasingly in the last decade or so of his life toward an emphasis on the third term, the knowing subject.

As part of his application to the Collège de France, Foucault had submitted a project of instruction and research, on "the knowledge [*savoir*] of heredity" as a system of thought. The choice of heredity as a research topic is fully in line with the work he had carried out in cooperation with Georges Canguilhem, the historian and philosopher of the life sciences with whom he was working during this period. The project's goal was to expand the analysis of natural history and biology, which Foucault had undertaken in *The Order of Things*. How did it happen, he asked, that a nonprestigious set of knowledges, such as those surrounding breeding, eventually took the form and function of a science—*une connaissance scientifique*—as important as genetics? In what specific fashion did this particular science "take up" more general historical events and enter into relations with other structures? The answers to these questions, Foucault held, would require philosophical concepts *and* detailed empirical inquiry. He wrote that, whenever possible, he would employ "a concrete example" to "serve as a testing ground for analysis." This deceptively simple rule of thumb provided him with a powerful means to counterbalance the weaknesses and to multiply the strengths of standard historical and philosophical approaches. He drew on existing resources, putting them to new uses. From the

*See p. 5 of this volume. Hereafter, all page citations given in parentheses are to this volume.

great French tradition of the *Annales* school of historical analysis, he retained an emphasis on long-term and impersonal economic and social trends; from the equally distinctive French lineage of the history of science, he adopted an emphasis on concepts and epistemological rupture points. One could say, to simplify, that he sought to work at the nexus where the history of practices met the history of concepts.

In 1966, Foucault had ended his most famous book, *The Order of Things*, impatiently awaiting the dispersal of the episteme of Man, thinking he discerned glimmers of an imminent reassemblage of language into a new form. In his inaugural lecture at the Collège, "The Order of Discourse," he looked back to the sixth century B.C. For him, it had been a time of "Greek poets [speaking] true discourse...inspiring respect and terror...meting out justice, weaving into the fabric of fate," before the tragic rupture, "a century later [when] Truth moved from the ritualized act—potent and just—to settle on what was enunciated: its meaning, its form, its object, and its relation to what it referred to."[3] He solemnly announced that his project—and the goal of his work—was "to question our will to truth, to restore to discourse its character as an event; to abolish the sovereignty of the signifier."[4] However, he would shortly abandon this nostalgia for a union of power, justice, and discourse. In order to rethink the goal of overcoming the will to truth, he would abandon his attempt to look back to the time of the Greek poets—just as he would forsake his state of alert, ever-attentive to signs of a coming episteme. Nevertheless, he continued to think about how to move beyond sovereign regimes of power and discourse to question the will to truth.

Earlier in the inaugural lecture, Foucault wondered, "what has been, what still is, throughout our discourse, this *will to truth* which has survived throughout so many centuries of our history; or if we ask what is, in its very general form, the kind of division governing our *will to knowledge*"? He answered, "we may discern something like a system of exclusion (historical, modifiable, institutionally constraining) in the process of development."[5] This formulation is vintage Foucault. From his earliest publications, he had identified and analyzed the functions of systems of exclusions variously linked to scientific categorizations. He continued to produce analyses of the will to knowledge, but they gradually came to be situated within a different framework. The will to truth, on the other hand, maintains a rather obscure presence throughout his work. At times, he strongly contrasts the will to truth with the will to knowledge; however, almost simultaneously, it frequently seems to be totally enveloped by it. Apparently, at this point, as he entered the Collège de France, Foucault had not established an adequate conceptual framework within which to develop this opposition.

The Courses

The submission of "course summaries" was one of the few bureaucratic requirements at the Collège. The summaries Foucault submitted are remarkably straightforward, even didactic. The courses themselves shared this pedagogical quality, although they were often presented with exuberant humor and theatrical flair. They provide a series of preliminary sketches of extraordinary vitality and lucidity. It is essential to emphasize that the courses at the Collège were works in progress— philosophical-historical expeditions in search of new objects and new ways of relating to things. The courses can best be seen as exercises, not final performances.

His inaugural course was entitled "The Will to Knowledge" (p. 11). He promised to explore, "fragment by fragment," the "morphology of the will to knowledge," through alternating historical inquiries and theoretical questioning. The first year's course would provide an initial test of the place and role played by the will to knowledge in the history of the systems of thought. He began by attempting to clarify a set of distinctions: "between knowledge [*savoir*] and learning [*connaissance*]; the differences between the will to knowledge [*savoir*] and the will to truth [*vérité*]; the position of the subject, or subjects, in relation to that will." His reference to "that will" is mysterious, given that he has just distinguished two types. Although grammatically the referent is "the will to truth," Foucault immediately turned the course to "the will to knowledge."[6]

This condensation of the two "wills" arises in part from the figures Foucault chose to compare, Aristotle and Nietzsche, and the manner in which he cast the comparison, as exemplars, extreme and opposed cases. Foucault interpreted Aristotle as representing the universal and naturalistic pole. For Aristotle, there is an essential pregiven harmony between sensation, pleasure, knowing, and truth. Our perceptual apparatus is constituted in such a way that it establishes a link of pleasure and of (above all visual) knowledge, even when such a link serves no direct utilitarian purpose. The same economy extends all the way up the hierarchy through to the highest form of knowing, contemplation. As posited in the famous opening lines of the *Metaphysics*, the desire to know is essential to who we are, and is ours "by nature." Our nature is to seek knowledge, and we take pleasure through doing so. He offers Nietzsche's *The Gay Science*, on the other hand, as a total contrast to Aristotle's naturalism. Nietzsche's knowledge (*connaissance*) is not an appropriation of universals but an invention that masks the basest instincts, interests, desires, and fears.[7] There is no preestablished harmony of these drives and the world—just the contingent, temporary, and malicious products of deceitful wills, striving for advantage, fighting for survival and engaged in a ceaseless effort to forcefully impose their will on each other. Knowledge is not a natural faculty but a series of struggles, a weapon in the universal war of domination and submission. Knowledge is always secondary to those more primary struggles. It is linked not to pleasure in flourishing but harnessed to hatred and struggle. Truth is our longest lie, our most intimate ally and enemy.

The interpretation Foucault gives of both thinkers at this moment, because it provides such an absolute contrast, does not allow for a fruitful distinction between the will to knowledge and the will to truth. He seems to affirm their functional identity in Western history, a distinction without a difference. Had Foucault chosen Aristotle's *Ethics* rather than his *Metaphysics* as his paradigmatic text, these same relations of pleasure, knowledge, and the body would have been present, but they would have taken a different form. Over the course of the next decade, he would reexamine the elements of his interpretation of both Aristotle and Nietzsche and recombine them differently. Later on Foucault would indeed come a good deal closer to posing the relations of pleasure, friendship, and practices of truth as a problem, in a way reminiscent of the *Ethics*, although he would never adopt Aristotle's answers, or his metaphysics.

The Move Toward Power

During the early seventies, for reasons his biographers have sought to explain in terms of his personal life, Foucault began to move away from these philosophical themes as well as the project on heredity. Rather, he devoted his courses to material directly related to technologies of power. These themes will be treated more fully in Volume Three of this series; however, it is vital to an understanding of his eventual thoughts on ethics to underline several key changes here. In 1975–76, he entitled his course "Society Must Be Defended" (p. 59). The course began with a despondent, almost despairing apology for what he characterized as his thinking's directionless drift. While he had intended to bring the work of recent years to completion in his current lectures, he was at a loss on how to do so. He lamented that "[t]hough these researches were very closely related to each other, they have failed to develop into any continuous or coherent whole."[8] This confession seems severe given the publication of *Discipline and Punish* in 1975 and in 1976 *The History of Sexuality*, vol. 1.

Obliged to continue teaching, Foucault decided to take up the question of power relations. According to him, we lacked an adequate understanding of power as something other than a reflection of economic structures. Two alternatives were available: one that equates mechanisms of power with repression, another that locates "the basis of the relationship of power in the hostile engagement of forces.... For convenience, I shall call this Nietzsche's hypothesis."[9] The first model, associated with the eighteenth-century *philosophes* and their precursors, proceeds from the social contract in which individuals give up their natural rights to a sovereign in a contractual agreement for peace and prosperity. The model contains explicit normative limits; when the sovereign extends his power beyond the contractual stipulations, then his use of power can be called oppression. Legitimate power is finite.[10] In the contrastive model (the couplet war–domination), power is understood as a perpetual relationship of force whose only goal is submission, the norm of power has no internal limitation: power seeks only victory. "It is obvious," Foucault told his audience, "that all my work in recent years has been couched in terms of" the second model. However, "I have been forced to reconsider [it] both because it is insufficient" and because its key notions "must be considerably modified if not ultimately abandoned." This forced reconsideration follows from the conclusion that "it is wholly inadequate to the analysis of the mechanisms and effects of power that it is so pervasively used to characterize today."[11]

A problem was coming into focus. By the end of the year, Foucault submitted a crisp course summary: "In order to conduct a concrete analysis of power relations, one would have to abandon the juridical model of sovereignty. That model assumes the individual as a subject of natural rights or original powers" (p. 59). Foucault never seriously entertained a view of the individual as bearer of natural rights. There is an analogy between the figure of the individual endowed with primitive powers and the Nietzschean subject Foucault had invoked as the contrastive and polar opposite to Aristotle in his first year of lectures at the Collège. To the extent that the Nietzschean subject had itself been insufficiently submitted to genealogical scrutiny, it needed to be rethought.

The questions Foucault posed in his 1975–76 lectures lend support to this reexamination. How and when, Foucault asked, did we moderns begin to interpret (*déchiffrer*) power relations as examples of warfare? Is warfare the general model for all social relations? How did an interpretation emerge that viewed the subject as endowed with primitive powers of antagonism, proclivities for war, mutual antagonism? When and where did a historico-political discourse of war substitute for a philosophico-juridical discourse of sovereignty? How is it that truths came to function as arms? How did it come to be that within such a discourse, there emerged a subject for whom universal truth and natural law (*droit général*) came to be seen as illusions or snares? How did this somber, critical, and intensely mythical form of self-understanding and practice emerge? Under what conditions did this figure arise who refuses the role of mediator, of neutral arbiter, a role philosophers have assigned to themselves from Solon to Kant to Habermas? How should we analyze a principle of interpretation that proceeds from violence, hatred, passions, revenge, that makes brute givens such as vigor, physique, force, and temperament the underpinnings of thought; that views history as a series of chance events? What has been the trajectory of such a historical discourse that can be advanced both by bearers of aristocratic nostalgia as well as popular revenge? Pursuing this line of inquiry would make it possible not only to answer the question of how von Clausewitz became possible but, more unexpectedly, to pose the question of how Nietzsche became possible.

By the publication of "The Will to Knowledge" in 1976, Foucault had reshaped his understanding of power relations. He was also on the road to transforming his understanding of knowledge and the subject. Foucault coined the phrase the "speaker's benefit" for those who combined "a discourse in which sex, the revelation of truth, the overturning of global laws, the proclamation of a new day to come, and the promise of a certain felicity are linked together."[12] Foucault's sarcasm about

this longing for a space of knowledge simultaneously outside formations of power and yet capable of undermining them all reaches its rue-
ful culmination in the closing lines of the first volume of *The History
of Sexuality*: "The irony of this deployment is in having us believe that
our 'liberation' is in the balance."[13] The highest form of irony is self-
irony. Although the main target of the speaker's benefit was the reigning militant orthodoxy in France, Foucault was equally looking back
over a path he himself had traveled. His true problem, he began to
think, was "the subject" and its relations to the will to truth.

Over the next four years, Foucault carried out a major recasting and
consolidation of his core conceptual tools. The details of this complex
rethinking will receive extended treatment in the introduction to Volume Three of this series. Nevertheless, it is again crucial to underline a
central shift in his views on power relations, for it situates the problems
that his later thought sought to address. During the courses of the late
seventies, Foucault further refined his view of power relations. Simply
and schematically, he concluded: "It seems to me we must distinguish
between power relations understood as strategic games between liberties—in which some try to control the conduct of others, who in turn
try to avoid allowing their conduct to be controlled or try to control the
conduct of others—and the states of domination that people ordinarily call 'power.' And between the two, between games of power and
states of domination, you have technologies of government—understood, of course, in a very broad sense...." To denote this broad understanding of government, Foucault used the term *governmentality*. It
implies, he continued, "the relationship of the self to itself, and...
[covers] the range of practices that constitute, define, organize and
instrumentalize the strategies which individuals in their freedom can
use in dealing with each other. I believe that the concept of governmentality makes it possible to bring out the freedom of the subject and
its relationship to others—which constitutes the very stuff [*matière*] of
ethics." Beginning from this premise, Foucault understands thought as
the exercise of freedom.[14]

SIGNS OF EXISTENCE

In 1979, Foucault reviewed *The Era of Ruptures* by his friend Jean
Daniel, the editor of a Parisian weekly, *Le Nouvel observateur*, to
which Foucault had regularly contributed political commentary. His

review, *"Pour une morale de l'inconfort"*[15] (best translated as "For an Ethic of Discomfort" for reasons that will be elucidated below), is a kind of editorial—a combination of praise, reflection, and advocacy—addressed to the journal's urbane, leftist audience at a time when their political and intellectual hopes were rather dampened. Foucault set forth several guiding principles and themes, to which he would return incessantly in the remaining years of his life, albeit in different contexts and using different forms (see, for example, "What is Enlightenment?" p. 303). He began by invoking a question posed in 1784 by the *Berlinische Monatsschrift* to a number of leading *Aufklärer*, including Kant: "What is Enlightenment?" The question, as well as Kant's response, would preoccupy Foucault over the next several years. These reflections provided him with a starting point from which to transform the newspaper's question and Kant's answer into a different question—"What is modernity?"—or, as he posed it in his book review, "who are we in the present, what is this fragile moment from which we can't detach our identity and which will carry that identity away with itself?"

Good journalism required a passion for stalking the elusive singularity of the present. More challenging yet was the task of observing oneself, with a certain distance, in the process of practicing this *métier*, midst the hurly-burly of everyday events, crises, deadlines, and myriad pressing demands. Foucault was intrigued by the fact that some journalists were better suited than philosophers and political activists for the task of sustaining a supple, yet critical, stance in the swirl of passing scenes, of resisting the temptation to always have a "position." Foucault praised Jean Daniel for his deft handling of this ever-renewed demand on the left to have a firm, well-defended, vantage point for anchoring one's analysis. *Vantage point*, after all, is a military term connoting an overall perspective from afar, the proverbial bird's-eye-view—but strategic advantage, however, does not necessarily provide understanding. For Foucault, in order to establish the right relationship to the present—to things, to others, to oneself—one must stay close to events, experience them, be willing to be effected and affected by them.

Foucault was not singing the praises of vacillation and indecision, or of a total refusal of perspective. Banality of thought, resolute opportunism, or a program of deconstruction and transgression as ends in themselves all seemed to him to be equally dubious. "The demand [*exigence*] for an identity," he insisted, "and the injunction to break that identity, both feel, in the same way, abusive."[16] Such demands are abusive because they assume in advance what one is, what one must do, what one always must be closed to, which side one must be on. He sought not so much to resist as to evade this installed dichotomy. One might say he refused the blackmail of having to choose between a unified, unchanging identity and a stance of perpetual and obligatory transgression. "One's way [*façon*] of no longer remaining the same," he wrote, "is, by definition, the most singular part of who I am." However, that singularity was never a blanket negation: if one knew in advance that everything, including one's self and the current state of affairs, was bad, what would there be to learn? What would be the sense of acting? Why think? A life without the possibility of error would not be conceivable. One might say, following Georges Canguilhem, such a life would not be alive.

Who one is, Foucault wrote, emerges acutely out of the problems with which one struggles. In the review, he phrased his approach in a manner so as to distance it from Sartre and his version of the committed intellectual: "Experience with...rather than engagement in..." Privileging experience over engagement makes it increasingly difficult to remain "absolutely in accord with oneself," for identities are defined by trajectories, not by position taking. Such an attitude is an uncomfortable one insofar as one risks being mistaken and is vulnerable to the perfect hindsight of those who adopt firm positions (especially after events have passed) or who speak assuredly of universals as though the singular were secondary. To that extent, one could say, adopting a distinction Foucault developed in his work leading up to the second volume of *The History of Sexuality*, *The Uses of Pleasure*, that this attitude is rooted in an ethics and not a morality, a practice rather than a vantage point, an active experience rather than a passive waiting.

The challenge is not to replace one certitude (*évidence*) with another but to cultivate an attention to the conditions under which things become "evident," ceasing to be objects of our attention and therefore seemingly fixed, necessary, and unchangeable. A few pages later in the review, Foucault approvingly invoked Maurice Merleau-Ponty's definition of the task of philosophy, "to never consent to be completely at ease with what seems evident to oneself." What seems so new, if we are attentive, often can be seen to have been around, at the back of our minds, at the corner of our vision, at the edge of things we almost, but never quite, saw or said. "The most fragile of passing moments has its antecedents. There is a whole ethics of an alert certitude [*évidence*] which doesn't exclude a rigorous economy of Truth and Falsity, far from it, but isn't summed up by that economy either."[17] Philosophy is a practice and an ethos, a state or condition of character, not detached observation and legislation. "What is philosophy after all? if not a means of reflecting on not so much on what is true or false but on our relation to truth? How, given that relation to truth, should we act?" ("The Masked Philosopher," p. 321) In this formulation, we see the thinker as nominalist engaged in a reexamination of knowledge, the conditions of knowledge, and the knowing subject.

The Masked Philosopher

Foucault's exasperation with what he continued to see and feel as political posturing and lack of imagination in France found another articulation in an anonymous interview he gave in April 1980 to the leading French daily, *Le Monde*, which was interviewing leading thinkers about their views on the current scene. He refused to join in this vogue of condemning "intellectuals," which was sweeping Paris as a part of rejection of the media and its supposed destructive influence on French political and intellectual culture: "I've never met any intellectuals. I have met people who write novels, and others who treat the sick; people who work in economics and others who compose electronic music. I've met people who teach, people who paint and people of whom I have never really understood what they do. But intellectuals? Never" (p. 322). His sarcasm was aimed at what he saw as the reigning style of criticism, one based on denunciation, condemnation, judgment of guilt, and attempts to silence and ultimately to destroy the object of criticism. He lyrically but pointedly evoked an alternative: "I can't help but dream about a kind of criticism that would try not to judge but to bring an oeuvre, a sentence, an idea to life; it would light fires, watch the grass grow, listen to the wind, and catch the sea foam in the breeze and scatter it. It would multiply not judgments but signs of existence; it would summon them, drag them from their sleep.... It would bear the lightning of possible storms." We should remember that he agreed to the interview on condition that he remain anonymous, that he be referred to simply as "the masked philosopher." Apparently not many readers guessed that Foucault—whom many thought of as "the nihilist," "the deconstructionist"—had spoken these words.

Well and good, the interviewer persisted, but isn't the present, after all, a time of mediocrity and lowered expectations? Foucault responded with an emphatic *no* to that commonplace as well. Quite the contrary, he insisted: it is a propitious time. "There is an overabundance of things to be known: fundamental, terrible, wonderful, funny, insignificant, and crucial at the same time. And there is an enormous curiosity, a need, a desire to know.... Curiosity is seen as futility. However,...it evokes "care"; it evokes the care one takes of what exists and what might exist; a sharpened sense of reality, but one that is never immobilized before it; a readiness to find what surrounds us strange and odd; a certain determination to throw off familiar ways of thought and to look at the same things in a different way; a passion for seizing what is happening now and what is disappearing; a lack of respect for traditional hierarchies of what is important and fundamental. I dream of a new age of curiosity. We have the technical means; the desire is there; there is an infinity of things to know; the people capable of doing such work exist" (p. 325). Curiosity: a simple little thing.

At this time, one of Foucault's cherished projects was to create a different kind of publishing in France. After Editions Gallimard, the prestigious house that published his major books in huge print runs, refused his offer to edit a small series of books, Foucault (along with Paul Veyne and François Wahl) succeeded in convincing another distinguished Parisian publisher, Les Editions du Seuil, to initiate a series entitled "Works" (*Des Travaux*). The purpose of the series was to publish works that might be considered too long and difficult—hence lacking an immediate audience—but that over time would show their importance, short pieces outlining the main points of future work to be developed over time, and translations of important foreign works with no large market in France. Foucault and friends provided a trenchant definition of "work" as "that which is susceptible of introducing a meaningful difference in the field of knowledge, albeit with a certain demand placed on the author and reader, but with the eventual recompense of a certain pleasure, that is to say of an access to another figure of truth."[18]

Arenas: Iran, Poland, USA

"Where are we today?" Foucault asked his readers to ask themselves in 1979.[19] At a moment of the globalization of the economy? "Certainly." At a moment of global geopolitics as well. But, he wondered, was thought also in a globalizing moment? It seemed to him that the answer was no: he discerned no indications of an emergent universal philosophy or political consciousness. In France, in his view, this contradictory conjuncture had yielded a stifling combination of ever-more empty rhetorical allegiance to the receding utopia of a universal revolution, accompanied by a pervasive social conservatism. How then, to "tear oneself away from" that predicament? His almost visceral rejection of French bourgeois *moeurs* was a long-standing one that he shared with other French writers he admired, such as Flaubert. A young Canadian interviewer's assertion that France held an enduring attraction for North Americans elicited this retort: "Yes, but now I don't think they come to Paris any longer for freedom. They come to have a taste of an old traditional culture. They come to France as painters went to Italy in the seventeenth century, to see a dying civilization" (p. 123). That is why, he explained, he had lived in Sweden, in Poland, in Germany, in Tunisia, and in the United States and had made repeated trips to Brazil and Japan.

During the late seventies and early eighties, Foucault's main areas of political and social activity were outside France. He went to Iran for an Italian newspaper as an eyewitness to the period leading up to the fall of the Shah and the triumph of the Khomeini regime. Surely he had in mind a maxim he had applied approvingly to Jean Daniel's work, that of not giving "our unhesitant support [*confiance*] to any revolution, even if one can understand each revolt."[20] He was fascinated by the type of political action taking place, the massive presence of an underarmed populace in the streets facing a police force and army among the world's most brutal and omnipresent. A revolution was taking place, but it was one that made the European Left uneasy. It was hard to identify class dynamics, social divisions, a vanguard party, or political ideology as the driving force; these "lacks" intrigued Foucault. He was intrigued by the question of the role of religion in political life, of the unexpected and resurgent role it was playing. He reminded his European readers that the sentence preceding Marx's famous phrase about religion being the opium of the people, spoke of "the spirit of a world without spirit." He saw or felt—or thought he saw—hints of such a spirit, and of a possible role it might have in forming the self in a different relationship to politics.

Foucault mused that until his visit to Iran he had only read about the collective will. In Iran, it seemed that he had encountered it in the streets, focused in determined opposition to the Shah. He wondered what to make of "the vocabulary, the ceremonial, the timeless drama into which one could fit the historical drama of a people that pitted its very existence against that of the sovereign."[21] Foucault was fascinated, perhaps above all, by what he saw as a demand for a new subjectivity. He felt he discerned an imperative that went beyond overthrowing yet another corrupt, Western-supported authoritarian regime, an imperative he formulated thus: "above all we have to change ourselves. Our way of being, our relationships with others, with things, with eternity, with God."[22] He grappled with this intuition, repeating a similar hypothesis on several occasions. "What is the meaning for these people, to seek out, at the price of their lives, that thing whose very possibility we Europeans have forgotten at least since the Renaissance and the period of the great crises of Christianity—a spirituality. I can hear the French laughing at these words, but they are making a mistake."[23] Foucault intended to examine this issue of political spirituality and its changing relationships with self-fashioning as soon as he finished the seemingly interminable rewriting of the "Greek and Christian books." In the early eighties, he proposed a two-pronged research project with colleagues and students at Berkeley—on political spirituality and self-fashioning in the fifteenth and sixteenth centuries, and the arts of socialist governmentality in the twenties.

The latter project was linked to a dialogue he had undertaken with representatives of the main noncommunist labor union, the Confédération Française des Travailleurs Démocratique (CFDT), on such matters as the future of the social security system. He was intrigued by the spirit of the seemingly futile efforts of Solidarity in Poland, which he actively supported and with whom the CFDT forged close ties. Foucault went to Poland on a number of occasions, not just to meet and discuss the situation with various participants but to seek out rather humble work as a bookkeeper. When martial law was imposed in December 1981, France's Socialist government made only perfunctory protests. Foucault, like many others, took to the streets. And as Iran faded from Western public attention, and Poland endured in the gray night of martial law, Foucault seriously considered working anonymously with the humanitarian group Médecins Sans Frontières (Doctors Without Borders), or of retiring to the countryside to practice spiritual exercises and tend his garden. Although he did not pursue either of these escape fantasies, his increasing preoccupation with the theme of "the care of the self" dovetailed with his efforts to bring the later volumes of *The History of Sexuality* to completion.

During this period, he made frequent visits to California and New York. Until the late seventies, he had been openly, if discreetly, homosexual in the then current French style.[24] In the context of his work on the care of the self, though, he began to rethink publicly homosexual and homosocial relationships, embarking on a distinctive series of explorations and reflections on emergent forms of pleasure, sociality, and thought. In California, his explorations and reflections on gay life in San Francisco are well known; less has been made of the fact that, when in California, he spent his days at the University of California in Berkeley, working in the libraries, talking with colleagues, holding seminars, and meeting students. It seems fair to say that Foucault was experimenting in his own life with the twin imperatives to "know thyself" and to "care for thyself."

A MODERN ETHOS

Max Weber, Foucault argued, had placed the following question on the historical, sociological, and ethical agenda: "If one wants to behave rationally and regulate one's action according to true principles, what part of one's self should one renounce? What is the ascetic price of reason?" He continued, "For my part, I have posed the opposite question: How have certain kinds of interdictions become the price required for attaining certain kinds of knowledge [*savoir*] about oneself? What must one know [*connaître*] about oneself in order to be willing to accept such renunciation?" The latter formulation is a guiding thread in Foucault's historical work in the second and third volumes of *The History of Sexuality*, as well as in the unpublished fourth volume, *Confessions of the Flesh*. Despite his reformulation of Weber's question, Foucault's core concern applies equally well to Foucault himself—what is the place of asceticism in a philosophic life? If asceticism is taken as "exercise" and not as renunciation (and this is precisely how Foucault takes it up in his later work), then the question becomes: How is reason exercised? How is reason practiced?

One of the main themes Foucault explored in the early eighties was "the care of the self." The nearly complete uncoupling of this imperative from its twin, "know yourself," is an essential element of his diagnosis of modernity, in which the latter imperative was gradually to eclipse the former as a philosophical object. From Descartes to Husserl, the imperative to "know thyself" increasingly predominated over that to "take care of thyself." As the "care of the self" had traditionally passed through or entailed relationships with others, this disproportionate weighting of knowledge has contributed to the "universal unbrotherliness" that caused Weber so much pain and which he lacked the tools to do more than decry. For Foucault the equation of philosophical *askēsis* with renunciation of feeling, solidarity, and care for one's self and for others—as the price of knowledge—was one of our biggest wrong turnings. However, reversing such a course is not merely a matter of willing or desiring it to be otherwise. What could be more self-delusional than the recent heralding of a reenchantment of the world, or that we have actually never been modern? As this trajectory became clearer to him, Foucault aimed at rethinking this separation. Rather than seek to force a reconciliation, he focused on whether the "universal unbrotherliness" produced by the will to knowledge, which had previously seemed like a necessary component of modernity—the price to be paid for knowledge and ethics—might well be more contingent than Weber had thought. He began thinking his way around this culturally coherent but humanly intolerable outcome by radically recasting what Weber would have called "a vocation"—something that Foucault called an "ethics" understood as an ethos.

Care of the Self

In an interview published as "The Ethic of the Concern for the Self as a Practice of Freedom" (p. 281), Foucault provides an unusually unqualified formulation of his philosophical and ethical work. He reiterates that his project has always been to untangle the relations between the subject and truth. Although his argument is not presented as a set of working premises, it is convenient and plausible to view it this way. *Premise one:* "what is ethics, if not the practice of freedom, the considered [*réfléchie*] practice of freedom" (p. 284). "Freedom is the ontological condition of ethics. But ethics is the considered form that freedom takes" (p. 284). Thus, a condition of liberty is the ontological starting point. *Premise two:* In the Western tradition, "taking care of oneself requires knowing [*connaître*] oneself" (p. 285). "To take care of the self is to equip oneself with these truths" (p. 285). It is through these tools and this conceptual linkage that "ethics is linked to the

game of truth" (p. 285). *Premise three:* Ethics is not just a theory—it is
equally a practice, an embodiment, a style of life. Hence, the problem
is to give liberty "shape in an ēthos" (p. 286). *Premise four:* the subject "is not a substance. It is a form, and this form is not primarily or
always identical to itself" (p. 290). "*Self* is a reflexive pronoun, and
it has two meanings. *Auto* means 'the same,' but it also conveys the
notion of identity. The latter meaning shifts the question from 'What
is this self?' to 'Departing from what ground shall I find my identity?'"
(p. 230). *Premise five:* The central arena of inquiry is the historical
constitution of these forms and their relation to "games of truth." A
game of truth is a "set of procedures that lead to a certain result,
which, on the basis of its principles and rules of procedure, may be
considered valid or invalid" (p. 297). [W]hy truth?... And why must the
care of the self occur only through the concern for truth? [This is] *the*
question for the West. How did it come about that all of Western culture began to revolve around this obligation of truth...?" (p. 295).
Given these premises, one must conclude equally that "one escaped
from a domination of truth" only by playing that game differently
(p. 295). *Premise six:* "the relationship between philosophy and politics is permanent and fundamental" (p. 293). By "politics" Foucault
means both power relations and the life of the city as understood in
the ancient world, the modern equivalent being "governmentality."
Premise seven: Philosophy, understood as a practice and a problem,
is a vocation. The manner in which liberty is taken up by the philosopher is distinctive, differing in "intensity" and "zeal" from other free
citizens (p. 293).

Since the Enlightenment, while demand for an ethics has been in-
cessant, the philosophical fulfillment of that demand has been notably
scarce. This impasse has led to many fundamentalist projects, none of
which has achieved any general acceptance, even among the philosophers and moralists. Such a meager harvest has also led to the categorical or partial rejection of such projects. Foucault himself argued in
The Order of Things that there could be no moral system in modernity, if by "moral system" one meant a philosophical anthropology that
produced firm foundations concerning the nature of Man and, thereby,
a basis for human action. Ultimately, though, Foucault may well be
remembered as one of the major ethical thinkers of modernity.

Foucault sets up two "ideal" types of moral systems: one that emphasizes the moral code, and another that emphasizes ethical practices.

Within systems of the first type, "the authority that enforces the code, [takes] a quasi-juridical form, the subject refers his conduct to a law, or set of laws."[25] The great monotheistic religious systems exemplify this type of moral system. In the second ideal-typical form, which Foucault associated with the ancient world, it is the "mode of subjectivation"—the way a subject freely relates to himself—that receives greater elaboration. In this type of system, the codes and explicit rules of behavior may be rudimentary, while greater attention is paid to the methods, techniques, and exercises directed at forming the self within a nexus of relationships. In such a system, authority would be self-referential and might take a therapeutic or philosophical form. He stressed that, in practice, these forms were not wholly distinct—subject-oriented practices have been widespread in Christianity, just as there were moral prohibitions in the ethical practices of the ancient world. Nonetheless, the contrast is an instructive one.

In Volumes Two and Three of *The History of Sexuality*, Foucault undertook a restorative historical analysis of the place of the self-formation as an "ethical subject" in the ancient world. He describes this process as one in which "the individual delimits that part of himself that will form the object of his moral practice, defines his position relative to the precept that he will follow, and decides on a certain mode of being that will serve his moral goal."[26] His goal in this analysis was not to "return" to some archaic mode of social order but, rather, to make visible a bygone way of approaching the self and others which might suggest possibilities for the present. He was seeking not to denaturalize the "subject of desire," not to invent a philosophic system per se, but to contribute to a mode of living. He thought that elements of that possible mode of living were already in existence: he sought to learn from and strengthen these, not to discover or "invent" others. In that spirit, it seems worthwhile to turn his ethical categories onto his own thought—something he himself did not do—in order to identity and illuminate his singular enterprise.

The Ethical Fourfold

Foucault saw ethical analysis as the free relationship to the self (*rapport à soi*)—a relationship that could be examined through four basic categories: ethical substance, mode of subjectivation, ethical work, and telos. Although he treats these categories as independent one from the other, he recognizes that, in any historical instance, they are always found in a specific configuration. In his genealogy of the subject of desire, he gives us historical examples of how such an analytics of ethics had been elaborated, of the internal systematicity, and of the differential mode of alteration over time. His goal in these historical analyses was to loosen the grip of our self-understanding as "subjects of desire," so as to make possible a different relationship to our thought, ourselves and others, as well as to our pleasures.

However, as he was wont to say, there is more. What if one was undertaking not only a history of sexuality but also a genealogy of ethics? How, then, would one cast the analytics of a free relationship to the self that a life of thinking entailed? In an interview in Berkeley ("On the Genealogy of Ethics," p. 253), he was asked why he was not intending to talk more about friendship in his forthcoming books. He responded, "don't forget *L'Usage des plaisirs* is a book about sexual ethics; it's not a book about love, or about friendship, or about reciprocity.... Friendship is reciprocal and sexual relations are not reciprocal" (p. 257). "What I want to ask is: Are we able to have an ethics of acts and their pleasures which would be able to take into account the pleasure of the other?" (p. 258).

There are two important points here. First, Foucault makes it clear that the content of the ethical discussion he provides in Volumes Two and Three of *The History of Sexuality* follow from the subject matter under discussion. As we shall see, the general categories of ethics he provides can be elaborated differently in the context of a different genealogy. At the end of the *Archaeology of Knowledge*, he stated that it would have been perfectly possible to construct other archaeologies of other objects, and that he was never talking about the spirit of an age or a unified understanding of being. Second, he is very clear that he is not advocating a "return" to the Greek model of sexual or human relations. Ancient Greek society was characterized by essential inequalities and nonreciprocities that moderns can only find intolerable. Consequently, what he identifies in the ancient world is a problematic, a way of thinking about ethical issues, and a form of practice—*askēsis*—integrally linked to that thought.

It should be stressed again, though, that when in 1984 Foucault was asked if he found the ancient Greeks admirable, he answered: "Not very.... They were stymied right away by what seems to be the point of contradiction of ancient morality: between, on the one hand, this obstinate search for a certain style of existence and, on the other hand, the effort to make it common to everyone, a style that they approached more or less obscurely with Seneca and Epictetus but which would find the possibility of realization only within a religious style. All of antiquity appears to me to have been a 'profound error' (*laughs*)."[27] It is not entirely clear what exactly he was laughing at: certainly not the obstinate search for a style of existence. Was it the religious stylization? Was it the effort to make a stylized life common? The offending term appears to be "common," understood as uniform. Foucault definitely rejected two possible interpretations of what "common" could mean: either that a class location or professional identity was the sine qua non of liberty and, hence, of ethics; or that everyone would have the same stylization. Foucault unequivocally equated the latter project with normalization and the will to knowledge, and there is no reason to believe he ever entertained the former (although the issue of "leisure" to pursue such questions remains unaddressed). This answer, perhaps appropriately, leaves entirely open how general and diverse Foucault thought such a project could be.

ETHICAL SUBSTANCE: THE WILL TO TRUTH. *The way that the individual has to constitute this or that part of himself as the prime material of his moral conduct*—Foucault[28]

For Foucault as a thinker, the ethical substance, the prime material of moral conduct, is the "will to truth." As we have seen, in the course summary of his first year at the Collège, he summarized his comparison between Aristotle and Nietzsche, discussed archaic practices of establishing the truth in the context of justice, and elucidated the general goal of his work. The primary, perhaps ultimate, task he had set for himself was to establish "the difference between the will to knowledge [*savoir*] and the will to truth [*vérité*]; the position of the subject, or subjects with respect to that will" (p. 12). The lion's share of Foucault's work centered on [t]he historical analysis of this rancorous will to knowledge."[29] He did not abandon his attention to the dangers of knowledge–power complexes, even as he cautiously moved away from a central focus on the "will to knowledge." He categorically refused appeals to "science, religion, or law" as the basis upon which a free person could shape his life. For him, whatever we were to become, it could not be legitimated by the will to knowledge. Still, of the will to truth he said very, very little. In his 1971 essay, "Nietzsche, Genealogy, History," he offered an utterly bleak picture of modernity: [T]he will to truth...

loses all sense of limitations and all claim to truth in its unavoidable sacrifice of the subject of knowledge."[31] In "The Order of Discourse," he had told his audience it was "[as] though the will to truth and its vicissitudes were masked by truth itself and its necessary unfolding."[31] The "as though" presents the smallest sliver of maneuvering space.

Thirteen years later, in the introduction to *The Uses of Pleasure*, Foucault formulated his problem thus: "How, why and in what forms is thinking constituted as a moral domain?"[32] A few paragraphs later he could ingenuously write, "As for what motivated me, it is quite simple; I would hope that in the eyes of some people it might be sufficient in itself. It was curiosity—the only kind of curiosity, in any case, that is worth acting upon with a degree of obstinacy; not the curiosity that seeks to assimilate what is proper for one to know, but that which enables one to get free of oneself."[34] Foucault presents curiosity as a modest impulse, but his qualification that curiosity is what enables one "to get free of oneself"—the telos of his ethics—signals that the stakes of this simple little thing could not be higher. "But, then, what is philosophy today—philosophical activity, I mean—if it is not the critical work that thought brings to bear on itself"[34]

In another version of the preface to *The Uses of Pleasure*, Foucault wrote, "It is easy to see how the reading of Nietzsche in the early fifties has given access to these kinds of questions." Nietzsche does indeed provide access to these kinds of questions. In *The Gay Science*, he had already specified the problem: "This unconditional will to truth—what is it? Is it the will *not to allow oneself to be deceived?* Or is it the will not to deceive?" He concludes: "Consequently 'will to truth' does not mean 'I will not allow myself to be deceived' but—there is no alternative—'I will not deceive, even myself'; *and with that we stand on moral ground*."[35] Nietzsche and Weber are clearly Foucault's precursors in making these topics into problems.

MODE OF SUBJECTIVATION: SELF-STYLIZATION OR FORM-GIVING. *The way in which the individual establishes his relation to the rule and recognizes himself as obligated to put it into practice.*—Foucault[36]

> M.F. What strikes me is the fact that, in our society, art has become something that is related only to objects and not to individuals or to life. That art is something which is specialized or done by experts who are artists. But couldn't everyone's life become a work of art? Why should the lamp or the house be an art object, but not our life?

Q. Of course, that kind of project is very common in places like Berkeley....

M.F. But I am afraid in most of those cases, most of the people think if they do what they do, if they live as they live, the reason is that they know the truth about desire, life, nature, body and so on. (pp. 261–262)

For Foucault, the challenge of the mode of subjectivation is not to base one's subjectivity, that multidimensional relationship (to others, to things, and to ourselves) on any science, nor on any previously established doctrine. In "What is Enlightenment?" he wrote: "I wonder whether we may not envisage modernity as an attitude rather than as a period of history. And by 'attitude,' I mean a mode of relating to contemporary reality; a voluntary choice made by certain people; in the end, a way of thinking and feeling; a way, too, of acting and behaving that at one and the same time marks a relation of belonging and presents itself as a task" (p. 309). This "belonging" is relation to the society in its historical and political determinations, with its embedded and embodied strictures, its sedimented orders of thought. The "task" is to determine what must be shown to be contingent, and what can be shown to be truly singular in the present. An essential aspect of doing this work is to take up a stylized relationship to things, to oneself, and to others. The question is, What form should such a relationship take?

In "What is Enlightenment?" Foucault presents two exemplary modes of subjectivation, one personified by Kant, the other by Baudelaire. Kant took up this question in an original way, by transforming it from an issue of epochs or of pure reason into a question of the thinker's relationship to the present—to temporality understood as memory.[37] Foucault restates Kant's question thus: "What difference does today introduce with respect to yesterday?" (p. 305). What difference does the present make to our thinking? For Kant, addressing this question put one on the road from an "immature" state marked by a lack of thought, or reflection upon dependency toward "maturity." Kant problematized the relationship between the will, authority, and reason. For him, thinking about the relationship of these terms was not only a process but, equally, a task and an obligation. We are responsible for our own maturity. Consequently, it is through the obligation to work on ourselves that we may discover the way to a proper relationship to the Enlightenment—we will "dare to know." Kant proposed a political contract with the "rational despot" Frederick II: an exchange of political subservience for the free use of the rational faculties. However, this contract was not something Foucault was willing to endorse.

Baudelaire also privileged a particular relationship to temporality—characterized by keen attentiveness to the passing moment. However, he transformed the Enlightenment attitude into one of "modernity." In his now-classic manifesto, *The Painter of Modern Life*, Baudelaire identified the modern artist's challenge as one of seizing the eternal within the "contingent, fleeting, volatile" present. What he sought was not behind or beyond the present but within it. The artist had not merely to observe the carnival parading in front of him with the disinterested, ironic, blasé attitude of the *flâneur* but rather to heroize the present by "taking hold" (*prendre*) of it. For Baudelaire, the artist has "no right to despise the present"; hence, it is his business—through an act of will—to seize hold of it.

This is only half the story, though. The point of seizing hold of the present is to transfigure it. As Foucault understands it, Baudelaire's "transfiguration entails not the annulling of reality but a difficult interplay between the truth of what is real and the exercise of freedom" (p. 311). Transfiguration is not transgression; *transgression* is a word Foucault does not employ in his later work.[38] Rather, Foucault sought in Baudelaire the means to invent a different attitude toward the world and the self, one more respectful and ultimately more difficult to achieve. Just as he drew from Kant an attention to the historical singularity of reason as a practice, so, in a parallel way—and one closer to the original text he was interpreting—he drew from Baudelaire a stylization of the self as an exercise "in which extreme attention to what is real is confronted with the practice of a liberty that simultaneously respects this reality and violates it" (p. 311).

Baudelaire gives form to the self in art. He never imagined, Foucault insists, that such stylization could operate on "society itself or on the body politic" (p. 312). Foucault proposes a stylization of the practices and exercises of the self taken as an attitude—a relationship—that clearly draws from the models of Kant and Baudelaire. However, unlike Kant, Foucault does not accept social and political conformity as the trade-off for freedom of thought; equally, he refuses Baudelaire's restriction of a modern ethos to the arena of art. Rather, Foucault hopes to invent a mode of subjectivation in which this ethos would be a practice of thought formed in direct contact with social and political realities. "Yet if we are not to settle for the affirmation or the empty dream of freedom, it seems to me that this historico-critical attitude must also be an experimental one. I mean that this work done at the limits of ourselves must, on the one hand, open up a realm of historical inquiry, and, on the other, put itself to a test of reality, of contemporary reality, both to grasp the points where change is possible and desirable, and to determine the precise form this change should take" (p. 316). The relation to the present is one that tests the limits of society, and of the self, a determination of what it is desirable and possible to change.

"This philosophical attitude may be characterized as a *limit-attitude*. We are not talking about a gesture of rejection. . . . Criticism indeed consists of analyzing and reflecting upon limits. But if the Kantian question was that of knowing [*savoir*] what limits knowledge [*connaissance*] must renounce exceeding [*franchir*], it seems to me that the critical question today must be turned back into a positive one: In what is given to us as universal, necessary, obligatory, what place is occupied by whatever is singular, contingent, and the product of arbitrary constraints? The point, in brief, is to transform the critique conducted in the form of a necessary limitation into a practical critique that takes the form of a possible crossing-over [*franchissement*]" (p. 315). Such a crossing-over or "clearing-away" will always be historically specific and partial. "This means that the historical ontology of ourselves must turn away from all projects that claim to be global or radical. . . . I prefer the very specific transformations that have proved to be possible in the last twenty years in a certain number of areas which concern our ways of being and thinking, relations to authority, relations between the sexes, the way in which we perceive insanity or illness; I prefer even these partial transformations, which have been made in the correlation of historical analysis and the practical attitude, to the programs for a new man that the worst political systems have repeated throughout the twentieth century. I shall thus characterize the philosophical ethos appropriate to the critical ontology of ourselves as a historico-practical test of the limits we may go beyond, and thus as work carried out by ourselves upon ourselves as free beings" (p. 316). What is that work?

ETHICAL WORK: CRITICAL ACTIVITY, THOUGHT EXPERIENCE. *The work one performs to attempt to transform oneself into the ethical subject of one's behavior. (What are the means by which we can change ourselves in order to become ethical subjects?)*—Foucault[39] What we are to do, either to moderate our acts, or to decipher what we are. . . .

The task of ethical work for Foucault is to establish the right relationship between intellect and character in the context of practical affairs. His clearest discussion of this relationship between "thought" and "experience" is found in a version of the preface to *The Uses of Pleasure*, where he states that his attempt in this work had been to develop a satisfactory means to analyze sexuality as "a historically singular form of experience." However, as he indicates elsewhere, his general remarks about sexuality apply as well to other "fundamental" experiences. Not surprisingly, he differentiated his approach from phenomenological or existential approaches based on the subject and its "primary experience." Rather, Foucault located experience (and the subject) within a complex site comprising "a domain of knowledge [*savoir*], a type of normativity, and a mode of relation to the self." Thus, he addressed experience as a historical product that emerges within a "field of knowledge [*connaissance*]...a collection of social rules... and a mode of relation between the individual and himself." Foucault identified this overall project as a nominalist philosophic anthropology, explicitly rejecting any basis in pregiven essence or nature. Without rejecting the possibility that some such constants can be found, he interprets experiences, such as those of sexuality, within the particular historical fields that shaped them, to which they were in part a reaction, and which both created and limited the form those experiences could take at a given historical moment.

Many analytical, political, and ethical problems could be developed from this nominalist understanding of experience, thought, and the subject. Foucault made this constellation the privileged domain of the history of thought. To do so, he provides a rich, if idiosyncratic definition of "thought": "By 'thought,' I mean what establishes, in a variety of possible forms, the play of true and false, and consequently constitutes the human being as a knowing subject [*connaissance*]...as social and juridical subjects...and as an ethical subject." This definition establishes a terrain for the history of thought which is far broader than the history of scientific disciplines or philosophic systems. It posits all forms of experience as potential objects of thought, and thus of the history of thought. The task of the history of thought is to identify and delimit the development and transformation of these domains of experience; as these domains and these experiences are diverse, it follows that so, too, are modes of thought.

Foucault's definition of thought as a modern practice is so broad that it comes close to equating thought not only with experience but with

action. However, it is important to avoid a misunderstanding here (as
in a parallel way with Foucault's definition of power). Since thought is
a defining aspect of any historically singular complex—a vital aspect
of its singularity—an analysis of such complexes is always possible for
a history of thought. But that does not mean that thought (or power
relations, which are also an unsurpassable part of such historical singularities) is totally coextensive with the object of analysis. As Foucault
put it, "The study of forms of experience can thus proceed from an
analysis of 'practices'... as long as one qualifies that word to mean the
different systems of action *insofar as* they are inhabited by thought."
Insofar, to the extent that, "qua" a classic and elementary philosophic
proviso that is often misunderstood today as totalization.

In this light, we can make sense of Foucault's claim that "thought
is...the very form of action." He is referring to a potential present
both in the object of analysis and for the analyst. "Thought is not what
inhabits a certain conduct and gives it its meaning; rather, it is what
allows one to step back from this way of acting or reacting, to present
it to oneself as an object of thought and to question it as to its meaning, its conditions, and its goals. Thought is freedom in relation to what
one does, the motion by which one detaches oneself from it, establishes it as an object, and reflects on it as a problem." Precisely because
thought is not a given, thought is an action; and actions arising from
experience and formed by thought are ethical ones.

This brings us to the question of ethical work; it will have both an
intellectual and a practical dimension, though, as we have just seen,
experience and action arise within complex assemblages. As a thinker,
the work Foucault performs "to transform himself into an ethical subject of one's behavior" is a distinctive form of intellectual practice, a
singular form of critical thought. He writes: criticism is "a historical
investigation into the events that have led us to constitute ourselves
and to recognize ourselves as subjects of what we are doing, thinking,
saying. In that sense, this criticism is not transcendental, and its goal
is not to that of making a metaphysics possible; it is genealogical in its
design and archaeological in its method.... [I]t will separate out, from
the contingency that has made us what we are, the possibility of no
longer being, doing, or thinking what we are, do, or think...it is seeking to give new impetus, as far and as wide as possible, to the undefined work of freedom." Such work would have multiple dimensions
but, qua ethical work, it would be a disentangling and re-forming of

the (power and thought) relationships within which and from which the self is shaped and takes shape.

Thus, Foucault came to conceive of the most general name for the practice he was seeking to identify: "problematization." "The proper task of a history of thought is: to define the conditions in which human beings 'problematize' what they are, what they do, and the world in which they live."[40] Or, again, in more philosophical language, he defines his object of analysis (and also his task) as: "the problematizations through which being [*l'être*] offers itself to be necessarily [*pouvant et devant*] thought and the practices on the basis of which these problematizations are formed."[41] It is vital to understand that, for Foucault, "being" is given through problematizations and practices; it is not prior to them. That is why it is both potentially and obligatorily—*pouvant et devant*—available for thought. As Foucault insisted, thought does not reside in the practices giving them their meaning; it is always a practice of freedom that could have taken (or could take in the future) a different form. Problematizations and practices can and must be thought vis-à-vis experience insofar as they concern our freedom. Ethical work makes them available in that form.

In interviews with the young editors of gay journals, Foucault presents a quasi manifesto of what he sees as his own ethical task, cast as the work of thought, pleasure, and invention. In these interviews, he is especially crisp in his formulations, speaking as a member of the community. The problem for gays now, he told his young interviewers, was not to uncover the truth of homosexual desire but to make homosexuality desirable; "Sex is not a fatality; it's a possibility for creative life" (p. 163). The search should be not for the secret of one's identity but for how to invent new modes of relationship and a new way of life. How, that is, to become homosexual rather than affirming that one already is so. "I am not sure we should create our *own* culture. We have to *create* a culture" (p. 164). Could such a quest lead to a way of life not based on social class and other existing divisions? One that could be shared among individuals of different ages, statuses, and so on? One that could "reopen affective and relational virtualities" (p. 138) and invent "the instruments for polymorphic, varied, and individually modulated relationships" (p. 139)? He thought this was possible; what needed to be problematized was the whole tissue of sociality. What was needed was not a means of making everyone the same but of creating new modes of being together.

Gays, Foucault told his interviewers, have come a long way in overcoming sexual renunciation, so perhaps they have an obligation, to themselves and to others, to invent "a homosexual ascesis," a manner of being that today seems improbable. Ascesis is "the work that one performs on oneself in order to transform oneself or make the self appear which, happily, one never attains. Can that be our problem today?" (p. 137). To make the self a continuous creative task, a social experience? For gays, the problem might be how "to make ourselves infinitely more susceptible to pleasure [*plaisirs*]. We must escape and help others to escape the two readymade formulas of the pure sexual encounter and the lovers' fusion of identities" (p. 137). Or, he asked in the same interview, "What is friendship?" His answer: "the sum of all those things through which [people] can give each other pleasure" (p. 136). A provocative answer, no doubt, but what he means by *pleasure* is not very well spelled out. A few things, however, can be said about his use of the term. First, he is opposing pleasure to desire, as surface to depth, as the body to the person. He is seeking to break open the equation of the forms of pleasure one enjoys and one's supposed identity. Second, his attention to pleasure does not entail embracing the doctrine of hedonism: pleasure is neither the unique nor the highest good but, rather, an accompaniment to other activities. Foucault's pleasure is embedded in a practice, an *askēsis*. One might say, it supervenes on other practices. For him, pleasure seems to function as a kind of ethical heuristic, in the sense that he suggests that where one encounters pleasures, one will be in the vicinity of experiences worthy of further reflection, experimentation, and reformulation.[42]

In another interview for a gay audience, Foucault insisted that gays should not privilege the model of individual rights or heterosexual marriage (that is, rights to inheritance and so on). As important as the struggles to obtain basic rights and legal protections for homosexuality were, Foucault argued, the real target was the general impoverishment of social relationships in contemporary society. Instead of treating the task as one of normalizing homosexuality in the heterosexual model, he urged his readers to try and invent something else. Such work, while arising within gay relationships, might be partially transposable to others, albeit with some imagination and tenacity. The problem, as he saw it, was to create new social forms: "We should fight against the impoverishment of the relational fabric" (p. 158). Why not imagine new practices (and eventually new forms of law) that were not restricted to individual rights but began from a premise of giving new forms to relational activities? This work is not only ethical, it is also political; but it is politics without a program.

TELOS: DISASSEMBLING THE SELF. *The place an action occupies in a pattern of conduct. It commits an individual…to a certain mode of being, a mode of being characteristic of the ethical subject.*—Foucault[43]

The mode of being to which Foucault was committed is captured in his ambiguous formula "to release oneself from one self" (*se déprendre de soi-même*). The difficulties of finding a correct translation for the phrase indicates some of the ambiguities that surround it. A falsely literal translation would be "to untake oneself, oneself"; but not only is this phrasing alien to English (and French), but if the goal were to "untake" oneself, how exactly had one previously "taken" (*prendre*) oneself? What self had one taken? And who had been doing the taking? The dictionary translation of *se déprendre* is to "free oneself,"[44] which captures the dimension of releasing oneself from a material entanglement. But "to free" obviously carries inappropriate philosophic baggage, for it implies a preexistent, essential, or true self already there to be freed. Another possibility might be "detaching oneself from one self." Although "detachment" can suggest (as it does for the Stoics) an emotional distancing from the things of the world, in English the phrase connotes an affectless noninvolvement. And, in fact, Foucault is pointing to a certain self-distancing, and he advocated an exercise of detaching and examining parts that need to be cared for and ultimately repaired or replaced. Thus, the most adequate (or least inadequate) rendering might well be "to disassemble the self, oneself"—a phrasing that highlights the material and relational aspects of this exercise, and introduces a notion of the self as a form-giving practice that operates with and upon heterogeneous parts and forms available at a given point in history.

Foucault reiterated that the goal—the mode of being—of ethics, as historically constrained, practical assembly and disassembly, when he asked: "But what then is philosophy—philosophical activity I mean—if it is not the critical work that thought brings to bear on itself? In what does it consist, if not in the endeavor to know how and to what extent it might be possible to think differently, instead of legitimating what is already known? [Thought] is entitled to explore what might be changed, through the practice of a knowledge that is foreign to it."[45]

Consequently, *se déprendre de soi-même* might be best understood as a form of continual self-*bricolage*.

Lévi-Strauss's classic description of the *bricoleur*, or "handyman," constantly tinkering with heterogeneous objects—objects in which there was no clear distinction between concrete thought, aesthetic form-giving, and a subject's material practice—is helpful up to a point. So, too, the *bricoleur*'s work on discarded and anonymous materials, reshaped and "customized" in a new way, seems apposite.[46] Foucault points at such a conception when he asserts that: "I insist that this change take the form neither of a sudden illumination that makes 'the scales fall from the eyes' nor an openness to every movement of the time. I would like it to be an elaboration of the self by the self, a studious transformation, a slow and arduous transformation through a constant care for the truth."[47] Of course, the constant focus on the self, the care for the truth, and its reflectiveness separates Foucault's ethics from the cultural constructions of the handyman.

But if we can indicate the way in which this activity should be engaged, the question of why we should do so remains. If Foucault was stingy in his explanations of the place and meaning of the "will to truth," he is only slightly more generous in providing material about the telos of his own thinking. There are, however, some scattered and suggestive indications. For example, he wonders, "What can the ethics of an intellectual be...if not...to render oneself permanently capable of self-detaching [*se déprendre de soi-même*] (which is the opposite of the attitude of conversion)?... To be at the same time an academic and an intellectual is to try to engage a type of knowledge and analysis that is taught and received in the university in a way so as to modify not only the thought of others but one's own as well. This work of modifying one's own thought and that of others seems to me to be the intellectual's reason for being."[48] Elsewhere: "After all, what would the value of the passion for knowledge be if it resulted only in a certain amount of knowledgeableness and not, in one way or another, and to the extent possible, in the knower straying afield from himself?"[49] The word he uses that is translated as "straying afield of oneself" is *égarement*.[50] The *Le Robert* dictionary gives the primary meaning of *égarement* as "an action of getting a distance from what is defined as morality, reason, and the norm, and the state that ensues." This definition has a certain resonance with Georges Canguilhem's conception of *errance*, to err, to wander, to stray from the norm. For Canguilhem, as one commentator put it, "We must move, err, adapt to survive. This condition of 'erring or drifting' is not merely accidental or external to life but its fundamental form."[51] Norms are active states; error is a condition of truth.

Disassembling the self suggests a modulated version of the second part of Lévi-Strauss's definition of *bricolage*, in fact the original meaning of the word, *un mouvement incident*, or a swerve. This "incidental movement" originally referred to the motion of a billiard ball caroming off a cushion, or a horse swerving to avoid an unexpected obstacle. Foucault's *égarement* is a slower and more meandering swerve, but nonetheless it is fair to take it as an unplanned, if reflective, avoidance or alteration of historical constituted obstacles, and as a patient disentanglement from the encumbrances of contingency. Foucault stresses the obligation to analyze historical forms that, with all their constraints and their diversity, make us what we are, and the patient labor required to reformulate them, fragment by fragment. In that work lies both the necessity and the pleasure of thought.

NOTES

1   For details, see Didier Eribon, *Michel Foucault*, (Cambridge, Mass.: Harvard University Press, 1991); the biography originally appeared in French in 1989.

2   Foucault has already defined these terms in great detail in two works: *The Archaeology of Knowledge*, (trans. A. M. Sheridan Smith |New York: Pantheon, 1972|) and *The Order of Things* (trans. Alan Sheridan |New York: Pantheon, 1972|), both of which preceded his nomination and election to the Collège de France. At the time of his lectures at the Collège, he was finishing "Nietzsche, Genealogy, History" (in *The Foucault Reader*, Rabinow, ed. |New York: Pantheon, 1984), an important statement of his understanding of these topics.

3   Foucault, "The Order of Discourse," trans. Rupert Sawyer, appendix to *The Archaeology of Knowledge* (New York: Pantheon, 1972), p. 229.

4   Idem.

5   Ibid., p. 217.

6   His use of *savoir* and *connaissance* also seems to be inconsistent in this text.

7   Again, Foucault at times distinguishes between *savoir* and *connaissance* but he seems not to do so with any great consistency.

8   Foucault, "Two Lectures," in Colin Gordon, ed., *Power/Knowledge* (New York: Pantheon, 1972), · p. 78.

9   Ibid., p. 91.

10 Idem. The English translation has "repression," but that is a confusion.

11 Ibid., p. 92.

12 *The History of Sexuality*, vol. 1: *An Introduction* (New York: Pantheon, 1978), p. 7.

13 Ibid., p. 159.

14 In a 1978 lecture, Foucault emphatically stated that these technologies did not simply replace one another, as one epoch supersedes another: "We need to see things not in terms of the replacement of a society of sovereignty by a disciplinary society by a society of governmentality, in reality one has a triangle, sovereignty-discipline-governmentality." Foucault, "Governmentality," in *The Foucault Effect: Studies in Governmentality*, Burchall, Gordon, Miller, eds. (Chicago: University of Chicago Press, 1991), p. 102.

15 Foucault, "Pour une morale de l'inconfort," in *Dits et écrits* (Paris: Gallimard, 1994), vol. 3, p. 784.

16 Idem.

17 Ibid., p. 787.

18 Foucault, "Des Travaux," in *Dits et écrits*, vol. 4, p. 367.

19 "Pour une Morale," p. 786.

20 Idem.

21 Foucault, "Iran: The Spirit of a World without Spirit," in *Michel Foucault: Politics, Philosophy, Culture*, Lawrence Kritzman, ed. (New York and London: Routledge, 1988), p. 214.

22 Ibid., p. 218.

23 Foucault, "A quoi rêvent les Iraniens?" in *Dits et écrits*, vol. 3, p. 694.

24 Cf. Didier Eribon, *Michel Foucault et ses contemporains* (Paris: 1995).

25 *The History of Sexuality*, vol. 2: *The Uses of Pleasure* (New York: Pantheon, 1985), p. 29.

26 Ibid., p. 28.

27 "Le retour de la morale," in *Dits et écrits*, vol. 4, p. 698.

28 *The History of Sexuality*, vol. 2, p. 26.

29 "Nietzsche, Genealogy, History," p. 162.

30 Ibid., p. 164.

31 "The Order of Discourse," p. 218.

32 *History of Sexuality*, vol. 2, p. x.

33 Ibid., p. 8.

34 Ibid., p. 9.

35 Friedrich Nietzsche, *The Gay Science*, trans. Walter Kaufmann (New York: Vintage, 1974), pp. 281–82.

36 *History of Sexuality*, vol. 2, p. 27.

37 Gilles Deleuze makes a point in many ways similar to this in *Foucault* (Minneapolis: University of Minnesota, 1988), pp. 94–123.

38 The term *transgression* appears only twice in all of *Dits et écrits*, vol. 4, and then only as historical examples.

39 *History of Sexuality*, vol. 2, p. 27.

40 Ibid., p. 10.

41 Ibid., p. 11.

42 I would like to thank James Faubion for the notion of an "ethical heuristic."

43 *History of Sexuality*, vol. 2, p. 28.

44 *Harrap's New Collegiate French and English Dictionary* (London: Harraps, 1982).

45 *History of Sexuality*, vol. 2, p. 9.

46 I would like to thank Robert Hurley for suggesting "customize" as a helpful gloss.

47 Foucault, "The Concern for Truth" in *Foucault Live* (New York: Semiotext(e), 1996), p. 461.

48 Idem.

49 *History of Sexuality*, vol. 2, p. 8.

50 I would like to thank Arpad Szakoloczai for bringing this word to my attention.

51 François Delaporte, ed., *A Vital Rationalist: Selected Writings from Georges Canguilhem* (New York: Zone Books, 1994), pp. 20–21.

NOTE ON TERMS AND TRANSLATIONS

This volume comprises texts written and published over a range of nearly two decades. A few were originally published in English. Several others have already been translated into English. The majority, however, appear in English here for the first time. The last category, which includes all the course summaries, and "Self Writing" are due to Robert Hurley, a distinguished translator of twentieth-century French social thought and the translator in particular of the second and third volumes of Foucault's *History of Sexuality*.

As a matter of principle, the editorial hand has been exercised lightly. Texts originally in English are accordingly subject to mechanical, but only to the most compelling stylistic, emendations. Translations are another, and more complex, matter. With only a few exceptions, extant translations have proved to be of sufficient quality to merit reprinting. Even so, they vary in any number of ways with their translators. Even the most polished of translations is, moreover, far from timeless. Certain words and phrases become standard at the cost that others become misleading or seem strange. Certain early words or phrases, certain early lexical distinctions emerge as crucial only in the light of the later oeuvre. Initially unexceptionable glosses emerge as controversial only in the light of retrospective discussion and debate.

James Faubion's review of the available translations was undertaken with such problems in mind. His emendations are of several different sorts. The first sort seeks to highlight or clarify Foucault's usage by inserting French terms in brackets after their English glosses (when the translator has not himself or herself inserted them). Such terms are relatively rare, but worth noting in advance. One is *épistémè*. It appears in English as "episteme"—an inevitable coinage, but a misleading one insofar as it conjures associations with such apparent cognates as "phoneme" or "lexeme." *Epistémè* is rather a transliteration of the Greek ἐπιστήμη, "science" or "systematic understanding" of a conceptual domain, or of an art or craft. The least troublesome of them is *savoir*, which can usually be glossed straightforwardly as "knowledge" (or in its verbal form, "to know"). Much more troublesome is *connaissance* and its related verb *connaître*. *Connaissance* can also frequently be glossed as "knowledge"—indeed, sometimes must be, even when its usage is not synonymous with *savoir*. English has no consistent way of registering the difference between that sort of knowledge that derives from "acquaintance" or familiarity with someone or something (*connaissance*) and that which is, or may be, purely "theoretical" or abstract (*savoir*). The lack of a register is all the more troublesome because Foucault's usage sometimes suggests that the distinction between *connaissance* and *savoir* is analytically pivotal. A more extended discussion of the distinction must, however, be reserved for Faubion's introduction to the second volume of the series.

Faubion has also undertaken a variety of more direct editorial interventions, more or fewer from one available translation to the next. In some cases, he corrects what seems to be an obvious error. In many others, however, he merely seeks to render more literally or more to the letter what the translator has rendered more freely or inventively. In general, his corrections have the purpose of clarifying the semantic content—in some cases, the semantic ambiguity—of assertions that allow of diverse English representations. In a few cases, he has appended footnotes (marked by lower-case Roman letters) that elaborate upon the context of some remark or allusion. Finally, he has standardized the gloss and the spelling of a few words and phrases that take on special thematic significance as Foucault's thought unfolds. Foucault himself sometimes writes of *problémisation*, sometimes of *problématisation*, but with no alteration of meaning from one instance to the next. Translations preserve the variation in English. In this volume, however, we render both terms throughout as *problematization* (after *problematic*). Especially in early translations, *asujettissement* is often brought into English as "subjugation," and its related verb, *asujettir*, as "to subjugate." Here, however, we opt for a neologism that signals Foucault's technical, and more positive, usage. Hence, *asujettissement* consistently appears as "subjectivation"; and *asujettir*, as "to subjectify." *Le souci de soi* might be—and has been—translated into English as "concern for" or "concern with the self," or as "self-concern." In this volume, however, it has consistently been rendered as "the care of the self."

Faubion has made virtually no changes to Robert Hurley's own translations. He was, however, able to review a draft of those translations, and to provide a list of questions and annotations that Hurley considered in the course of making revisions. Hurley reciprocally provided Faubion with linguistic analyses and editorial advice. It is hoped that the result is a volume that might, among other things, go far in clarifying many of those aspects of Foucault's modes of expression and thought that have been lost or obscured, if not within single translations then often enough between them.

PART ONE

THE COURSES

———

PREVIOUS WORK

In the *Histoire de la folie à l'âge classique*,[a] I tried to determine what might be known about mental illness in a given epoch. A knowledge of this sort is manifested, of course, in the medical theories that name and classify the different pathological types and attempt to explain them; one also sees it appearing in phenomena of opinion—in that old fear which madmen give rise to, in the operation of the credulities that surround them, in the way they are depicted in the theater or in literature. Here and there, analyses done by historians could serve me as guides. Yet one dimension appeared to be unexplored: I needed to try to discover how the mad were recognized, set apart, excluded from society, interned, and treated; what institutions were assigned to receive and hold them—care for them at times; what authorities decided about their madness, and according to what criteria; what methods were employed to constrain them, punish them, or cure them; in short, in what network of institutions and practices the madman was both enmeshed and defined. Now, this network appears very coherent and well adapted to its purpose when one looks at its functioning and the justifications it was given at the time: a whole exact and articulated knowledge was involved in it. So an object took shape for me: the knowledge invested in complex institutional systems. And a method asserted itself: instead of running through the library of scientific literature, as one was apt to do, and stopping at that, I would need to examine a collection of archives comprising official orders, statutes, hospital or prison records, court proceedings, and so on. It was at the Arsenal and the

Archives Nationales that I undertook the analysis of a knowledge whose visible body is not theoretical or scientific discourse, nor literature either, but a regulated, everyday practice. The example of madness appeared to me, however, to be insufficiently topical; in the seventeenth and eighteenth centuries, psychopathology was still too rudimentary for one to be able to distinguish it from a mere elaboration of traditional opinions; it seemed to me that clinical medicine at the time of its birth posed the problem in more rigorous terms; indeed, at the beginning of the nineteenth century it was connected with constituted sciences or ones in the process of being constituted, such as biology, physiology, and pathological anatomy; but it was also connected with a set of institutions such as hospitals, welfare services, and teaching clinics, as well as with practices such as administrative surveys. I wondered how, between these two reference points, a knowledge could have come into being, transformed itself and developed, offering to scientific theory new fields of observation, fresh problems, and objects unperceived until then; but how, on the other hand, scientific knowledge [*des connaissances scientifiques*] had been introduced into it, had taken on a prescriptive value and become a source of ethical standards. The practice of medicine is not limited to combining a rigorous science and an uncertain tradition to form an unstable blend; it is built as a knowledge system that has its own balance and coherence.

So one could grant the existence of domains of knowledge that were not exactly identifiable with sciences yet were not just mental habits either. Thus, in *Les Mots et les choses*[b] I tried an opposite experiment: neutralize the whole practical and institutional side but without giving up the idea of going back to it one day; consider, for a given period, several of these domains of knowledge (natural classifications, general grammar, and the analysis of wealth in the seventeenth and eighteenth centuries) and examine them in turn to define the type of problems they raise, of concepts they bring into play, the theories they put to the test. Not only could one define the internal "archaeology" of each of these domains taken one by one, but from one to the other there were discernible identities, analogies, sets of differences that must be described. An overall configuration emerged. To be sure, it was far from characterizing the classical mind in general, but it organized in a coherent way a whole area of empirical knowledge.

I was thus presented with two very distinct groups of results: on the one hand, I had established the specific and relatively autonomous existence of "vested knowledges"; on the other, I had noted systematic relations in the architecture peculiar to each one of them. A clarification became necessary. I outlined it in *L'Archéologie du savoir*[c]: between opinion and science [*connaissance scientifique*] one can recognize the existence of a particular level that we may call the level of knowledge [*savoir*]. This knowledge is embodied not only in theoretical texts or empirical instruments but also in a whole set of practices and institutions; however, it is not the pure and simple result, the half-conscious expression, of these. In point of fact, it comprises rules that properly belong to it, characterizing its existence, its operation, and its history. Some of these rules are peculiar to a single domain, others are common to several; and there are rules that may be general to a whole epoch. Finally, the development of this knowledge [*savoir*] and its transformations involve complex relations of causality.

TEACHING PROJECT

The work to come is subject to two imperatives: never lose sight of the reference of a concrete example that may serve as a testing ground for the analysis; frame the problems that I have come across or will no doubt encounter.

1. The sector chosen as a privileged example, which I will adhere to for a certain time, is the knowledge of heredity. It developed throughout the nineteenth century, starting from breeding techniques, on through attempts to improve species, experiments with intensive cultivation, efforts to combat animal and plant epidemics, and culminating in the establishment of a genetics whose birth date can be placed at the beginning of the twentieth century. On the one hand, this knowledge responded to quite particular economic needs and historical conditions. Changes in the dimensions and forms of cultivation of rural properties, in the equilibrium of markets, in the required standards of profitability, and in the system of colonial agriculture deeply transformed this knowledge; they altered not only the nature of its information but also its quantity and scale. On the other hand, this knowledge was receptive to new developments in sciences such as chemistry or plant and animal physiology. (Witness the use of nitrate fertilizer or the technique of hybridization, which had been made possible by the theory of plant fertilization, defined in the eighteenth century.) But this dual dependence does not deprive it of its characteristics and its inter-

nal regulation. It gave rise both to adapted techniques (such as those of Vilmorin for species improvement) and epistemologically productive concepts (such as that of hereditary trait, explained in detail if not defined by Naudin). Darwin was not mistaken when he found in this human practice the model enabling him to understand the natural evolution of species.

2. As for the theoretical problems that will have to be worked out, it seems to me that they can be assembled into three groups.

It will be necessary first to try to assign a status to this knowledge: where to place it, between what boundaries, and what tools to select for describing it. (In the example I've put forward, one sees that the material is enormous, going from almost silent habits transmitted by tradition to duly transcribed experimentations and precepts.) It will also be necessary to try to identify its instruments and its channels of dissemination, and to see whether it spread evenly through all the social groups and all the areas. Lastly, it will be necessary to try to determine the different levels of such a knowledge, its degrees of consciousness, its possibilities of adjustment and correction. Thus, the theoretical problem that appears is that of an anonymous social knowledge [*savoir*] which does not take individual conscious learning [*connaissance*] as a model or foundation.

Another group of problems has to do with the elaboration of this knowledge into a scientific discourse. In a sense, these crossings, these transformations, and these thresholds constitute the genesis of a science. But instead of seeking—as was done in certain projects of the phenomenological type—the primary origin of a science, its fundamental project, and its root conditions of possibility, I will try to witness the insidious and manifold beginnings of a science. It is sometimes possible to rediscover and date the decisive text that constitutes a science's birth certificate and its initial charter, so to speak (in the domain that I will use as my example, the texts of Naudin, Mendel, De Vries, or Morgan may claim this role by turns); but the important thing is to determine what transformation must have been carried out prior to them, around them, or in them for a knowledge to be able to take on the status and function of a science. In short, this is the theoretical problem of the constitution of a science when one aims to analyze it not in transcendental terms but in terms of history.

The third group of problems concerns causality in the order of knowledge. General correlations between events and discoveries, or between economic necessities and the development of a domain of knowledge, have been established for a long time, of course. (We know, for example, how important the great plant epidemics of the nineteenth century were in the study of varieties, of their adaptive capacity and their stability.) But we need to determine much more precisely how—by what channels and according to what codes—knowledge registers (not without choice or modification) phenomena that had remained exterior to it up to that point; how it becomes receptive to processes that are foreign to it; how, finally, an alteration that occurred in one of its areas or at one of its levels can be transmitted elsewhere and take effect there.

The analysis of these three groups of problems should bring knowledge to light in its threefold appearance: it characterizes, groups together, and coordinates a set of practices and institutions; it is the constantly shifting locus of the constitution of sciences; it is the constituent element of a complex causality in which the history of science is caught up. To the extent that, in a given period, it has clearly specified forms and domains, it can be broken down into several systems of thought. Obviously, it is by no means a matter of determining *the* system of thought of a particular epoch, or something like its "worldview." Rather, it is a matter of identifying the different ensembles that are each bearers of a quite particular type of knowledge; that connect behaviors, rules of conduct, laws, habits, or prescriptions; that thus form configurations both stable and capable of transformation. It is also a matter of defining relations of conflict, proximity, or exchange. Systems of thought are forms in which, during a given period of time, the knowledges [*savoirs*] individualize, achieve an equilibrium, and enter into communication.

In its most general formulation, the problem I have encountered bears some analogy, perhaps, with that which philosophy raised a few decades ago. Between a reflexive tradition of pure consciousness and an empiricism of sensation, philosophy gave itself the task of finding not the genesis, not the connection, not even the surface of contact, but a third dimension, that of perception and the body. Today, the history of thought requires, perhaps, a readjustment of the same order: between the constituted sciences (whose history has often been written) and the phenomena of opinion (which historians know how to deal with), it would be necessary to undertake the history of systems of thought. By bringing out the specificity of knowledge [*savoir*] in this way, one not only defines a level of analysis that has been overlooked up to now, but one might well be forced to reexamine knowledge [*connaissance*], its conditions, and the status of the knowing subject.

NOTES

a   *Madness and Civilization: A History of Insanity in the Age of Reason*, trans. Richard Howard (New York: Vintage, 1973), is an abridged translation of the work that Foucault cites.

b   *The Order of Things: An Archaeology of the Human Sciences* (New York: Vintage, 1973).

c   *The Archaeology of Knowledge*, trans. A. M. Sheridan Smith (New York: Harper Colophon, 1972).

———

This year's course begins a series of analyses that attempt to piece together, fragment by fragment, a "morphology of the will to knowledge." Sometimes this theme of the will to knowledge will be invested in specific historical inquiries; sometimes it will be treated for itself and in its theoretical implications.

The aim this year was to determine its place and define its role in a history of systems of thought; to decide, at least provisionally, upon an initial model of analysis, and to test its effectiveness on a first batch of examples.

1. Previous research had made it possible to recognize a peculiar level among all those which enable one to analyze systems of thought—that of discursive practices. There one finds a type of systematicity which is neither logical nor linguistic. Discursive practices are characterized by the demarcation of a field of objects, by the definition of a legitimate perspective for a subject of knowledge, by the setting of norms for elaborating concepts and theories. Hence, each of them presupposes a play of prescriptions that govern exclusions and selections.

Now, these sets of regularities do not coincide with individual works. Even if they are manifested through the latter, even if they happen to stand out, for the first time, in one of them, they extend well beyond such works and often group together a considerable number of them. But neither do they coincide necessarily with what are usually called "sciences" or "disciplines," although their boundaries may sometimes be provisionally the same. More often, it happens that a discursive practice brings together various disciplines or sciences, or it passes through a number of them and gathers several of their areas into a sometimes-inconspicuous cluster.

Discursive practices are not purely and simply modes of manufacture of discourse. They take shape in technical ensembles, in institutions, in behavioral schemes, in types of transmission and dissemination, in pedagogical forms that both impose and maintain them.

Finally, they have specific modes of transformation. One cannot reduce these transformations to a precise individual discovery; and yet one cannot merely characterize them as an overall change of outlook [*mentalité*], of collective attitude or state of mind. The transformation of a discursive practice is tied to a whole, often quite complex set of modifications which may occur either outside it (in the forms of production, in the social relations, in the political institutions), or within it (in the techniques for determining objects, in the refinement and adjustment of concepts, in the accumulation of data), or alongside it (in other discursive practices). And it is linked to them in the form not simply of an outcome but of an effect that maintains its own autonomy and a set of precise functions relative to what determines the transformation.

These principles of exclusion and selection—whose presence is multifarious, whose efficacy is concretely demonstrated in practices, and whose transformations are relatively autonomous—do not refer to a (historical or transcendental) subject of knowledge that would invent them one after another or would found them at an original level; they point, rather, to an anonymous and polymorphous will to knowledge, capable of regular transformations and caught up in an identifiable play of dependence.

Empirical studies, dealing with psychopathology, with clinical medicine, with natural history, and so on, had made it possible to isolate the level of discursive practices. The general features of these practices and the appropriate methods for analyzing them had been inventoried under the name of archaeology. Research concerning the will to knowledge should now be able to give a theoretical justification to this ensemble. For the moment, one can indicate in a very general way the directions in which it will need to advance, involving the distinction between knowledge [*savoir*] and learning [*connaissance*]; the difference between the will to knowledge [*savoir*] and the will to truth [*vérité*]; the position of the subject, or subjects, with respect to that will.

2. Few conceptual tools for analyzing the will to knowledge have

been developed up to now. Most of the time, rather crude notions are used. "Anthropological" or psychological notions: curiosity, the need to master or appropriate through learning [*connaissance*], anguish in the face of the unknown, reactions to the threats of the undifferentiated. Historical generalities, like the spirit of an epoch, its sensibility, its types of interest, its conception of the world, its system of values, its basic needs. Philosophical themes such as that of a horizon of rationality which becomes explicit through time. Nothing, finally, allows one to think that the still quite rudimentary formulations of psychoanalysis on the position of the subject and the object in desire and knowledge might be imported unaltered into the field of historical studies. No doubt, it must be admitted that the instruments enabling us to analyze the will to knowledge will have to be made up and defined as we go along, according to the requirements and possibilities that are revealed by concrete studies.

The history of philosophy offers theoretical models of this will to knowledge, and analysis of them may enable us to get our bearings. Among all those who will need to be studied and tested (Plato, Spinoza, Schopenhauer, Aristotle, Nietzsche, and so on), the last two were selected first and studied this year, seeing that they constitute two extreme and opposite forms.

The Aristotelian model has been analyzed essentially on the basis of the texts of the *Metaphysics*, the *Nichomachean Ethics*, and *De Anima*.[1] It is brought to bear starting at the level of sensation. It establishes:

- a link between sensation and pleasure;

- the independence of this link with regard to the vital usefulness sensation can entail;

- a direct ratio between the intensity of pleasure and the quantity of knowledge delivered by the sensation;

- the incompatibility between the truth of pleasure and the error of sensation.

Visual perception, as a remote sensing of multiple objects which are given simultaneously and are not immediately related to the usefulness of the body, manifests the link between knowledge, pleasure, and truth in the satisfaction it carries. This same relationship is found again, transposed to the other extreme, in the happiness of theoretical contemplation. The desire to know, which the first lines of the *Metaphysics* posit as both universal and natural, is based on that primary belonging which sensation already manifests.[2] And it is this desire which ensures the continuous passage from that first type of knowledge to the ultimate type expressed in philosophy. In Aristotle, the desire to know presupposes and transposes the prior relationship of knowledge, truth, and pleasure.

In *The Gay Science*, Nietzsche defines an altogether different set of relations:

- knowledge is an "invention"[3] behind which there is something quite distinct from it: an interplay of instincts, impulses, desires, fear, will to appropriation. It is on the stage where they clash that knowledge comes into being;

- it arises not as an effect of their harmony, of their successful equilibrium, but of their hatred, of their dubious and provisional compromise, of a fragile pact they are always prepared to betray. It is not a permanent faculty; it is an event or at least a series of events;

- it is always servile, dependent, alert to advantages (not to its own, but to what might interest the instinct or instincts that dominate it);

- and if it professes to be a knowledge of the truth, this is because it produces the truth through the action of a primordial and renewed falsification that establishes the distinction between the true and the untrue.

Interest is thus posited radically prior to the knowledge that it subordinates as a mere instrument; the dissociated knowledge of pleasure and happiness is linked to strife, aversion, and malevolence exerted against themselves to the point of renouncing themselves through a supplement of strife, aversion, and malevolence; its original link to truth is undone, since in it truth is only an effect—an effect, moreover, of a falsification that calls itself opposition of the true and the untrue. This model of a fundamentally interested knowledge, produced as an event of the will and determining the effect of truth through falsification, is doubtless as far as it could be from the postulates of classical metaphysics. It is the one that has been freely adapted and used, in this year's course, with regard to a series of examples.

3. This series of examples was borrowed from archaic Greek history and institutions. They all belong to the domain of justice. It was a matter of following a development that occurred from the seventh to the fifth centuries. This transformation concerns the administration of justice, the concept of the just, and social reactions to crime.

Studied in turn were:

• the practice of the oath in judicial disputes and the evolution that goes from the defiance oath of litigants exposing themselves to the vengeance of the gods to the assertoric oath of the witness who is supposed to affirm what is true from having seen it and been present to it;

• the search for a just measure not only in commercial exchanges but in social relations inside the city-state, through the institution of money;

• the search for a *nomos*, a just law of distribution ensuring the order of the city-state by making an order reign therein which is the order of the world.

• the rituals of purification after killings.

During the whole period under consideration, the distribution of justice was the focus of significant political struggles. They ultimately gave rise to a form of justice linked to a knowledge [*savoir*] in which truth was posited as visible, easily established, obedient to laws like those governing the order of the world, and whose discovery holds a purificatory value for oneself. This type of affirmation of truth was to be decisive in the history of Western knowledge.

This year's seminar was generally confined to the study of penality in France in the nineteenth century. It dealt this year with the first developments of a penal psychiatry in the period of the Restoration. The material used was largely the text of the medico-legal experts' opinions submitted by the contemporaries and disciples of Esquirol.

NOTES

1 Aristotle, *Métaphysique*, trans. J. Tricot (Paris: Vrin, 1956); *Éthique à Nicomaque*, trans. J. Tricot (Paris: Vrin, 1959); *De l'Ame*, trans. E. Barbotin (Paris: Belles Lettres, 1966).

2 Aristotle, *Métaphysique*, trans. J. Tricot (Paris: Vrin, 1956). [Aristotle, *Metaphysics*, A.I.980a21: "All men by nature desire to know. An indication of this is the delight we take in our senses; for even apart from their usefulness they are loved for themselves; and above all others the sense of sight," in *The Basic Works of Aristotle*, Richard McKeon, ed. (New York: Random House, 1941), p. 689.]

3 F. Nietzsche, *Die fröliche Wissenschaft* (Chemnitz, 1882); the subtitle *La Gaya scienza* does not appear until the edition of 1887 (*Le Gai Savoir*, trans. P. Klossowski, in *Oeuvres philosophiques complètes* [Paris: Gallimard, 1967], vol. 5) [*The Gay Science*, trans. Walter Kaufmann (New York: Vintage, 1974)].

PENAL THEORIES AND INSTITUTIONS

———

This year's course was meant to serve as a historical preliminary to the study of penal institutions (more generally, of social controls and punitive systems) in French society of the nineteenth century. That study itself fits within a broader project, outlined the previous year: to trace the formation of certain types of knowledge [*savoir*] out of the juridico-political matrices that gave birth to them and act as their support. The working hypothesis is this: power relations (together with the struggles that traverse them or the institutions that maintain them) do not simply play a facilitating or obstructing role with respect to knowledge; they do not merely encourage or stimulate it, distort or restrict it; power and knowledge are not bound to each other solely through the action of interests and ideologies; so the problem is not just to determine how power subordinates knowledge and makes it serve its ends or how it superimposes itself on it, imposing ideological contents and limitations. No knowledge is formed without a system of communication, registration, accumulation, and displacement that is in itself a form of power, linked in its existence and its functioning to other forms of power. No power, on the other hand, is exercised without the extraction, appropriation, distribution, or restraint of a knowledge. At this level there is not knowledge [*connaissance*] on one side and society on the other, or science and the state, but the basic forms of "power-knowledge" ["*pouvoir-savoir*"].

Measure [*mesure*] had been studied, the previous year, as a form of "power-knowledge" tied to the construction of the Greek city-state. This year the *inquiry* was studied in the same manner as it related to the formation of the medieval state; next year the *examination* will be considered, as a form of power-knowledge linked to systems of control, exclusion, and punishment characteristic of industrial societies. In their historical formation, *measure, inquiry*, and *examination* were all means of exercising power and, at the same time, rules for establishing knowledge. *Measure*: a means of establishing or restoring order, the right order, in the combat of men or the elements; but also a matrix of mathematical and physical knowledge. The *inquiry*: a means of establishing or restoring facts, events, actions, properties, rights; but also a matrix of empirical knowledge and natural sciences. The *examination*: a means of setting or reinstating the standard, the rule, the distribution, the qualification, the exclusion; but also a matrix of all the psychologies, sociologies, psychiatries—in short, of what is called the "human sciences." To be sure, *measure, inquiry*, and *examination* are brought into play simultaneously in many scientific practices, as so many pure and simple methods or strictly controlled instruments. It is also true that at this level and in this role they are detached from their relationship with the forms of power. Before appearing together, in this clarified form, inside definite epistemological domains, they were connected to a setting in place of a political power; they were both its effect and its instrument, serving a function of order in the case of *measure*, of centralization in the case of the *inquiry*, of selection and exclusion in the case of the *examination*.

So the course for the year 1971–1972 was divided into two parts.

The first was devoted to studying the *inquiry* and its development during the Middle Ages. Special attention was given to the conditions of its emergence in the domain of penal practice. A transition from the system of revenge to that of punishment; from accusatory practice to inquisitory practice; from the injury that provokes the litigation to the infraction that determines the prosecution; from the decision upon testing to the judgment upon proof; from the combat that designates the victor and shows the just cause to the official report that establishes the fact by relying on the evidence. This whole set of transformations is tied to the birth of a State that tends to take stricter and stricter control of the administration of penal justice; and this insofar as the functions of maintaining order become concentrated in its hands and as the fiscalization of justice by the feudal system has inserted judicial practice in the great circuits of transfer of wealth. The judicial form of the *inquiry* was perhaps borrowed from what remained of the forms of

Carolingian administration; but much more surely from models of ecclesiastical administration and control. To this set of practices belong: the questions characteristic of the inquiry (Who did what? Is the act publicly known? Who saw it and can testify about it? What is the evidence, what are the proofs? Is there a confession?); the phases of the inquiry (the one that establishes the facts, the one that determines the guilty party, the one that establishes the circumstances of the act); the characters of the inquiry (the one who prosecutes, the one who accuses, the one who denies or admits; the one who must judge and make the decision). This judicial model of the *inquiry* rests on a whole system of power; it is this system that defines what must be constituted as knowledge; how, from whom, and by whom it is extracted; in what manner it moves about and is transmitted; at what point it accumulates and gives rise to a judgment or a decision.

This "inquisitorial" model, displaced and gradually transformed, will constitute, starting in the fourteenth century, one of the factors that shapes the empirical sciences. The inquiry, connected with experimentation and voyage or not, but strongly opposed to the authority of tradition and to the decision of the symbolic text, will be utilized in scientific practices (magnetism, for example, or natural history), theorized in methodological reflection (Bacon, that administrator), transposed into discursive types (the *inquiry* as opposed to the *essay*, the *meditation*, the *treatise*). We belong to an inquisitorial civilization that, for centuries now, practices, according to forms of varying complexity but all derived from the same model, the extraction, displacement, and accumulation of knowledge. The inquisition: a form of power-knowledge essential to our society. The truth of experience is a daughter of the inquisition—of the political, administrative, judicial power to ask questions, extract answers, collect testimonies, verify assertions, establish facts—just as the truth of measures and proportions was a daughter of *Dikē*. A day came, quite early, when empiricism forgot and covered over its beginning. *Pudenda origo*. It set the serenity of the inquiry against the tyranny of the inquisition, disinterested learning [*connaissance*] against the passion of the inquisitorial system; and, in the name of the truths of experience, that system was blamed for giving birth, in its tortures, to the demons it claimed to be driving out; but the inquisition was only one—and for a long time the most perfected one—of the forms of the inquisitorial system that is one of the most important political matrices of our knowledge.

The other part of the course was devoted to the emergence, in sixteenth-century France, of new forms of social controls. The massive practice of confinement, the development of the police apparatus, the supervision of populations prepared for the construction of a new type of power-knowledge which would take the form of the examination. A study of this new type, of the functions and forms that it took in the nineteenth century, will be undertaken in the course for the year 1972–1973.

In the Monday seminar we continued the study of medico-legal practices and concepts of the nineteenth century. One case was singled out for a detailed analysis and a subsequent publication.

Pierre Rivière, a little-known murderer of the nineteenth century: at the age of twenty he had slaughtered his mother, his brother, and his sister; after his arrest, he had written a memoir that was handed over to his judges and to the doctors charged with preparing a psychiatric report. Rivière's statement, partially published in 1836 in a medical journal, was rediscovered in its entirety by Jean-Pierre Peter, along with most of the documents from the dossier. It is this set that was prepared for publication, with the participation of Robert Castel, Gilles Deleuze, Alexandre Fontana, Jean-Pierre Peter, Phillippe Riot, and Maryvonne Saison.

Among all the dossiers of penal psychiatry that we have at our disposal, this one captured our attention for various reasons: the existence, certainly, of the statement written by the murderer, a young Norman peasant who seemed to be regarded by his entourage as bordering on imbecility; the content of that statement (the first part is taken up with an extremely meticulous account of all the contracts, conflicts, arrangements, promises, breaks that managed to bind together the families of his father and mother or set them at odds, beginning with their marriage plan—a remarkable document of peasant ethnology; in the second part of his text, Pierre Rivière explains the "reasons" for his act); the relatively detailed deposition of the witnesses, all of them inhabitants of the hamlet, giving their impressions concerning the "oddities" of Pierre Rivière; a series of psychiatric reports representing each of the well-defined strata of medical knowledge: one was drafted by a country doctor, another by a physician from Caen, others by the great Parisian psychiatrists of the day (Esquirol, Orfila, and so on); the date, finally, of the event (the beginning of criminological psychiatry, great public debates between psychiatrists and jurists about the concept of monomania, the extension of mitigating circumstances in judicial practice, the publication of Lacenaire's *Mémoires* and the appearance of the great criminal in literature).

THE PUNITIVE SOCIETY

In the penal system of the Classical period, one reencounters, mixed together, four great forms of punitive tactics—four forms having different historical origins, each having played if not an exclusive role then a privileged one:

1. exile, cast out, banish, expel beyond the borders, forbid certain places, destroy the home, obliterate the birthplace, confiscate the possessions and properties;

2. arrange a compensation, impose a redemption, convert the damage caused into a debt to repay, turn the offense into a financial obligation;

3. expose, mark, wound, amputate, make a scar, stamp a sign on the face or the shoulder, impose an artificial and visible handicap, torture—in short, seize hold of the body and inscribe upon it the marks of power;

4. confine.

As a hypothesis we may distinguish, in terms of the types of punishment they privileged, banishment societies (Greek society), redemption societies (Germanic societies), marking societies (Western societies at the end of the Middle Ages), and confinement societies—our own?

Ours, but only since the end of the eighteenth century. For one thing is certain: detention and imprisonment do not form part of the European penal system before the great reforms of the years 1780–1820. The jurists of the eighteenth century are unanimous on this point: "Prison is not regarded as a penalty according to our civil law...although the princes, for reasons of State, sometimes go so far as to inflict this penalty, these are decisive blows, and civil courts do not make use of these kinds of sentences" (Serpillon, *Code criminel*, 1767).[1] But it can already be said that such an insistence on denying that imprisonment has any penal character indicates a growing uncertainty. In any case, the confinements that are practiced in the seventeenth and eighteenth century remain on the fringe of the penal system, even if they are close by and drawing ever closer.

- surety confinement, employed by the courts during the investigation of a criminal matter, by the creditor until repayment of the debt, or by the royal power when it fears an enemy. This is not so much a matter of punishing an offense as of making sure of a person.

- substitute confinement, imposed on someone who doesn't come under criminal justice (either because of the nature of his offenses, which are only moral or behavioral in nature; or due to a privileged status: the ecclesiastical courts, which since 1629 no longer have the right to pass prison sentences in the strict sense, may order the guilty to withdraw to a monastery; the *lettre de cachet* is often a means for the privileged to escape criminal justice; women are sent to houses of detention for mistakes that men will pay for on the convict ships).

It should be noted, except in this last case, that this substitute confinement is characterized in general by the fact that it is not decided by judicial authority, that its duration is not set once and for all, and that it depends on a hypothetical purpose—correction. Punishment rather than penalty.

Now, fifty years or so after the great monuments of Classical criminal law (Serpillon, Jousse,[2] Muyart de Vouglans[3]), prison became the general form of penality.

In 1831, Rémusat, in a speech to the Chamber, said: "What is the penal system authorized by the new law? It is incarceration in all its forms. Compare in fact the four main penalties that remain in the Penal Code. Forced labor is a form of incarceration. Penal servitude is an open-air prison. Detention, hard labor, and correctional imprisonment are in a way just different names for the same act of punishment."[4] And Van Meenen, opening the Third Penitentiary Conference at Brussels, recalled the time of his youth when the land was still covered with "wheels, gibbets, gallows, and pillories," with "skeletons hideously spread."[5] It looks as if prison, parapenal punishment, had, at the end of the eighteenth century, made its entry into penal practice and had very quickly occupied the entire space. The Austrian Criminal Code, drafted under Joseph II, offers the most obvious evidence of this immediately triumphant invasion.

The organization of a penal system of confinement is not simply recent, it is enigmatic.

At the very time of its planning, it was the object of vehement criticism—criticism formulated in terms of basic principles; but also formulated with a view to the dysfunctions that prison might induce in the penal system and in society as a whole.

1. Prison prevents judicial authority from supervising and verifying the application of penalties. The law does not penetrate into the prisons, said Decazes in 1818.

2. Prison, by intermingling convicts who are both different and isolated, forms a homogeneous community of criminals who become comrades in confinement and who will remain such on the outside. Prison manufactures a veritable army of domestic enemies.

3. By giving convicts shelter, food, clothing, and often work, prison provides them with a condition preferable at times to that of workers. Not only may it fail to have a disuasive effect, but it fosters delinquency.

4. Leaving prison are people who are doomed by their habits and by the infamy with which they are stamped to a life of crime.

Right away, then, prison is denounced as an instrument that, in the margins of justice, manufactures those whom that justice will send or send back to prison. The carceral circle is clearly denounced as early as the years 1815–1830. To this criticism there were three successive replies:

- imagine an alternative to prison which retains its positive effects (the segregation of criminals, their removal from circulation in society) and eliminates its dangerous consequences (their return to circulation). One will take up the old system of transport, which the British had suspended at the time of the War of Independence and reinstated after 1790, in the direction of Australia. The great debates about Botany Bay took place in France around the years 1824–1830. In actual fact, deportation-colonization will never take the place of imprisonment; during the period of the great colonial conquests, it will play a complex role in the controlled circuits of delinquency. A whole ensemble constituted by the groups of more or less voluntary colonists, the colonial regiments, the batallions of Africa, the Foreign Legion, and Cayenne will come to function, during the nineteenth century, in correlation with a penal practice that will remain essentially carceral.

• reform the internal system of the prison so that it stops manufacturing that army of domestic perils. This is the goal that was pointed to throughout Europe as "penitentiary reform." We can give as chronological markers for it the *Lessons on Prisons* by Julius (1828),[6] on the one hand, and on the other the Brussels Conference in 1847. This reform includes three main aspects: complete or partial isolation of prisoners inside the prisons (debates about the systems of Auburn and Pennsylvania); moral reform of convicts through work, instruction, religion, rewards, sentence reductions; development of parapenal institutions of prevention, or cooptation, or supervision. Now, these reforms, which the revolutions of 1848 put an end to, did not have the slightest effect on the prison dysfunctions that were denounced in the preceding period;

• finally, give an anthropological status to the carceral circle; replace the old project of Julius and of Charles Lucas[7] (to establish a "science of prisons" capable of giving the architectural, administrative, and pedagogical principles of a "correctional" institution) with a "science of criminals" that would be able to characterize them in their specificity and define the modes of social reaction suited to their case. The class of delinquents, to which the carceral circuit gave at least part of its autonomy and whose isolation and closure it ensured, appears then as a psychosociological deviation. A deviation that comes under a "scientific" discourse (into which will rush psychopathological, psychiatric, psychoanalytic, and sociological analyses); a deviation about which people will wonder if prison constitutes a response or an appropriate treatment.

What prison was reproached for in other terms at the beginning of the nineteenth century (its forming a "marginal" population of "delinquents") is now considered as an inevitability. Not only is it accepted as a fact, but it is constituted as a primary assumption. The "delinquency" effect produced by prison becomes a delinquency problem to which prison must give a suitable response. A criminological turning of the carceral circle.

It must be asked how such a turning was possible; how effects that were denounced and criticized managed, after all, to be assumed as fundamental data for a scientific analysis of criminality; how it came about that prison, a recent, unstable, criticizable and criticized institution, was planted so deep in the institutional field that the mechanism of its effects could be posited as an anthropological constant; what prison's ultimate reason for being was; what functional requirement it happened to meet.

It is all the more necessary to pose the question and, beyond that, all the more difficult to answer it, as one has trouble seeing the "ideological" genesis of the institution. One might think, in fact, that prison was indeed denounced, and very early on, in its practical consequences, but that it was so firmly tied to the new penal theory (the one presiding over the drafting of the nineteenth-century code) that it had to be accepted along with the theory; or, further, that this theory would have to be reworked, from top to bottom, if one aimed to formulate a radical prison policy.

Now, from this viewpoint, an examination of the penal theories of the second half of the eighteenth century yields rather surprising results. None of the great reformers, whether they were theoreticians like Beccaria, jurists like Servan, legislators like Le Peletier de Saint-Fargeau, or both at the same time like Brissot, recommend prison as a universal or even a major penalty. In a general way, in all these formulations, the criminal is defined as society's enemy. In this respect, the reformers take up and transform what had been the result of a whole political and institutional evolution since the Middle Ages: the replacement of litigation settlement by public prosecution. By intervening, the king's prosecutor designates the infraction not just as an attack on a person or a private interest but as an attempt upon the king's sovereignty. Commenting on the English laws, Blackstone said that the public prosecutor defends both the sovereignty of the king and the interests of society.[8] In short, a large majority of the reformers, starting with Beccaria, sought to define the notion of crime, the role of the public party, and the necessity of punishment solely on the basis of the interest of society or the need to protect it. The criminal injures society first of all; breaking the social compact, he sets himself up in society as a domestic enemy. A certain number of consequences derive from this general principle.

1. Each society will have to adjust the scale of penalties according to

its particular needs. Since the punishment does not derive from the transgression itself but from the harm caused to society or from the danger to which it exposes society, the weaker the society is, the more mindful of its security it will have to be, and the more severe it will need to show itself. Hence, no universal model of penal practice, and an essential relativity of penalties.

2. If the penalty were expiation, there would be no harm in its being too harsh; in any case, it would be difficult to establish a just proportion between it and the crime. Yet if it is a matter of protecting society, one can calculate it in such a way that it ensures exactly that function: any additional severity becomes an abuse of power. The justice of the penalty is in its economy.

3. The role of the penalty is entirely oriented toward the exterior and toward the future: to prevent crime from recommencing. Logically, a crime that one knew for certain to be the last would not need to be punished. Hence, make the guilty incapable of further harm and dissuade the innocent from any similar infraction. Here, the certainty of the penalty, its inevitability, more than any severity, constitutes its effectiveness.

Now, from such principles it is not possible to deduce what will actually come to pass in penal practice, namely, the universalization of prison as the general form of punishment. On the contrary, one sees the emergence of very different punitive models:

- one of these is geared to dishonor, that is, to the effects of public opinion. Dishonor is a perfect penalty, since it is the immediate and spontaneous reaction of society itself; it varies with each society; it is graduated according to the harmfulness of each crime; it can be revoked by a public rehabilitation; lastly, it affects only the guilty person. It is therefore a penalty that is adjusted to the crime without having to go by way of a code, without having to be applied by a court, and without risk of being misused by a political power. It is exactly attuned to the principles of penal practice. "The triumph of a good legislation is when public opinion is strong enough to punish offenses by itself.... Fortunate is the people in whom the sense of honor can be the only law. It has little need of legislation. Dishonor, there is its penal code";[9]

- another model employed in the plans for reform is that of retaliation. By sentencing the guilty individual to a punishment of the same type and of the same gravity as the crime, one is sure of obtaining a penalty that is both graduated and exactly proportional. The penalty takes the form of a counterattack. And, provided the latter is quick and inevitable, it almost automatically nullifies the advantages expected by the lawbreaker, rendering the crime useless. The benefit of the offense is abruptly brought back to zero. Doubtless, the retaliation model was never proposed in a detailed form; but it often enabled one to define some types of punishment. Beccaria, for example: "Attacks against persons ought to be punished by corporal penalties"; "personal injuries against honor ought to be pecuniary." One also finds it in the form of a "moral retaliation": punish the crime not by turning its effects around but by turning back toward the beginnings and the vices that are its cause.[10] Le Peletier de Saint-Fargeau recommends to the National Assembly (21 May 1791): physical pain to punish heinous crimes; hard labor to punish crimes originating in idleness; and dishonor to punish crimes inspired by an "abject and degraded" soul;[11]

• lastly, a third model, enslavement for the benefit of society. Such a penalty can be graduated, in its intensity and duration, according to the harm done to the community. It is connected with the transgression through that damaged interest. Beccaria, apropos of thieves: "Temporary slavery places the labor and the person of the guilty individual in the service of society so that this state of total dependence compensates it for the unjust despotism that he practiced by violating the social compact."[12] Brissot: "By what should the death penalty be replaced? By slavery which makes the guilty incapable of harming society; by labor which makes him useful; by long and continuous suffering which frightens those who might be tempted to imitate him."[13]

Of course, in all these plans, prison often figures as one of the possible penalties: either as a condition of forced labor, or as a retaliation penalty for those who have interfered with the liberty of others. But it does not appear as the general form of penalty, nor as the condition for a psychological and moral transformation of the delinquent.

It is in the first years of the nineteenth century that one will see the theoreticians grant this role to prison. "Imprisonment is the preeminent penalty in civilized societies. Its tendency is moral when it is

accompanied by the obligation of labor" (P. Rossi, 1829).[14] But during this period the prison will already exist as a major instrument of
penality. Prison as a place of improvement is a reinterpretation of a
practice of imprisonment that had spread in the preceding years.

Thus, prison practice was not implied in penal theory. It was born elsewhere and was formed for other reasons. And it was imposed from the
outside, as it were, on penal theory, which would be obliged to justify
it after the fact. For example, this is what Livingston would do, in 1820,
when he said that the prison penalty had the fourfold advantage of
being divisible into as many degrees as there were degrees of serious-
ness in the offenses; of preventing recurrence; of enabling correction;
of being mild enough so that juries would not hesitate to punish and
the people would not rebel against the law.[15]

To understand how prison really functioned, beneath its apparent
dysfunction, and how deeply successful it was beneath its surface failures, we must go back, no doubt, to those parapenal agencies of control
in which it figured, as we have seen, in the seventeenth and especially
the eighteenth centuries.

In those instances, confinement plays a role that includes three distinct features.

- It intervenes, in the spatial distribution of individuals, through
  the temporary imprisonment of beggars and vagabonds. No doubt,
  ordinances (end of seventeenth and eighteenth century) sentence
  them to the convict ships, at least in the case of repeat offenses; but
  confinement remains in fact the most frequent punishment. Now,
  if they are confined, it is not so much to keep them where they are
  held as to move them: make the cities off-limits to them, send them
  into the countryside, or also prevent them from roaming in an area,
  force them to go where they can be given work. This is at least a
  negative way of controlling their location relative to the apparatus
  of farm and factory production; a way of acting upon the population flow, taking into account the needs of production and of the
  job market.

- Confinement also intervenes at the level of individual conduct. It
  penalizes at an infrapenal level ways of living, types of discourse,
  political projects or intentions, sexual behaviors, rejections of author-

ity, defiances of opinion, acts of violence, and so on. In short, it intervenes not so much on behalf of law as on behalf of order and regularity. The irregular, the unsettled, the dangerous, and the dishonorable are the object of confinement; whereas penality punishes the infraction, it penalizes disorder.

• Lastly, while it is true that it is in the hands of political power, that it totally or partly escapes the control of regular justice (in France it is almost always decided by the king, the ministers, the administrators, the subdelegates), it is not by any means the instrument of arbitrariness and absolutism. An analysis of the *lettres de cachet* (of both their functioning and their motivation) shows that the great majority of them were solicited by family men, by minor notables, by local, religious, and professional communities against individuals who in their estimation cause disturbance and disorder. The *lettre de cachet* rises from the bottom to the top (in the form of a request) before going back down the power apparatus in the form of an order bearing the royal seal. It is the instrument of a local and, so to speak, capillary control.

A similar analysis could be done concerning associations in England from the end of the seventeenth century onward. Often led by "dissidents," they aim to denounce, exclude, and bring action against individuals for delinquencies, refusals of work, and everyday disorders. Between this form of control and that ensured by the *lettres de cachet* the differences, obviously, are enormous. This one alone would suffice: the English associations (at least in the first part of the eighteenth century) are independent of any state apparatus; moreover, rather popular in their recruitment, they direct their attack, in general terms, against the immorality of the rich and the powerful; finally, the strictness they show toward their own members is doubtless also a way of helping them to escape an extremely strict penal justice (English penal laws, a "bloody chaos," included more capital cases than any other European code). In France, by contrast, the forms of control were closely connected with a state apparatus that had organized Europe's first great police force, which the Austria of Joseph II, then England, undertook to imitate. As to England, it should be noted in fact that in the last years of the eighteenth century (essentially after the Gordon Riots, and at the time of the great popular movements more or less contemporaneous with the French Revolution), new moral reform associations sprang up, much more aristocratic in their recruitment (some of them militarily equipped): they requested royal intervention, the promulgation of a new set of laws, and the organization of a police force. The work and the person of Colquhoun are at the center of this process.

What transformed penality at the turn of the century was the adjustment of the judicial system to a mechanism of oversight and control. It is their joint integration into a centralized state apparatus—but also the establishment and development of a whole series of (parapenal and at times nonpenal) institutions—that serves the main apparatus as a point of support, as forward positions, or reduced forms. A general system of oversight and confinement penetrates all layers of society, taking forms that go from the great prisons built on the panopticon model to the charitable societies, and that find their points of application not only among the delinquents, but among abandoned children, orphans, apprentices, high school students, workers, and so on. In a passage of his *Lessons On Prisons*, Julius contrasted civilizations of the spectacle (civilizations of sacrifice and ritual, where it is a matter of giving everyone the spectacle of a unique event and the major architectural form is the theater) with civilizations of supervision (where it is a matter of ensuring an uninterrupted control by a few over the greatest number; its privileged architectural form—the prison). And he added that European society, which had replaced religion with the state, offered the first example of a civilization of supervision.[16]

The nineteenth century founded the age of panopticism.

What needs did this transformation meet?

It seems to have provided new forms and new rules in the practice of illegality. New threats, above all.

The example of the French Revolution (but also of many other movements in the last twenty years of the eighteenth century) shows that the political apparatus of a nation is vulnerable to popular rebellions. A food riot, a revolt against taxes or rents, resistance to conscription are no longer those localized and limited movements which may well reach (and physically so) the representative of political power while leaving its structures and its distribution out of range. They may challenge the possession and exercise of political power. But further, and perhaps above all, the development of industry places the production apparatus in the grasp of those who must operate it. The small-scale craft units, the factories with limited and relatively simple equipment, the low-capacity warehouses supplying local markets did not offer much of an opportunity for gross depredations or large-scale acts of destruction; but mechanization, the organization of great factories, with large stocks of raw materials, the globalization of the market, and the appearance of great centers for the redistribution of commodities place wealth within reach of endless attacks. And these attacks come not from the outside—from those deprived or poorly assimilated individuals who, in the cast-off garb of the beggar or the vagabond, caused such fear in the eighteenth century—but from within, as it were, from the very people who must handle the machines to make them productive. From the daily pillaging of stored products to the great collective smashings by machine operators, a constant danger threatens the wealth that is invested in the productive apparatus. The whole series of measures taken at the end of the eighteenth century and the beginning of the nineteenth to protect the ports, docks, and arsenals of London and to dismantle the networks of black market dealers can serve as an example.

In the countryside, an apparently inverse situation produces analogous effects. The parceling out of rural property, the more or less complete disappearance of the commons, and the bringing of fallow land into cultivation solidify appropriation and make rural society intolerant of a whole set of minor illegalities that people had to accept—like it or not—in the system of great undercultivated estates. The margins disappeared where the poorest and the most mobile had managed to subsist, taking advantage of tolerance and neglect, of forgotten regulations and established facts. The tightening of property ties or, rather, the new status of landed property and its new cultivation transforms many established illegalities into offenses. The importance, more political than economic, of rural offenses in the France of the Directoire and the Consulat (offenses that are connected either to struggles in the form of civil wars or to draft resistance); the importance, too, of resistances in Europe against the forest codes of the beginning of the nineteenth century.

But perhaps the most important form of the new illegality is elsewhere. It concerns not so much the body of the production apparatus or that of landed property as the very body of the worker and the way in which it is applied to apparatuses of production. Inadequate wages, disqualification of labor by the machine, excessive labor hours, multiple regional or local crises, prohibition of associations, mechanism of indebtment—all this leads workers into behaviors such as absenteeism, breaking of the "hiring contract," migration, and "irregular" living. The problem is then to attach workers firmly to the production apparatus, to settle them or move them where it needs them to be, to subject them to its rhythm, to impose the constancy or regularity on them that it requires—in short, to constitute them as a labor force. Hence a set of laws creating new offenses (the passbook order, the law concerning drinking establishments, the lottery prohibition); hence a whole series of measures that, without being absolutely binding, bring about a division between the good and the bad worker, and seek to ensure a behavioral rectification (the savings bank, the encouragement of marriage, and later, the workers' housing projects [*cités ouvrières*]); hence the appearance of organizations exercising control or pressure (philanthropic societies, rehabilitation associations); hence, finally, a whole immense worker moralization campaign. This campaign defines what it wants to exorcize as "dissipation" and what it wants to establish as "regularity": a working body that is concentrated, diligent, adjusted to the time of production, supplying exactly the force required. It gives the marginalization effect that is due to the control mechanisms a psychological and moral status of importance.

A certain number of conclusions can be drawn from all this.

1. The forms of penality that one sees appearing between the years 1760 and 1840 are not linked to a renewal of moral perception. The essential nature of the infractions defined by the code scarcely changed (we may note, however, the gradual or sudden disappearance of religious offenses); the appearance of certain economic or professional offenses; and while the regimen of penalties grew considerably milder, the infractions themselves remained nearly identical. What brought the great renewal of the epoch into play was a problem of bodies and materiality, a question of physics: a new form of materiality taken by the production apparatus, a new type of contact between that apparatus and the individual who makes it function; new requirements imposed on individuals as productive forces. The history of penality at the beginning of the nineteenth century does not belong essentially to a history of moral ideas; it is a chapter in the history of the body. Or let us put it another way: By questioning moral ideas in light of penal institutions and practice, one discovers that the evolution of morals is, above all, the history of the body, of bodies, rather. This being the case, it is understandable that:

• prison became the general form of punishment, replacing torture. The body no longer has to be marked; it must be trained and retrained; its time must be measured out and fully used; its forces must be continuously applied to labor. The prison form of penality corresponds to the wage form of labor;

• medicine, as a science of the normality of bodies, found a place at the center of penal practice (the penalty must have healing as its purpose).

2. The transformation of penality does not belong simply to a history of bodies; it belongs more specifically to a history of relations between political power and bodies. The coercion of bodies, their control, their subjectivation, the way in which that power is exerted on them directly or indirectly, the way in which they are adapted, set in place, and used are at the root of the change we have examined. A *Physics* of power would need to be written, showing how that physics was modified relative to its earlier forms, at the beginning of the nineteenth century, at the time of the development of state structures.

A new *optics*, first of all: an organ of generalized and constant oversight; everything must be observed, seen, transmitted: organization of a police force; instituting of a system of records (with individual files), establishment of a *panopticism*.

A new *mechanics*: isolation and regrouping of individuals, localization of bodies; optimal utilization of forces; monitoring and improvement of the output; in short, the putting into place of a whole *discipline* of life, time, and energies.

A new *physiology*: definition of standards, exclusion and rejection of everything that does not meet them, mechanism of their reestablishment through corrective interventions that are ambiguously therapeutic and punitive.

3. Delinquency plays an important role in this "physics." But there should be no misunderstanding about the term *delinquency*. It is not a matter of delinquents, a kind of psychological and social mutant, who would be the object of penal repression. Delinquency should be understood, rather, as the coupled penality–delinquent system. The penal institution, with prison at its center, manufactures a category of individuals who form a circuit with it: prison does not correct—it endlessly calls the same ones back; little by little, it constitutes a marginalized

population that is used to exert pressure on the "irregularities" or "illegalities" that cannot be tolerated. And it exerts this pressure on illegalities via delinquency in three ways: by gradually leading the irregularity or illegality toward the infraction, with the help of a whole process of exclusions and parapenal sanctions (a mechanism that we may call "indiscipline leads to the gallows"); by incorporating delinquents into its own instruments for supervising illegality (recruitment of provocateurs, informers, detectives; a mechanism that we may call "every thief can become Vidocq"); by channeling the infractions of delinquents toward populations that need watching the most (the principle here: "a poor person is always easier to rob than a rich one").

So, to return to the question posed right at the start—"Why this strange institution of the prison, why this choice of a penality whose dysfunction was denounced so early?"—perhaps the answer should be sought along these lines: prison has the advantage of producing delinquency, an instrument of control over and pressure on illegality, a substantial component in the exercise of power over bodies, an element of that physics of power which gave rise to the psychology of the subject.

This year's seminar was devoted to preparing the Pierre Rivière dossier for publication.

NOTES

1   F. Serpillon, *Code criminel, ou commentaire sur l'ordonnance de 1670* (Lyon: Perisse, 1767), vol. 2, title 35: *Des sentences, jugements et arrêts*, art. 13, §33, p. 1095.

2   D. Jousse, *Traité de la justice criminelle de France* (Paris: Debure, 1771), 4 vols.

3   P. Muyart de Vouglans, *Institutes au droit criminel, ou Principes généraux en ces matières* (Paris: Breton, 1757).

4   C. Rémusat, "Discussion du projet de loi relatif à des réformes dans la législation pénale" (Chambre des deputés, December 1, 1831), *Archives parlementaires*, 2d ser. (Paris: Dupont, 1889), p. 185.

5   Van Meenen (Presiding Judge of the Supreme Court of Appeals of Brussels), "Discours d'ouverture du IIe congrès international pénitentiaire" (September 20–23, 1847, Brussels), *Débats du Congrès pénitentiare de Bruxelles* (Deltombe, 1847), p. 20.

6   N. H. Julius, *Vorselungen über die Gefängnisskunde* (Berlin: Stuhr, 1828): *Leçons sur les prisons, présentées en forme de cours au public de Berlin en l'année 1827*, trans. Lagarmitte (Paris: Levrault, 1831), 2 vols.

7   C. Lucas, *De la Réforme des prisons, ou de la théorie de l'emprisonnement, de ses principes, de ses moyens et de ses conditions pratiques* (Paris: Legrand and Bergouinioux, 1836–1838), 3 vols.

8   Sir W. Blackstone, *Commentaries on the Law of England* (Oxford: Clarendon, 1758): *Commentaire sur le code criminel d'Angleterre*, trans. abbé Goyer (Paris: Knapen, 1776).

9   J. Brissot de Warville, *Théorie des lois criminelles* (Berlin), ch. 2, sec. 2, p. 187.

10 C. de Beccaria, *Dei Delitti e delle Pene* (Milan, 1764): *Traité des délits et des peines*, trans. Collin de Plancy (Paris: Flammarion, 1979), ch. 27, p. 118; ch. 28, p. 121; ch. 30, p. 125.

11 Le Peletier de Saint-Fargeau, "Rapport sur le projet de Code pénal" (Assemblée nationale, 23 mai 1791), *Archives parlementaires de 1787 à 1860: recueil complet des débats législatifs et politiques des Chambres françaises* (Paris: Dupont, 1887), 1st ser., vol. 26, p. 322.

12 Beccaria, *Traité des délits*, p. 125.

13 Brissot de Warville, *Théories des lois*, p. 147.

14 P. L. Rossi, *Traité de droit pénal*, bk. 3, ch. 8, "De l'emprisonnement" (Paris: Sautelet, 1829), p. 169.

15 E. Livingston, *Introductory Report to the System of Penal Law Prepared for the State of Louisiana* (New Orleans, 1820): *Rapport fait à l'Assemblée générale de l'Etat de Louisiane sur le projet d'un code pénal* (New Orleans: Levy, 1822).

16 Julius, *Leçons sur les prisons*, vol. 1, pp. 384–86.

PSYCHIATRIC POWER

For a long time, medicine, psychiatry, penal justice, and criminology remained—and in large part still remain—within the limits of a manifestation of truth inside the norms of knowledge and a production of truth in the form of the test, the second of these always tending to hide beneath and getting its justification from the first. The current crisis in these "disciplines" does not simply call into question their limits or uncertainties in the sphere of knowledge; it calls knowledge into question, the form of knowledge, the "subject–object" norm; it questions the relations between our society's economic and political structures and knowledge (not in its true and untrue contents but in its "power-knowledge" functions). A historico-political crisis, then.

Consider, first, the example of medicine, with the space connected to it, namely, the hospital. The hospital was still an ambiguous place quite late, a place of investigation for a hidden truth and of testing for a truth to be produced.

A direct action upon illness: not just enable it to reveal its truth to the physician's gaze but to produce that truth. The hospital, a place where the true illness blossoms forth. It was assumed, in fact, that the sick person left at liberty—in his "milieu," in his family, in his circle of friends, with his regimen, his habits, his prejudices, his illusions— could not help but be affected by a complex, mixed, and tangled disease, a kind of unnatural illness that was both the blend of several diseases and the impediment preventing the true disease from being produced in the authenticity of its nature. So the hospital's role was, by clearing away that parasitic vegetation, those aberrant forms, not only to bring to light the disease as it was but to produce it finally in its heretofore-enclosed and blocked truth. Its peculiar nature, its essential characteristics, its specific development would be able at last, through the effect of hospitalization, to become a reality.

The eighteenth-century hospital was supposed to create the conditions that would allow the truth of the sickness to break out. Thus, it was a place of observation and demonstration, but also of purification and testing. It constituted a sort of complex setup designed both to bring out and actually to produce the illness: a botanical place for the contemplation of species, a still-alchemical place for the elaboration of pathological substances.

It is this dual function that was taken charge of for a long time yet by the great hospital structures established in the nineteenth century. And, for a century (1760–1860), the theory and practice of hospitalization, and generally speaking, the conception of illness, were dominated by this ambiguity: should the hospital, a reception structure for illness, be a space of knowledge or a place of testing?

Hence a whole series of problems that traversed the thought and practice of physicians. Here are a few of them:

1. Therapy consists in suppressing sickness, in reducing it to nonexistence; but if this therapy is to be rational, if it is to be based on truth, must it not allow the disease to develop? When must one intervene, and in what way? Must one intervene at all? Must one act so that the disease develops or so that it stops? To diminish it or to guide it to its term?

2. There are diseases and alterations of diseases. Pure and impure, simple and complex diseases. Is there not ultimately just one disease, of which all the others would be the more or less distantly derived forms, or must irreducible categories be granted? (The debate between Broussais and his adversaries concerning the notion of irritation. The problem of essential fevers.)

3. What is a normal disease? What is a disease that follows its course? A disease that leads to death, or one that heals spontaneously once its development is completed? These are the terms in which Bichat reflected on the position of disease between life and death.

We are aware of the prodigious simplification that Pasteurian biology brought to all these problems. By determining the agent of the sickness and by pinpointing it as a single organism, it enabled the hospital to become a place of observation, of diagnosis, of clinical and experimental identification, but also of immediate intervention, of counter-attack against the microbial invasion.

As to the testing function, one sees that it may disappear. The place where the disease is produced will be the laboratory, the test tube; but there, the disease does not develop in a crisis; its process is reduced to an amplified mechanism; it is brought down to a verifiable and controllable phenomenon. For the patient, the hospital milieu no longer must be the place that favors a decisive event; it simply enables a reduction, a transfer, an amplification, a verification; the test is transformed into a proof in the technical structure of the laboratory and in the physician's report.

If one were to write an "ethno-epistemology" of the medical personage, it would be necessary to say that the Pasteurian revolution deprived him of his role—an ancient one no doubt—in the ritual production and testing of the disease. And the disappearance of that role was dramatized, of course, by the fact that Pasteur did not merely show that the physician did not have to be the producer of the disease "in its truth," but even that, through ignorance of the truth, he had made himself, thousands of times, its propagator and reproducer: the hospital physician going from bed to bed was one of the main agents of contagion. Pasteur delivered a formidable narcissistic wound to physicians, something for which they took a long time to forgive him: those hands that must glide over the patient's body, palpate it, examine it, those hands that must uncover the disease, bring it forth, Pasteur pointed to as carriers of disease. Up to that moment, the hospital space and the physician's body had had the role of producing the "critical" truth of disease; now the physician's body and the overcrowded hospital appeared as producers of disease's reality.

By asepticizing the physician and the hospital, one gave them a new innocence, from which they drew new powers, and a new status in men's imagination. But that is another story.

These few notations may help us to understand the position of the madman and the psychiatrist in the space of the asylum.

There is doubtless a historical correlation between two facts: before the eighteenth century, madness was not systematically interned; and it was considered essentially as a form of error or illusion. At the beginning of the Classical age, madness was still seen as belonging to the world's chimeras; it could live in the midst of them, and it didn't have to be separated from them until it took extreme or dangerous forms. Under these conditions, it is understandable that the privileged place where madness could and must shine forth in its truth could not be the artificial space of the hospital. The therapeutic places that were recognized were in nature, first of all, since nature was the visible form of truth; it held the power to dissipate error, to make the chimera melt away. So the prescriptions given by doctors were apt to be travel, rest, walking, retirement, breaking with the artificial and vain world of the city. Esquirol will remember this when, in planning a psychiatric hospital, he will recommend that each courtyard open expansively onto a garden view. The other therapeutic place put to use was the theater, nature's opposite: the patient's own madness was acted out for him on the stage; it was lent a momentary fictive reality; one pretended, with the help of props and disguises, as if it were true, but in such a way that, caught in this trap, the delusion would finally reveal itself to the very eyes of its victim. This technique had not completely disappeared, either, in the nineteenth century; Esquirol, for example, would recommend that proceedings be instituted against melancholics to stimulate their taste for fighting back.

The practice of internment at the beginning of the nineteenth century coincides with the moment when madness is perceived less in relation to delusion than in relation to regular, normal behavior; when it appears no longer as disturbed judgment but as a disorder in one's way of acting, of willing, of experiencing passions, of making decisions, and of being free; in short, when it is no longer inscribed on the axis truth– error–consciousness but on the axis passion–will–freedom—the moment of Hoffbauer and Esquirol. "There are madmen whose delirium is scarcely visible; there are none whose passions, whose moral affections are not confused, perverted, or reduced to nothing.... The lessening of the delirium is a sure sign of recovery only when the madmen return to their first affections."[1] What is the process of recovery in fact? The movement by which the delusion is dissipated and the truth is newly brought to light? Not at all; rather, "the return of the moral affections within their proper bounds, the desire to see one's friends, one's children, again, the tears of sensibility, the need to pour out one's heart, to be in the midst of one's family again, to resume one's habits."[2]

What might be the role of the asylum, then, in this new orientation toward regular behaviors? Of course, first it will have the function that was attributed to hospitals at the end of the eighteenth century:

make it possible to uncover the truth of the mental illness, brush aside everything in the patient's milieu that may mask it, muddle it, give it aberrant forms, or sustain it and give it a new impetus. But even more than a place of unveiling, the hospital for which Esquirol supplied the model is a scene of confrontation: madness, a disturbed will, a perverted passion, must encounter there a sound will and orthodox passions. Their confrontation, their unavoidable (and in fact desirable) collision will produce two effects: the diseased will, which could very well remain beyond grasp so long as it did not express itself in any delirium, will produce illness in broad daylight through the resistance it offers against the healthy will of the physician, moreover, the struggle that is engaged as a result should lead, if it is properly conducted, to the victory of the sound will, to the submission, the renunciation of the troubled will. A process of opposition, then, of struggle and domination. "We must apply a perturbing method, to break the spasm by means of the spasm.... We must subjugate the whole character of some patients, subdue their transports, break their pride, while we must stimulate and encourage the others."[3]

In this way, the quite curious function of the nineteenth-century psychiatric hospital was set into place; a place of diagnosis and classification, a botanical rectangle where the species of diseases are distributed over courtyards whose layout brings to mind a vast kitchen garden; but also an enclosed space for a confrontation, the scene of a contest, an institutional field where it is a question of victory and submission. The great asylum physician—whether it is Leuret, Charcot, or Kraepelin—is both the one who can tell the truth of the disease through the knowledge [*savoir*] he has of it and the one who can produce the disease in its truth and subdue it in its reality, through the power that his will exerts on the patient himself. All the techniques or procedures employed in asylums of the nineteenth century—isolation, private or public interrogations, punishment techniques such as cold showers, moral talks (encouragements or reprimands), strict discipline, compulsory work, rewards, preferential relations between the physician and his patients, relations of vassalage, of possession, of domesticity, even of servitude between patient and physician, at times—all this was designed to make the medical personage the "master of madness": the one who makes it appear in its truth (when it conceals itself, when it remains hidden and silent) and the one who dominates it, pacifies it, absorbs it after astutely unleashing it.

Let us say, then, in a schematic way, that in the Pasteurian hospital the "truth-producing" function of the disease continues to fade; the physician as truth-producer disappears into a knowledge structure. On the other hand, in the hospital of Esquirol or Charcot the "truth-production" function hypertrophies, intensifies around the figure of the physician. And this occurs in a process revolving around the inflated power of the physician. Charcot, the miracle worker of hysteria, is undoubtedly the figure most highly symbolic of this type of functioning.

Now, this heightening occurs at a time when medical power finds its guarantees and its justifications in the privilege of expertise [*connaissance*]; the doctor is qualified, the doctor knows the diseases and the patients, he possesses a scientific knowledge that is of the same type as that of the chemist or the biologist, and that is what authorizes him to intervene and decide. So the power that the asylum gives to the psychiatrist will have to justify itself (and mask itself at the same time as a primordial superpower) by producing phenomena that can be integrated into medical science. One understands why the technique of hypnosis and suggestion, the problem of simulation, and diagnosis differentiating between organic disease and psychological disease were, for so many years (from 1860 to 1890 at least), at the center of psychiatric theory and practice. The point of perfection, of a too-miraculous perfection, was reached when patients in the service of Charcot began to reproduce, at the behest of medical power-knowledge, a symptomatology normed on epilepsy—that is, capable of being deciphered, known, and recognized in terms of an organic disease.

A crucial episode where the two functions of the hospital (testing and truth production, on the one hand; recording and understanding of phenomena, on the other) are redistributed and superimposed. Henceforth, the physician's power enables him to produce the reality of mental illness characterized by the ability to reproduce phenomena completely accessible to knowledge. The hysteric was the perfect patient since she *provided material for knowledge* [*donnait à connaître*]: she herself would retranscribe the effects of medical power into the forms that the physician could describe according to a scientifically acceptable discourse. As for the power relation that made this whole operation possible, how could it have been detected in its decisive role, since— supreme virtue of hysteria, unparalleled docility, veritable epistemological sanctity—the patients themselves took charge of it and accepted responsibility for it: it appeared in the symptomatology as a morbid suggestibility. Everything would spread out henceforth in the limpidness of knowledge cleansed of all power, between the knowing subject and the known object.

A hypothesis: the crisis was opened, and the still imperceptible age of antipsychiatry began, when people developed the suspicion, then the certainty, that Charcot actually produced the hysterical fit he described. There one has the rough equivalent of the discovery made by Pasteur that the physician transmitted the diseases he was supposed to combat.

It seems to me, in any case, that all the big jolts that have shaken psychiatry since the end of the nineteenth century have essentially questioned the power of the physician—his power and the effect that he produced on the patient, more than his knowledge and the truth he told concerning the illness. Let us say more exactly that, from Bernheim to Laing or Basaglia, in question was the way in which the physician's power was involved in the truth of what he said and, conversely, the way in which the truth could be manufactured and compromised by his power. Cooper has said: "At the heart of our problem is violence."[4] And Basaglia: "The characteristic of these institutions (schools, factories, hospitals) is a clear-cut separation between those who hold the power and those who don't."[5] All the great reforms, not only of psychiatric power but of psychiatric thought, are focused on this power relation: they constitute so many attempts to displace it, mask it, eliminate it, nullify it. The whole of modern psychiatry is fundamentally pervaded by antipsychiatry, if one understands by this everything that calls back into question the role of the psychiatrist formerly charged with *producing the truth of illness in the hospital space.*

One might speak, then, of the antipsychiatries that have traversed the history of modern psychiatry. Yet perhaps it would be better to distinguish carefully between two processes that are completely distinct from the historical, epistemological, and political point of view.

First, there was the "depsychiatrization" movement. It is what appears immediately after Charcot. And it is then not so much a question of neutralizing the physician's power as of displacing it on behalf of a more exact knowledge, of giving it a different point of application and new measures. Depsychiatrize mental medicine in order to restore to its true effectiveness a medical power that Charcot's shamelessness (or ignorance) had wrongly caused to produce illnesses, hence false illnesses.

1. A first form of depsychiatrization begins with Basinski, in whom it finds its critical hero. Instead of trying to produce the truth of illness theatrically, it would be better to try to reduce it to its strict reality, which is often nothing more than the capacity for letting itself be dramatized—pithiatism. Henceforth, not only will the relation of domination by the doctor over the patient lose none of its rigor, but its rigor will be directed toward *reducing* the illness to its strict minimum: the signs necessary and sufficient for it to be diagnosable as a mental illness, and the techniques absolutely necessary in order for these manifestations to disappear.

The object is to Pasteurize the psychiatric hospital, as it were, to obtain the same simplification effect for the asylum that Pasteur had forced upon the hospitals: link diagnosis and therapy, knowledge of the nature of the illness and the suppression of its manifestations, directly to one another. The moment of testing, when the illness appears in its truth and is fully expressed, no longer must figure in the medical process; the hospital can become a silent place where the form of medical power is maintained in its strictest aspect, but without its having to encounter or confront madness itself. Let us call this "aseptic" and "asymptomatic" form of depsychiatrization "zero-production psychiatry." Psychosurgery and pharmacological psychiatry are its most notable forms.

2. Another form of depsychiatrization, the exact opposite of the preceding one. Here it is a matter of making the production of madness in its truth as intense as possible, but in such a way that the power relations between doctor and patient are invested exactly in that production; they remain adequate to it and do not allow themselves to be overrun by it, and they keep control of it.

The first condition for this maintenance of "depsychiatrized" medical power is the discrediting of all the effects peculiar to the space of the asylum. Above all, one must avoid the trap into which Charcot's thaumaturgy fell: one must make sure that hospital allegiance does not mock medical authority and that, in this place of collusions and obscure collective knowledge [*savoirs*], the physician's sovereign science does not get caught up in mechanisms that it may have unintentionally produced. Hence a rule of private consultation; hence a rule of free contract between physician and patient; hence a rule of limitation of all the effects the relationship at the discourse level alone ("I only ask one thing of you, which is to speak, but to tell me effectively everything that crosses your mind"); hence a rule of discursive freedom ("You won't be able to boast about fooling your doctor any more, since you will no longer be answering questions put to you; you will say what occurs to you, without even needing to ask me what I think about it, and should you try to fool me by breaking this rule, I will not really be fooled; you will be caught in your own trap, because you will have interfered with the production of truth, and added several sessions to the total you owe me"); hence a rule of the couch that grants reality only to the results produced in that privileged place and during that single hour when the doctor's power is exercised—a power that cannot be drawn into any countereffect, since it is completely withdrawn into silence and invisibility.

Psychoanalysis can be deciphered historically as the other great form of depsychiatrization that was provoked by Charcot's traumatism: a withdrawal outside the asylum space in order to obliterate the effects of psychiatric superpower; but a reconstitution of medical power as truth-producer, in a space arranged so that that production would always remain perfectly adapted to that power. The notion of transference, as a process essential to the treatment, is a way of conceptualizing this adequation in the form of knowledge [*connaissance*]; the payment of money, the monetary counterpart of transference, is a way of preventing the production of truth from becoming a counterpower that traps, annuls, overturns the power of the physician.

These two great forms of depsychiatrization—both of which are power-conserving, the first because it annuls the production of truth, the second because it tries to ensure an exact fit between truth production and medical power—become the target of antipsychiatry. Rather than a withdrawal outside the asylum space, it is a question of its systematic destruction through an internal effort; and it is a matter of transferring to the patient himself the power to produce his madness and the truth of his madness, instead of trying to reduce it to zero. This being the case, one can understand, I believe, what is at issue in antipsychiatry, which is not at all the truth value of psychiatry in terms of knowledge (of diagnostic correctness or therapeutic effectiveness).

At the heart of antipsychiatry, the struggle with, in, and against the institution. When the great asylum structures were put into place at the beginning of the nineteenth century, they were justified by a marvelous harmony between the requirements of the social order (which demanded to be protected against the disorder of madmen) and the needs of therapeutics (which called for the isolation of patients).[6] In justifying the isolation of madmen, Esquirol gave five main reasons for the practice: (1) to ensure their safety and that of their families; (2) to free them from outside influences; (3) to overcome their personal resistances; (4) to subject them to a medical regimen; (5) to impose new intellectual and moral habits on them. Obviously, everything is a matter of power; subdue the power of the madman, neutralize the external powers that may be brought to bear on him; establish a power of therapy and rectification—of "orthopedics"—over him. Now, it is clearly the institution—as a place, a form of distribution, and a mechanism of these power relations—that antipsychiatry attacks. Beneath the rationale of an internment that would make it possible, in a purified place, to determine what's what and to intervene when, where, and however necessary, it gives rise to the relations of domination that characterize the institutional setup: "The sheer power of the doctor increases," says Basaglia, observing the effects of Esquirol's prescriptions in the twentieth century, "and the power of the patient diminishes at the same vertiginous rate; the patient, from the mere fact that he is interned, becomes a citizen without rights, delivered over to the arbitrariness of the doctor and the orderlies, who can do what they please with him without any possibility of appeal."[7] It seems to me that one could situate the different forms of antipsychiatry according to their strategies with respect to these institutional power games: escape from them in the form of a two-party contract freely agreed to by both sides (Szasz[8]); arrange a privileged place where they must be suspended or rooted out if they manage to reconstitute themselves (Kingsley Hall[9]); identify them one by one and gradually destroy them inside an institution of the classic type (Cooper, at Villa 21[10]); connect them to other power relations outside the asylum which may have already brought about the segregation of an individual as a mental patient (Gorizia[11]). Power relations constituted the a priori of psychiatric practice. They conditioned the operation of the mental institution; they distributed relationships between individuals within it; they governed the forms of medical intervention. The characteristic reversal of antipsychiatry consists in placing them, on the contrary, at the center of the problematic field and in questioning them in a primary way.

Now, what was essentially involved in these power relations was the absolute right of nonmadness over madness. A right transcribed into terms of competence brought to bear on an ignorance, of good sense (access to reality) correcting errors (delusions, hallucinations, fantasies), of normality imposing itself on disorder and deviance. It is this threefold power that constituted madness as an object of possible knowledge for a medical science, that constituted it as an illness, at the very moment when the "subject" stricken with this illness found himself disqualified as insane—which is to say, stripped of any power and any knowledge concerning his illness: "We know enough about your suffering and your special condition (things that you have no inkling of) to recognize that it is a disease; but we are familiar enough with this disease to know that you can't exercise any right over it or with respect to it. Our science enables us to call your madness a disease, and consequently we doctors are qualified to intervene and diagnose a madness in you that prevents you from being a patient like others: so you will be a mental patient." This game involving a power relation that gives rise to a knowledge, which in return founds the rights of the power in question, characterizes "classical" psychiatry. It is this circle that antipsychiatry undertakes to undo: giving the individual the right to take his madness to the limit, to see it through, in an experience to which others may contribute, but never in the name of a power that would be conferred on them by their reason or their normality; detaching the behaviors, the suffering, the desires from the medical status that had been conferred on them, freeing them from a diagnosis and a symptomatology that had not simply a value of classification but also one of decision and decree; invalidating, finally, the great retranscription of madness into mental illness which had been initiated in the seventeenth century and completed in the nineteenth.

The demedicalization of madness is correlative with that fundamental questioning of power in antipsychiatric practice. A fact that allows us to gauge the latter's opposition to "depsychiatrization," which appears to characterize psychoanalysis as well as psychopharmacology: both seem to derive from an overmedicalization of madness. And now, at last, the problem is posed of the eventual freeing of madness from that singular form of power-knowledge which is expertise [*connaissance*]. Is it possible that the truth production of madness might be carried out in forms that are not those of the knowledge relation? A fictitious problem, it will be said, a question that has its place only in utopia. In actual fact, it is posed concretely every day in connection with the role of the doctor—of the official subject of knowledge—in the depsychiatrization movement.

The seminar was devoted alternately to two topics: the history of the hospital institution and hospital architecture in the eighteenth century; and the study of medico-legal appraisal in psychiatric cases since 1820.

NOTES

1   J. E. D. Esquirol, *De la Folie* (1816), §1: "Symptômes de la folie," in *Des Maladies mentales considérées sous les rapports médical, hygiènique, et médico-légal* (Paris: Baillière, 1838), vol. 1, p. 16 (repub. Paris: Frénésie, 1989).

2   Ibid.

3   Esquirol, *De la Folie*, §5: "Traitement de la folie," pp. 132–33.

4   D. Cooper, *Psychiatry and Antipsychiatry* (London: Tavistock, 1967), p. 17: *Psychiatrie et antipsychiatrie*, trans. M. Braudeau (Paris: Seuil, 1970), ch. 1: "Violence et psychiatrie," p. 33.

5   F. Basaglia, ed., *L'Instituzione negata: rapporto da un ospedale psichiatrico* (Turin: Nuovo politecnico, 1968): *Les Institutions de la violence*, in F. Basaglia, ed., *L'Institution en négation: rapport sur l'hôpital psychiatrique de Gorizia*, trans. L. Bonalumi (Paris: Seuil, 1970), p. 105.

6   See the pages of Robert Castel on this subject, in *Le Psychanalysme* (Paris: Maspero, 1973), pp. 150–53.

7   Basaglia, *L'Institution en négation*, p. 111.

8   Thomas Stephen Szasz, American psychiatrist and psychoanalyst born in Budapest in 1920. Professor of psychiatry at Syracuse University, he was the only American psychiatrist to join the "antipsychiatric" movement that developed in the sixties. His work carries out a critique of psychiatric institutions based on a liberal humanistic conception of the subject and human rights. See his collection of articles titled *Ideology and Insanity* (London: Calder and Boyars, 1970): *Idéologie et folie: Essais sur la négation des valeurs humaines dans la psychiatrie d'aujourd'hui*, trans. P. Sullivan (Paris: P.U.F., 1976); *The Myth of Mental Illness* (New York: Harper and Row, 1961): *Le Mythe de la maladie mentale*, trans. D. Berger (Paris: Payot, 1975).

9   Kingsley Hall is one of the three reception centers created in the sixties. Located in a working-class neighborhood of London's East End, it is known through the account given by Mary Barnes, who spent five years there, and her therapist, Joe Berke, in the book *Mary Barnes, un voyage autour de la folie*, trans. M. Davidovici (Paris: Seuil, 1973) [Mary Barnes and Joseph Berke, *Two Accounts of a Journey Through Madness* (London: MacGibbon and Kee, 1971)].

10   The experience of Villa 21, begun in January 1962 in a psychiatric hospital in northwest London, inaugurated the series of communal psychiatric projects, Kingsley Hall being one of the best known. David Cooper, the director until 1966, writes about it in his *Psychiatry and Antipsychiatry*.

11   Italian public psychiatric hospital located in northern Trieste. Its institutional transformation was undertaken by Franco Basaglia and his team starting in 1963. *L'Institution en négation* describes this anti-institutional struggle that set an example. Basaglia resigned as director of Gorizia in 1968 in order to develop his experience in Trieste.

THE ABNORMALS

The great indefinite and confused family of "abnormals," the fear of which will haunt the end of the nineteenth century, does not simply mark a phase of indecision or a somewhat unfortunate episode in the history of psychopathology; it was formed in correlation with a whole set of institutions of control, a whole series of mechanisms of supervision and distribution; and when it will have been almost completely covered over by the category of "degeneration," it will give rise to ridiculous theoretical constructions but with harshly real effects.

The group of abnormals was formed out of three elements whose own formation was not exactly synchronic.

1. The human monster. An ancient notion whose frame of reference is law. A juridical notion, then, but in the broad sense, as it referred not only to social laws but to natural laws as well; the monster's field of appearance is a juridico-biological domain. The figures of the half-human, half-animal being (valorized especially in the Middle Ages), of double individualities (valorized in the Renaissance), of hermaphrodites (who occasioned so many problems in the seventeenth and eighteenth centuries) in turn represented that double violation; what makes a human monster a monster is not just its exceptionality relative to the species form; it is the disturbance it brings to juridical regularities (whether it is a question of marriage laws, canons of baptism, or rules of inheritance). The human monster combines the impossible and the forbidden. One needs to study from this viewpoint the great trials of hermaphrodites in which jurists and physicians clashed from the Rouen affair[1] (beginning of the seventeenth century) to the trial of

Anne Grandjean[2] (in the middle of the following century); and also works like Cangiamila's *Sacred Embryology*,[3] published and translated in the eighteenth century.

From this history one can understand a number of ambiguities that will continue to haunt the analysis and the status of the abnormal man, even when he will have reduced and appropriated the peculiar traits of the monster. In the first rank of these ambiguities one would have to place the unnatural act and the illegal offense. They cease to be super-imposed without ceasing to be reciprocally related. The "natural" devi-ation from "nature" alters the juridical effects of the transgression yet does not obliterate them entirely; it does not refer purely and simply to the law but does not suspend it either; it snares the law, provoking effects, triggering mechanisms, calling in parajudicial and marginally medical institutions. We have been able to study in this regard the evo-lution of medico-legal appraisals in penal cases, from the "monstrous" act problematized at the beginning of the nineteenth century (with the Cornier, Léger, and Papavoine affairs[4]) to the emergence of that notion of the "dangerous" individual—to which it is not possible to give a medical sense or a juridical status—and which is nonetheless the fun-damental notion of contemporary experts' assessments. By asking the doctor the properly senseless question "Is this individual dangerous?" (a question that contradicts a penal law based solely on the condem-nation of acts, and postulates a natural connection between illness and infraction), the courts revive, through transformations that need ana-lyzing, the uncertainties of the age-old monsters.

2. The individual to be corrected. This is a more recent figure than the monster. It is the correlative not so much of the imperatives of the law as of training techniques with their own requirements. The emer-gence of the "incorrigible" is contemporaneous with the putting into place of disciplinary techniques during the seventeenth and eighteenth centuries, in the army, the schools, the workshops, then, a little later, in families themselves. The new procedures for training the body, behavior, and aptitudes open up the problem of those who escape that normativity which is no longer the sovereignty of the law.

"Interdiction" constituted the judicial measure by which an individ-ual was at least partially disqualified as a legal subject. This juridical and negative frame will be partly filled, partly replaced by a set of tech-niques and methods by which the authorities will undertake to train those who resist training and correct the incorrigibles. The "confinement" that was practiced on a wide scale starting in the seventeenth century may appear as a kind of intermediate formula between the negative judicial interdiction and the positive methods of rectification. Confinement does in fact exclude, and it functions outside the laws, but as justification it asserts the need to correct, to improve, to lead to repentance, to restore to "better feelings." Starting from this mixed but historically decisive form, it is necessary to study the appearance, at precise historical dates, of the different institutions of rectification and the categories of individuals to which they are directed. Technico-institutional births of blindness and deaf-muteness, of imbeciles, of the retarded, the nerve-disordered, the unbalanced.

A vulgarized and faded monster, the nineteenth-century abnormal is also a descendant of those incorrigibles who appeared on the fringes of modern "training" techniques.

3. The onanist. A completely new figure in the eighteenth century. It appears in connection with the new relations between sexuality and family organization, with the new position of the child at the center of the parental group, with the new importance given to the body and to health. The appearance of the sexual body of the child.

In actual fact, this emergence has a long prehistory: the joint development of the techniques of direction of conscience (in the new pastoral springing from the Reformation and the Council of Trent) and the institutions of education. From Gerson to Alfonso da Ligouri, a whole discursive partitioning of sexual desire, the sensual body, and the sin of *mollities* is ensured by the obligation of penitential confession and a highly coded practice of subtle interrogations. We can say, schematically, that the traditional control of forbidden relations (adultery, incest, sodomy, bestiality) was duplicated by the control of the "flesh" in the basic impulses of concupiscence.

But the crusade against masturbation breaks out of this background. It begins noisily in England first, in the years around 1710, with the publication of *Onania*,[5] then in Germany, before getting underway in France, in about 1760, with the book by Tissot.[6] Its raison d'être is enigmatic, but its effects are innumerable. None of these can be determined without taking into consideration some of the essential features of the campaign. It would not be enough, in fact, to see it—in a perspective close to Reich, who recently inspired the work of Van Ussel[7]—only as a process of repression linked to the new requirements of industrialization: the productive body as against the pleasure body. In reality, this crusade does not take, at least in the eighteenth century, the form of a general sexual discipline: it is directed primarily if not exclusively toward adolescents and children, and even more specifically toward those of wealthy or comfortably off families. It places sexuality, or at least the sexual use of one's own body, at the origin of an indefinite series of physical disorders that may make their effects felt in all forms and at all ages of life. Sexuality's limitless etiological power, at the level of bodies and diseases, is one of the most constant themes not only in the texts of that new medical ethics but also in the most serious works of pathology. If the child thus becomes responsible for his own body and his own life, in the "abuse" he makes of sexuality, the parents are denounced as the real culprits: lack of supervision, neglect, and, above all, lack of interest in their children, their children's bodies, and their conduct, which leads them to entrust their children to wet nurses, domestic servants, tutors, all those intermediaries regularly denounced as initiators into vice (Freud will take up this theme in his first theory of "seduction"). What emerges through this campaign is the imperative of a new parents–children relationship, and more broadly as a new economy of intrafamilial relations: a solidification and intensification of father–mother–children relations (at the expense of the multiple relations that characterized the large "household"); a reversal of the system of family obligations (which formerly went from children to parents but now tend to make the child the primary and ceaseless object of the duties of the parents, who are assigned complete moral and medical responsibility for their progeny); the emergence of the health principle as a basic law governing family ties; the distribution of the family cell around the body—and the sexual body—of the child; the organization of an immediate physical bond, a body-to-body relationship of parents and children, knitting together desire and power in a complex way; the necessity, finally, for a control and an external medical knowledge to arbitrate and regulate these new relations between the parents' obligatory vigilance and the children's ever so fragile, irritable, and excitable body. The crusade against masturbation reflects the setting-up of the restricted family (parents, children) as a new knowledge-power apparatus. The questioning of the child's sexuality, and of all the anomalies it was thought to be responsible for, was one of the means by which this new contrivance [*dispositif*] was put together. The little incestuous family, the tiny, sexually saturated familial space in which we were raised and in which we live, was formed there.

The "abnormal" individual that so many institutions, discourses, and knowledges have concerned themselves with since the end of the nineteenth century is derived from the juridico-natural exceptionality of the monster, from the multitude of incorrigibles caught up in the mechanisms of rectification, and from the universal secrecy of children's sexualities. In actual fact, the three figures of the monster, the incorrigible, and the onanist will not exactly merge together. Each one will be taken into autonomous systems of scientific reference: the monster, into a teratology and an embryology that found its first great scientific coherence with Geoffroy Saint-Hilaire;[8] the incorrigible, into a psychophysiology of sensations, motricity, and capacities; the onanist, into a theory of sexuality that is slowly elaborated starting with Kaan's *Psychopathia Sexualis*.[9]

Yet the specificity of these references must not lead us to overlook three essential phenomena, which cancel it in part, or at least modify it: the construction of a general theory of "degeneration," which, starting with the book by Morel (1857),[10] will serve for more than a half century as a theoretical framework, as well as a social and moral justification, for all the techniques of identification, classification, and intervention applied to abnormals; the setting-up of a complex institutional network that, within the limits of medicine and justice, serves as a "reception" structure for abnormals and an instrument for society's defense; lastly, the movement by which the historically most recent problem to appear, that of children's sexuality, will overlay the two others, to become, in the twentieth century, the most productive principle for explaining all abnormalities.

The Antiphysis, which terror of the monster brought to the light of an exceptional day, is the universal sexuality of children, which now slips it under the little everyday anomalies.

Since 1970, the series of courses has dealt with the slow formation of a knowledge and power of normalization based on the traditional juridical procedures of punishment. The course for the year 1975–1976 will end this cycle with a study of the mechanisms by which, since the end of the nineteenth century, people claim to "defend society."

This year's seminar was devoted to an analysis of the transformations of psychiatric expert opinion in penal cases from the great affairs of criminal monstrosity (prime case: Henriette Cornier) to the diagnosis of "abnormal" delinquents.

NOTES

1   This concerns the case of Marie Le Marcis. Born in 1581 and baptized as a girl, she eventually adopted men's dress, took the first name of Marin, and undertook to marry a widow, Jeanne Le Febvre. Arrested, she was given a death sentence on May 4, 1601, for "the crime of sodomy." The report by the doctor Jacques Duval saved her from being burned at the stake. She was sentenced to remain a girl. See J. Duval, *Des hermaphrodites* (Rouen: Geuffroy, 1612); *Réponse au discours fait par le sieur Riolan, docteur en médecine, contre l'histoire de l'hermaphrodite de Rouen* (Rouen: Courant, n.d.).

2   Anne Grandjean, born in 1732 at Grenoble, dressed as a man and married Françoise Lambert at Chambéry, on June 24, 1761. Informed against and accused, she was summoned before the court of Lyon, where she was first sentenced to the iron collar and banishment for desecrating the marriage tie. A judgment from the Tournelle, on January 10, 1765, cleared her of the accusation but ordered her to change back to women's dress. See the memoir by her lawyer, Mme. Vermeil, *Mémoire pour Anne Grandjean, connu sous le nom de Jean-Baptiste Grandjean, accusé et appelant contre L. le Procureur général, accusateur* (Lyon, 1765), in C. Champeaux, *Réflexions sur les hermaphrodites relativement à Anne Grandjean, qualifiée telle dans un mémoire de Mme. Vermeil, avocat au parlement* (Lyon: Jacquenod, 1765).

3   F. E. Cangiamila, *Sacra Embryologia, sive De officio sacerdotum, medicorum, et aliorum circa aeternam parvulorum in utero existentium salutem* (Panormi: Valenza, 1758): *Embryologie sacrée, ou Traité du devoir des prêtres, des médecins et autres sur le salut éternel des enfants qui sont dans le ventre de leur mère*, trans. J. A. Dinouart and A. Roux (Paris, 1766).

4   On November 4, 1825, Henriette Cornier cut off the head of Fanny Belon, nineteen months old, who was in her care. Her lawyers asked Charles Marc for a medico-legal consultation. See C. Marc, *Consultation médicale pour Henriette Cornier, accusée d'homicide commis volontairement et avec préméditation* (1826), in *De la Folie considérée dans ses rapports avec les questions médico-judiciaires* (Paris: Baillière, 1840), vol. 2, pp. 71–130.

    Antoine Léger, twenty-nine-year-old vine grower, was summoned before the assize court of Versailles on November 23, 1824, for indecent assault with violence and homicide upon Jeanne Debully, twelve and a half years old. Reported first in the *Journal de débats* of November 24, 1824, the affair was reviewed by Etienne Georget in his book *Examen des procès criminels des nommés Léger, Feldtmann, Lecouffe, Jean-Pierre et Papavoine, dans lesquels l'aliénation mentale a été alléguée comme moyen de défense* (Paris: Migneret, 1825), pp. 2–16.

    Louis Auguste Papavoine, ex-navy clerk, forty-one years old, was summoned on February 23, 1825, before the assize court of Paris for the murder of two young children, committed in the Bois de Vincennes: ibid., pp. 39–65.

5   Bekker (attrib.), *Onania, or the Heinous Sin of Self Pollution, and All Its Frightful Consequences in Both Sexes, Considered with Spiritual and Physical Advice to Those Who Have Already Injured Themselves by This Abominable Practice* (London: Crouch, 1710).

6   First published in 1758 subsequent to *Dissertatio de febribus biliosis, seu Historia epidemiae biliosae Lausannensis*, the *Tentamen de morbis ex manustupratione* by Simon Tissot appeared in a revised and enlarged version under the title *L'Onanisme, ou Dissertation physique sur les maladies produites par la masturbation* (Lausanne: Chapuis, 1760).

7   J. Van Ussel, *Sexualunterdrückung* (Hamburg: Rowohlt, 1970): *Histoire de la répression sexuelle*, trans. C. Chevalot (Paris: Laffont, 1972).

8   E. Geoffroy Saint-Hilaire, *La Philosophie anatomique* (Paris: Rignoux, 1822), vols. 2 and 3: *Des Monstruosités humaines: Considérations générales sur les monstres, comprenant une théorie des phénomènes de la monstruosité* (Paris: Tastu, 1826). See also idem, *Histoire générale et par-*

ticulière des anomalies de l'organisation chez l'homme et les animaux, ou Traité de tératologie (Paris: Baillière, 1832–1837), 4 vols.

9 H. Kaan, *Psychopathia sexualis* (Leipzig: Voss, 1844).

10 B. A. Morel, *Traité des dégénérescences physiques, intellectuelles et morales de l'espèce humaine et des causes qui produisent ces variétés maladives* (Paris: Baillière, 1857).

In order to conduct a concrete analysis of power relations, one would have to abandon the juridical notion of sovereignty. That model presupposes the individual as a subject of natural rights or original powers; it aims to account for the ideal genesis of the state; and it makes law the fundamental manifestation of power. One would have to study power not on the basis of the primitive terms of the relation but starting from the relation itself, inasmuch as the relation is what determines the elements on which it bears: instead of asking ideal subjects what part of themselves or what powers of theirs they have surrendered, allowing themselves to be subjectified [*se laisser assujettir*], one would need to inquire how relations of subjectivation can manufacture subjects. Similarly, rather than looking for the single form, the central point from which all the forms of power would be derived by way of consequence or development, one must first let them stand forth in their multiplicity, their differences, their specificity, their reversibility: study them therefore as relations of force that intersect, interrelate, converge, or, on the contrary, oppose one another or tend to cancel each other out. Finally, instead of privileging law as a manifestation of power, it would be better to try and identify the different techniques of constraint that it brings into play.

If it is necessary to avoid reducing the analysis of power to the scheme suggested by the juridical constitution of sovereignty, if it is necessary to think about power in terms of force relations, must it be deciphered, then, according to the general form of war? Can war serve as an effective analyzer of power relations?

This question overlays several others:

• Should war be considered as a primary and fundamental state of things in relation to which all the phenomena of social domination, differentiation, and hierarchization are considered as secondary?

• Do the processes of antagonism, confrontation, and struggle between individuals, groups, or classes belong, in the last instance, to the general processes of warfare?

• Can the set of notions derived from strategy or tactics constitute a valid and adequate instrument for analyzing power relations?

• Are military and war-related institutions and, in a general way, the methods utilized for waging war, immediately or remotely, directly or indirectly, the nucleus of political institutions?

• But perhaps the question that needs to be asked first of all is this one: How, since when and how, did people begin to imagine that it is war that functions in power relations, that an uninterrupted combat undermines peace, and that the civil order is basically an order of battle?

That is the question that was posed in this year's course. How was war perceived in the background of peace? Who looked in the din and confusion of war, in the mud of battles, for the principle of intelligibility of order, institutions, and history? Who first thought that politics was war pursued by other means?

A paradox appears at a glance. With the evolution of states since the beginning of the Middle Ages, it seems that the practices and institutions of war pursued a visible development. Moreover, they tended to be concentrated in the hands of a central power that alone had the right and the means of war; owing to that very fact, they withdrew, albeit slowly, from the person-to-person, group-to-group relationship, and a line of development led them increasingly to be a state privilege. Furthermore and as a result, war tends to become the professional and technical prerogative of a carefully defined and controlled military apparatus. In short, a society pervaded by warlike relations was slowly replaced by a state equipped with military institutions.

Now, this transformation had scarcely been completed when there appeared a certain type of discourse on the relations of society and war. A historico-political discourse—very different from the philosophico-juridical discourse organized around the problem of sovereignty—makes war the permanent basis of all the institutions of power. This discourse appeared shortly after the end of the wars of religion and at the beginning of the great English political struggles of the seventeenth century. According to this discourse, which was illustrated in England by Coke or Lilburne, in France by Boulainvilliers and later by Du Buat-Nançay,[1] it was war that presided over the birth of states: not the ideal war imagined by the philosophers of the state of nature but real wars and actual battles; laws are born in the middle of expeditions, conquests, and burning cities; but war also continues to rage within the mechanisms of power—or, at least, to constitute the secret driving force of institutions, laws, and order. Beneath the omissions, illusions, and lies that make us believe in the necessities of nature or the functional requirements of order, we are bound to reencounter war: it is the cipher of peace. It continuously divides the entire social body; it places each of us in one camp or the other. And it is not enough to find this war again as an explanatory principle; we must reactivate it, make it leave the mute, larval forms in which it goes about its business almost without our being aware of it, and lead it to a decisive battle that we must prepare for if we intend to be victorious.

Through this thematic, which I have characterized loosely thus far, one can understand the importance of this form of analysis.

1. The subject who speaks in this discourse cannot occupy the position of the universal subject. In that general struggle of which he speaks, he is necessarily on one side or the other; he is in the battle, he has adversaries, he fights for a victory. No doubt, he tries to make right prevail, but the right in question is his particular right, marked by a relation of conquest, domination, or antiquity: rights of triumphant invasions or millennial occupations. And if he also speaks of truth, it is that perspectival and strategic truth that enables him to win the victory. So, in this case, we have a political and historical discourse that lays claim to truth and right, while explicitly excluding itself from juridico-philosophical universality. Its role is not the one that lawmakers and philosophers dreamed of, from Solon to Kant: to take a position between the adversaries, at the center of and above the conflict, and impose an armistice, establish an order that brings reconciliation. It is a matter of positing a right stamped with dissym-

metry and functioning as a privilege to be maintained or reestablished, of asserting a truth that functions as a weapon. For the subject who speaks this sort of discourse, universal truth and general right are illusions and traps.

2. We are dealing, moreover, with a discourse that turns the traditional values of intelligibility upside down. An explanation from below, which is not the simplest, the most elementary, the clearest explanation but, rather, the most confused, the murkiest, the most disorderly, the most haphazard. What is meant to serve as a principle of decipherment is the confusion of violence, passions, enmities, revenges; it is also the web of petty circumstances that decide defeats and victories. The dark, elliptical god of battles must illuminate the long days of order, labor, and peace. Fury must account for harmonies. Thus, at the beginning of history and law one will posit a series of brute facts (physical vigor, force, character traits), a series of chance happenings (defeats, victories, successes or failures of conspiracy, rebellions or alliances). And only above this tangle will a growing rationality take shape, that of calculations and strategies—a rationality that, as one rises and it develops, becomes increasingly fragile, more and more spiteful, more closely tied to illusion, to fancy, to mystification. So we have the complete opposite of those traditional analyses which attempt to rediscover, beneath the visible brutality of bodies and passions, a fundamental, abiding rationality, linked by nature to the just and the good.

This type of discourse develops entirely within the historical dimension. It undertakes not to measure history, unjust governments, abuses, and acts of violence with the ideal principle of a reason or a law but, rather, to awaken, beneath the form of institutions or laws, the forgotten past of real struggles, of masked victories or defeats, the dried blood in the codes. It takes as its field of reference the undefined movement of history. But at the same time it is possible for it to draw support from the traditional mythical forms (the lost age of great ancestors, the imminence of new times and millennial revenge, the coming of a new kingdom that will wipe out the ancient defeats): it is a discourse that will be able to carry both the nostalgia of decaying aristocracies and the ardor of popular revenges.

In summary, as against the philosophico-juridical discourse organized in terms of the problem of sovereignty and law, this discourse which deciphers the continued existence of war in society is essentially a historico-political discourse, a discourse in which truth functions as a weapon for a partisan victory, a discourse at once darkly critical and intensely mythical.

This year's course was devoted to the emergence of that form of analysis: how was war (and its different aspects—invasion, battle, conquest, victory, relations of victors and vanquished, pillage and appropriation, uprisings) used as an analyzer of history and, in a general way, of social relations?

1. One must first set aside some false paternities—that of Hobbes, in particular. What Hobbes calls the "war of all against all" is not in any way a real historical war but a game of representations by which each measures the danger that each represents for him, estimates the others' will to fight, and calculates the risk he himself would be taking if he resorted to force. Sovereignty—whether it involves a "commonwealth by institution" or a "commonwealth by acquisition"—is established not by an act of bellicose domination but, rather, by a calculation that allows war to be avoided. For Hobbes it is nonwar that founds the State and gives it its form.[2]

2. The history of wars as wombs of states was doubtless outlined in the sixteenth century at the end of the wars of religion (in France, for example, in the work of Hotman[3]). But it was mostly in the seventeenth century that this type of analysis was developed. In England, first, in the parliamentary opposition and among the Puritans, with the idea that English society, since the eleventh century, was a society of conquest: monarchy and aristocracy, with their characteristic institutions, were seen as Norman imports, while the Saxon people preserved, not without difficulty, a few traces of their original freedoms. Against this background of martial domination, English historians such as Coke or Selden[4] restored the chief episodes of England's history; each of these is analyzed either as a consequence or as a resumption of that historically primary state of war between two hostile races with different institutions and interests. The revolution of which these historians are the contemporaries and sometimes the protagonists would thus be the last battle and the revenge of that ancient war.

An analysis of the same type is also found in France, but at a later date and, above all, in the aristocratic circles of the end of the reign of Louis XIV. Boulainvilliers will give it the most rigorous formulation; but this time the story is told, and the rights are asserted, in the name of the victor. By giving itself a Germanic origin, the French aristocracy lays claim to the right of conquest, hence of eminent possession, upon all the lands of the realm and of absolute dominion over all the Gallic or Roman inhabitants; but it also claims prerogatives with respect to royal power, which would have been established originally only by its consent, and which should always be kept within the limits established back then. The history written in this way is no longer, as in England, that of the perpetual confrontation of the vanquished and the victors, with uprising and extracted concessions as a basic category; it will be the history of the king's usurpations or betrayals with regard to the nobility from which he descended, and of his unnatural collusions with a bourgeoisie of Gallo-Roman origin. This scheme of analysis, taken up again by Freret[5] and especially Du Buat-Nançay, was the object of a whole series of polemical exchanges and the occasion of substantial historical research up to the Revolution.

The important point is that the principle of historial analysis was sought in the duality and the war of races. Starting from there and going via the works of Augustin[6] and Amédée Thierry[7], two types of decipherment of history will develop in the nineteenth century: one will be linked to class struggle, the other to biological confrontation.

This year's seminar was devoted to a study of the category of "the dangerous individual" in criminal psychiatry. The notions connected with the theme of "social defense" were compared with the notions connected with the new theories of civil responsibility, as they appeared at the end of the nineteenth century.

NOTES

1   Sir E. Coke, *Argumentum Anti-Normannicum, or an Argument Proving, from Ancient Stories and Records, that William, Duke of Normandy, Made No Absolute Conquest of England by the Word* (London: Derby, 1682); J. Lilburne, *English Birth Right Justified Against All Arbitrary Usurpation* (London, 1645); *An Anatomy of the Lord's Tiranny and Injustice* (London, 1646); Count H. de Boulainvilliers, *Mémoire pour la noblesse de France contre les ducs et pairs* (n.p., 1717); *Histoire de l'ancien gouvernement de la France, avec XIV lettres historiques sur les parlements ou états généraux* (The Hague: Gesse et Neaulne, 1727), 3 vols.; *Essai sur la noblesse de France, contenant une dissertation sur son origine et son abaissement* (Amsterdam, 1732). Count L.-G. Du Buat-Nançay, *Les Origines ou l'Ancien Gouvernement de la France, de l'Italie, de l'Allemagne* (Paris: Didot, 1757), 4 vols.; *Histoire ancienne des peuples de l'Europe* (Paris: Desaint, 1772), 12 vols.

2   T. Hobbes, *Leviathan, or the Matter, Form and Power of a Commonwealth Ecclesiastical and Civil* (London: Crooke, 1651): *Léviathan: Traité de la matière, de la forme et du pouvoir de la république ecclésiastique et civile*, trans. F. Tricaud (Paris: Sirey, 1971).

3   F. Hotman, *Discours simple et véritable des rages exercés par la France, des horribles et indignes meurtres commis es personnes de Gaspar de Coligny et de plusieurs grands seigneurs* (Basel: Vaullemand, 1573); *La Gaule françoise* (Cologne: Bertulphe, 1574).

4   J. Selden, *England's epinomis* (1610), in *Opera omnia* (London: Walthoe, 1726), vol. 3: *De Jure naturali et gentium juxta disciplinam Ebraerorum libri septem* (London: Bishopius, 1640); *An Historical Discourse of the Uniformity of the Government of England* (London: Walbancke, 1647).

5   N. Freret, *Recherches historiques sur les moeurs et le gouvernement des Français, dans les divers temps de la monarchie: De l'origine des Francs et de leur établissement dans les Gaules*, in *Oeuvres complètes*, vols. 5–6 (Paris: Moutardier, 1796); *Vues générales sur l'origine et le mélange des anciennes nations et sur la manière d'en étudier l'histoire*, ibid., vol. 18.

6   A. J. Thierry, *Histoire de la conquête de l'Angleterre par les Normands, de ses causes et de ses suites jusqu'a nos jours* (Paris: Tessier, 1825), 2 vols.; *Récits des temps mérovingiens, précédés de considérations sur l'histoire de France* (Paris: Tessier, 1840), 2 vols.

7   A. J. Thierry, *Histoire des Gaulois, depuis les temps les plus reculés jusqu'à l'entière soumission de la Gaulle à la domination romaine* (Paris: Sautelet, 1828), 3 vols.

———

The course dealt with the genesis of a political knowledge that was to place at the center of its concerns the notion of population and the mechanisms capable of ensuring its regulation. A transition from a "territorial state" to a "population state"? No, one would have to say, because what occurred was not a replacement but, rather, a shift of accent and the appearance of new objectives, and hence of new problems and new techniques.

To follow that genesis, we took up the notion of government as our leading thread.

1. One would need to do an in-depth inquiry concerning the history not merely of the notion but even of the procedures and means employed to ensure, in a given society, the "government of men." In a very first approach, it seems that for the Greek and Roman societies the exercise of political power did not involve the right or the possibilities of a "government" understood as an activity that undertakes to conduct individuals throughout their lives by placing them under the authority of a guide responsible for what they do and for what happens to them. Following the indications furnished by Paul Veyne, it seems that the idea of a pastor-sovereign, a king or judge-shepherd of the human flock, is rarely found outside the archaic Greek texts or except in certain authors of the imperial epoch. On the other hand, the metaphor of the shepherd watching over the sheep is accepted when it comes to characterizing the activity of the educator, the doctor, the gymnastics teacher. An analysis of the *Politics* would confirm this hypothesis.

It was in the East that the theme of pastoral power was fully developed—above all, in Hebrew society. A certain number of traits mark this theme: the shepherd's power is exercised not so much over a fixed territory as over a multitude in movement toward a goal; it has the role of providing the flock with its sustenance, watching over it on a daily basis, and ensuring its salvation; lastly, it is a matter of a power that individualizes by granting, through an essential paradox, as much value to a single one of the sheep as to the entire flock. It is this type of power that was introduced into the West by Christianity and took an institutional form in the ecclesiastical pastorate: the government of souls was constituted in the Christian Church as a central, knowledge-based activity indispensable for the salvation of each and every one.

Now, the fifteenth and sixteenth centuries saw a general crisis of the pastorate open up and develop, but in a much more complex fashion: a search for other modes (and not necessarily less strict ones) of spiritual direction and new types of relations between pastor and flock; but also inquiries concerning the right way to "govern" children, a family, a domain, a principality. The general questioning of government and self-government, of guidance and self-guidance, accompanies, at the end of feudalism, the birth of new forms of economic and social relations and new political structurations.

2. We next analyzed some aspects of the formation of a political "governmentality": that is, the way in which the behavior of a set of individuals became involved, more and more markedly, in the exercise of sovereign power. This important transformation is expressed in the different "arts of governing" that were written at the end of the sixteenth century and the first half of the seventeenth. No doubt, it is linked to the emergence of the "reason of state." One goes from an art of governing whose principles were borrowed from the traditional virtues (wisdom, justice, liberality, respect for divine laws and human customs) or from the common abilities (prudence, thoughtful decisions, taking care to surround oneself with the best adviser) to an art of governing whose rationality has its principles and its specific domain of application in the state. The "reason of state" is not the imperative in the name of which one can or must upset all the other rules; it is the new matrix of rationality according to which the prince must exercise his sovereignty in governing men. One is far from the virtue of the sovereign of justice—far, too, from that virtue which is proper to Machiavelli's hero.

The development of the reason of state is correlative with the fad-

ing away of the imperial theme. Rome finally disappears. A new historical perception takes form; it is no longer polarized around the end
of time and the consolidation of all the particular sovereignties into the
empire of the last days; it is open to an indefinite time in which the
states have to struggle against one another to ensure their own survival.
And more than the problems of a sovereign's legitimate dominion over
a territory, what will appear important is the knowledge and development of a state's forces: in a space (European and global at once) of
competition between states, very different from that in which dynastic
rivals confront each other, the major problem is that of a dynamic of
the forces and the rational techniques which enable one to intervene
in those forces.

Thus, the reason of state, apart from the theories that formulated
and justified it, takes shape in two great ensembles of political knowledge and technology: a diplomatico-military technology that consists
in ensuring and developing the forces of a state through a system of
alliances, and the organizing of an armed apparatus. The search for a
European equilibrium, which was one of the guiding principles of the
treaties of Westphalia, is a consequence of this political technology.
The second is constituted by "policy" [*police*], in the sense given to the
word then: that is, the set of means necessary to make the forces of
the state increase from within. At the junction point of these two great
technologies, and as a shared instrument, one must place commerce
and monetary circulation between the states: enrichment through commerce offers the possibility of increasing the population, the manpower,
production, and export, and of endowing oneself with large, powerful armies. During the period of mercantilism and cameralistics, the
population–wealth pair was the privileged object of the new governmental reason.

3. The working-out of this population–wealth problem (in its different concrete aspects: taxation [*fiscalité*], scarcity, depopulation,
idleness–beggary–vagabondage) constitutes one of the conditions of
formation of political economy. The latter develops when it is realized
that the resources–population relationship can no longer be fully managed through a coercive regulatory system that would tend to raise the
population in order to augment the resources. The physiocrats are not
antipopulationist in opposition to the mercantilists of the preceding
epoch; they frame the population problem in a different way. For them,
the population is not simply the sum of subjects who inhabit a terri-

tory, a sum that would be the result of each person's desire to have children or of laws that would promote or discourage births—it is a variable dependent on a number of factors. These are not all natural by any means (the tax system, the activity of circulation, and the distribution of profit are essential determinants of the population rate). But this dependence can be rationally analyzed, in such a way that the population appears as "naturally" dependent on multiple factors that may be artificially alterable. So there begins to appear, branching off from the technology of "policy" and in correlation with the birth of economic thought, the political problem of population. The latter is not conceived as a collection of legal subjects, nor as a mass of human arms intended for labor; it is analyzed as a set of elements that, first, is connected with the general system of living beings (population in this sense falls in the category of "the human race" [*l'espèce humaine*]; the notion, new at the time, is to be distinguished from "mankind" [*le genre humain*]) and, second, may offer a purchase for concerted interventions (through laws, but also through changes of attitude, of ways of acting and living that can be obtained through "campaigns").

SEMINAR

The seminar was devoted to a few aspects of what the Germans, in the eighteenth century, called *Polizeiwissenschaft*—that is, the theory and analysis of everything "that tends to affirm and increase the power of the state to make good use of its forces, to obtain the welfare of its subjects," and, above all, "the maintenance of order and discipline, the regulations that tend to make their lives comfortable and to provide them with the things they need for their livelihood."

We tried to show what problems this "policy" was meant to address; how the role it was assigned was different from the one that would later devolve upon the police institution; what results were expected of it in order to bring about the growth of the state, and this in terms of two objectives—enable it to mark out and improve its position in the game of rivalry and competition between European states, and to guarantee internal order by ensuring the "welfare" of individuals. Development of the competitive state (economically and militarily), development of the *Wohlfahrt* state (wealth–tranquility–happiness): it is these two principles that "policy," understood as a rational art of governing, must be able to coordinate. It was conceived during this period as a sort of "technology of state forces." Among the main objects with which this technology needed to be concerned was population, in which the mercantilists saw a principle of enrichment and in which everyone recognized an essential component of the strength of states. And the management of this population required, among other things, a health policy capable of diminishing infant mortality, preventing epidemics, and bringing down the rates of endemic diseases, of intervening in living conditions in order to alter them and impose standards on them (whether this involved nutrition, housing, or urban planning), and of ensuring adequate medical facilities and services. The development, starting in the second half of the eighteenth century, of what was called *medizinische Polizei*, public health, or social medicine, must be written back into the general framework of a "biopolitics"; the latter tends to treat the "population" as a mass of living and coexisting beings who present particular biological and pathological traits and who thus come under specific knowledge and technologies. And this "biopolitics" itself must be understood in terms of a theme developed as early as the seventeenth century: the management of state forces.

Papers were read on the notion of *Polizeiwissenschaft* (Pasquale Pasquino), on the antismallpox campaigns in the eighteenth century (Anne-Marie Moulin), on the Paris cholera epidemic in 1832 (François Delaporte), on the legislation dealing with work-related accidents, and the development of insurance in the nineteenth century (François Ewald).

———————

As it turned out, this year's course was devoted in its entirety to what was to have formed only its introduction. The theme addressed was "biopolitics." By that I meant the endeavor, begun in the eighteenth century, to rationalize the problems presented to governmental practice by the phenomena characteristic of a group of living human beings constituted as a population: health, sanitation, birthrate, longevity, race... We are aware of the expanding place these problems have occupied since the nineteenth century, and of the political and economic issues they have constituted up to the present day.

It seemed to me that these problems could not be dissociated from the framework of political rationality within which they appeared and developed their urgency. "Liberalism" enters the picture here, because it was in connection with liberalism that they began to have the look of a challenge. In a system anxious to have the respect of legal subjects and to ensure the free enterprise of individuals, how can the "population" phenomenon, with its specific effects and problems, be taken into account? On behalf of what, and according to what rules, can it be managed? The debate that took place in England in the middle of the nineteenth century concerning public health legislation can serve as an example.

What should we understand by "liberalism"? I relied on Paul Veyne's reflections concerning historical universals and the need to test a nominalist method in history. And taking up a number of choices of method already made, I tried to analyze "liberalism" not as a theory or an ideology—and even less, certainly, as a way for "society" to "represent itself..."—but, rather, as a practice, which is to say, as a "way of doing things" oriented toward objectives and regulating itself by means of a sustained reflection. Liberalism is to be analyzed, then, as a principle and a method of rationalizing the exercise of government, a rationalization that obeys—and this is its specificity—the internal rule of maximum economy. While any rationalization of the exercise of government aims at maximizing its effects while diminishing, as far as possible, its cost (understood in the political as well as the economic sense), liberal rationalization starts from the assumption that government (meaning not the institution "government," of course, but the activity that consists in governing human behavior in the framework of, and by means of, state institutions) cannot be its own end. It does not have its reason for being in itself, and its maximization, even under the best possible conditions, should not be its regulative principle. On this point, liberalism breaks with that "reason of state" which, since the end of the nineteenth century, had sought, in the existence and strengthening of the state, the end capable both of justifying a growing governmentality and of regulating its development. The *Polizeiwissenschaft* developed by the Germans in the eighteenth century—either because they lacked a large state form, or also because the narrowness of their territorial partitions gave them access to much more easily observable units, given the technical and conceptual tools of the time—always subscribed to the principle: One is not paying enough attention, too many things escape one's control, too many areas lack regulation and supervision, there's not enough order and administration. In short, one is governing too little. *Polizeiwissenschaft* is the form taken by a governmental technology dominated by the principle of the reason of state, and it is in a "completely natural way," as it were, that it attends to the problems of population, which ought to be the largest and most active possible—for the strength of the state. Health, birthrate, sanitation find an important place in it, therefore, without any problem.

For its part, liberalism resonates with the principle: "One always governs too much"—or, at any rate, one always must suspect that one governs too much. Governmentality should not be exercised without a "critique" far more radical than a test of optimization. It should inquire not just as to the best (or least costly) means of achieving its effects but also concerning the possibility and even the lawfulness of its scheme for achieving effects. The suspicion that one always risks governing too much is inhabited by the question: Why, in fact, must one govern? This explains why the liberal critique barely detaches itself from a problematic, new at the time, of "society": it is on the latter's behalf that one will try to determine why there has to be a government, to what extent it can be done without, and in which cases it is needless or harmful for it to intervene. The rationalization of governmental practice, in terms of a reason of state, implied its maximization in optimal circumstances insofar as the existence of the state immediately assumes the exercise of government. Liberal thought starts not from the existence of the state, seeing in the government the means for attaining that end it would be for itself, but rather from society, which is in a complex relation of exteriority and interiority with respect to the state. Society, as both a precondition and a final end, is what enables one to no longer ask the question: How can one govern as much as possible and at the least possible cost? Instead, the question becomes: Why must one govern? In other words, what makes it necessary for there to be a government, and what ends should it pursue with regard to society in order to justify its existence? The idea of society enables a technology of government to be developed based on the principle that it itself is already "too much," "in excess"—or at least that it is added on as a supplement which can and must always be questioned as to its necessity and its usefulness.

Instead of making the distinction between state and civil society into a historical universal that allows us to examine all the concrete systems, we can try to see it as a form of schematization characteristic of a particular technology of government.

It cannot be said, then, that liberalism is a utopia never realized—unless the core of liberalism is taken to be the projections it has been led to formulate out of its analyses and criticisms. It is not a dream that comes up against a reality and fails to find a place within it. It constitutes— and this is the reason for both its polymorphism and its recurrences—a tool for criticizing the reality: (1) of a previous governmentality that one tries to shed; (2) of a current governmentality that one attempts to reform and rationalize by stripping it down; (3) of a governmentality that one opposes and whose abuses one tries to limit. So that we will be able to find liberalism, in different but simultaneous forms, as a regulative scheme of governmental practice and as the theme of a sometimes-radical opposition. English political thought, at the end of the eighteenth century and in the first half of the nineteenth, is highly characteristic of these multiple uses of liberalism. And even more specifically, the developments and ambiguities of Bentham and the Benthamites.

There is no doubt that the market as a reality and political economy as a theory played an important role in the liberal critique. But, as P. Rosanvallon's important book has confirmed, liberalism is neither the consequence nor the development of these;[1] rather, the market played, in the liberal critique, the role of a "test," a locus of privileged experience where one can identify the effects of excessive governmentality and even weigh their significance: the analysis of the mechanisms of "dearth" or more generally, of the grain trade in the middle of the eighteenth century, was meant to show the point at which governing was always governing too much. And whether it is a question of the physiocrats' Table or Smith's "invisible hand"; whether it is a question, therefore, of an analysis aiming to make visible (in the form of "evidence") the formation of the value and circulation of wealth—or, on the contrary, an analysis presupposing the intrinsic invisibility of the connection between individual profit-seeking and the growth of collective wealth—economics, in any case, shows a basic incompatibility between the optimal development of the economic process and a maximization of governmental procedures. It is by this, more than by the play of ideas, that the French or English economists broke away from mercantilism and cameralism; they freed reflection on economic practice from the hegemony of the "reason of state" and from the saturation of governmental intervention. By using it as a measure of "governing too much," they placed it "at the limit" of governmental action.

Liberalism does not derive from juridical thought any more than it does from an economic analysis. It is not the idea of a political society founded on a contractual tie that gave birth to it; but in the search for a liberal technology of government, it appeared that regulation through the juridical form constituted a far more effective tool than the wisdom or moderation of the governors. (Rather, the physiocrats tended, out of a distrust of law and the juridical institution, to look for that regulation in the recognition, by a despot with institutionally limited power, of the economy's "natural" laws, impressing themselves upon him as an evident truth.) Liberalism sought that regulation in "the law," not through a legalism that would be natural to it but because the law defines forms of general intervention excluding particular, individual, or exceptional measures; and because the participation of the governed in the formulation of the law, in a parliamentary system, constitutes the most effective system of governmental economy. The "state of right," the *Rechtsstaat*, the rule of law, the organization of a "truly represent-ative" parliamentary system was, therefore, during the whole beginning of the nineteenth century, closely connected with liberalism, but just as political economy—used at first as a test of excessive governmental-ity—was not liberal either by nature or by virtue, and soon even led to antiliberal attitudes (whether in the *Nationaloekonomie* of the nine-teenth century or in the planning economies of the twentieth), so the democracies of the state of right were not necessarily liberal, nor was liberalism necessarily democratic or devoted to the forms of law.

Rather than a relatively coherent doctrine, rather than a politics pur-suing a certain number of more or less clearly defined goals, I would be tempted to see in liberalism a form of critical reflection on govern-mental practice. That criticism can come from within or without, it can rely on this or that economic theory, or refer to this or that juridical system without any necessary and one-to-one connection. The ques-tion of liberalism, understood as a question of "too much government," was one of the constant dimensions of that recent European phenom-enon, having appeared first in England, it seems—namely, "political life." Indeed, it is one of the constituent elements of it, if it is the case that political life exists when governmental practice is limited in its pos-sible excess by the fact that it is the object of public debate as to its "good or bad," its "too much or too little."

Of course, the above reflections constitute not an "interpretation" of liberalism which would claim to be exhaustive but, rather, a plan of possible analysis—of "governmental reason," that is, of those types of rationality which are brought into play in the methods by which human behavior is directed via a state administration. I have tried to carry out such an analysis concerning two contemporary examples: German lib-eralism of the years 1948–62, and American liberalism of the Chicago school. In both cases, liberalism presented itself, in a definite context, as a critique of the irrationality peculiar to "excessive government" and as a return to a technology of "frugal government," as Franklin would have said.

In Germany, that excess was the regime of war, Nazism, but, beyond that, a type of directed and planned economy developing out of the

1914–18 period and the general mobilization of resources and men; it was also "state socialism." In point of fact, German liberalism of the second postwar period was defined, programmed, and even to a certain extent put into practice by men who, starting in the years 1928–1930, had belonged to the Freiburg school (or at least had been inspired by it) and who had later expressed themselves in the journal *Ordo*. At the intersection of neo-Kantian philosophy, Husserl's phenomenology, and Weber's sociology, on certain points close to the Viennese economists, concerned about the historical correlation between economic processes and juridical structures, men like Eucken, W. Roepke, Franz Böhm, and Von Rustow had conducted their critiques on three different political fronts: Soviet socialism, National Socialism, and interventionist policies inspired by Keynes. But they addressed what they considered as a single adversary: a type of economic government systematically ignorant of the market mechanisms that were the only thing capable of price-forming regulation. Ordo-liberalism, working on the basic themes of the liberal technology of government, tried to define what a market economy could be, organized (but not planned or directed) within an institutional and juridical framework that, on the one hand, would offer the guarantees and limitations of law, and, on the other, would make sure that the freedom of economic processes did not cause any social distortion. The first part of this course was devoted to the study of this Ordo-liberalism, which had inspired the economic choice of the general policy of the German Federal Republic during the time of Adenauer and Ludwig Erhard.

The second part was devoted to a few aspects of what is called "American neoliberalism": that liberalism which is generally associated with the Chicago school and which also developed in reaction against the "excessive government" exhibited in its eyes, starting with Simons, by the New Deal, war-planning, and the great economic and social programs generally supported by postwar Democratic administrations. As in the case of the German Ordo-liberals, the critique carried out in the name of economic liberalism cited the danger represented by the inevitable sequence: economic interventionism, inflation of governmental apparatuses, overadministration, bureaucracy, and rigidification of all the power mechanisms, accompanied by the production of new economic distortions that would lead to new interventions. But what was striking in this American neoliberalism was a movement completely contrary to what is found in the social economy of the market in Ger-

many: where the latter considers regulation of prices by the market—
the only basis for a rational economy—to be in itself so fragile that
it must be supported, managed, and "ordered" by a vigilant internal
policy of social interventions (involving assistance to the unemployed,
health care coverage, a housing policy, and so on), American neoliberalism seeks rather to extend the rationality of the market, the
schemes of analysis it proposes, and the decisionmaking criteria it suggests to areas that are not exclusively or not primarily economic. For
example, the family and birth policy, or delinquency and penal policy.

What would need to be studied now, therefore, is the way in which
the specific problems of life and population were raised within a technology of government which, without always having been liberal—far
from it—was always haunted since the end of the eighteenth century
by liberalism's question.

The seminar was devoted this year to the crisis of juridical thought in
the last years of the nineteenth century. Papers were read by François
Ewald (on civil law), Catherine Mevel (on public and administrative
law), Eliane Allo (on the right to life in legislation concerning children),
Nathalie Coppinger and Pasquale Pasquino (on penal law), Alexandre
Fontana (on security measures), François Delaporte and Anne-Marie
Moulin (on health policy and health politics).

NOTE

1 P. Rosanvallon, *Le Capitalisme utopique: critique de l'idéologie économique* (Paris: Seuil, 1979).

This year's course drew support from the analyses done the pre-ceding years on the subject of "government," this notion being under-stood in the broad sense of techniques and procedures for directing human behavior. Government of children, government of souls and consciences, government of a household, of a state, or of oneself. Inside this very general framework, we studied the problem of self-examination and confession.

Speaking of the sacrament of penance, Tomaso de Vio called the con-fession of sins an "act of truth."[1] Let us retain this phrase, with the meaning that Cajetan gave to it. The question raised is this one, then: How is it that in Western Christian culture the government of men demands, on the part of those who are led, not only acts of obedience and submission but also "acts of truth," which have the peculiar re-quirement not just that the subject tell the truth but that he tell the truth about himself, his faults, his desires, the state of his soul, and so on? How was a type of government of men formed in which one is required not simply to obey but to reveal what one is by stating it?

After a theoretical introduction concerning the notion of "truth regime," the longest part of the course was devoted to the procedures of examination of souls and of confession in early Christianity. Two con-cepts have to be recognized, each of which corresponds to a particular practice: *exomologēsis* and *exagoreusis*. A study of *exomologēsis* shows that this term is often employed in a very broad sense: it designates an act meant to reveal both a truth and the subject's adherence to that truth; to do the exomologesis of one's belief is not merely to affirm what one believes but to affirm the fact of that belief; it is to make the act of affirmation an object of affirmation, and hence to authenticate it either for oneself or with regard to others. Exomologesis is an emphatic affirmation whose emphasis relates above all to the fact that the subject binds himself to that affirmation and accepts the consequences.

Exomologesis as an "act of faith" is indispensable to the Christian, for whom the revealed and taught truths are not simply a matter of beliefs that he accepts but of obligations by which he commits himself—to uphold his beliefs, to accept the authority that authenticates them, to profess them publicly if need be, to live in accordance with them, and so on. Yet a different type of exomologesis is found very early on: the exomologesis of sins. There, too, distinctions must be made. Recognizing that one has committed sins is an obligation laid either on catechumens who are candidates for baptism or on Christians who have been prone to a few lapses. To the latter, the *Didascalia* prescribes that they perform the exomologesis of their sins to the congregation.[2] Now, this "confession" seems not to have taken, at the time, the form of a detailed public statement of the transgressions committed but, rather, of a collective rite in the course of which each individual acknowledged in his heart that he was a sinner before God. It was concerning serious offenses—in particular, idolatry, adultery, and homicide, as well as on the occasion of persecutions and apostasy—that the specific character of the exomologesis of wrongs was manifested: it became a condition for reinstatement, and it was connected with a complex public ritual.

The history of penitential practices from the second to the fifth centuries shows that exomologesis did not have the form of a verbal confession examining the different offenses along with their circumstances, and that it did not obtain remission from the fact that it was enacted in the canonical form before the person who had received the authority to remit them. Penance was a state into which one entered after a ritual, and it was ended (sometimes on the deathbed) after a second ceremonial. Between these two moments, the penitent did the exomologesis of his faults through his mortifications, his austerities, his way of living, his garments, his manifest attitude of repentance—in short, through a whole dramaticity in which the verbal expression did not have the main role, and in which the analytical statement of specific wrongs seems to have been absent. It may be that before the reconciliation a special rite took place, and that the term *exomologesis* was applied to it more particularly. Yet even in that case it was still a mat-

ter of a dramatic and synthetic expression by which the sinner acknowledged in the presence of all the fact of having sinned; he attested this
acknowledgment in a manifestation that at the same time visibly bound
him to a sinner's state and prepared his deliverance. Verbalization of
the confession of sins in canonical penance will be done systematically
only later—first with the practice of penance at a price, then from the
twelfth and thirteenth centuries onward, when the sacrament of penance would be organized.

In the monastic institutions, the practice of confession took quite different forms (which did not exclude recourse to forms of exomologesis
in front of the assembled community when the monk had committed
transgressions of a certain importance). To study these confessional
practices in monastic life, we resorted to a more detailed study of
Cassian's *Conferences* and *Institutes of the Cenobites*,[3] with a view to
the techniques of spiritual direction. Three aspects in particular were
analyzed: the mode of dependence with respect to the elder or teacher,
the way of conducting the examination of one's own conscience, and the
obligation to describe one's mental impulses in a formulation that aims
to be exhaustive—the *exagoreusis*. Considerable differences appear on
these three points, in comparison with ancient philosophy. Schematically, we can say that in the monastic institution the relation to the
teacher takes the form of an unconditional and steadfast obedience that
concerns every aspect of life and, in principle, does not leave the nov-
ice any margin of initiative; that while the value of this relationship
depends on the teacher's qualification, it is nonetheless true that by
itself the form of obedience, whatever its object, holds a positive value;
and finally, that while obedience is absolutely necessary for the nov-
ices and, as a rule, the teachers are elders, the age differential is not
sufficient in itself to justify such a relationship—both because the ability to direct is a charisma and the obedience must constitute, in the
form of humility, a permanent relationship with oneself and others.

The examination of conscience is also very different from the one
recommended in the philosophical schools of antiquity. Like the latter, of course, it comprises two great forms: the evening recollection
of the day gone by and continual vigilance concerning oneself. It is this
second form that is most important in the monasticism described by
Cassian. Its procedures show clearly that it is not a matter of deciding
what must be done to keep from committing a transgression or even
to recognize whether one may have committed a transgression in what

one has done. It is a matter of taking hold of the thought occurrence (*cogitatio = logismos*), of probing rather deeply in order to grasp its origin and determine where it comes from (from God, from oneself, from the Devil) and do a sorting-out (which Cassian describes by using several metaphors, the most important of which is that of the money-changer who inspects the coins). Cassian devotes one of the most interesting *Conferences* to "inconstancy of the mind"—relating the views of Abbot Serenus—which forms the domain of a self-examination that clearly has the role of making possible the unity and continuity of contemplation.[4]

As for the confession prescribed by Cassian, it is not simply a statement of wrongs committed, nor a general exposition of the state of one's soul; it must tend toward the continuous verbalization of all the impulses of thought. This confession enables the director to give counsel and render a diagnosis: Cassian thus relates examples of consultation; sometimes several elders take part and give their opinions. But verbalization also involves intrinsic effects which it owes simply to the fact that it transforms the impulses of the mind into statements addressed to another. In particular, the "sorting-out," which is one of the aims of the examination, is performed through verbalization with the help of a threefold mechanism of shame that makes one blush at expressing any bad thought, the material realization of what is happening in the mind through the words spoken, and the incompatibility between the Devil, who tempts and deceives while hiding in the recesses of consciousness, and the light that exposes them to view. Hence, understood in this way, confession involves a continuous externalization through words of the "arcana" of consciousness.

Unconditional obedience, uninterrupted examination, and exhaustive confession form an ensemble with each element implying the other two; the verbal manifestation of the truth that hides in the depths of oneself appears as an indispensable component of the government of men by each other, as it was carried out in monastic—and especially Cenobitic—institutions beginning in the fourth century. But it must be emphasized that this manifestation was not for the purpose of establishing one's sovereign mastery over oneself; what was expected, rather, was humility and mortification, detachment toward oneself and the constitution of a relation with oneself tending toward the destruction of the form of the self.

This year's seminar was devoted to certain aspects of liberal thought in the nineteenth century. Papers were read by N. Coppinger on economic development at the end of the century, by D. Deleule on the Scottish historical school, P. Rosanvallon on Guizot, F. Ewald on Saint-Simon and the Saint-Simonians, P. Pasquino on the place of Menger in the history of liberalism, A. Schutz on Menger's epistemology, and C. Mevel on the notions of the general will and the general interest.

N O T E S

1 Father T. De Vio, *De Confessione questiones*, in *Opuscula* (Paris: Regnault, 1530).

2 *Didascalia*, the teaching of the twelve apostles and their disciples, an ecclesiastical document from the third century whose original, in Greek, is lost. There remains only an adaptation of it in the first six books of the *Apostolic Constitutions*: *Constitutions apostoliques: Didascalie, c'est-à-dire l'enseignement catholique des douze apôtres et des saints disciples de Notre Saveur*, trans. abbé F. Nau (Paris: Firmin Didot, 1902).

3 J. Cassian, *Institutions cénobitiques*, trans. J.-C. Guy (Paris: Cerf, 1965). *Conférences*, trans. Dom E. Pichery (Paris: Cerf): vol. 1 (1966), vol. 2 (1967), vol. 3 (1971) [*The Institutes of the Coenobia and Conferences*, trans. Edgar C. S. Gibson, in *A Select Library of Nicene and Post-Nicene Fathers* (Grand Rapids, Mich.: Eerdman's, 1978), vol. 11].

4 Cassian, *Première conférence de l'abbé Serenus, de la mobilité de l'âme et des ésprits du mal*, in *Conférences*, vol. 1, pp. 242–77.

SUBJECTIVITY AND TRUTH

This year's course is to be the object of a forthcoming publication, so it will be enough for now to give a brief summary.

Under the general title of "Subjectivity and Truth," it is a question of beginning an inquiry concerning the instituted models of self-knowledge and their history: How was the subject established, at different moments and in different institutional contexts, as a possible, desirable, or even indispensable object of knowledge? How were the experience that one may have of oneself and the knowledge that one forms of oneself organized according to certain schemes? How were these schemes defined, valorized, recommended, imposed? It is clear that neither the recourse to an original experience nor the study of the philosophical theories of the soul, the passions, or the body can serve as the main axis in such an investigation. The guiding thread that seems the most useful for this inquiry is constituted by what one might call the "techniques of the self," which is to say, the procedures, which no doubt exist in every civilization, suggested or prescribed to individuals in order to determine their identity, maintain it, or transform it in terms of a certain number of ends, through relations of self-mastery or self-knowledge. In short, it is a matter of placing the imperative to "know oneself"—which to us appears so characteristic of our civilization—back in the much broader interrogation that serves as its explicit or implicit context: What should one do with oneself? What work should be carried out on the self? How should one "govern oneself" by performing actions in which one is oneself the objective of those actions, the domain in which they are brought to bear, the instrument they employ, and the subject that acts?

Plato's *Alcibiades* can be taken as the starting point:[1] the question of the "care of oneself"—*epimeleia heautou*—appears in this text as the general framework within which the imperative of self-knowledge acquires its significance. The series of studies that can be envisaged starting from there could form a history of the "care of oneself," understood as an experience, and thus also as a technique elaborating and transforming that experience. Such a project is at the intersection of two themes treated previously: a history of subjectivity and an analysis of the forms of "governmentality." The history of subjectivity was begun by studying the social divisions brought about in the name of madness, illness, and delinquency, along with their effects on the constitution of a rational and normal subject. It was also begun by attempting to identify the modes of objectification of the subject in knowledge disciplines [*dans ses savoirs*] such as those dealing with language, labor, and life. As for the study of "governmentality," it answered a dual purpose: doing the necessary critique of the common conceptions of "power" (more or less confusedly conceived as a unitary system organized around a center that is at the same time its source, a system that is driven by its internal dynamic always to expand); analyze it rather as a domain of strategic relations focusing on the behavior of the other or others, and employing various procedures and techniques according to the case, the institutional frameworks, social groups, and historical periods in which they develop. The studies already published concerning confinement and the disciplines, the courses devoted to the reason of state and the "art of governing," and the volume in preparation, with the collaboration of Arlette Farge, on the *lettres de cachet* in the eighteenth century,[2] constitute elements in this analysis of "governmentality."

The history of the "care" and the "techniques" of the self would thus be a way of doing the history of subjectivity; no longer, however, through the divisions between the mad and the nonmad, the sick and nonsick, delinquents and nondelinquents, nor through the constitution of fields of scientific objectivity giving a place to the living, speaking, laboring subject; but, rather, through the putting in place, and the transformations in our culture, of "relations with oneself," with their technical armature and their knowledge effects. And in this way one could take up the question of governmentality from a different angle: the government of the self by oneself in its articulation with relations with others (such as one finds in pedagogy, behavior counseling, spiritual direction, the prescription of models for living, and so on).

The study done this year delimited this general framework in two ways. A historical limitation: we studied what had developed in Hellenic and Roman culture as a "technique of living," a "technique of existence" in the philosophers, moralists, and doctors in the period stretching from the first century B.C. to the second century A.D. And a limitation of domain: these techniques of living were considered only in their application to that type of act which the Greeks called *aphrodisia*, and for which our notion of "sexuality" obviously constitutes a completely inadequate translation. The problem raised was the following, then: How did the philosophical and medical techniques of living, on the eve of Christianity's development, define and regulate the practice of sexual acts—the *khrēsis aphrodisiōn*? One sees how far one is from a history of sexuality organized around the good old repressive hypothesis and its customary questions (how and why is desire repressed?). It is a matter of acts and pleasures, not of desire. It is a matter of the formation of the self through techniques of living, not of repression through prohibition and law. We shall try to show not how sex was kept in check but how that long history began which, in our societies, binds together sex and the subject.

It would be completely arbitrary to connect a particular moment in time to the emergence of the "care of oneself" in regard to sexual acts; but the proposed demarcation (around the techniques of the self in the centuries immediately preceding Christianity) has its justification. In fact, it is certain that the "technology of the self"—reflection on modes of living, on choices of existence, on the way to regulate one's behavior, to attach oneself to ends and means—experienced an extensive development in the Hellenistic and Roman period, to the point of having absorbed a large portion of philosophical activity. This development cannot be dissociated from the growth of urban society, from the new distribution of political power, or from the importance assumed by the new service aristocracy in the Roman Empire. This government of the self, with the techniques that are peculiar to it, takes its place "between" pedagogical institutions and the religions of salvation. This should not be taken to mean a chronological succession, even if it is true that the question of the education of future citizens seems to have occasioned more interest and reflection in classical Greece, and the question of an afterlife and a hereafter caused more anxiety in later periods. Nor should it be thought that pedagogy, government of the self, and salvation constituted three utterly distinct domains, employing different notions and methods; in reality there were numerous cross-overs and a definite continuity between the three. The fact remains that the technology of the self intended for the adult can be analyzed in the specificity and breadth it took on during this period, provided it is pulled out of the retrospective shadow cast on it by pedagogical institutions and the salvation religions.

Now, this art of self-government as it developed in the Hellenistic and Roman period is important for the ethic of sexual acts and its history. Indeed, it is there—and not in Christianity—that the principles of the famous conjugal arrangement, whose history has been so long, were formulated: the exclusion of any sexual activity outside the relation between spouses, the procreative purpose of these acts, at the expense of pleasure as an end, the emotional function of sexual relations in the marriage partnership. But that is not all; it is also in this technology of the self that one observes the development of a form of uneasiness about sexual acts and their effects, an uneasiness whose origin is too readily attributed to Christianity (when it is not attributed to capitalism or "bourgeois morality"!). Of course, the question of sexual acts was far from having the importance then that it would subsequently have in the Christian problematic of the flesh and its lusts; the question, for example, of anger or reversal of fortune undoubtedly looms larger than sexual relations for the Hellenistic and Roman moralists; but even if the place of sexual relations in the order of concerns is rather far from being the first, it is important to note the way in which these techniques of the self connect the order of sexual acts to the whole of existence.

In this year's course we focused on four examples of these techniques of the self in their relation with the regimen of the *aphrodisia*.

1. The interpretation of dreams. Artemidorus's *Oneirocritica*,[3] in Book One, Chapters 78–80, constitutes the basic text in this area. The question raised there does not directly concern the practice of sexual acts but, rather, the use to be made of the dreams in which they are represented. In this text, it is a matter of determining the prognostic value they should be given in everyday life: what auspicious or inauspicious events may one expect according to whether the dream has presented this or that type of sexual relation? A text of this sort obviously does not prescribe any morals, but it does reveal, through the play of positive or negative significations that it ascribes to the dream

images, a whole set of correlations (between sexual acts and social life) and a whole system of differential valuations (hierarchizing the sexual acts relative to one another).

2. The medical regimens. These aim directly to assign a "measure" to sexual acts. It is noteworthy that this measure almost never concerns the form of the sexual act (natural or not, normal or not), but its frequency and its moment. Quantitative and circumstantial values are all that is taken into consideration. A study of Galen's great theoretical edifice shows clearly the connection established in medical and philosophical thought between sexual acts and the death of individuals. (Because each living being is destined to die, but the species must live eternally, nature invented the mechanism of sexual reproduction.) It also clearly shows the connection established between the sexual act and the substantial, violent, paroxysmal, and dangerous expenditure of the vital principle that it involves. A study of regimens properly speaking (in Rufus of Ephesus, Athenaeus, Galen, Soranus) shows, through the endless precautions they recommended, the complexity and tenuousness of the relations established between sexual acts and the life of the individual: the sexual act's extreme sensitivity to all external and internal circumstances that might make it harmful; the immense range of effects of every sexual act on all parts and components of the body.

3. Married life. The treatises on marriage were quite numerous in the period under study. What remains of the work of Musonius Rufus, Antipater of Tarsus, or Hierocles, as well as the works of Plutarch, shows not only the valorization of marriage (which seems to correspond to a social phenomenon, according to the historians) but also a new conception of the marital relationship: added to the traditional principles of the complementarity of the two sexes necessary for the order of the "household" is the ideal of a dual relation, involving every aspect of the life of the two partners, and establishing personal emotional ties in a definitive way. Sexual acts must find their exclusive place inside this relationship (a condemnation of adultery therefore, understood, by Musonius Rufus, no longer as an infringement on a husband's privileges but as a breach of the marriage tie, which binds the husband as well as the wife[4]). So they must be directed toward procreation, since that is the end given by the nature of marriage. And, finally, they must comply with an internal regulation required by modesty, mutual affection, and respect for the other (Plutarch offers the most numerous and valuable indications on this last point).

4. The choice of loves. The standard comparison between the two loves—the love for women and the love for boys—left two important texts for the period studied: Plutarch's *Dialogue on Love* and Lucian's *Amores*.[5] An analysis of these two texts attests to the persistence of a problem with which the classical period was very familiar: the difficulty of giving a status and a justification to sexual relations in the pederastic relationship. Lucian's dialogue concludes ironically with a precise reminder of those acts which the erotics of boys sought to elide in the name of friendship, virtue, and pedagogy. Plutarch's much more elaborate text brings out the mutual consent to pleasure as an essential element in the *aphrodisia*; it shows that this kind of reciprocity in pleasure can only exist between a man and a woman; better still, in the marriage relationship, where it regularly serves to renew the marriage covenant.

NOTES

1   Plato, *Alcibiade*, trans. M. Croiset (Paris: Belles Lettres, 1925). [Plato, *Alcibiades*, trans. W. R. M. Lamb, in *Plato* (Cambridge, Mass.: Harvard, 1967), vol. 12].

2   M. Foucault and A. Farge, *Le Désordre des familles: Lettres de cachet des archives de la Bastille au VIIIᵉ siècle* (Paris: Gallimard-Julliard, 1982).

3   Artemidorus, *La Clef des songes: Onirocriticon*, trans. A. J. Festugière (Paris: Vrin, 1975), bk. 1, chs. 78–80, pp. 84–93. [Artemidorus, *The Interpretation of Dreams: Oneirocritica*, trans. R. J. White (Park Ridge, N.J.: Noyes, 1975), bk. 1, pp. 58–66].

4   C. Musonius Rufus, *Reliquiae, XII: Sur les aphrodisia*, ed. O. Hense (Leipzig: Teubner, 1905), pp. 65–67.

5   Lucian (attrib.), *Amores: Affairs of the Heart*, trans. M. D. Macleod, in *Works* (London: Loeb Classical Library, 1967), no. 53, pp. 230–33; Plutarch, *Dialogue sur l'amour*, trans. R. Flacelière, in *Oeuvres morales* (Paris: Belles Lettres, 1980), vol. 10, §769b, p. 101 [Plutarch, *The Dialogue on Love*, trans. Edwin Minor, Jr., F. H. Sandbach, and W. C. Helmbold (Cambridge, Mass.: Harvard University Press, 1961), vol. 9, pp. 427–28].

THE HERMENEUTIC OF THE SUBJECT

———————

This year's course was devoted to the formation of the theme of the hermeneutic of the self. The object was not just to study it in its theoretical formulations but to analyze it in relation to a set of practices that were very important in classical and late antiquity. These practices had to do with what was often called in Greek *epimeleia heautou*, and in Latin *cura sui*. This principle that one needs to "attend to oneself," to "take care of oneself," is doubtless obscured by the radiance of the *gnōthi seauton*. Yet, one must bear in mind that the rule of having to know oneself was regularly associated with the theme of care of the self. Through all the culture of antiquity it is easy to find evidence of the importance given to "concern with oneself" and its connection with the theme of self-knowledge.

To start with, in Socrates himself. In the *Apology*, one sees Socrates presenting himself to his judges as the teacher of self-concern.[1] He is the man who accosts passersby and says to them: You concern yourself with your wealth, your reputation, and with honors, but you don't worry about your virtue and your soul. Socrates is the man who takes care that his fellow citizens "take care of themselves." Now, concerning this role, Socrates says three important things, a little farther on in this same *Apology*: it is a mission that was conferred on him by the deity, and he will not give it up before his last breath; it is a disinterested task for which he doesn't ask any payment, he performs it out of pure benevolence; and it is a useful service to the city-state, more useful even than an athlete's victory at Olympia, for by teaching citizens to attend to themselves (rather than to their possessions), one also teaches them to attend to the city-state itself (rather than its material affairs). Instead of sentencing him, his judges would do better to reward Socrates for having taught others to care for themselves.

Eight centuries later, the same notion of *epimeleia heautou* appears with an equally important role in Gregory of Nyssa. He applies this term to the impulse that moves one to renounce marriage, detach oneself from the flesh, and, through the virginity of one's heart and body, regain the immortality from which one had fallen. In another passage of the *Treatise on Virginity* he makes the parable of the lost drachma the model of the care of the self:[2] for a lost drachma one must light the lamp, ransack the house, explore every nook, until one sees the metal of the coin shining in the darkness; in the same way, in order to rediscover the effigy that God imprinted on our soul and that the body has covered with grime, one must "take care of oneself," lighting the lamp of reason and exploring all the recesses of the soul. So it is clear that Christian asceticism, like ancient philosophy, places itself under the sign of the care of the self and makes the obligation to know oneself one of the elements of this essential care.

Between these two extreme references—Socrates and Gregory of Nyssa—one can ascertain that the care of the self constituted not just a principle but a constant practice. We can consider two other examples, very far apart this time in their way of thinking and their type of ethic. An Epicurean text, the *Letter to Menoeceus*, begins in this way: "Let no one when young delay to study philosophy, nor when he is old grow weary of his study. For no one can come too early or too late to secure the health of his soul."[3] Philosophy is assimilated to the care of the soul (the term is quite precisely medical: *hugiainein*), and this care is a task that must be carried on throughout one's life. In the treatise *On the Contemplative Life*, Philo thus designates a certain practice of the Theraputae as an *epimeleia* of the soul.[4]

We cannot stop there, however. It would be a mistake to think that the care of the self was an invention of philosophical thinking and that it constituted a precept peculiar to the philosophical life. It was actually a precept of living that, in a general way, was very highly valued in Greece. Plutarch cites a Lacedaemonian aphorism that is very significant in this regard.[5] One day Anaxandrides was asked why his fellow countrymen, the Spartans, entrusted the cultivation of their lands to slaves instead of reserving this activity for themselves. This was the response: "It was by not taking care of the fields, but of ourselves, that we acquired those fields." Attending to oneself is a privilege; it is the mark of a social superiority, as against those who must attend to others in order to serve them or attend to a trade in order to live. The advantage afforded by wealth, status, and birth is expressed by the fact that one has the possibility of attending to oneself. We may note that the Roman concept of the *otium* has some relation to this theme: the "leisure" designated by the word is, above all, the time that one spends attending to oneself. In this sense, philosophy, in Greece as in Rome, has only incorporated into its own requirements a much more widespread social ideal.

In any case, even after becoming a philosophical principle, the care of the self remained a form of activity. The very term *epimeleia* does not merely designate an attitude of awareness or a form of attention that one would focus on oneself; it designates a regulated occupation, a work with its methods and objectives. Xenophon, for example, employs the word *epimeleia* to designate the work of the master of the household who supervises its farming. It is a word also used to designate the ritual respects that are paid to the gods and to the dead. The activity of the sovereign who looks after his people and leads the city-state is called *epimeleia* by Dio of Prusa. It should be understood, then, that when the philosophers and moralists will recommend care of oneself (*epimeleisthai heautō*) they are not advising simply to pay attention to oneself, to avoid mistakes or dangers or to stay out of harm's way; they are referring to a whole domain of complex and regulated activities. We may say that in all of ancient philosophy the care of the self was considered as both a duty and a technique, a basic obligation and a set of carefully worked-out procedures.

The quite natural starting point for a study focused on the care of the self is the *Alcibiades*.[6] Three questions appear in it, relating to the connection of the care of the self with politics, pedagogy, and self-knowledge. A comparison of the *Alcibiades* with the texts of the first and second centuries reveals several important transformations.

1. Socrates advised Alcibiades to take advantage of his youth to look after himself: "At fifty you would be too old." But Epicurus said: "When young one must not hesitate to study philosophy, and when old, one must not hesitate to study philosophy. It is never too early or too late to take care of one's soul." It is this principle of constant care throughout life that clearly prevails. Musonius Rufus, for example: "One must

always take care of oneself if one wishes to live in a wholesome way." Or Galen: "To become an accomplished man, each individual needs to exercise, as it were, his whole life through," even if it is true that it would be better "to have looked after his soul from his earliest years."

It is a fact that the friends to whom Seneca or Plutarch offer their advice are no longer those ambitious adolescents to whom Socrates spoke: they are men, sometimes young (like Serenus), sometimes fully mature (like Lucilius, who served as the procurator of Sicily when Seneca and he exchanged a long spiritual correspondence). Epictetus, who ran a school, had students who were still quite young, but he, too, occasionally challenged adults—and even "statesmen"—to turn their attention back to themselves.

Attending to oneself is therefore not just a momentary preparation for living; it is a form of living. Alcibiades realized that he must take care of himself if he meant to attend to others. Now it becomes a matter of attending to oneself, for oneself: one should be, for oneself and throughout one's existence, one's own object.

Hence the idea of conversion to oneself (*ad se convertere*), the idea of an existential impulse by which one turns in upon oneself (*eis heauton epistrephein*). Of course, the theme of the *epistrophē* is a typically Platonic one. But, as one may have already seen in the *Alcibiades*, the impulse by which the soul turns to itself is an impulse by which one's gaze is drawn "aloft"—toward the divine element, toward the essences and the supracelestial world where they are visible. The turning that Seneca, Plutarch, and Epictetus urge people to accomplish is a kind of turning in place: it has no other end or outcome than to settle into oneself, to "take up residence in oneself" and to remain there. The final objective of the conversion to oneself is to establish a certain number of relations with oneself. These relations are sometimes conceived on the jurido-political model: to be sovereign over oneself, to exert a perfect mastery over oneself, to be completely "self-possessed" (*fieri suum*, Seneca often says). They are also often represented on the model of positive enjoyment: to enjoy oneself, to take one's pleasure with oneself, to delight in the self alone.

2. A second major difference concerns pedagogy. In the *Alcibiades*, care of the self was essential because of the deficiencies of education; it was a matter of perfecting the latter or of taking charge of it oneself—in any case, of providing a "formation."

From the moment that applying oneself to oneself became an adult practice that must be carried out one's entire life, its pedagogical role tended to fade and other functions came to the fore.

a) A critical function, first of all. The practice of the self must enable one to get rid of all the bad habits, all the false opinions that one can get from the crowd or from bad teachers, but also from parents and associates. To "unlearn" (*de-discere*) is one of the important tasks of self-cultivation.

b) But it also has a function of struggle. The practice of the self is conceived as a permanent battle. It is not simply a matter of shaping a man of valor for the future. The individual must be given the weapons and the courage that will enable him to fight all his life. We know how frequently two metaphors appeared: that of the athletic contest (in life one is like a wrestler who has to dispose of his successive opponents and who must be training when he is not fighting) and that of warfare (the mind must be deployed like an army that an enemy is always liable to attack).

c) But, above all, this self-cultivation has a curative and therapeutic function. It is much closer to the medical model than to the pedagogical model. Of course, one must bear in mind certain facts that are very ancient in Greek culture: the existence of a notion such as *pathos*, which denotes both mental passion and physical illness; the breadth of a metaphorical field that allows one to apply to the body and the mind expressions such as "nurse," "heal," "amputate," "scarify," "purge." One should also recall the principle—familiar to the Epicureans, the Cynics, the Stoics—that philosophy's role is to heal the diseases of the soul. Plutarch was able one day to declare that philosophy and medicine constituted *mia khōra*, a single area, a single domain. Epictetus did not want his school to be regarded merely as a place of education but also as a "medical clinic," an *iatreion*; he intended it to be a "dispensary for the soul"; he wanted his students to arrive thinking of themselves as patients: "One man has a dislocated shoulder, another an abcess, another a headache."

3. In the first and second centuries, the relation to the self is always considered as needing to rely on the relation to a teacher, to a director, or in any case to another person. Yet this presupposed a growing independence from the love relation.

It was a generally accepted principle that one could not attend to oneself without the help of another. Seneca said that no one was ever strong enough on his own to get out of the state of *stultitia* he was in:

"He needs someone to extend him a hand and pull him free." In the same way, Galen said that man loves himself too much to be able to cure himself of his passions by himself; he had often seen men "stumble" who had not been willing to rely on one another's authority. This principle is true for beginners but also for what follows, and even to the end of one's life. Seneca's attitude, in his correspondence with Lucilius, is characteristic: no matter that he is aged, having given up all his activities, he gives counsel to Lucilius but asks him for advice in return and is thankful for the help he finds in this exchange of letters.

What is remarkable in this soul practice is the variety of social relations that can serve as its support.

- There are the strictly educational organizations: Epictetus's school can serve as an example. Temporary auditors were given a place next to students who remained for a longer course of study; but instruction was also given to those who aspired to become philosophers and soul directors themselves. Some of the *Discourses* collected by Arrian are technical lessons for future practitioners of self-cultivation.[7]

- One also finds private counselors, especially in Rome: installed in the entourage of a great personage, being part of his group of clientele, they would give political opinions, supervise the education of the young people, and provide assistance in the important circumstances of life. For example, Demetrius in the entourage of Thrasea Pactus; when the latter was led to take his own life, Demetrius served him as a kind of suicide counselor and braced his final moments with a discourse on immortality.

- But there are many other forms in which this soul direction is carried out. The latter joins and animates a whole set of other relations: family relations (Seneca writes a consolation to his mother on the occasion of his own exile); relations of protection (the same Seneca looks after both the career and the soul of the young Serenus, a provincial cousin newly arrived at Rome); relations of friendship between two persons rather close in age, culture, and situation (Seneca with Lucilius); relations with a highly placed personage to whom one pays homage by offering him useful advice (thus Plutarch with Fundanus, to whom he rushes the notes he himself has taken concerning the tranquility of the soul).

In this way there is constituted what one might call a "soul service," which is performed through multifarious social relations. Traditional eros play an occasional role in it at best. This is not to say that affective relations were not intense; they often were. Our modern categories of friendship and love are completely inadequate for interpreting them. The correspondence of Marcus Aurelius with Fronto can serve as an example of that intensity and complexity.

This cultivation of the self comprised a set of practices designated by the general team *askēsis*. It is appropriate first to analyze its objectives. In a passage cited by Seneca, Demetrius resorts to the very common metaphor of the athlete; the athlete does not learn all the possible moves, he does not attempt to do useless feats; he practices the few moves that he needs to triumph over his opponents in the wrestling match. In the same way, we do not have to perform feats on ourselves (philosophical ascesis looks with suspicion on those figures who point to the marvels of their abstinences, their fasts, their foreknowledge of the future). Like a good wrestler, we must learn only what will enable us to bear up against events that may occur; we must learn not to let ourselves be thrown by them, and not to let ourselves be overwhelmed by the emotions they may give rise to in ourselves.

Now, what do we need in order to keep our control in the face of the events that may take place? We need "discourses": *logoi*, understood as true discourses and rational discourses. Lucretius speaks of the *veridica dicta* that enable us to thwart our fears and not allow ourselves to be disheartened by what we believe to be misfortunes. The equipment we need in order to confront the future consists of true discourses; they are what enables us to face reality.

Three questions about them are raised.

1. The question of their nature. There were numerous discussions on this point between the philosophical schools and within the same currents. The main controversy had to do with the need for theoretical knowledge. On this point, the Epicureans were all in agreement: knowing the principles that govern the world, the nature of the gods, the causes of the wonders, the laws of life and death, and so on is absolutely necessary, in their view, if one is to prepare for the possible events of existence. The Stoics were divided according to their proximity to cynical tenets: some attributed the greatest significance to the *dogmata*, the theoretical principles that complete the practical prescrip-

tions; others assigned the most important place to those concrete rules of behavior. Seneca's Letters 90–91 lay out the opposing arguments very clearly.[8] What should be noted here is that those true discourses we need relate only to what we are in our connection with the world, in our place in the natural order, and in our dependence or independence with respect to the events that occur. They are in no way a decipherment of our thoughts, our representations, our desires.

2. The second question raised concerns how these true discourses exist inside us. To say that they are necessary for our future is to say that we must be able to have recourse to them when the need is felt. When an unforeseen event or misfortune presents itself, we must be able to call upon the relevant true discourses in order to protect ourselves; they must be at our disposal within us. The Greeks have a common expression for this, *prokheiron ekhein*, which the Latins translate as *habere in manu, in promptu habere*—to have near at hand.

One needs to understand that this involves something very different from a simple memory that would be recalled when the occasion arose. Plutarch, for example, calls on several metaphors to characterize the presence in us of these true discourses. He compares them to a medicine (*pharmakon*) we should be supplied with for protection against all the vicissitudes of existence. (Marcus Aurelius compares them to the instrument kit that a surgeon must always have near at hand.) Plutarch also speaks of them as being like those friends "the surest and best of which are those whose useful presence in adversity lends assistance to us." Elsewhere he evokes them as an inner voice that insists on being heard when the passions stir: these discourses must be in us "like a master whose voice is enough to hush the growling of the dogs." In a passage of the *De Beneficiis*, one finds a gradation of this sort, going from the instrument at one's disposal to the automatism of a discourse that would speak within us of its own volition.[9] Concerning advice given by Demetrius, Seneca says that one must "grasp it with both hands" (*utraque manu*) and never let go; but also "cling" to it, attach (*adfigere*) it to one's mind, "making it a part of oneself" (*partem sui facere*), and finally, "by daily meditation reach the point where these wholesome maxims occur of their own accord."

Here we see a movement very different from the one prescribed by Plato when he asks the soul to turn back on itself to rediscover its true nature. What Plutarch and Seneca suggest instead is the absorption of a truth imparted by a teaching, a reading, or a piece of advice; and one assimilates it so thoroughly that it becomes a part of oneself, an abiding, always-active, inner principle of action. In a practice such as this, one does not rediscover a truth hidden deep within oneself through an impulse of recollection; one internalizes accepted texts through a more and more thorough appropriation.

3. So a series of technical questions crops up concerning the methods of this appropriation. Obviously, memory plays a large role in it—though not in the Platonic form of the soul rediscovering its original nature and its homeland but, rather, in the form of progressive exercises of memorization. I would merely like to indicate some of the salient points in this "ascesis" of truth:

- the importance of listening. Whereas Socrates questioned people and tried to get them to say what they knew (without knowing that they knew it), for the Stoics or the Epicureans (as in the Pythagorean sects) the disciple must at first keep silent and listen. One finds in Plutarch, or in Philo of Alexandria, a whole set of rules for proper listening (the physical posture to take, how to direct one's attention, the way to retain what has been said);

- the importance, too, of writing. In this period, there was a cultivation of what might be called "personal writing": taking notes on the readings, conversations, and reflections that one hears or has or does; keeping notebooks of one sort or another on important subjects (what the Greeks called *hupomnēmata*), which must be reread from time to time in order to reactualize what they contain;

- and the importance of habitual self-reflection, but in the sense of exercises for committing to memory the things that one has learned. That is the exact technical meaning of the expression *anakhōrēsis eis heauton*, as Marcus Aurelius uses it: to come back inside oneself and examine the "riches" that one has deposited there; one must have within oneself a kind of book that one rereads from time to time. This corresponds to the practice of the arts of memory that Frances Yates has studied.

So we have a whole set of techniques whose purpose is to link together truth and the subject. But there should be no misunderstanding: it is not a matter of uncovering a truth in the subject or of making the soul the place where truth resides, through an essential kinship or an original law, the truth; nor is it a matter of making the soul the object of a true discourse. We are still very far from what would be a hermeneutic of the subject. The object, rather, is to arm the subject with a truth it did not know, one that did not reside in it; what is wanted is to make this learned, memorized truth, progressively put into practice, a quasi subject that reigns supreme in us.

One can distinguish between those exercises carried out in a real situation, which basically constitute training in endurance and abstinence, and those which constitute training in thought by means of thought.

1. The most famous of these thought exercises was the *praemeditatio malorum*, a meditation on future ills. It was also one of the most disputed: the Epicureans rejected it, saying that it was useless to suffer in advance ills that had not yet come to pass, and that it was better to practice calling up the memory of past pleasures as a protection against present ills. The strict Stoics, such as Seneca or Epictetus, but also men like Plutarch, whose attitude toward Stoicism is very ambivalent, practice the *praemeditatio malorum* assiduously. One needs to be clear about what it consists in: it appears to be a somber, pessimistic anticipation of the future. In reality, it is something quite different.

In the first place, it is a matter not of visualizing the future as it is likely to be but, rather, very systematically imagining the worst that might happen, even if it is not at all likely to happen. Seneca says concerning a fire that had destroyed the town of Lyons: this example ought to teach us to regard the worst as always certain.

  • Further, these things should not be considered as a possibility in the relatively distant future, but envisioned as already present, already occurring. Let us imagine, for example, that we are already exiled, already subjected to torture.

  • Finally, if one pictures them in their actuality, this is not in order to experience beforehand the pain or suffering they would cause us but to persuade ourselves that they are not in any sense real troubles, and that only the opinion we have of them lets them be taken for true misfortunes.

Clearly then, this exercise consists not in contemplating a possible future of real evils, as a way of getting used to it, but in neutralizing both the future and the evil. The future, since one envisions it as already given in an extreme actuality; the evil, since one practices no longer thinking of it as such.

2. At the other end of these exercises, one finds those carried out in reality. These exercises had a long tradition behind them: they were practices of abstinence, privation, or physical resistance. They could have a purificatory value or attest the "demonic" strength of the person who practiced them. Yet in the cultivation of the self, these exercises have another meaning: it is a matter of establishing and testing the individual's independence relative to the external world.

Two examples. The first in Plutarch, *On the Daemon of Socrates.*[10] One of the speakers alludes to a practice, whose origin, moreover, he attributes to the Pythagoreans: first, one engages in athletic activities that whet the appetite; then one takes his place before tables laden with the most savory dishes; and, after gazing upon them, one gives them to the servants while taking the simple and frugal nourishment of a poor man for oneself.

In Letter 18, Seneca relates that the whole town is getting ready for the Saturnalia. He plans, for reasons of expediency, to take part in the festivities, at least after a fashion; but his preparation will for several days consist in wearing a coarse cloak, sleeping on a pallet, and nourishing himself only with hard bread. This is not in order to build an appetite for the feasts—it is to establish both that poverty is not an evil and that he is fully capable of bearing it. Other passages, in Seneca himself or in Epicurus, evoke the usefulness of these short periods of voluntary trials. Musonius Rufus also recommends periods spent in the country where one lives like the peasants, devoting oneself to farm work as they do.

3. Between the pole of the *meditatio*, where one practices in thought, and the pole of the *exercitatio*, where one trains in reality, there is a whole series of other possible practices designed for proving oneself.

In particular, Epictetus gives examples of these in the *Discourses*. They are interesting because quite similar ones will be found again in Christian spirituality. They are especially concerned with what one might call the "control of representations."

Epictetus insists that one must be in an attitude of constant supervision over the representations that may enter the mind. He expresses this attitude in two metaphors: that of the night watchman who does not let just anyone come into the town or the house; and that of the moneychanger or inspector—the *arguronomos*—who, when presented with a coin, examines it, weighs it in his hand, and checks the metal and the effigy. The principle that one must be like a moneychanger with respect to one's own thoughts is found again in Evagrius Ponticus and in Cassian; but, in their case, it's a matter of prescribing a hermeneutic attitude toward oneself: decipher what there may be that is lustful in our seemingly innocent thoughts, recognize those coming from God and those coming from the Tempter. In Epictetus something else is at issue: one needs to determine whether or not one is affected or moved by the thing that is represented, and what reason one has for being or not being affected in that way.

With this in view, Epictetus recommends to his students an exercise of control inspired by the Sophistic challenges that were so highly regarded in the schools; but instead of tackling one or another of the questions difficult to resolve, one will address types of situations that demand a reaction: "Someone's son has died.—Respond: That is beyond our power, so it is not an evil.—Someone's father has disinherited him. What do you think about it?—It is beyond our power, it is not an evil...—He was distressed about it.—That does concern us, it is an evil.—He bore it courageously.—That concerns us, it is a good."

One can see that this control of representations is not aimed at uncovering, beneath appearances, a hidden truth that would be that of the subject itself; rather, it finds in these representations, as they present themselves, the occasion for recalling to mind a certain number of true principles—concerning death, illness, suffering, political life, and so on; and by means of this reminder one can see if he is able to respond in accordance with such principles—if they have really become, according to Plutarch's metaphor, that voice of the master which is raised as soon as the passions growl and is able to silence them.

4. At the apex of all these exercises, one finds the famous *meletē thanatou*—a meditation on death or, rather, a training for it. Indeed, it does not consist of the mere reminder, even the insistent reminder, that one is fated to die; it is a way of making death actual in life. Among all the Stoics, Seneca was especially given to this practice. It tends to make one live each day as if it were the last.

To fully understand the exercise that Seneca proposes, one needs to recall the correspondences traditionally established between the different time cycles: the times of the day from dawn to dusk are related symbolically to the seasons of the year from spring to winter; and these seasons are related in turn to the ages of life from childhood to old age. The death exercise as it is evoked in certain letters of Seneca consists in living the long span of life as if it were as short as a day, and in living each day as if one's entire life depended on it; every morning one ought to be in the childhood of his life, but one ought to live the whole day as if the evening would be the moment of death. In Letter 12, he says: "Let us go to our sleep with joy and gladness; let us say; I have lived." It is this same type of exercise that Marcus Aurelius was thinking of when he wrote that "moral perfection requires that one spend each day as if it were the last" (7.69). He would even have it that every action he performed be done "as if it were the last" (2.5).

What accounts for the particular value of the death meditation is not just the fact that it anticipates what is generally held to be the greatest misfortune; it is not just that it enables one to convince oneself that death is not an evil; it offers the possibility of looking back, in advance as it were, on one's life. By thinking of oneself as being about to die, one can judge each action that one is performing in terms of its own value. Death, said Epictetus, takes hold of the laborer in the midst of his labor, the sailor in the midst of his sailing: "And you, in the midst of what occupation do you want to be taken?" And Seneca envisaged the moment of death as one in which an individual would be able to become a sort of judge of himself and assess the moral progress he will have made, up to his final day. In Letter 26, he wrote: "I shall leave it to Death to determine what progress I have made.... I am making ready for the day when I am to pass judgment on myself— whether I am merely declaiming brave sentiments or whether I really feel them."

NOTES

1 Plato, *Apologie de Socrate*, trans. M. Croiset (Paris: Belles Lettres, 1925), 29e, pp. 157–66 [*The Apology*, trans. Harold North Fowler (Cambridge, Mass.: Harvard University Press, 1990)].

2 Gregory of Nyssa, *Traité de la virginité*, trans. Michel Aubineau (Paris: Cerf, 1966), pp. 411–17 and 422–31 [*Treatise on Virginity*, trans. V. W. Callahan, in *St. Gregory of Nyssa: Ascetical Works* (Washington, D.C.: Catholic Universities of America Press, 1966), pp. 46–48 and p. 57].

3 Epicurus, *Lettre à Ménécée*, trans. M. Coche, in *Lettres et Maximes* (Villiers-sur-Mer: Mégare, 1977), §122, p. 217 ["Letter to Menoeceus," trans. Cyril Bailey, in *Epicurus: The Extant Remains* (Oxford: Oxford University Press, 1926), p. 83].

4 Philo of Alexandria, *De la Vie contemplative*, trans. F. Daumas and P. Miquel, in *Oeuvres* (Paris: Cerf, 1963), §29, p. 105 ["On the Contemplative Life," trans. F. H. Colson, in *Philo in Ten Volumes* (Cambridge, Mass.: Harvard University Press, 1985)].

5 Plutarch, *Apophthegmata laconica,* 217a: *Apophtègmes laconiens,* trans. F. Fuhrmann, in *Oeuvres morales* (Paris: Belles Lettres, 1988), vol. 3, pp. 171–72 ["Sayings of Spartans," trans. Frank Cole Babbitt, in *Plutarch's Moralia* (New York: Putnam's, 1931), p. 297].

6 Plato, *Alcibiade,* trans. M. Croiset (Paris: Belles Lettres, 1985), p. 99 [*The First Alcibiades,* trans. B. Jowett, in *The Dialogues of Plato* (New York: Macmillan, 1892), p. 496].

7 Epictetus, *Entretiens* 3.23.30, trans. J. Souilhé (Paris: Belles Lettres, 1963), vol. 3, p. 92 [*The Discourses and Manual,* trans. P. E. Matheson, bk. 3, ch. 23 (Oxford: Oxford University Press, 1916), p. 83].

8 Seneca, *Lettres à Lucilius,* trans. H. Noblot (Paris: Belles Lettres, 1945–64), vol. 4, pp. 27–50 [*Ad Lucilium Epistulae Morales,* trans. Richard M. Gummere (Cambridge, Mass.: Harvard University Press, 1962), vol. 2, pp. 395–449].

9 Seneca, *De Beneficiis* 2.2: *Des bienfaits,* trans. F. Préchac (Paris: Belles Lettres, 1927), vol. 2, p. 77) [*De Beneficiis,* trans. R. M. Gummere, in *Moral Essays* (Cambridge, Mass.: Harvard University Press, 1964), vol. 3, §2, p. 259].

10 Plutarch, *Le Démon de Socrate* 585a, trans. J. Hani, in *Oeuvres morales* (Paris: Belles Lettres, 1980), vol. 8, p. 95 [*On the Sign of Socrates* 585a, trans. Phillip H. De Lacy and Benedict Einarsan, in *Plutarch's Moralia* (New York: Putnam's, 1931), vol. 7].

PART TWO

ETHICS

POLEMICS, POLITICS, AND PROBLEMATIZATIONS:
AN INTERVIEW WITH MICHEL FOUCAULT*

P.R. Why is it that you don't engage in polemics?

M.F. I like discussions, and when I am asked questions, I try to answer them. It's true that I don't like to get involved in polemics. If I open a book and see that the author is accusing an adversary of "infantile leftism," I shut it again right away. That's not my way of doing things; I don't belong to the world of people who do things that way. I insist on this difference as something essential: a whole morality is at stake, the morality that concerns the search for the truth and the relation to the other.

In the serious play of questions and answers, in the work of reciprocal elucidation, the rights of each person are in some sense immanent in the discussion. They depend only on the dialogue situation. The person asking the questions is merely exercising the right that has been given him: to remain unconvinced, to perceive a contradiction, to require more information, to emphasize different postulates, to point out faulty reasoning, and so on. As for the person answering the questions, he too exercises a right that does not go beyond the discussion itself; by the logic of his own discourse, he is tied to what he has said earlier, and by the acceptance of dialogue he is tied to the questioning of the other. Questions and answers depend on a game—a game that is at once pleasant and difficult—in which each of the two partners

---
*This interview was conducted by Paul Rabinow in May, 1984, just before Foucault's death, to answer questions frequently asked by American audiences. It was translated by Lydia Davis. Special thanks are due Thomas Zummer for his help in preparing it.

takes pains to use only the rights given him by the other and by the accepted form of the dialogue.

The polemicist, on the other hand, proceeds encased in privileges that he possesses in advance and will never agree to question. On principle, he possesses rights authorizing him to wage war and making that struggle a just undertaking; the person he confronts is not a partner in the search for the truth but an adversary, an enemy who is wrong, who is harmful, and whose very existence constitutes a threat. For him, then, the game consists not of recognizing this person as a subject having the right to speak but of abolishing him, as interlocutor, from any possible dialogue; and his final objective will be not to come as close as possible to a difficult truth but to bring about the triumph of the just cause he has been manifestly upholding from the beginning. The polemicist relies on a legitimacy that his adversary is by definition denied.

Perhaps, someday, a long history will have to be written of polemics, polemics as a parasitic figure on discussion and an obstacle to the search for the truth. Very schematically, it seems to me that today we can recognize the presence in polemics of three models: the religious model, the judiciary model, and the political model. As in heresiology, polemics sets itself the task of determining the intangible point of dogma, the fundamental and necessary principle that the adversary has neglected, ignored, or transgressed; and it denounces this negligence as a moral failing; at the root of the error, it finds passion, desire, interest, a whole series of weaknesses and inadmissible attachments that establish it as culpable. As in judiciary practice, polemics allows for no possibility of an equal discussion: it examines a case; it isn't dealing with an interlocutor, it is processing a suspect; it collects the proofs of his guilt, designates the infraction he has committed, and pronounces the verdict and sentences him. In any case, what we have here is not on the order of a shared investigation; the polemicist tells the truth in the form of his judgment and by virtue of the authority he has conferred on himself. But it is the political model that is the most powerful today. Polemics defines alliances, recruits partisans, unites interests or opinions, represents a party; it establishes the other as an enemy, an upholder of opposed interests against which one must fight until the moment this enemy is defeated and either surrenders or disappears.

Of course, the reactivation, in polemics, of these political, judiciary, or religious practices is nothing more than theater. One gesticulates: anathemas, excommunications, condemnations, battles, victories, and dcfcats are no more than ways of speaking, after all. And yet, in the order of discourse, they are also ways of acting which are not without consequence. There are the sterilizing effects. Has anyone ever seen a new idea come out of a polemic? And how could it be otherwise, given that here the interlocutors are incited not to advance, not to take more and more risks in what they say, but to fall back continually on the rights that they claim, on their legitimacy, which they must defend, and on the affirmation of their innocence? There is something even more serious here: in this comedy, one mimics war, battles, annihilations, or unconditional surrenders, putting forward as much of one's killer instinct as possible. But it is really dangerous to make anyone believe that he can gain access to the truth by such paths and thus to validate, even if in a merely symbolic form, the real political practices that could be warranted by it. Let us imagine, for a moment, that a magic wand is waved and one of the two adversaries in a polemic is given the ability to exercise all the power he likes over the other. One doesn't even have to imagine it: one has only to look at what happened during the debates in the USSR over linguistics or genetics not long ago. Were these merely aberrant deviations from what was supposed to be the correct discussion? Not at all—they were the real consequences of a polemic attitude whose effects ordinarily remain suspended.

P.R. You have been read as an idealist, as a nihilist, as a "new philosopher," an anti-Marxist, a new conservative, and so on... Where *do* you stand?

M.F. I think I have in fact been situated in most of the squares on the political checkerboard, one after another and sometimes simultaneously: as anarchist, leftist, ostentatious or disguised Marxist, nihilist, explicit or secret anti-Marxist, technocrat in the service of Gaullism, new liberal, and so on. An American professor complained that a crypto-Marxist like me was invited to the USA, and I was denounced by the press in Eastern European countries for being an accomplice of the dissidents. None of these descriptions is important by itself; taken together, on the other hand, they mean something. And I must admit that I rather like what they mean.

It's true that I prefer not to identify myself, and that I'm amused by the diversity of the ways I've been judged and classified. Something tells me that by now a more or less approximate place should have been found for me, after so many efforts in such various directions; and since I obviously can't suspect the competence of the people who are get-

ting muddled up in their divergent judgments, since it isn't possible
to challenge their inattention or their prejudices, I have to be convinced
that their inability to situate me has something to do with me.

And no doubt fundamentally it concerns my way of approaching
political questions. It is true that my attitude isn't a result of the form
of critique that claims to be a methodical examination in order to reject
all possible solutions except for the one valid one. It is more on the
order of "problematization"—which is to say, the development of a
domain of acts, practices, and thoughts that seem to me to pose problems for politics. For example, I don't think that in regard to madness
and mental illness there is any "politics" that can contain the just and
definitive solution. But I think that in madness, in derangement, in
behavior problems, there are reasons for questioning politics; and politics must answer these questions, but it never answers them completely.
The same is true for crime and punishment: naturally, it would be
wrong to imagine that politics has nothing to do with the prevention
and punishment of crime, and therefore nothing to do with a certain
number of elements that modify its form, its meaning, its frequency;
but it would be just as wrong to think that there is a political formula
likely to resolve the question of crime and put an end to it. The same
is true of sexuality: it doesn't exist apart from a relationship to political structures, requirements, laws, and regulations that have a primary
importance for it; and yet one can't expect politics to provide the forms
in which sexuality would cease to be a problem.

It is a question, then, of thinking about the relations of these different experiences to politics, which doesn't mean that one will seek in
politics the main constituent of these experiences or the solution that
will definitively settle their fate. The problems that experiences like
these pose to politics have to be elaborated. But it is also necessary to
determine what "posing a problem" to politics really means. Richard
Rorty points out that in these analyses I do not appeal to any "we"—to
any of those "*we*s" whose consensus, whose values, whose traditions
constitute the framework for a thought and define the conditions in
which it can be validated. But the problem is, precisely, to decide if it
is actually suitable to place oneself within a "we" in order to assert the
principles one recognizes and the values one accepts; or if it is not,
rather, necessary to make the future formation of a "we" possible by
elaborating the question. Because it seems to me that the "we" must
not be previous to the question; it can only be the result—and the nec-

essarily temporary result—of the question as it is posed in the new terms in which one formulates it. For example, I'm not sure that at the time when I wrote the history of madness, there was a preexisting and receptive "we" to which I would only have had to refer in order to write my book, and of which this book would have been the spontaneous expression. Laing, Cooper, Basaglia, and I had no community, nor any relationship; but the problem posed itself to those who had read us, as it also posed itself to some of us, of seeing if it were possible to establish a "we" on the basis of the work that had been done, a "we" that would also be likely to form a community of action.

I have never tried to analyze anything whatsoever from the point of view of politics, but always to ask politics what it had to say about the problems with which it was confronted. I question it about the positions it takes and the reasons it gives for this; I don't ask it to determine the theory of what I do. I am neither an adversary nor a partisan of Marxism; I question it about what it has to say about experiences that ask questions of it.

As for the events of May 1968, it seems to me they depend on another problematic. I wasn't in France at that time; I only returned several months later. And it seemed to me one could recognize completely contradictory elements in it: on the one hand, an effort, which was very widely asserted, to ask politics a whole series of questions that were not traditionally a part of its statutory domain (questions about women, about relations between the sexes, about medicine, about mental illness, about the environment, about minorities, about delinquency); and, on the other hand, a desire to rewrite all these problems in the vocabulary of a theory that was derived more or less directly from Marxism. But the process that was evident at that time led not to taking over the problems posed by the Marxist doctrine but, on the contrary, to a more and more manifest powerlessness on the part of Marxism to confront these problems. So that one found oneself faced with interrogations that were addressed to politics but had not themselves sprung from a political doctrine. From this point of view, such a liberation of the act of questioning seemed to me to have played a positive role: now there was a plurality of questions posed to politics rather than the reinscription of the act of questioning in the framework of a political doctrine.

P.R. Would you say that your work centers on the relations among ethics, politics, and the genealogy of truth?

M.F. No doubt one could say that in some sense I try to analyze the relations among science, politics, and ethics; but I don't think that would be an entirely accurate representation of the work I set out to do. I don't want to remain at that level; rather, I am trying to see how these processes may have interfered with one another in the formation of a scientific domain, a political structure, a moral practice. Let's take psychiatry as an example: no doubt, one can analyze it today in its epistemological-structure—even if that is still rather loose; one can also analyze it within the framework of the political institutions in which it operates; one can also study it in its ethical implications, as regards the person who is the object of the psychiatry as much as the psychiatrist himself. But my goal hasn't been to do this; rather, I have tried to see how the formation of psychiatry as a science, the limitation of its field, and the definition of its object implicated a political structure and a moral practice: in the twofold sense that they were presupposed by the progressive organization of psychiatry as a science, and that they were also changed by this development. Psychiatry as we know it couldn't have existed without a whole interplay of political structures and without a set of ethical attitudes; but inversely, the establishment of madness as a domain of knowledge [*savoir*] changed the political practices and the ethical attitudes that concerned it. It was a matter of determining the role of politics and ethics in the establishment of madness as a particular domain of scientific knowledge [*connaissance*], and also of analyzing the effects of the latter on political and ethical practices.

The same is true in relation to delinquency. It was a question of seeing which political strategy had, by giving its status to criminality, been able to appeal to certain forms of knowledge [*savoir*] and certain moral attitudes; it was also a question of seeing how these modalities of knowledge [*connaissance*] and these forms of morality could have been reflected in, and changed by, these disciplinary techniques. In the case of sexuality it was the development of a moral attitude that I wanted to isolate; but I tried to reconstruct it through the play it engaged in with political structures (essentially in the relation between self-control [*maîtrise de soi*] and domination of others) and with the modalities of knowledge [*connaissance*] (self-knowledge and knowledge of different areas of activity).

So that in these three areas—madness, delinquency, and sexuality—I emphasized a particular aspect each time: the establishment of a certain objectivity, the development of a politics and a government of the

self, and the elaboration of an ethics and a practice in regard to oneself. But each time I also tried to point out the place occupied here by
the other two components necessary for constituting a field of experience. It is basically a matter of different examples in which the three
fundamental elements of any experience are implicated: a game of
truth, relations of power, and forms of relation to oneself and to others. And if each of these examples emphasizes, in a certain way, one
of these three aspects—since the experience of madness was recently
organized as primarily a field of knowledge [*savoir*], that of crime as
an area of political intervention, while that of sexuality was defined as
an ethical position—each time I have tried to show how the two other
elements were present, what roles they played, and how each one was
affected by the transformations in the other two.

P.R. You have recently been talking about a "history of problematics." What is a history of problematics?

M.F. For a long time, I have been trying to see if it would be possible to describe the history of thought as distinct both from the history of ideas (by which I mean the analysis of systems of representation)
and from the history of mentalities (by which I mean the analysis of
attitudes and types of action [*schémas de comportement*]). It seemed
to me there was one element that was capable of describing the history
of thought—this was what one could call the element of problems or,
more exactly, problematizations. What distinguishes thought is that it
is something quite different from the set of representations that under-
lies a certain behavior; it is also something quite different from the
domain of attitudes that can determine this behavior. Thought is not
what inhabits a certain conduct and gives it its meaning; rather, it is
what allows one to step back from this way of acting or reacting, to
present it to oneself as an object of thought and to question it as to its
meaning, its conditions, and its goals. Thought is freedom in relation
to what one does, the motion by which one detaches oneself from it,
establishes it as an object, and reflects on it as a problem.

To say that the study of thought is the analysis of a freedom does
not mean one is dealing with a formal system that has reference only
to itself. Actually, for a domain of action, a behavior, to enter the field
of thought, it is necessary for a certain number of factors to have made
it uncertain, to have made it lose its familiarity, or to have provoked a
certain number of difficulties around it. These elements result from
social, economic, or political processes. But here their only role is that

of instigation. They can exist and perform their action for a very long time, before there is effective problematization by thought. And when thought intervenes, it doesn't assume a unique form that is the direct result or the necessary expression of these difficulties; it is an original or specific response—often taking many forms, sometimes even contradictory in its different aspects—to these difficulties, which are defined for it by a situation or a context, and which hold true as a possible question.

To one single set of difficulties, several responses can be made. And most of the time different responses actually are proposed. But what must be understood is what makes them simultaneously possible: it is the point in which their simultaneity is rooted; it is the soil that can nourish them all in their diversity and sometimes in spite of their contradictions. To the different difficulties encountered by the practice regarding mental illness in the eighteenth century, diverse solutions were proposed: Tuke's and Pinel's are examples. In the same way, a whole group of solutions was proposed for the difficulties encountered in the second half of the eighteenth century by penal practice. Or again, to take a very remote example, the diverse schools of philosophy of the Hellenistic period proposed different solutions to the difficulties of traditional sexual ethics.

But the work of a history of thought would be to rediscover at the root of these diverse solutions the general form of problematization that has made them possible—even in their very opposition; or what has made possible the transformations of the difficulties and obstacles of a practice into a general problem for which one proposes diverse practical solutions. It is problematization that responds to these difficulties, but by doing something quite other than expressing them or manifesting them: in connection with them, it develops the conditions in which possible responses can be given; it defines the elements that will constitute what the different solutions attempt to respond to. This development of a given into a question, this transformation of a group of obstacles and difficulties into problems to which the diverse solutions will attempt to produce a response, this is what constitutes the point of problematization and the specific work of thought.

It is clear how far one is from an analysis in terms of deconstruction (any confusion between these two methods would be unwise). Rather, it is a question of a movement of critical analysis in which one tries to see how the different solutions to a problem have been constructed; but also how these different solutions result from a specific form of problematization. And it then appears that any new solution which might be added to the others would arise from current problematization, modifying only several of the postulates or principles on which one bases the responses that one gives. The work of philosophical and historical reflection is put back into the field of the work of thought only on condition that one clearly grasps problematization not as an arrangement of representations but as a work of thought.

MICHEL FOUCAULT:
AN INTERVIEW BY STEPHEN RIGGINS*

————

S.R. One of the many things that a reader can unexpectedly learn from your work is to appreciate silence. You write about the freedom it makes possible, its multiple causes and meanings. For instance, you say in your last book that there is not one but many silences. Would it be correct to infer that there is a strongly autobiographical element in this?

M.F. I think that any child who has been educated in a Catholic milieu just before or during the Second World War had the experience that there were many different ways of speaking as well as many forms of silence. There were some kinds of silence which implied very sharp hostility and others which meant deep friendship, emotional admiration, even love. I remember very well that when I met the filmmaker Daniel Schmidt who visited me, I don't know for what purpose, we discovered after a few minutes that we really had nothing to say to each other. So we stayed together from about three o'clock in the afternoon to midnight. We drank, we smoked hash, we had dinner. And I don't think we spoke more than twenty minutes during those ten hours. From that moment a rather long friendship started. It was for me the first time that a friendship originated in strictly silent behavior.

Maybe another feature of this appreciation of silence is related to the obligation of speaking. I lived as a child in a petit bourgeois, provincial milieu in France and the obligation of speaking, of making con-

*Michel Foucault was interviewed for *Ethos* in English by Stephen Riggins on June 22, 1982, in Toronto, where he was teaching a course at the third International Summer Institute for Semiotic and Structural Studies.

versation with visitors, was for me something both very strange and very boring. I often wondered why people had to speak. Silence may be a much more interesting way of having a relationship with people.

S.R. There is in North American Indian culture a much greater appreciation of silence than in English-speaking societies and I suppose in French-speaking societies as well.

M.F. Yes, you see, I think silence is one of those things that has unfortunately been dropped from our culture. We don't have a culture of silence; we don't have a culture of suicide either. The Japanese do, I think. Young Romans or young Greeks were taught to keep silent in very different ways according to the people with whom they were interacting. Silence was then a specific form of experiencing a relationship with others. This is something that I believe is really worthwhile cultivating. I'm in favor of developing silence as a cultural ethos.

S.R. You seem to have a fascination with other cultures, and not only from the past; for the first ten years of your career you lived in Sweden, West Germany, and Poland. This would seem a very atypical career for a French academic. Can you explain why you left France and why, when you returned in about 1961, from what I have heard, you would have preferred to live in Japan?

M.F. There is a snobbism about antichauvinism in France now. I hope what I say is not associated with those kinds of people. Maybe if I were an American or a Canadian, I would suffer from some features of North American culture. Anyway, I have suffered and I still suffer from a lot of things in French social and cultural life. That was the reason why I left France in 1955. Incidentally, in 1966 and 1968 I also spent two years in Tunisia for purely personal reasons.

S.R. Could you give some examples of the aspects of French society that you suffered from?

M.F. Well, I think that, at the moment when I left France, freedom for personal life was very sharply restricted there. At this time, Sweden was supposed to be a much freer country. And there I had the experience that a certain kind of freedom may have, not exactly the same effects, but as many restrictive effects as a directly restrictive society. That was an important experience for me. Then I had the opportunity of spending one year in Poland where, of course, the restrictions and oppressive power of the Communist Party are really something quite different. In a rather short period of time I had the experience of an old traditional society, as France was in the late forties and early fifties, and the new free society that was Sweden. I won't say I had the total experience of all the political possibilities, but I had a sample of what the possibilities of Western societies were at that moment. That was a good experience.

s.r. Hundreds of Americans went to Paris in the twenties and thirties for exactly the same reasons you left in the fifties.

m.f. Yes, but now I don't think they come to Paris any longer for freedom. They come to have a taste of an old traditional culture. They come to France as painters went to Italy in the seventeenth century, to see a dying civilization. Anyway, you see, we very often have the experience of much more freedom in foreign countries than in our own. As foreigners we can ignore all those implicit obligations which are not in the law but in the general way of behaving. Secondly, merely changing your obligations is felt or experienced as a kind of freedom.

s.r. If you don't mind, let us return for a while to your early years in Paris. I understand that you worked as a psychologist at the Hôpital Ste. Anne in Paris.

m.f. Yes, I worked there a little more than two years, I believe.

s.r. And you have remarked that you identified more with the patients than the staff. Surely that's a very atypical experience for anyone who is a psychologist or psychiatrist. Why did you feel, partly from that experience, the necessity of radically questioning psychiatry when so many other people were content to try to refine the concepts that were already prevalent?

m.f. Actually, I was not officially appointed. I was studying psychology in the Hôpital Ste. Anne. It was the early fifties. There was no clear professional status for psychologists in a mental hospital. So, as a student in psychology (I studied first philosophy and then psychology), I had a very strange status there. The *chef de service* was very kind to me and let me do anything I wanted. But nobody worried about what I should be doing; I was free to do anything. I was actually in a position between the staff and the patients, and it wasn't my merit, it wasn't because I had a special attitude—it was the consequence of this ambiguity in my status which forced me to maintain a distance from the staff. I am sure it was not my personal merit, because I felt all that at the time as a kind of malaise. It was only a few years later when I started writing a book on the history of psychiatry that this malaise, this personal experience, took the form of a historical criticism or a structural analysis.

S.R. Was there anything unusual about the Hôpital Ste. Anne? Would it have given an employee a particularly negative impression of psychiatry?

M.F. Oh, no. It was as typical a large hospital as you could imagine, and I must say it was better than most of the large hospitals in provincial towns that I visited afterward. It was one of the best in Paris. No, it was not terrible. That was precisely the thing that was important. Maybe if I had been doing this kind of work in a small provincial hospital I would have believed its failures were the result of its location or its particular inadequacies.

S.R. As you have just mentioned the French provinces, which is where you were born, in a sort of derogatory way, do you, nevertheless, have fond memories of growing up in Poitiers in the thirties and forties?

M.F. Oh, yes. My memories are rather, one could not exactly say strange, but what strikes me now when I try to recall those impressions is that nearly all the great emotional memories I have are related to the political situation. I remember very well that I experienced one of my first great frights when Chancellor Dollfuss was assassinated by the Nazis in, I think, 1934. It is something very far from us now. Very few people remember the murder of Dollfuss. I remember very well that I was really scared by that. I think it was my first strong fright about death. I also remember refugees from Spain arriving in Poitiers. I remember fighting in school with my classmates about the Ethiopian War. I think that boys and girls of this generation had their childhood formed by these great historical events. The menace of war was our background, our framework of existence. Then the war arrived. Much more than the activities of family life, it was these events concerning the world which are the substance of our memory. I say "our" because I am nearly sure that most boys and girls in France at this moment had the same experience. Our private life was really threatened. Maybe that is the reason why I am fascinated by history and the relationship between personal experience and those events of which we are a part. I think that is the nucleus of my theoretical desires. [*Laughs*]

S.R. You remain fascinated by the period even though you don't write about it.

M.F. Yes, sure.

S.R. What was the origin of your decision to become a philosopher?

M.F. You see, I don't think I ever had the project of becoming a philosopher. I had not known what to do with my life. And I think that is also something rather typical for people of my generation. We did not know when I was ten or eleven years old whether we would become German or remain French. We did not know whether we would die or not in the bombing and so on. When I was sixteen or seventeen, I knew only one thing: school life was an environment protected from exterior menaces, from politics. And I have always been fascinated by living protected in a scholarly environment, in an intellectual milieu. Knowledge is for me that which must function as a protection of individual existence and as a comprehension of the exterior world. I think that's it. Knowledge as a means of surviving by understanding.

s.r. Could you tell me a bit about your studies in Paris? Is there anyone who had a special influence upon the work that you do today or any professors you are grateful to for personal reasons?

m.f. No, I was a pupil of Althusser, and at that time the main philosophical currents in France were Marxism, Hegelianism, and phenomenology. I must say, I have studied these but what gave me for the first time the desire of doing personal work was reading Nietzsche.

s.r. An audience that is non-French is likely to have a very poor understanding of the aftermath of the May rebellion of '68, and you have sometimes said that it resulted in people being more responsive to your work. Can you explain why?

m.f. I think that before '68, at least in France, you had to be as a philosopher a Marxist, or a phenomenologist or a structuralist, and I adhered to none of these dogmas. The second point is that at this time in France studying psychiatry or the history of medicine had no real status in the political field. Nobody was interested in that. The first thing that happened after '68 was that Marxism as a dogmatic framework declined and new political, new cultural interests concerning personal life appeared. That's why I think my work had nearly no echo, with the exception of a very small circle, before '68.

s.r. Some of the works you refer to in the first volume of *The History of Sexuality*, such as the Victorian book *My Secret Life*, are filled with sexual fantasies. It is often impossible to distinguish between fact and fantasy. Would there be a value in your focusing explicitly upon sexual fantasies and creating an archaeology of them rather than one of sexuality?

m.f. [*Laughs*] No, I don't try to write an archaeology of sexual fantasies. I try to make an archaeology of discourse about sexuality, which is really the relationship between what we do, what we are obliged to do, what we are allowed to do, what we are forbidden to do in the field of sexuality, and what we are allowed, forbidden, or obliged to say about our sexual behavior. That's the point. It's not a problem of fantasy; it's a problem of verbalization.

S.R. Could you explain how you arrived at the idea that the sexual repression that characterized eighteenth- and nineteenth-century Europe and North America, and which seemed so well documented historically, was in fact ambiguous, and that there were beneath it forces working in the opposite direction?

M.F. Indeed, it is not a question of denying the existence of repression. It's one of showing that repression is always a part of a much more complex political strategy regarding sexuality. Things are not merely repressed. There is about sexuality a lot of defective regulations in which the negative effects of inhibition are counterbalanced by the positive effects of stimulation. The way in which sexuality in the nineteenth century was both repressed but also put in light, underlined, analyzed through techniques like psychology and psychiatry shows very well that it was not simply a question of repression. It was much more a change in the economics of sexual behavior in our society.

S.R. In your opinion, what are some of the most striking examples that support your hypothesis?

M.F. One of them is children's masturbation. Another is hysteria and all the fuss about hysterical women. These two examples show, of course, repression, prohibition, interdiction, and so on; but the fact that the sexuality of children became a real problem for the parents, an issue, a source of anxiety, had a lot of effects upon the children and upon the parents. To take care of the sexuality of their children was not only a question of morality for the parents but also a question of pleasure.

S.R. A pleasure in what sense?

M.F. Sexual excitement and sexual satisfaction.

S.F. For the parents themselves?

M.F. Yes. Call it rape, if you like. There are texts that are very close to a systemization of rape. Rape by the parents of the sexual activity of their children. To intervene in this personal, secret activity, which masturbation was, does not represent something neutral for the parents. It is not only a matter of power, or authority, or ethics; it's also a pleasure. Don't you agree with that? Yes, there is enjoyment in intervening. The fact that masturbation was so strictly forbidden for children was naturally the cause of anxiety. It was also a reason for the intensification of this activity, for mutual masturbation and for the pleasure of secret communication between children about this theme. All this has given a certain shape to family life, to the relationship between children and parents, and to the relations between children. All that has, as a result, [brought about] not only repression but an intensification both of anxieties and of pleasures. I don't want to say that the pleasure of the parents was the same as that of the children, or that there was no repression. I tried to find the roots of this absurd prohibition.

One of the reasons why this stupid interdiction of masturbation was maintained for such a long time was because of this pleasure and anxiety and all the emotional network around it. Everyone knows very well that it's impossible to prevent a child from masturbating. There is no scientific evidence that it harms anybody. [*Laughs*] One can be sure that it is at least the only pleasure that really harms nobody. Why has it been forbidden for such a long time then? To the best of my knowledge, you cannot find more than two or three references in all the Greco-Latin literature about masturbation. It was not relevant. It was supposed to be, in Greek and Latin civilization, an activity either for slaves or for satyrs. [*Laughs*] It was not relevant to speak about it for free citizens.

S.R. We live at a point in time when there is great uncertainty about the future. One sees apocalyptic visions of the future reflected widely in popular culture. Louis Malle's *My Dinner with André*, for example. Isn't it typical that, in such a climate, sex and reproduction come to be a preoccupation and thus writing a history of sexuality would be symptomatic of the time?

M.F. No, I don't think I would agree with that. First, the preoccupation with the relationship between sexuality and reproduction seems to have been stronger, for instance, in the Greek and Roman societies and in the bourgeois society of the eighteenth and nineteenth centuries. No. What strikes me is the fact that now sexuality seems to be a question without direct relation with reproduction. It is your sexuality as your personal behavior which is the problem.

Take homosexuality, for instance. I think that one of the reasons why homosexual behavior was not an important issue in the eighteenth century was due to the view that if a man had children, what he did besides that had little importance. During the nineteenth century, you begin to see that sexual behavior was important for a definition of the individual self. And that is something new. It is very interesting to see that, before the nineteenth century, forbidden behavior—even if it was very severely judged—was always considered to be an excess, a "libertinage," as something too much. Homosexual behavior was only considered to be a kind of excess of natural behavior, an instinct that is difficult to keep within certain limits. From the nineteenth century on, you see that behavior like homosexuality came to be considered an abnormality. When I say that it was libertinage, I don't say that it was tolerated.

I think that the idea of characterizing individuals through their sexual behavior or desire is not to be found, or very rarely, before the nineteenth century. "Tell me your desires, I'll tell you who you are." This question is typical of the nineteenth century.

S.R. It would not seem any longer that sex could be called *the* secret of life. Has anything replaced it in this respect?

M.F. Of course it is not *the* secret of life now, since people can show at least certain general forms of their sexual preferences without being plagued or condemned. But I think that people still consider, and are invited to consider, that sexual desire is able to reveal what is their deep identity. Sexuality is not *the* secret, but it is still a symptom, a manifestation of what is the most secret in our individuality.

S.R. The next question I would like to ask may at first seem odd, and if it does I'll explain why I thought it was worth asking. Does beauty have special meaning for you?

M.F. I think it does for everyone. [*Laughs*] I am nearsighted but not blind to the point that it has no meaning for me. Why do you ask? I'm afraid I have given you proof that I am not insensitive to beauty.

S.R. One of the things about you that is very impressive is the sort of monachal austerity in which you live. Your apartment in Paris is almost completely white; you also avoid all the objets d'art that decorate so many French homes. While in Toronto during the past month you have on several occasions worn clothes as simple as white pants, a white T-shirt and a black leather jacket. You suggested that perhaps the reason you like the color white so much is that in Poitiers during the thirties and forties it was impossible for the exterior of houses to be genuinely white. You are staying here in a house whose white walls are decorated with black cut-out sculptures, and you remarked that you especially appreciated the straightforwardness and strength of pure black and white. There is also a noteworthy phrase in *The History of*

Sexuality: "that austere monarchy of sex." You do not fit the image of the sophisticated Frenchman who makes an art out of living well. Also, you are the only French person I know who has told me he prefers American food.

M.F. Yes. Sure. [*Laughs*] A good club sandwich with a Coke. That's my pleasure. It's true. With ice cream. That's true.

Actually, I think I have real difficulty in experiencing pleasure. I think that pleasure is a very difficult behavior. It's not as simple as that to enjoy one's self. [*Laughs*] And I must say that's my dream. I would like and I hope I'll die of an overdose of pleasure of any kind. [*Laughs*] Because I think it's really difficult, and I always have the feeling that I do not feel *the* pleasure, the complete total pleasure, and, for me, it's related to death.

S.R. Why would you say that?

M.F. Because I think that the kind of pleasure I would consider as *the* real pleasure would be so deep, so intense, so overwhelming that I couldn't survive it. I would die. I'll give you a clearer and simpler example. Once I was struck by a car in the street. I was walking. And for maybe two seconds I had the impression that I was dying and it was really a very, very intense pleasure. The weather was wonderful. It was seven o'clock during the summer. The sun was descending. The sky was very wonderful and blue and so on. It was, it still is now, one of my best memories. [*Laughs*]

There is also the fact that some drugs are really important for me because they are the mediation to those incredibly intense joys that I am looking for, and that I am not able to experience, to afford by myself. It's true that a glass of wine, of good wine, old and so on, may be enjoyable, but it's not for me. A pleasure must be something incredibly intense. But I think I am not the only one like that.

I'm not able to give myself and others those middle-range pleasures that make up everyday life. Such pleasures are nothing for me, and I am not able to organize my life in order to make place for them. That's the reason why I'm not a social being, why I'm not really a cultural being, why I'm so boring in my everyday life. [*Laughs*] It's a bore to live with me.

S.R. A frequently quoted remark of Romain Rolland is that the French Romantic writers were " 'visuels' for whom music was only a noise." Despite the remark being an obvious exaggeration, most recent scholarship tends to support it. Many references to paintings occur in some of your books, but few to music. Are you also representative of this characteristic of French culture that Rolland called attention to?

M.F. Yes, sure. Of course French culture gives no place to music, or nearly no place. But it's a fact that in my personal life music played a great role. The first friend I had when I was twenty was a musician. Then afterward, I had another friend who was a composer and who is dead now. Through him I know all the generation of Boulez. It has been a very important experience for me. First, because I had contact with the kind of art which was, for me, really enigmatic. I was not competent at all in this domain; I'm still not. But I felt beauty in something that was quite enigmatic for me. There are some pieces by Bach and Webern I enjoy, but what is, for me, real beauty is a "phrase musicale, un morceau de musique," that I cannot understand, something I cannot say anything about. I have the opinion—maybe it's quite arrogant or presumptuous—that I could say something about any of the most wonderful paintings in the world. For this reason they are not absolutely beautiful. Anyway, I have written something about Boulez. What has been for me the influence of living with a musician for several months. Why it was important even in my intellectual life.

S.R. If I understand correctly, artists and writers responded to your work more positively at first than philosophers, sociologists, or other academics.

M.F. Yes, that's right.

S.R. Is there a special kinship between your kind of philosophy and the arts in general?

M.F. Well, I think I am not in a position to answer. You see, I hate to say it, but it's true that I am not a really good academic. For me, intellectual work is related to what you could call "aestheticism," meaning transforming yourself. I believe my problem is this strange relationship between knowledge, scholarship, theory, and real history. I know very well, and I think I knew it from the moment when I was a child, that knowledge can do nothing for transforming the world. Maybe I am wrong. And I am sure I am wrong from a theoretical point of view, for I know very well that knowledge has transformed the world.

But if I refer to my own personal experience, I have the feeling knowledge can't do anything for us, and that political power may destroy us. All the knowledge in the world can't do anything against that. All this is related not to what I think theoretically (I know that's wrong), but I speak from my personal experience. I know that knowledge can transform us, that truth is not only a way of deciphering the world (and maybe what we call truth doesn't decipher anything), but that if I know the truth I will be changed. And maybe I will be saved. Or maybe I'll die, but I think that is the same anyway for me. [*Laughs*]

You see, that's why I really work like a dog, and I worked like a dog all my life. I am not interested in the academic status of what I am doing because my problem is my own transformation. That's the reason also why, when people say, "Well, you thought this a few years ago and now you say something else," my answer is...[*Laughs*] "Well, do you think I have worked like that all those years to say the same thing and not to be changed?" This transformation of one's self by one's own knowledge is, I think, something rather close to the aesthetic experience. Why should a painter work if he is not transformed by his own painting?

s.r. Beyond the historical dimension, is there an ethical concern implied in *The History of Sexuality*? Are you not in some ways telling us how to act?

m.f. No. If you mean by ethics a code that would tell us how to act, then of course *The History of Sexuality* is not an ethics. But if by ethics you mean the relationship you have to yourself when you act, then I would say that it intends to be an ethics, or at least to show what could be an ethics of sexual behavior. It would be one that would not be dominated by the problem of the deep truth of the reality of our sex life. The relationship that I think we need to have with ourselves when we have sex is an ethics of pleasure, of intensification of pleasure.

s.r. Many people look at you as someone who is able to tell them the deep truth about the world and about themselves. How do you experience this responsibility? As an intellectual, do you feel responsible toward this function of seer, of shaper of mentalities?

m.f. I am sure I am not able to provide these people with what they expect. [*Laughs*] I never behave like a prophet—my books don't tell people what to do. And they often reproach me for not doing so (and maybe they are right), and at the same time they reproach me for behaving like a prophet. I have written a book about the history of psychiatry from the seventeenth century to the very beginning of the nineteenth.[1] In this book, I said nearly nothing about the contemporary situation, but people still have read it as an antipsychiatry position. Once, I was invited to Montreal to attend a symposium about psychiatry. At first, I refused to go there, since I am not a psychiatrist, even if I have some experience—a very short experience as I told you earlier. But they assured me that they were inviting me only as a historian of psychiatry to give an introductory speech. Since I like Quebec, I went. And I was really trapped because I was presented by the president as *the* representative in France of antipsychiatry. Of course, there were nice people there who had never read a line of what I had written and they were convinced that I was an antipsychiatrist.

I have done nothing other than write the history of psychiatry to the beginning of the nineteenth century. Why should so many people, including psychiatrists, believe that I am an antipsychiatrist? It's because they are not able to accept the real history of their institutions, which is, of course, a sign of psychiatry being a pseudoscience. A real science is able to accept even the shameful, dirty stories of its beginning. [*Laughs*]

So you see, there really is a call for prophetism. I think we have to get rid of that. People have to build their own ethics, taking as a point of departure the historical analysis, sociological analysis, and so on that one can provide for them. I don't think that people who try to decipher the truth should have to provide ethical principles or practical advice at the same moment, in the same book and the same analysis. All this prescriptive network has to be elaborated and transformed by people themselves.

S.R. For a philosopher to have made the pages of *Time* magazine, as you did in November 1981, is an indication of a certain kind of popular status. How do you feel about that?

M.F. When newsmen ask me for information about my work, I consider that I have to accept. You see, we are paid by society, by the taxpayers, to work. [*Laughs*] And really I think that most of us try to do our work the best we can. I think it is quite normal that this work, as far as it is possible, is presented and made accessible to everybody. Naturally, a part of our work cannot be accessible to anybody because it is too difficult. The institution I belong to in France (I don't belong to the university but the Collège de France) obliges its members to make public lectures, open to anyone who wants to attend, in which we have to explain our work. We are at once researchers and people who have to explain publicly our research. I think there is in this very old institution—it dates from the sixteenth century—something very interesting. The deep meaning is, I believe, very important. When a newsman comes and asks for information about my work, I try to provide it in the clearest way I can.

Anyway, my personal life is not at all interesting. If somebody thinks that my work cannot be understood without reference to such and such a part of my life, I accept to consider the question. [*Laughs*] I am ready to answer if I agree. As far as my personal life is uninteresting, it is not worthwhile making a secret of it. [*Laughs*] By the same token, it may not be worthwhile publicizing it.

NOTE

1   *Madness and Civilization* (London: Tavistock, 1967).

FRIENDSHIP AS A WAY OF LIFE*

Q. You're in your fifties. You're a reader of *Le Gai Pied*, which has been in existence now for two years. Is the kind of discourse you find there something positive for you?

M.F. That the magazine exists is the positive and important thing. In answer to your question, I could say that I don't have to read it to voice the question of my age. What I could ask of your magazine is that I do not, in reading it, have to pose the question of my age. Now, reading it...

Q. Perhaps the problem is the age group of those who contribute to it and read it; the majority are between twenty-five and thirty-five.

M.F. Of course. The more it is written by young people the more it concerns young people. But the problem is not to make room for one age group alongside another but to find out what can be done in relation to the quasi identification between homosexuality and the love among young people.

Another thing to distrust is the tendency to relate the question of homosexuality to the problem of "Who am I?" and "What is the secret of my desire?" Perhaps it would be better to ask oneself, "What relations, through homosexuality, can be established, invented, multiplied, and modulated?" The problem is not to discover in oneself the truth of one's sex, but, rather, to use one's sexuality henceforth to arrive at a multiplicity of relationships. And, no doubt, that's the real reason why

*R. de Ceccaty, J. Danet, and J. Le Bitoux conducted this interview with Foucault for the French magazine *Gai Pied*. It appeared in April 1981. The text that appears here, translated by John Johnston, has been amended.

homosexuality is not a form of desire but something desirable. Therefore, we have to work at becoming homosexuals and not be obstinate
in recognizing that we are. The development toward which the problem of homosexuality tends is the one of friendship.

Q. Did you think so at twenty, or have you discovered it over the
years?

M.F. As far back as I remember, to want guys [*garçons*] was to want
relations with guys. That has always been important for me. Not necessarily in the form of a couple but as a matter of existence: how is it
possible for men to be together? To live together, to share their time,
their meals, their room, their leisure, their grief, their knowledge, their
confidences? What is it to be "naked" among men, outside of institutional relations, family, profession, and obligatory camaraderie? It's a
desire, an uneasiness, a desire-in-uneasiness that exists among a lot
of people.

Q. Can you say that desire and pleasure, and the relationships one
can have, are dependent on one's age?

M.F. Yes, very profoundly. Between a man and a younger woman,
the marriage institution makes it easier: she accepts it and makes it
work. But two men of noticeably different ages—what code would allow
them to communicate? They face each other without terms or convenient words, with nothing to assure them about the meaning of the
movement that carries them toward each other. They have to invent,
from A to Z, a relationship that is still formless, which is friendship:
that is to say, the sum of everything through which they can give each
other pleasure.

One of the concessions one makes to others is not to present homosexuality as anything but a kind of immediate pleasure, of two young
men meeting in the street, seducing each other with a look, grabbing
each other's asses and getting each other off in a quarter of an hour.
There you have a kind of neat image of homosexuality without any possibility of generating unease, and for two reasons: it responds to a reassuring canon of beauty, and it cancels everything that can be troubling
in affection, tenderness, friendship, fidelity, camaraderie, and companionship, things that our rather sanitized society can't allow a place for
without fearing the formation of new alliances and the tying together
of unforeseen lines of force. I think that's what makes homosexuality
"disturbing": the homosexual mode of life, much more than the sexual act itself. To imagine a sexual act that doesn't conform to law or

nature is not what disturbs people. But that individuals are beginning to love one another—there's the problem. The institution is caught in a contradiction; affective intensities traverse it which at one and the same time keep it going and shake it up. Look at the army, where love between men is ceaselessly provoked [*appelé*] and shamed. Institutional codes can't validate these relations with multiple intensities, variable colors, imperceptible movements and changing forms. These relations short-circuit it and introduce love where there's supposed to be only law, rule, or habit.

Q. You were saying a little while ago: "Rather than crying about faded pleasures, I'm interested in what we ourselves can do." Could you explain that more precisely?

M.F. Asceticism as the renunciation of pleasure has bad connotations. But ascesis is something else: it's the work that one performs on oneself in order to transform oneself or make the self appear which, happily, one never attains. Can that be our problem today? We've rid ourselves of asceticism. Yet it's up to us to advance into a homosexual ascesis that would make us work on ourselves and invent—I do not say discover—a manner of being that is still improbable.

Q. That means that a young homosexual must be very cautious in regard to homosexual imagery; he must work at something else?

M.F. What we must work on, it seems to me, is not so much to liberate our desires but to make ourselves infinitely more susceptible to pleasure [*plaisirs*]. We must escape and help others to escape the two readymade formulas of the pure sexual encounter and the lovers' fusion of identities.

Q. Can one see the first fruits of strong constructive relationships in the United States, in any case in the cities where the problem of sexual misery seems under control?

M.F. To me, it appears certain that in the United States, even if the basis of sexual misery still exists, the interest in friendship has become very important; one doesn't enter a relationship simply in order to be able to consummate it sexually, which happens very easily. But toward friendship, people are very polarized. How can a relational system be reached through sexual practices? Is it possible to create a homosexual mode of life?

This notion of mode of life seems important to me. Will it require the introduction of a diversification different from the ones due to social class, differences in profession and culture, a diversification that would also be a form of relationship and would be a "way of life"? A way of life can be shared among individuals of different age, status, and social activity. It can yield intense relations not resembling those that are institutionalized. It seems to me that a way of life can yield a culture and an ethics. To be "gay," I think, is not to identify with the psychological traits and the visible masks of the homosexual but to try to define and develop a way of life.

Q. Isn't it a myth to say: Here we are enjoying the first fruits of a socialization between different classes, ages, and countries?

M.F. Yes, like the great myth of saying: There will no longer be any difference between homo- and heterosexuality. Moreover, I think that it's one of the reasons that homosexuality presents a problem today. Many sexual liberation movements project this idea of "liberating yourself from the hideous constraints that weigh upon you." Yet the affirmation that to be a homosexual is for a man to love another man—this search for a way of life runs counter to the ideology of the sexual liberation movements of the sixties. It's in this sense that the mustached "clones" are significant. It's a way of responding: "Have nothing to fear; the more one is liberated, the less one will love women, the less one will founder in this polysexuality where there are no longer any differences between the two." It's not at all the idea of a great community fusion.

Homosexuality is a historic occasion to reopen affective and relational virtualities, not so much through the intrinsic qualities of the homosexual but because the "slantwise" position of the latter, as it were, the diagonal lines he can lay out in the social fabric allow these virtualities to come to light.

Q. Women might object: What do men together have to win compared to the relations between a man and a woman or between two women?

M.F. There is a book that just appeared in the U.S. on the friendships between women.[1] The affection and passion between women is well documented. In the preface, the author states that she began with the idea of unearthing homosexual relationships—but perceived that not only were these relationships not always present but that it was uninteresting whether relationships could be called "homosexual" or not. And by letting the relationship manifest itself as it appeared in words and gestures, other very essential things also appeared: dense, bright, marvelous loves and affections or very dark and sad loves. The book shows the extent to which woman's body has played a great role, and the importance of physical contact between women: women do each other's hair, help each other with make up, dress each other. Women have had access to the bodies of other women: they put their arms around each other, kiss each other. Man's body has been forbidden to other men in a much more drastic way. If it's true that life between women was tolerated, it's only in certain periods and since the nineteenth century that life between men not only was tolerated but rigorously necessary: very simply, during war.

And equally in prison camps. You had soldiers and young officers who spent months and even years together. During World War I, men lived together completely, one on top of another, and for them it was nothing at all, insofar as death was present and finally the devotion to one another and the services rendered were sanctioned by the play of life and death. And apart from several remarks on camaraderie, the brotherhood of spirit, and some very partial observations, what do we know about these emotional uproars and storms of feeling that took place in those times? One can wonder how, in these absurd and grotesque wars and infernal massacres, the men managed to hold on in spite of everything. Through some emotional fabric, no doubt. I don't mean that it was because they were each other's lovers that they continued to fight; but honor, courage, not losing face, sacrifice, leaving the trench with the captain—all that implied a very intense emotional tie. It's not to say: "Ah, there you have homosexuality!" I detest that kind of reasoning. But no doubt you have there one of the conditions, not the only one, that has permitted this infernal life where for weeks guys floundered in the mud and shit, among corpses, starving for food, and were drunk the morning of the assault.

I would like to say, finally, that something well considered and voluntary like a magazine ought to make possible a homosexual culture, that is to say, the instruments for polymorphic, varied, and individually modulated relationships. But the idea of a program of proposals is dangerous. As soon as a program is presented, it becomes a law, and there's a prohibition against inventing. There ought to be an inventiveness special to a situation like ours and to these feelings, this need that Americans call "coming out," that is, showing oneself. The program must be wide open. We have to dig deeply to show how things have been historically contingent, for such and such reason intelligible but not necessary. We must make the intelligible appear against a background of emptiness and deny its necessity. We must think that what exists is far from filling all possible spaces. To make a truly unavoidable challenge of the question: What can be played?

NOTE

1 Lilian Faderman, *Surpassing the Love of Men* (New York: Morrow, 1980).

SEXUAL CHOICE, SEXUAL ACT*

J.O'H. Let me begin by asking you to respond to John Boswell's recent book on the history of homosexuality from the beginning of the Christian era through the Middle Ages.[1] As an historian yourself, do you find his methodology valid? To what extent do you think the conclusions he draws contribute to a better understanding of what homosexuality is today?

M.F. This is certainly a very important study whose originality is already evident from the way in which it poses the question. Methodologically speaking, the rejection by Boswell of the categorical opposition between homosexual and heterosexual, which plays such a significant role in the way our culture conceives of homosexuality, represents an advance not only in scholarship but in cultural criticism as well. His introduction of the concept of "gay" (in the way he defines it) provides us both with a useful instrument of research and, at the same time, a better comprehension of how people actually conceive of themselves and their sexual behavior. On the level of investigative results, this methodology has led to the discovery that what has been called the "repression" of homosexuality does not date back to Christianity properly speaking but developed within the Christian era at a much later date. In this type of analysis it is important to be aware of the way in which people conceived of their own sexuality. Sexual behavior is not, as is too often assumed, a superimposition of, on the one hand, desires

*This interview was conducted in French and translated by James O'Higgins; it first appeared in the "Homosexuality: Sacrilege, Vision, Politics" special issue of *Salmagundi* 58–59 (Fall 1982–Winter 1983), pp. 10–24.

that derive from natural instincts, and, on the other hand, of permissive or restrictive laws that tell us what we should or shouldn't do. Sexual behavior is more than that. It is also the consciousness one has of what one is doing, what one makes of the experience, and the value one attaches to it. It is in this sense that I think the concept "gay" contributes to a positive (rather than a purely negative) appreciation of the type of consciousness in which affection, love, desire, sexual rapport with people have a positive significance.

J.O'H. I understand that your own recent work has led you to a study of sexuality as it was experienced in ancient Greece.

M.F. Yes, and precisely Boswell's book has provided me with a guide for what to look for in the meaning people attached to their sexual behavior.

J.O'H. Does this focus on cultural context and people's discourse about their sexual behavior reflect a methodological decision to bypass the distinction between innate predisposition to homosexual behavior and social conditioning? Or do you have any conviction one way or the other on this issue?

M.F. On this question I have absolutely nothing to say. "No comment."

J.O'H. Does this mean you think the question is unanswerable, or bogus, or does it simply not interest you?

M.F. No, none of these. I just don't believe in talking about things that go beyond my expertise. It's not my problem, and I don't like talking about things that are not really the object of my work. On this question I have only an opinion; since it is only an opinion, it is without interest.

J.O'H. But opinions can be interesting, don't you agree?

M.F. Sure, I could offer my opinion, but this would only make sense if everybody and anybody's opinions were also being consulted. I don't want to make use of a position of authority while I'm being interviewed to traffic in opinions.

J.O'H. Fair enough. We'll shift direction then. Do you think it is legitimate to speak of a class consciousness in connection with homosexuals? Ought homosexuals to be encouraged to think of themselves as a class in the way that unskilled laborers or black people are encouraged to in some countries? How do you envision the political goals of homosexuals as a group?

M.F. In answer to the first question, I would say that the homosexual consciousness certainly goes beyond one's individual experience and includes an awareness of being a member of a particular social group. This is an undeniable fact that dates back to ancient times. Of course, this aspect of their collective consciousness changes over time and varies from place to place. It has, for instance, on different occasions taken the form of membership in a kind of secret society, membership in a cursed race, membership in a segment of humanity at once privileged and persecuted—all kinds of different modes of collective consciousness, just as, incidentally, the consciousness of unskilled laborers has undergone numerous transformations. It is true that more recently certain homosexuals have, following the political model, developed or tried to create a certain class consciousness. My impression is that this hasn't really been a success, whatever the political consequences it may have had, because homosexuals do not constitute a social class. This is not to say that one can't imagine a society in which homosexuals would constitute a social class. But in our present economic and social mode of organization, I don't see this coming to pass.

As for the political goals of the homosexual movement, two points can be made. First, there is the question of freedom of sexual choice which must be faced. I say "freedom of sexual *choice*" and not "freedom of sexual *acts*" because there are sexual acts like rape which should not be permitted whether they involve a man and a woman or two men. I don't think we should have as our objective some sort of absolute freedom or total liberty of sexual action. However, where freedom of sexual choice is concerned, one has to be absolutely intransigent. This includes the liberty of expression of that choice. By this I mean the liberty to manifest that choice or not to manifest it. Now, there has been considerable progress in this area on the level of legislation, certainly progess in the direction of tolerance, but there is still a lot of work to be done.

Second, a homosexual movement could adopt the objective of posing the question of the place in a given society which sexual choice, sexual behavior, and the effects of sexual relations between people could have with regard to the individual. These questions are fundamentally obscure. Look, for example, at the confusion and equivocation that surround pornography, or the lack of elucidation which characterizes the question of the legal status that might be attached to the liaison between two people of the same sex. I don't mean that the legalization of marriage among homosexuals should be an objective; rather, that we are dealing here with a whole series of questions concerning the insertion and recognition—within a legal and social framework—of diverse relations among individuals which must be addressed.

J.O'H. I take it, then, your point is that the homosexual movement should not only give itself the goal of enlarging legal permissiveness but should also be asking broader and deeper questions about the strategic roles played by sexual preferences and how they are perceived. Is it your point that the homosexual movement should not stop at liberalizing laws relating to personal sexual choice but should also be provoking society at large to rethink its own presuppositions regarding sexuality? In other words, it isn't that homosexuals are deviants who should be allowed to practice in peace but, rather, that the whole conceptual scheme that categorizes homosexuals as deviants must be dismantled. This throws an interesting light on the question of homosexual educators. In the debate that arose in California, regarding the right of homosexuals to teach primary and secondary school, for example, those who argued against permitting homosexuals to teach were concerned not only with the likelihood of homosexuals constituting a threat to innocence, in that they may be prone to seducing their students, but also that they might preach the gospel of homosexuality.

M.F. The whole question, you see, has been wrongly formulated. Under no circumstances should the sexual choice of an individual determine the profession he is allowed, or forbidden, to practice. Sexual practices simply fall outside the pertinent factors related to the suitability for a given profession. "Yes," you might say, "but what if the profession is used by homosexuals to encourage others to become homosexual?"

Well, let me ask you this: Do you believe that teachers who for years, for decades, for centuries, explained to children that homosexuality is intolerable; do you believe that the textbooks that purged literature and falsified history in order to exclude various types of sexual behavior, have not caused ravages at least as serious as a homosexual teacher who speaks about homosexuality and who can do no more harm than explain a given reality, a lived experience?

The fact that a teacher is a homosexual can only have electrifying and intense effects on the students to the extent that the rest of society refuses to admit the existence of homosexuality. A homosexual teacher should not present any more of a problem than a bald teacher, a male teacher in an all-female school, a female teacher in an all-male school, or an Arab teacher in a school in the 16th district in Paris.

As for the problem of a homosexual teacher who actively tries to seduce his students, all I can say is that in all pedagogical situations the possibility of this problem is present; one finds instances of this kind of behavior much more rampant among heterosexual teachers— for no other reason than that there are a lot more heterosexual teachers.

J.O'H. There is a growing tendency in American intellectual circles, particularly among radical feminists, to distinguish between male and female homosexuality. The basis of this distinction is twofold. If the term *homosexuality* is taken to denote not merely a tendency toward affectional relations with members of the same sex but an inclination to find members of the same sex erotically attractive and gratifying, then it is worth insisting on the very different physical things that happen in the one encounter and the other. The second basis for the distinction is that lesbians seem in the main to want from other women what one finds in stable heterosexual relationships: support, affection, long-term commitment, and so on. If this is not the case with male homosexuals, then the difference may be said to be striking, if not fundamental. Do you think the distinction here a useful and viable one? Are there discernible reasons for the differences noted so insistently by many prominent radical feminists?

M.F. [*Laughs*] All I can do is explode with laughter.

J.O'H. Is the question funny in a way I don't see, or stupid, or both?

M.F. Well, it is certainly not stupid, but I find it very amusing, perhaps for reasons I couldn't give even if I wanted to. What I will say is that the distinction offered doesn't seem to be convincing, in terms of what I observe in the behavior of lesbian women. Beyond this, one would have to speak about the different pressures experienced by men and women who are coming out or are trying to make a life for themselves as homosexuals. I don't think that radical feminists in other countries are likely to see these questions quite in the way you ascribe to such women in American intellectual circles.

J.O'H. Freud argued in "Psychogenesis of a Case of Hysteria in a Woman" that all homosexuals are liars.[2] We don't have to take this assertion seriously to ask whether there is not in homosexuality a tendency to dissimulation that might have led Freud to make his statement. If we substitute for the word "lie" such words as *metaphor* or *indirection*, may we not be coming closer to the heart of the homosexual style? Or is there any point in speaking of a homosexual style or sensibility? Richard Sennett, for one, has argued that there is no more a homosexual style than there is a heterosexual style. Is this your view as well?

M.F. Yes, I don't think it makes much sense to talk about a homosexual style. Even on the level of nature, the term *homosexuality* doesn't have much meaning. I'm reading right now, as a matter of fact, an interesting book that came out recently in the U.S. called *Proust and the Art of Love.*[3] The author shows us how difficult it is to give meaning to the proposition "Proust was a homosexual." It seems to me that it is finally an inadequate category—inadequate, that is, in that we can't really classify behavior, on the one hand, and the term can't restore a type of experience, on the other. One could perhaps say there is a "gay style," or at least that there is an ongoing attempt to recreate a certain style of existence, a form of existence or art of living, which might be called "gay."

In answer to the question about dissimulation, it is true that, for instance, during the nineteenth century it was, to a certain degree, necessary to hide one's homosexuality. But to call homosexuals liars is equivalent to calling the resisters under a military occupation liars. It's like calling Jews "moneylenders," when it was the only profession they were allowed to practice.

J.O'H. Nevertheless, it does seem evident, at least on a sociological level, that there are certain characteristics one can discern in the gay style, certain generalizations which (your laughter a moment ago notwithstanding) recall such stereotypifications as promiscuity, anonymity between sexual partners, purely physical relationships, and so on.

M.F. Yes, but it's not quite so simple. In a society like ours, where homosexuality is repressed, and severely so, men enjoy a far greater degree of liberty than women. Men are permitted to make love much more often and under less restrictive conditions. Houses of prostitution exist to satisfy their sexual needs. Ironically, this has resulted in a certain permissiveness with regard to sexual practices between men. Sexual desire is considered more intense for men and therefore in greater need of release; so, along with brothels, one saw the emergence of baths where men could meet and have sex with each other. The Roman baths were exactly this, a place for heterosexuals to engage in sexual acts. It wasn't until the sixteenth century, I believe, that these baths were closed as places of unacceptable sexual debauchery. Thus, even homosexuality benefited from a certain tolerance toward sexual practices, as long as it was limited to a simple physical encounter. And not only did homosexuality benefit from this situation but, by a curious twist—often typical of such strategies—it actually reversed the standards in such a way that homosexuals came to enjoy even more freedom in their physical relations than heterosexuals. The effect has been that homosexuals now have the luxury of knowing that in a certain number of countries—Holland, Denmark, the United States, and even as provincial a country as France—the opportunities for sexual encounters are enormous. There has been, you might say, a great increase in consumption on this level. But this is not necessarily a natural condition of homosexuality, a biological given.

J.O'H. The American sociologist Philip Rieff, in an essay on Oscar Wilde entitled "The Impossible Culture," sees Wilde as a forerunner of modern culture.[4] The essay begins with an extensive quotation from the transcript of the trial of Oscar Wilde, and goes on to raise questions about the viability of a culture in which there are no prohibitions, and therefore no sense of vital transgression. Consider, if you will, the following:

"A culture survives the assault of sheer possibility against it only so far as the members of a culture learn, through their membership, how to narrow the range of choices otherwise open."

"As culture sinks into the psyche and becomes character, what Wilde prized above all else is constrained: individuality. A culture in crisis favors the growth of individuality; deep down things no longer weigh so heavily to slow the surface play of experience. Hypothetically, if a culture could grow to full crisis, then everything would be expressed and nothing would be true."

"Sociologically, a truth is whatever militates against the human capacity to express everything. Repression is truth."

Is Rieff's response to Wilde and to the idea of culture Wilde embodied at all plausible?

M.F. I'm not sure I understand Professor Rieff's remarks. What does he mean, for instance, by "Repression is truth?"

J.O'H. Actually, I think this idea is similar to claims you make in your own books about truth being the product of a system of exclusions, a network, or *episteme* [*épistémè*], which defines what can and cannot be said.

M.F. Well, the important question here, it seems to me, is not whether a culture without restraints is possible or even desirable but whether the system of constraints in which a society functions leaves individuals the liberty to transform the system. Obviously, constraints of any kind are going to be intolerable to certain segments of society. The necrophiliac finds it intolerable that graves are not accessible to him. But a system of constraint becomes truly intolerable when the individuals who are affected by it don't have the means of modifying it. This can happen when such a system becomes intangible as a result of its being considered a moral or religious imperative, or a necessary consequence of medical science. If Rieff means that the restrictions should be clear and well defined, I agree.

J.O'H. Actually, Rieff would argue that a true culture is one in which the essential truths have been sunk so deep in everyone that there would be no need to articulate them. Clearly, in a society of law, one would need to make explicit a great variety of things that were not to be done, but the main credal assumptions would for the most part remain inaccessible to simple articulation. Part of the thrust of Rieff's work is directed against the idea that it is desirable to do away with credal assumptions in the name of a perfect liberty, and also the idea that restrictions are by definition what all must aim to clear away.

M.F. There is no question that a society without restrictions is inconceivable, but I can only repeat myself in saying that these restrictions have to be within the reach of those affected by them so that they at least have the possibility of altering them. As to credal assumptions, I don't think that Rieff and I would agree on their value or on their meaning or on the devices by which they are taught.

J.O'H. You're no doubt right about that. In any case, we can move now from the legal and sociological spheres to the realm of letters. I would like to ask you to comment on the difference between the erotic as it appears in heterosexual literature and the manner in which sex emerges in homosexual literature. Sexual discourse, as it appears in the great heterosexual novels of our culture—I realize that the designation "heterosexual novels" is itself dubious—is characterized by a certain modesty and discretion that seems to add to the charm of the works. When heterosexual writers treat sex too explicitly, it seems to lose some of the mysteriously evocative quality, some of the potency we find in novels like *Anna Karenina*. The point is made with great cogency in a number of essays by George Steiner, as a matter of fact. In contrast to the practice of the major heterosexual novelists, we have the example of various homosexual writers. I'm thinking for example of Cocteau's *The White Paper*, where he succeeds in retaining the poetic enchantment, which heterosexual writers achieve through veiled allusion, while depicting sexual acts in the most graphic terms.[5] Do you think such a difference does exist between these two types of literature, and if so, how would you account for it?

M.F. That's a very interesting question. As I mentioned earlier, over the past few years I have been reading a lot of Latin and Greek texts that describe sexual practices both between men and between men and women; and I've been struck by the extreme prudishness of these texts (with certain exceptions, of course). Take an author like Lucian. Here we have an ancient writer who talks about homosexuality but in an almost bashful way. At the end of one of his dialogues, for instance, he evokes a scene where a man approaches a boy, puts his hand on the boy's knee, slides his hand under his tunic and caresses the boy's chest; then the hand moves down to the boy's stomach and suddenly the text stops there. Now, I would attribute this prudishness, which generally characterizes homosexual literature in ancient times, to the greater freedom then enjoyed by men in their homosexual practices.

J.O'H. I see. So the more free and open sexual practice is, the more one can afford to be reticent or oblique in talking about it. This would explain why homosexual literature is more explicit in our culture than heterosexual literature. But I'm still wondering how one could use this explanation to account for the fact that the former manages to achieve the same effect in the imagination of the reader as the latter achieves with the exact opposite tools.

M.F. Let me try to answer your question another way. The experience of heterosexuality, at least since the Middle Ages, has always consisted of two axes; on the one hand, the axis of courtship in which the man seduces the woman; and, on the other hand, the axis of sexual act itself. Now, the great heterosexual literature of the West has had to do essentially with the axis of amorous courtship, that is, above all, with that which precedes the sexual act. All the work of intellectual and cultural refinement, all the aesthetic elaboration of the West, were aimed at courtship. This is the reason for the relative poverty of literary, cultural, and aesthetic appreciation of the sexual act as such.

In contrast, the modern homosexual experience has no relation at all to courtship. This was not the case in ancient Greece, however. For the Greeks, courtship between men was more important than between men and women. (Think of Socrates and Alcibiades.) But in Christian culture of the West, homosexuality was banished and therefore had to concentrate all its energy on the act of sex itself. Homosexuals were not allowed to elaborate a system of courtship because the cultural expression necessary for such an elaboration was denied them. The wink on the street, the split-second decision to get it on, the speed with which homosexual relations are consummated: all these are products of an interdiction. So when a homosexual culture and literature began to develop it was natural for it to focus on the most ardent and heated aspect of homosexual relations.

J.O'H. I'm reminded of Cassanova's famous expression that "the best moment in life is when one is climbing the stairs." One can hardly imagine a homosexual today making such a remark.

M.F. Exactly. Rather, he would say something like: "the best moment of love is when the lover leaves in the taxi."

J.O'H. I can't help thinking that this describes more or less precisely Swann's relations with Odette in the first volume of Proust's great novel.

M.F. Well, yes, that is true. But though we are speaking there of a relationship between a man and a woman, we should have to take into account in describing it the nature of the imagination that conceived it.

J.O'H. And we would also then have to take into account the pathological nature of the relationship as Proust himself conceives it.

M.F. The question of pathology I would as well omit in this context. I prefer simply to return to the observation with which I began this part of our exchange, namely, that for a homosexual, the best moment of love is likely to be when the lover leaves in the taxi. It is when the act is over and the guy [*garçon*] is gone that one begins to dream about the warmth of his body, the quality of his smile, the tone of his voice. It is the recollection rather than the anticipation of the act that assumes a primary importance in homosexual relations. This is why the great homosexual writers of our culture (Cocteau, Genet, Burroughs) can write so elegantly about the sexual act itself, because the homosexual imagination is for the most part concerned with reminiscing about the act rather than anticipating it. And, as I said earlier, this is all due to very concrete and practical considerations and says nothing about the intrinsic nature of homosexuality.

J.O'H. Do you think this has any bearing on the so-called proliferation of perversions one sees today? I am speaking of phenomena like the S&M scene, golden showers, scatological amusements, and the like.

We know these practices have existed for some time but they seem much more openly practiced these days.

M.F. I would say they are much more widely practiced also.

J.O'H. Do you think this general phenomenon and the fact that homosexuality is "coming out of the closet," making public its form of expression, have anything to do with each other?

M.F. I would advance the following hypothesis: In a civilization that for centuries considered the essence of the relation between two people to reside in the knowledge of whether one of the two parties was going to surrender to the other, all the interest and curiosity, the cunning and manipulation of people was aimed at getting the other to give in, to go to bed with them. Now, when sexual encounters become extremely easy and numerous, as is the case with homosexuality nowadays, complications are introduced only after the fact. In this type of casual encounter, it is only after making love that one becomes curious about the other person. Once the sexual act has been consummated, you find yourself asking your partner, "By the way, what was your name?"

What you have, then, is a situation where all the energy and imagination, which in the heterosexual relationship were channeled into courtship, now become devoted to intensifying the act of sex itself. A whole new art of sexual practice develops which tries to explore all the internal possibilities of sexual conduct. You find emerging in places like San Francisco and New York what might be called laboratories of sexual experimentation. You might look upon this as the counterpart of the medieval courts where strict rules of proprietary courtship were defined.

It is because the sexual act has become so easy and available to homosexuals that it runs the risk of quickly becoming boring, so that every effort has to be made to innovate and create variations that will enhance the pleasure of the act.

J.O'H. Yes, but why have these innovations taken the specific form they have? Why the fascination with excretory functions, for instance?

M.F. I find the S&M phenomenon in general to be more surprising than that. That is to say, sexual relations are elaborated and developed by and through mythical relations. S&M is not a relationship between he (or she) who suffers and he (or she) who inflicts suffering, but between the master and the one on whom he exercises his mastery. What interests the practitioners of S&M is that the relationship is at the same time regulated and open. It resembles a chess game in the sense that one can win and the other lose. The master can lose in the S&M game if he finds he is unable to respond to the needs and trials of his victim. Conversely, the servant can lose if he fails to meet or can't stand meeting the challenge thrown at him by the master. This mixture of rules and openness has the effect of intensifying sexual relations by introducing a perpetual novelty, a perpetual tension and a perpetual uncertainty, which the simple consummation of the act lacks. The idea is also to make use of every part of the body as a sexual instrument.

Actually this is related to the famous phase *animal triste post coitum.* Since in homosexuality coitus is given immediately, the problem becomes "what can be done to guard against the onset of sadness?"

J.O'H. Would you venture an explanation for the fact that bisexuality among women today seems to be much more readily accepted by men than bisexuality among men?

M.F. This probably has to do with the role women play in the imagination of heterosexual men. Women have always been seen by them as their exclusive property. To preserve this image, a man had to prevent his woman from having too much contact with other men, so women were restricted to social contact with other women and more tolerance was exercised with regard to the physical rapport between women. By the same token, heterosexual men felt that if they practiced homosexuality with other men this would destroy what they think is their image in the eyes of their women. They think of themselves as existing in the minds of women as master. They think that the idea of their submitting to another man, of being under another man in the act of love, would destroy their image in the eyes of women. Men think that women can only experience pleasure in recognizing men as masters. Even the Greeks had a problem with being the passive partner in a love relationship. For a Greek nobleman to make love to a passive male slave was natural, since the slave was by nature an inferior; but when two Greek men of the same social class made love it was a real problem because neither felt he should humble himself before the other.

Today homosexuals still have this problem. Most homosexuals feel that the passive role is in some way demeaning. S&M has actually helped alleviate this problem somewhat.

J.O'H. Is it your impression that the cultural forms growing up in the gay community are directed very largely to young people in that community?

M.F. I think that is largely the case, though I'm not sure there is much to make of it. Certainly, as a fifty-year-old man, when I read certain publications produced by and for gays, I find that I am not being taken into account at all, that I somehow don't belong. This is not something on the basis of which I would criticize such publications, which after all do what their writers and readers are interested in. But I can't help observing that there is a tendency among articulate gays to think of the major issues and questions of lifestyle as involving people in their twenties typically.

J.O'H. I don't see why this might not constitute the basis of a criticism—not only of particular publications but of gay life generally.

M.F. I didn't say that one *might* not find grounds for criticism, only that I don't choose to or think it useful.

J.O'H. Why not consider in this context the worship of the youthful male body as the very center of the standard homosexual fantasy, and go on to speak of the denial of ordinary life processes entailed in this, particularly aging and the decline of desire?

M.F. Look, these are not new ideas you're raising, and you know that. As to the worship of youthful bodies, I'm not convinced that it is peculiar at all to gays or in any way to be regarded as a pathology. And if that is the intention of your question, then I reject it. But I would also remind you that gays are not only involved in life processes, necessarily, but very much aware of them in most cases. Gay publications may not devote as much space as I would like to questions of gay friendship and to the meaning of relationship when there are no established codes or guidelines. But more and more gay people are having to face these questions for themselves. And, you know, I think that what most bothers those who are not gay about gayness is the gay lifestyle, not sex acts themselves.

J.O'H. Are you referring to such things as gays fondling or caressing one another in public, or their wearing flashy clothing, or adopting clone outfits?

M.F. These things are bound to disturb some people. But I was talking about the common fear that gays will develop relationships that are intense and satisfying even though they do not at all conform to the ideas of relationship held by others. It is the prospect that gays will create as yet unforeseen kinds of relationships that many people cannot tolerate.

J.O'H. You are referring to relationships that don't involve possessiveness or fidelity—to name only two of the common factors that might be denied?

M.F. If the relationships to be created are as yet unforeseeable, then we can't really say this feature or that feature will be denied. But you can see how, in the military for example, love between men can develop and assert itself in circumstances where only dead habits and rules were supposed to prevail. And it is possible that changes in established routines will occur on a much broader scale as gays learn to express their feelings for one another in more various ways and develop new lifestyles not resembling those which have been institutionalized.

J.O'H. Do you see it as your role to address the gay community especially on matters of general importance such as you have been raising?

M.F. I am, of course, regularly involved in exchanges with other members of the gay community. We talk, we try to find ways of opening ourselves to one another. But I am wary of imposing my own views, or of setting down a plan, or program. I don't want to discourage invention, don't want gay people to stop feeling that it is up to them to adjust their own relationships by discovering what is appropriate in their situations.

J.O'H. You don't think there is some special advice, or a special perspective, that a historian or archaeologist of culture like yourself can offer?

M.F. It is always useful to understand the historical contingency of things, to see how and why things got to be as they are. But I am not the only person equipped to show these things, and I want to avoid suggesting that certain developments were necessary or unavoidable. Gays have to work out some of these matters themselves. Of course, there are useful things I can contribute, but again, I want to avoid imposing my own scheme or plan.

J.O'H. Do you think that, in general, intellectuals are more tolerant toward, or receptive to, different modes of sexual behavior than other people? If so, is this due to a better understanding of human sexuality? If not, how do you think that you and other intellectuals can improve this situation? In what way can the rational discourse on sex best be reoriented?

M.F. I think that where tolerance is concerned we allow ourselves a lot of illusions. Take incest, for example. Incest was a popular practice, and I mean by this, widely practiced among the populace, for a very long time. It was toward the end of the nineteenth century that various social pressures were directed against it. And it is clear that the great interdiction of incest is an invention of the intellectuals.

J.O'H. Are you referring to figures like Freud and Lévi-Strauss, or to the class of intellectuals as a whole?

M.F. No, I'm not aiming at anyone in particular. I'm simply pointing out that if you look for studies by sociologists or anthropologists of the nineteenth century on incest you won't find any. Sure, there were some scattered medical reports and the like, but the practice of incest didn't really seem to pose a problem at the time.

It is perhaps true that in intellectual circles these things are talked about more openly, but that is not necessarily a sign of greater tolerance. Sometimes it means the reverse. I remember ten or fifteen years ago, when I used to socialize within the bourgeois milieu, that it was rare indeed for an evening to go by without some discussion of homosexuality and pederasty—usually even before dessert. But these same people who spoke so openly about these matters were not likely to tolerate their sons being pederasts.

As for prescribing the direction rational discourse on sex should take, I prefer not to legislate such matters. For one thing, the expression "intellectual discourse on sex" is too vague. There are very stupid things said by sociologists, sexologists, psychiatrists, doctors, and moralists, and there are very intelligent things said by members of those same professions. I don't think it's a question of intellectual discourse on sex but a question of asinine discourse and intelligent discourse.

J.O'H. And I take it that you have lately found a number of works that are moving in the right direction?

M.F. More, certainly, than I had any reason to expect I would some years ago. But the situation on the whole is still less than encouraging.

NOTES

1   John Boswell, *Christianity, Social Tolerance and Homosexuality: Gay People in Western Europe from the Christian Era to the Fourteenth Century* (Chicago: University of Chicago Press, 1980). According to Boswell the urban culture of Roman society did not distinguish homosexuals from others. The literature of the early Christian Church also did not oppose gay behavior. But hostility to the sexuality of gay people became more evident at the time of the dissolution of the Roman state and its urban centers. The eleventh century brought a renaissance of urban life and with it the reappearance of a more visible gay culture, which was only to be threatened a century later by theological and legal prejudices. The intolerance of the late Middle Ages continued to have an effect on European culture for centuries to come. To understand the nature of gay relationships, Boswell insists that they must be studied within temporal boundaries according to the customs of their day.

2   See *Standard Edition of the Complete Psychological Works of Sigmund Freud*, trans. James Strachey (London: Hogarth Press, 1955), vol. 2.

3   J. C. Rivers, *Proust and the Art of Love: The Aesthetics of Sexuality in the Life, Times, and Art of Marcel Proust* (New York: Columbia University Press, 1980).

4   Philip Rieff, "The Impossible Culture," *Salmagundi* 58–59 (Fall 1982–Winter 1983), 406–26.

5   Jean Cocteau, *Le Livre Blanc* (Paris: Quatre-Chemins, 1928) [*The White Paper*, pref. and ills. by Jean Cocteau (New York: Macaulay, 1958)].

THE SOCIAL TRIUMPH OF THE SEXUAL WILL*

G.B. Today we no longer speak of sexual liberation in vague terms; we speak of women's rights, homosexual rights, gay rights, but we don't know exactly what is meant by "rights" and "gay." In countries where homosexuality as such is outlawed, everything is simpler since everything is yet to be done, but in northern European countries where homosexuality is no longer officially prohibited, the future of gay rights is posed in different terms.

M.F. I think we should consider the battle for gay rights as an episode that cannot be the final stage. For two reasons: first because a right, in its real effects, is much more linked to attitudes and patterns of behavior than to legal formulations. There can be discrimination against homosexuals even if such discriminations are prohibited by law. It is therefore necessary to struggle to establish homosexual lifestyles, existential choices [des choix d'existence] in which sexual relations with people of the same sex will be important. It's not enough as part of a more general way of life, or in addition to it, to be permitted to make love with someone of the same sex. The fact of making love with someone of the same sex can very naturally involve a whole series of choices, a whole series of other values and choices for which there are not yet real possibilities. It's not only a matter of integrating this strange little practice of making love with someone of the same sex into preexisting cultures; it's a matter of constructing [créer] cultural forms.

*This interview was conducted in French and translated by Brendan Lemon. Given on October 20, 1981, it was published in *Christopher Street* 6:4 (May 1982), pp. 36–41. The text that appears here has been slightly amended.

G.B. But there are always things in the course of daily life which obstruct the creation of these ways of living.

M.F. Yes, but that's where there's something new to be done. That in the name of respect for individual rights someone is allowed to do as he wants, great! But if what we want to do is to create a new way of life [*mode de vie*], then the question of individual rights is not pertinent. In effect, we live in a legal, social, and institutional world where the only relations possible are extremely few, extremely simplified, and extremely poor. There is, of course, the relation of marriage, and the relations of family, but how many other relations should exist, should be able to find their codes not in institutions but in possible supports, which is not at all the case!

G.B. The essential question is that of supports, because the relations exist—or at least they try to exist. The problem comes because certain things are decided not by law-making bodies but by executive order. In Holland, certain legal changes have lessened the power of families and have permitted the individual to feel stronger in the relations he wishes to form. For example, inheritance laws [*droits*] between people of the same sex not tied by blood are the same as those of a married heterosexual couple.

M.F. That's an interesting example, but it represents only a first step, because if you ask people to reproduce the marriage bond for their personal relationship to be recognized, the progress made is slight. We live in a relational world that institutions have considerably impoverished. Society and the institutions which frame it have limited the possibility of relationships because a rich relational world would be very complex to manage. We should fight against the impoverishment of the relational fabric. We should secure recognition for relations of provisional coexistence, adoption....

G.B. Of children.

M.F. Or—why not?—of one adult by another. Why shouldn't I adopt a friend who's ten years younger than I am? And even if he's ten years older? Rather than arguing that rights are fundamental and natural to the individual, we should try to imagine and create a new relational right that permits all possible types of relations to exist and not be prevented, blocked, or annulled by impoverished relational institutions.

G.B. More concretely, shouldn't the legal, financial, and social advantages enjoyed by a married heterosexual couple be extended to all types of relationships? That's an important practical question, isn't it?

M.F. Certainly, but once again I think that's hard work, though very, very interesting. Right now I'm fascinated by the Hellenistic and Roman world before Christianity. Take, for example, relations of friendship. They played an important part, but there was a supple institutional framework for them—even if it was sometimes constraining—with a system of obligations, tasks, reciprocal duties, a hierarchy between friends, and so on. I don't think we should reproduce that model. But you can see how a system of supple and relatively codified relations could exist for a long time and support a certain number of important and stable relations, which we now have great difficulty defining. When you read an account of two friends from the period, you always wonder what it really is. Did they make love together? Did they have common interests? No doubt, it's neither of those things, or both.

G.B. In Western societies, the only notion upon which legislation is based is that of the citizen, or of the individual. How do we reconcile the desire to validate relations which have no legal sanction with a law-making body which confirms that all citizens have equal rights? There are still questions with no answers—that of the single person, for example.

M.F. Of course. The single person must be recognized as having relations with others quite different from those of a married couple, for example. We often say that the single person suffers from solitude because he is suspected of being an unsuccessful or rejected husband.

G.B. Or someone with "questionable morals."

M.F. Yes, someone who couldn't get married. When in reality the life of solitude is often the result of the poverty of possible relationships in our society, where institutions make insufficient and necessarily rare all relations that one could have with someone else and could be intense, rich—even if they were provisional—even and especially if they took place outside the framework of marriage.

G.B. All that makes us foresee that the gay movement has a future which goes beyond gays themselves. In Holland, it is surprising to see at what point gay rights interest more than homosexuals, because people want to direct their own lives and their relationships.

M.F. Yes, I think that there is an interesting part to play, one that fascinates me: the question of gay culture—which not only includes novels written by pederasts about pederasty, I mean culture in the large sense, a culture that invents ways of relating, types of existence, types of values, types of exchanges between individuals which are really new and are neither the same as, nor superimposed on, existing cultural forms. If that's possible, then gay culture will be not only a choice of homosexuals for homosexuals—it would create relations that are, at certain points, transferable to heterosexuals. We have to reverse things a bit. Rather than saying what we said at one time, "Let's try to re-introduce homosexuality into the general norm of social relations," let's say the reverse—"No! Let's escape as much as possible from the type of relations that society proposes for us and try to create in the empty space where we are new relational possibilities." By proposing a new relational *right*, we will see that nonhomosexual people can enrich their lives by changing their own schema of relations.

G.B. The word *gay* itself is a catalyst that has the power to negate what the word "homosexuality" stood for.

M.F. That's important because by getting away from the categorization homosexuality–heterosexuality, I think that gays have taken an important, interesting step: they define their problems differently by trying to create a culture that makes sense only in relation to a sexual experience and a type of relation that is their own. By taking the pleasure of sexual relations away from the area of sexual norms and its categories, and in so doing making the pleasure the crystallizing point of a new culture—I think that's an interesting approach.

G.B. That's what interests people, actually.

M.F. Today the important questions are no longer linked to the problem of repression, which doesn't mean that there aren't still many repressed people, and above all doesn't mean that we should overlook that and not struggle so that people stop being oppressed; of course I don't mean that. But the innovative direction we're moving in is no longer the struggle against repression.

G.B. The development of what used to be called a "ghetto," which now consists of bars, cafés, and baths, has perhaps been a phenomenon as radical and innovative as the struggle against discriminatory legislation. Of course, some people would say that the former would exist without the latter, and they're probably right.

M.F. Yes, but I don't think we should have an attitude toward the last ten or fifteen years which consists of stamping out the past as if it were a long error that we're finally leaving behind. A lot of change has come about in behavior, and this took courage, but we should no longer have only one model of behavior and one set of problems.

G.B. The fact that bars have—for many—stopped being private clubs indicates what transformations are taking place in the way homosexuality is lived. The dramatic part of the phenomenon—making it exist—has become a relic.

M.F. Absolutely, but from another point of view, I think that's due to the fact that we've reduced the guilt involved in making a very clear separation between the life of men and the life of women, the "monosexual" relation. With the universal condemnation of homosexuality, there was also a lessening of the monosexual relation—it was permitted only in places like prisons and army barracks. It's curious to note that homosexuals were also uneasy about monosexuality.

G.B. How so?

M.F. For a while, people were saying that when everyone started having homosexual relations, we could all finally have good relations with women.

G.B. Which was of course a fantasy.

M.F. That idea seemed to imply a difficulty in admitting that a monosexual relation was possible, and could be perfectly satisfying and compatible with relating to women—if we wanted that. That condemnation of monosexuality is disappearing, and we see women also affirming their right and desire for monosexuality. We shouldn't be afraid of that, even if it reminds us of college dorms, seminaries, army barracks, or prisons. We should acknowledge that "monosexuality" can be something rich.

G.B. In the sixties, the integration of the sexes was seen as the only civilized arrangement, and this created, in effect, a lot of hostility about "monosexual" groups like schools or private clubs.

M.F. We were right to condemn institutional monosexuality that was constricting, but the promise that we would love women as soon as we were no longer condemned for being gay was utopian. And a utopia in the dangerous sense, not because it promised good relations with women but because it was at the expense of monosexual relations. In the often-negative response some French people have toward certain types of American behavior, there is still that disapproval of monosexuality. So occasionally we hear: "What? How can you approve of those macho models? You're always with men, you have mustaches and leather jackets, you wear boots, what kind of masculine image is that?" Maybe in ten years we'll laugh about it all. But I think in the schema of a man affirming himself as a man, there is a movement toward redefining the monosexual relation. It consists of saying, "Yes, we spend our time with men, we have mustaches, and we kiss each other," without one of the partners having to play the nelly [*éphèbe*] or the effeminate, fragile boy.

G.B. Thus, the criticism of the machismo of the new gay man is an attempt to make us feel guilty and is full of the same clichés that have plagued homosexuality up to now?

M.F. We have to admit this is all something very new and practically unknown in Western societies. The Greeks never admitted love between two *adult men*. We can certainly find allusions to the idea of love between young men, when they were soldiers, but not for any others.

G.B. This would be something absolutely new?

M.F. It's one thing to be permitted sexual relations, but the very recognition by the individuals themselves of this type of relation, in the sense that they give them necessary and sufficient importance—that they acknowledge them and make them real—in order to invent other ways of life, yes, that's new.

G.B. Why has the idea of a relational right, stemming from "gay rights," come about first in Anglo-Saxon countries?

M.F. That's linked to many things, certainly to the laws regarding sexuality in Latin countries. We see for the first time a negative aspect of the Greek heritage, the fact that the love of one man for another is only valid in the form of classic pederasty. We should also take into consideration another phenomenon: in countries that are largely Protestant, associative rights were much more developed for obvious religious reasons. I would add, however, that relational rights are not exactly associative rights—the latter are an advance of the late nineteenth century. The relational right is the right to gain recognition in an institutional sense for the relations of one individual to another individual, which is not necessarily connected to the emergence of a group. It's very different. It's a question of imagining how the relation of two individuals can be validated by society and benefit from the same advantages as the relations—perfectly honorable—which are the only ones recognized: marriage and the family.

SEX, POWER, AND
THE POLITICS OF IDENTITY*

———

Q. You suggest in your work that sexual liberation is not so much the uncovering of secret truths about one's self or one's desire as it is a part of the process of defining and constructing desire. What are the practical implications of this distinction?

M.F. What I meant was that I think what the gay movement needs now is much more the art of life than a science or scientific knowledge (or pseudoscientific knowledge) of what sexuality is. Sexuality is a part of our behavior. It's a part of our world freedom. Sexuality is something that we ourselves create—it is our own creation, and much more than the discovery of a secret side of our desire. We have to understand that with our desires, through our desires, go new forms of relationships, new forms of love, new forms of creation. Sex is not a fatality: it's a possibility for creative life.

Q. That's basically what you're getting at when you suggest that we should try to become gay—not just to reassert ourselves as gay.

M.F. Yes, that's it. We don't have to discover that we are homosexuals.

Q. Or what the meaning of that is?

M.F. Exactly. Rather, we have to create a gay life. To *become*.

Q. And this is something without limits?

M.F. Yes, sure, I think when you look at the different ways people have experienced their own sexual freedoms—the way they have created their works of art—you would have to say that sexuality, as we now know it, has become one of the most creative sources of our society and

*This interview was conducted by B. Gallagher and A. Wilson in Toronto in June 1982. It appeared in *The Advocate* 400 (7 August 1984), pp. 26–30 and 58.

our being. My view is that we should understand it in the reverse way: the world regards sexuality as the secret of the creative cultural life; it is, rather, a process of our having to create a new cultural life underneath the ground of our sexual choices.

Q. Practically speaking, one of the effects of trying to uncover that secret has meant that the gay movement has remained at the level of demanding civil or human rights around sexuality. That is, sexual liberation has remained at the level of demanding sexual tolerance.

M.F. Yes, but this aspect must be supported. It is important, first, to have the possibility—and the right—to choose your own sexuality. Human rights regarding sexuality are important and are still not respected in many places. We shouldn't consider that such problems are solved now. It's quite true that there was a real liberation process in the early seventies. This process was very good, both in terms of the situation and in terms of opinions, but the situation has not definitely stabilized. Still, I think we have to go a step further. I think that one of the factors of this stabilization will be the creation of new forms of life, relationships, friendships in society, art, culture, and so on through our sexual, ethical, and political choices. Not only do we have to defend ourselves, not only affirm ourselves, as an identity but as a creative force.

Q. A lot of that sounds like what, for instance, the women's movement has done, trying to establish their own language and their own culture.

M.F. Well, I'm not sure that we have to create our *own* culture. We have to *create* culture. We have to realize cultural creations. But, in doing so, we come up against the problem of identity. I don't know what we would do to form these creations, and I don't know what forms these creations would take. For instance, I am not at all sure that the best form of literary creations by gay people is gay novels.

Q. In fact, we would not even want to say that. That would be based on an essentialism that we need to avoid.

M.F. True. What do we mean for instance, by "gay painting"? Yet, I am sure that from the point of departure of our ethical choices, we can create something that will have a certain relationship to gayness. But it must not be a translation of gayness in the field of music or painting or what have you, for I do not think this can happen.

Q. How do you view the enormous proliferation in the last ten or fifteen years of male homosexual practices: the sensualization, if you

like, of neglected parts of the body and the articulation of new pleasures? I am thinking, obviously, of the salient aspects of what we call
the ghetto—porn movies, clubs for S&M or fistfucking, and so forth.
Is this merely an extension into another sphere of the general proliferation of sexual discourses since the nineteenth century, or do you
see other kinds of developments that are peculiar to this present historical context?

M.F. Well, I think what we want to speak about is precisely the *innovations* those practices imply. For instance, look at the S&M subcul-
ture, as our good friend Gayle Rubin would insist. I don't think that
this movement of sexual practices has anything to do with the disclosure or the uncovering of S&M tendencies deep within our unconscious, and so on. I think that S&M is much more than that; it's the
real creation of new possibilities of pleasure, which people had no idea
about previously. The idea that S&M is related to a deep violence, that
S&M practice is a way of liberating this violence, this aggression, is stupid. We know very well what all those people are doing is not aggres-
sive; they are inventing new possibilities of pleasure with strange parts
of their body—through the eroticization of the body. I think it's a kind
of creation, a creative enterprise, which has as one of its main features
what I call the desexualization of pleasure. The idea that bodily pleasure should always come from sexual pleasure as the root of *all* our possible pleasure—I think *that's* something quite wrong. These practices
are insisting that we can produce pleasure with very odd things, very
strange parts of our bodies, in very unusual situations, and so on.

Q. So the conflation of pleasure and sex is being broken down.

M.F. That's it precisely. The possibility of using our bodies as a
possible source of very numerous pleasures is something that is very
important. For instance, if you look at the traditional construction of
pleasure, you see that bodily pleasure, or pleasures of the flesh, are
always drinking, eating, and fucking. And that seems to be the limit
of the understanding of our body, our pleasures. What frustrates me,
for instance, is the fact that the problem of drugs is always envisaged
only as a problem of freedom and prohibition. I think that drugs must
become a part of our culture.

Q. As a pleasure?

M.F. As a pleasure. We have to study drugs. We have to experience
drugs. We have to do *good* drugs that can produce very intense pleasure.
I think this puritanism about drugs, which implies that you can either

be for drugs or against drugs, is mistaken. Drugs have now become a part of our culture. Just as there is bad music and good music, there are bad drugs and good drugs. So we can't say we are "against" drugs any more than we can say we're "against" music.

Q. The point is to experiment with pleasure and its possibilities.

M.F. Yes. Pleasure also must be a part of our culture. It is very interesting to note, for instance, that for centuries people generally, as well as doctors, psychiatrists, and even liberation movements, have always spoken about desire, and never about pleasure. "We have to liberate our desire," they say. *No!* We have to create new pleasure. And then maybe desire will follow.

Q. Is it significant that there are, to a large degree, identities forming around new sexual practices, like S&M? These identities help in exploring such practices and defending the right to engage in them. But are they also limiting in regards to the possibilities of individuals?

M.F. Well, if identity is only a game, if it is only a procedure to have relations, social and sexual—pleasure relationships that create new friendships, it is useful. But if identity becomes the problem of sexual existence, and if people think that they have to "uncover" their "own identity," and that their own identity has to become the law, the principle, the code of their existence; if the perennial question they ask is "Does this thing conform to my identity?" then, I think, they will turn back to a kind of ethics very close to the old heterosexual virility. If we are asked to relate to the question of identity, it must be an identity to our unique selves. But the relationships we have to have with ourselves are not ones of identity, rather, they must be relationships of differentiation, of creation, of innovation. To be the same is really boring. We must not exclude identity if people find their pleasure through this identity, but we must not think of this identity as an ethical universal rule.

Q. But up to this point, sexual identity has been politically very useful.

M.F. Yes, it has been very useful, but it limits us, and I think we have—and can have—a right to be free.

Q. We want some of our sexual practices to be ones of resistance in a political and social sense. Yet how is this possible, given that control can be exercised by the stimulation of pleasure? Can we be sure that these new pleasures won't be exploited in the way advertising uses the stimulation of pleasure as a means of social control?

M.F. We can never be sure. In fact, we can always be sure *it will happen*, and that everything that has been created or acquired, any ground that has been gained will, at a certain moment be used in such a way. That's the way we live, that's the way we struggle, that's the way of human history. And I don't think that is an objection to all those movements or all those situations. But you are quite right in underlining that we always have to be quite careful and to be aware of the fact that we must move on to something else, that we' have other needs as well. The S&M ghetto in San Francisco is a good example of a community that has experimented with, and formed an identity around, pleasure. This ghettoization, this identification, this procedure of exclusion and so on—all of these have, as well, produced their countereffects. I dare not use the word *dialectics*—but this comes rather close to it.

Q. You write that power is not just a negative force but a productive one; that power is always there; that where there is power, there is resistance; and that resistance is never in a position of externality vis-à-vis power. If this is so, then how do we come to any other conclusion than that we are always trapped inside that relationship—that we can't somehow break out of it.

M.F. Well, I don't think the word *trapped* is a correct one. It is a struggle, but what I mean by *power relations* is the fact that we are in a strategic situation toward each other. For instance, being homosexuals, we are in a struggle with the government, and the government is in a struggle with us. When we deal with the government, the struggle, of course, is not symmetrical, the power situation is not the same; but we are in this struggle, and the continuation of this situation can influence the behavior or nonbehavior of the other. So we are not trapped. We are always in this kind of situation. It means that we always have possibilities, there are always possibilities of changing the situation. We cannot jump *outside* the situation, and there is no point where you are free from all power relations. But you can always change it. So what I've said does not mean that we are always trapped, but that we are always free—well, anyway, that there is always the possibility of changing.

Q. So resistance comes from within that dynamic?

M.F. Yes. You see, if there was no resistance, there would be no power relations. Because it would simply be a matter of obedience. You have to use power relations to refer to the situation where you're not doing what you want. So resistance comes first, and resistance remains superior to the forces of the process; power relations are obliged to change with the resistance. So I think that *resistance* is the main word, *the key word*, in this dynamic.

Q. Politically speaking, probably the most important part of looking at power is that, according to previous conceptions, "to resist" was simply to say no. Resistance was conceptualized only in terms of negation. Within your understanding, however, to resist is not simply a negation but a creative process; to create and recreate, to change the situation, actually to be an active member of that process.

M.F. Yes, that is the way I would put it. To say no is the minimum form of resistance. But, of course, at times that is very important. You have to say no as a decisive form of resistance.

Q. This raises the question of in what way, and to what degree, can a dominated subject (or subjectivity) actually create its own discourse. In traditional power analysis, the omnipresent feature of analysis is the dominant discourse, and only as a subsidiary are there reactions to, or within, that discourse. However, if what we mean by resistance in power relations is more than negation, then aren't some practices like, say, lesbian S&M, actually ways for dominated subjects to formulate their own languages?

M.F. Well, you see, I think that resistance is a part of this strategic relationship of which power consists. Resistance really always relies upon the situation against which it struggles. For instance, in the gay movement the medical definition of homosexuality was a very important tool against the oppression of homosexuality in the last part of the nineteenth century and in the early twentieth century. This medicalization, which was a means of oppression, has always been a means of resistance as well—since people could say, "If we are sick, then why do you condemn us, why do you despise us?" and so on. Of course, this discourse now sounds rather naïve to us, but at the time it was very important.

I should say, also, that I think that in the lesbian movement, the fact that women have been, for centuries and centuries, isolated in society, frustrated, despised in many ways, and so on, has given them the real possibility of constituting a society, of creating a kind of social relation between themselves, outside the social world that was dominated by males. Lillian Faderman's book *Surpassing the Love of Men* is very interesting in this regard. It raises the question: What kind of emotional experience, what kind of relationships, were possible in a world where women in society had no social, no legal, and no political power? And she argues that women used that isolation and lack of power.

Q. If resistance is a process of breaking out of discursive practices, it would seem that the case that has a prima facie claim to be truly oppositional might be something like lesbian S&M. To what degree can such practices and identities be seen as challenging the dominant discourse?

M.F. What I think is interesting now, in relation to lesbian S&M, is that they can get rid of certain stereotypes of femininity which have been used in the lesbian movement—a strategy that the movement has erected from the past. This strategy has been based on their oppression. But now, maybe, these tools, these weapons are obsolete. We can see that lesbian S&M tried to get rid of all those old stereotypes of femininity, of antimale attitude and so on.

Q. What do you think we can learn about power and, for that matter, about pleasure from the practice of S&M—that is, the explicit eroticization of power?

M.F. One can say that S&M is the eroticization of power, the eroticization of strategic relations. What strikes me with regard to S&M is how it differs from social power. What characterizes power is the fact that it is a strategic relation which has been stabilized through institutions. So the mobility in power relations is limited, and there are strongholds that are very, very difficult to suppress because they have been institutionalized and are now very pervasive in courts, codes, and so on. All this means that the strategic relations of people are made rigid.

On this point, the S&M game is very interesting because it is a strategic relation, but it is always fluid. Of course, there are roles, but everybody knows very well that those roles can be reversed. Sometimes the scene begins with the master and slave, and at the end the slave has become the master. Or, even when the roles are stabilized, you know very well that it is always a game. Either the rules are transgressed, or there is an agreement, either explicit or tacit, that makes them aware of certain boundaries. This strategic game as a source of bodily pleasure is very interesting. But I wouldn't say that it is a reproduction, inside the erotic relationship, of the structures of power. It is an acting-out of power structures by a strategic game that is able to give sexual pleasure or bodily pleasure.

Q. How does this strategic relation in sex differ for that in power relations?

M.F. The practice of S&M is the creation of pleasure, and there is an identity with that creation. And that's why S&M is really a subcul-

ture. It's a process of invention. S&M is *the use* of a strategic relationship as a source of pleasure (physical pleasure). It is not the first time
that people have used strategic relations as a source of pleasure. For
instance, in the Middle Ages there was the institution of "courtly love,"
the troubadour, the institutions of the love relationships between the
lady and the lover, and so on. That, too, was a strategic game. You even
find this between boys and girls when they are dancing on Saturday
night. They are acting out strategic relations. What is interesting is that,
in this heterosexual life, those strategic relations come before sex: It's
a strategic relation in order to obtain sex. And in S&M those strategic
relations are inside sex, as a convention of pleasure within a particular situation.

In the one case, the strategic relations are purely social relations, and
it is your social being that is involved; while, in the other case, it is your
body that is involved. And it is this transfer of strategic relations from
the court(ship) to sex that is very interesting.

Q. You mentioned in an interview in *Gai Pied* a year or two ago that
what upsets people most about gay relations is not so much sexual acts
per se but the potential for affectional relationships carried on outside
the normative patterns. These friendships and networks are unforeseen. Do you think what frightens people is the unknown potential of
gay relations, or would you suggest that these relations are seen as posing a direct threat to social institutions?

M.F. One thing that interests me now is the problem of friendship.
For centuries after antiquity, friendship was a very important kind of
social relation: a social relation within which people had a certain freedom, certain kind of choice (limited of course), as well as very intense
emotional relations. There were also economic and social implications
to these relationships—they were obliged to help their friends, and
so on. I think that in the sixteenth and seventeenth centuries, we see
these kinds of friendships disappearing, at least in the male society.
And friendship begins to become something other than that. You can
find, from the sixteenth century on, texts that explicitly criticize friendship as something dangerous.

The army, bureaucracy, administration, universities, schools, and so
on—in the modern senses of these words—cannot function with such
intense friendships. I think there can be seen a very strong attempt in
all these institutions to diminish or minimize the affectional relations.
I think this is particularly important in schools. When they started

grade schools with hundreds of young boys, one of the problems was how to prevent them not only from having sex, of course, but also from developing friendships. For instance, you could study the strategy of Jesuit institutions about this theme of friendship, since the Jesuits knew very well that it was impossible for them to suppress this. Rather, they tried to use the role of sex, of love, of friendship, and at the same time to limit it. I think now, after studying the history of sex, we should try to understand the history of friendship, or friendships. That history is very, very important.

And one of my hypotheses, which I am sure would be borne out if we did this, is that homosexuality became a problem—that is, sex between men became a problem—in the eighteenth century. We see the rise of it as a problem with the police, within the justice system, and so on. I think the reason it appears as a problem, as a social issue, at this time is that friendship had disappeared. As long as friendship was something important, was socially accepted, nobody realized men had sex together. You couldn't say that men *didn't* have sex together—it just didn't matter. It had no social implication, it was culturally accepted. Whether they fucked together or kissed had no importance. Absolutely no importance. Once friendship disappeared as a culturally accepted relation, the issue arose: "What is going on between men?" And that's when the problem appears. And if men fuck together, or have sex together, that now appears as a problem. Well, I'm sure I'm right, that the disappearance of friendship as a social relation and the declaration of homosexuality as a social/political/medical problem are the same process.

Q. If the important thing now is to explore anew the possibilities of friendships, we should note that, to a large degree, all the social institutions are designed for heterosexual friendships and structures, and the denial of homosexual ones. Isn't the real task to set up new social relations, new value structures, familial structures, and so on? One of the things gay people don't have is easy access to all the structures and institutions that go along with monogamy and the nuclear family. What kinds of institutions do we need to begin to establish, in order not just to defend ourselves but also to create new social forms that are really going to be alternative?

M.F. Institutions. I have no precise idea. I think, of course, that to use the model of family life, or the institutions of the family, for this purpose and this kind of friendship would be quite contradictory. But

it is quite true that since some of the relationships in society are protected forms of family life, an effect of this is that the variations which
are not protected are, at the same time, often much richer, more interesting and creative than the others. But, of course, they are much more
fragile and vulnerable. The question of what kinds of institutions we
need to create is an important and crucial issue, but one that I cannot
give an answer to. I think that we have to try to build a solution.

Q. To what degree do we want, or need, the project of gay liberation today to be one that refuses to chart a course and instead insists
on opening up new venues? In other words, does your approach to sexual politics deny the need for a program and insist on experimentation with new kind of relations?

M.F. I think that one of the great experiences we've had since the
last war is that all those social and political programs have been a great
failure. We have come to realize that things never happen as we expect
from a political program, and that a political program has always, or
nearly always, led to abuse or political domination from a bloc—be it
from technicians or bureaucrats or other people. But one of the developments of the sixties and seventies which I think has been a good
thing is that certain institutional models have been experimented with
without a program. Without a program does not mean blindness—to
be blind to thought. For instance, in France there has been a lot of criticism recently about the fact that there are no programs in the various
political movements about sex, about prisons, about ecology, and so
on. But in my opinion, being without a program can be very useful
and very original and creative, if it does not mean without proper
reflection about what is going on, or without very careful attention to
what's possible.

Since the nineteenth century, great political institutions and great
political parties have confiscated the process of political creation; that
is, they have tried to give to political creation the form of a political
program in order to take over power. I think what happened in the sixties and early seventies is something to be preserved. One of the things
that I think should be preserved, however, is the fact that there has
been political innovation, political creation, and political experimentation outside the great political parties, and outside the normal or ordinary program. It's a fact that people's everyday lives have changed from
the early sixties to now, and certainly within my own life. And surely
that is not due to political parties but is the result of many movements.

These social movements have really changed our whole lives, our mentality, our attitudes, and the attitudes and mentality of other people—people who do not belong to these movements. And that is something very important and positive. I repeat, it is not the normal and old traditional political organizations that have led to this examination.

In a work consecrated to the moral treatment of madness and published in 1840, a French psychiatrist, Leuret,[a] tells of the manner in which he treated one of his patients—treated and of course, as you may imagine, cured. One morning he placed Mr. A., his patient, in a shower room. He makes him recount in detail his delirium. "But all that," said the doctor, "is nothing but madness. Promise me not to believe in it anymore." The patient hesitates, then promises. "That is not enough," replies the doctor. "You have already made me similar promises and you haven't kept them." And he turns on the cold shower above the patient's head. "Yes, yes! I am mad!" the patient cries. The shower is turned off; the interrogation is resumed. "Yes. I recognize that I am mad," the patient repeats. "But," he adds, "I recognize it because you are forcing me to do so." Another shower. "Well, well," says Mr. A., "I admit it. I am mad, and all that was nothing but madness."

To make somebody suffering from mental illness recognize that he is mad is a very ancient procedure in traditional therapy. In the works of the seventeenth and eighteenth centuries, one finds many examples of what one might call "truth therapies." But the technique used by Leuret is altogether different. Leuret is not trying to persuade his patient that his ideas are false or unreasonable. What happens in the head of Mr. A. is a matter of perfect indifference to Leuret. The doctor wishes to obtain a precise act, the explicit affirmation: "I am mad." Since I first read this passage of Leuret, about twenty years ago, I kept in mind the project of analyzing the form and the history of such a bizarre practice. Leuret is satisfied when and only when his patient says, "I am mad," or: "That was madness." Leuret's assumption is that madness as a reality disappears when the patient asserts the truth and says he is mad.

We have, then, the reverse of the performative speech act. The affirmation destroys in the speaking subject the reality that made the same affirmation true. What conception of truth of discourse and of subjectivity is taken for granted in this strange and yet widespread practice? In order to justify the attention I am giving to what is seemingly so specialized a subject, let me take a step back for a moment. In the years that preceded the Second World War, and even more so after the war, philosophy in continental Europe and in France was dominated by the philosophy of subject. I mean that philosophy took as its task par excellence the foundation of all knowledge and the principle of all signification as stemming from the meaningful subject. The importance given to this question was due to the impact of Husserl, but the centrality of the subject was also tied to an institutional context, for the French university, since philosophy began with Descartes, could only advance in a Cartesian manner. But we must also take into account the political conjunct. Given the absurdity of wars, slaughters, and despotism, it seemed to be up to the individual subject to give meaning to his existential choices. With the leisure and distance that came after the war, this emphasis on the philosophy of subject no longer seemed so self-evident. Hitherto-hidden theoretical paradoxes could no longer be avoided. This philosophy of consciousness had paradoxically failed to found a philosophy of knowledge, and especially of scientific knowledge. Also, this philosophy of meaning had failed to take into account the formative mechanisms of signification and the structure of systems of meaning.

With the all too easy clarity of hindsight—of what Americans call the "Monday-morning quarterback"—let me say that there were two possible paths that led beyond this philosophy of subject. The first of these was the theory of objective knowledge as an analysis of systems of meaning, as semiology. This was the path of logical positivism. The second was that of a certain school of linguistics, psychoanalysis, and anthropology—all grouped under the rubric of Structuralism. These were not the directions I took. Let me announce once and for all that I am not a structuralist, and I confess, with the appropriate chagrin, that I am not an analytic philosopher. Nobody is perfect. But I have tried to explore another direction. I have tried to get out from the phi-

losophy of the subject, through a genealogy of the modern subject as a
historical and cultural reality—which means as something that can
eventually change. That, of course, is politically important. One can
proceed with this general project in two ways. In dealing with modern theoretical constructions, we are concerned with the subject in general. In this way, I have tried to analyze the theories of the subject as a
speaking, living, working being in the seventeenth and eighteenth centuries. One can also deal with the more practical understanding found
in those institutions where certain subjects became objects of knowledge and of domination: asylums, prisons, and so on.

I wished to study those forms of understanding which the subject
creates about himself. But since I started with this last type of problem, I have been obliged to change my mind on several points. Let me
introduce a kind of auto-critique. It seems, according to some suggestions of Jürgen Habermas, that one can distinguish three major types
of technique: the techniques that permit one to produce, to transform,
to manipulate things; the techniques that permit one to use sign systems; and finally, the techniques that permit one to determine the conduct of individuals, to impose certain ends or objectives. That is to say,
techniques of production, techniques of signification or communication,
and techniques of domination. But I became more and more aware that
in all societies there is another type of technique: techniques that permit individuals to effect, by their own means, a certain number of operations on their own bodies, their own souls, their own thoughts, their
own conduct, and this in a manner so as to transform themselves, modify themselves, and to attain a certain state of perfection, happiness,
purity, supernatural power. Let us call these techniques "technologies
of the self."

If one wants to analyze the genealogy of the subject in Western civilization, one must take into account not only techniques of domination
but also techniques of the self. One must show the interaction between
these types of technique. When I was studying asylums, prisons, and
so on, I perhaps insisted too much on the techniques of domination.
What we call "discipline" is something really important in this kind
of institution; but it is only one aspect of the art of governing people
in our societies. Having studied the field of power relations taking techniques of domination as a point of departure, I would like, in the years
to come, to study power relations starting from the techniques of the
self. In every culture, I think, this self technology implies a set of truth

obligations: discovering the truth, being enlightened by truth, telling the truth. All these are considered important either for the constitution of, or the transformation of, the self.

Now, what about truth as a duty in our Christian societies? As everybody knows, Christianity is a confession. This means that Christianity belongs to a very special type of religion—those which impose obligations of truth on the practitioners. Such obligations in Christianity are numerous. For instance, there is the obligation to hold as truth a set of propositions that constitute dogma, the obligation to hold certain books as a permanent source of truth, and obligations to accept the decisions of certain authorities in matters of truth. But Christianity requires another form of truth obligation. Everyone in Christianity has the duty to explore who he is, what is happening within himself, the faults he may have committed, the temptations to which he is exposed. Moreover, everyone is obliged to tell these things to other people, and thus to bear witness against himself.

These two ensembles of obligation—those regarding the faith, the book, the dogma, and those regarding the self, the soul, and the heart—are linked together. A Christian needs the light of faith when he wants to explore himself, Conversely, his access to the truth can't be conceived of without the purification of his soul. The Buddhist, too, must go to the light and discover the truth about himself; but the relation between these two obligations is quite different in Buddhism and in Christianity. In Buddhism, it is the same type of enlightenment which leads you to discover what you are and what is the truth. In this simultaneous enlightenment of yourself and the truth, you discover that your self was only an illusion. I would like to underline that the Christian discovery of the self does not reveal the self as an illusion. It gives place to a task that cannot be anything else but undefined. This task has two objectives. First, there is the task of clearing up all the illusions, temptations, and seductions that can occur in the mind, and of discovering the reality of what is going on within ourselves. Second, one must get free from any attachment to this self, not because the self is an illusion but because the self is much too real. The more we discover the truth about ourselves, the more we must renounce ourselves; and the more we want to renounce ourselves, the more we need to bring to light the reality of ourselves. That is what we would call the spiral of truth formulation and reality renouncement which is at the heart of Christian techniques of the self.

Recently, Professor Peter Brown stated to me that what we have to understand is why it is that sexuality became, in Christian cultures, the seismograph of our subjectivity. It is a fact, a mysterious fact, that in this indefinite spiral of truth and reality in the self sexuality has been of major importance since the first centuries of our era. It has become more and more important. Why is there such a fundamental connection between sexuality, subjectivity, and truth obligation? This is the point at which I met Richard Sennett's work.

Our point of departure in the seminar has been a passage of St. François de Sales. Here is the text in a translation made at the beginning of the seventeenth century: "I will tell you a point of the elephant's honesty. An elephant never changes his mate. He loves her tenderly. With her he couples not, but from three years to three years. And that only for five days, and so secretly that he is never seen in the act. But the sixth day, he shows himself abroad again, and the first thing he does is to go directly to some river and wash his body, not willing to return to his troupe of companions till he be purified. Be not these goodly and honest qualities in a beast by which he teaches married folk not to be given too much to carnal and sensual pleasures?"[b]

Everybody may recognize here the pattern of decent sexual behavior: monogamy, faithfulness, and procreation as the main, or maybe the single, justification for the sexual acts—sexual acts that remain, even in such conditions, intrinsically impure. Most of us are inclined, I think, to attribute this pattern either to Christianity or to modern Christian society as it developed under the influence of capitalist or so-called bourgeois morality. But what struck me when I started studying this pattern is the fact that one can also find it in Latin and even Hellenistic literature. One finds the same ideas, the same words, and eventually the same reference to the elephant. It is a fact that the pagan philosophers in the centuries before and after the death of Christ proposed a sexual ethics that was very similar to the alleged Christian ethics. In our seminar, it was very convincingly stressed that this philosophical pattern of sexual behavior, this elephant pattern, was not at that time the only one to be known and put into practice; it was in competition with several others. Yet this pattern soon became predominant because it was related to a social transformation involving the disintegration of the city-states, the development of the imperial bureaucracy, and the increasing influence of the provincial middle class.

During this period, we may witness an evolution toward the nuclear family, real monogamy, faithfulness between married people, and distress about sexual acts. The philosophical campaign in favor of the elephant pattern was both an effect and an adjunct of this transformation. If these assumptions are correct, we must concede that Christianity did not invent this code of sexual behavior. Christianity accepted it, reinforced it, and gave it a much larger and more widespread strength than it had before. But the so-called Christian morality is nothing more than a piece of pagan ethics inserted into Christianity. Shall we say then that Christianity did not change the state of things? Early Christians introduced important changes, if not in the sexual code itself, at least in the relationships everyone has to his own sexual activity. Christianity proposed a new type of experience of oneself as a sexual being.

To make things clearer, I will compare two texts—one written by Artemidorus, a pagan philosopher of the third century, and the other the well-known fourteenth book of *The City of God* by Augustine. Artemidorus wrote a book about the interpretation of dreams in the third century after the death of Christ, but he was a pagan. Three chapters of this book are devoted to sexual dreams. What is the meaning, or, more precisely, what is the prognostic value, of a sexual dream? It is significant that Artemidorus interpreted dreams in a way contrary to Freud, and gives an interpretation of sexual dreams in terms of economics, social relations, success and reverses in political activity and everyday life. For instance, if you dream that you have sex with your mother, that means that you will succeed as a magistrate, since your mother is obviously the symbol of your city or country.

It is also significant that the social value of the dream depends not on the nature of the sexual act but mainly on the social status of the partners. For instance, for Artemidorus it is not important in your dream whether you had sex with a girl or with a boy. The problem is to know if the partner was rich or poor, young or old, slave or free, married or not. Of course, he takes into account the question of the sexual act, but he sees it only from the point of view of the male. The only act he knows or recognizes as sexual is penetration. For him, penetration is not only a sexual act but part of the social role of a man in a city. I would say that for Artemidorus sexuality is relational, and that sexual relations cannot be dissociated from social relations.

Now let us turn to Augustine's text, whose meaning is the point at which we want to arrive in our analysis. In *The City of God*, and later on in the *Contra Julian*, Augustine gives a rather horrifying description of the sexual act. He sees the sexual act as a kind of spasm. All the body, says Augustine, is shaken by terrible jerks; one entirely loses control of oneself. "This sexual act takes such a complete and passionate possession of the whole man, both physically and emotionally, that what results is the keenest of all pleasures on the level of sensations, and at the crisis of excitement it practically paralyzes all power of deliberate thought." It is worthwhile to note that this description is not an invention of Augustine: you can find the same in the medical and pagan literature of the previous century. Moreover, Augustine's text is almost the exact transcription of a passage written by the pagan philosopher, Cicero, in the *Hortensius*.

The surprising point is not that Augustine would give such a classical description of the sexual act, but the fact that, having given such a horrible description, he then admits that sexual relations could have taken place in Paradise before the Fall. This is all the more remarkable since Augustine is one of the first Christian Fathers to admit the possibility. Of course, sex in Paradise could not have the epileptic form that we unfortunately know now. Before the Fall, Adam's body, every part of it, was perfectly obedient to the soul and the will. If Adam wanted to procreate in Paradise, he could do it in the same way and with the same control as he could, for instance, sow seeds in the earth. He was not involuntarily excited. Every part of his body was like the fingers, which one can control in all their gestures. Sex was a kind of hand gently sowing the seed. But what happened with the Fall? He rose up against God with the first sin; he tried to escape God's will and to acquire a will of his own, ignoring the fact that the existence of his own will depended entirely on the will of God. As a punishment for this revolt, and as a consequence of this will to will independently from God, Adam lost control of himself. He wanted to acquire an autonomous will and lost the ontological support for that will. That then became mixed in an indissociable way with involuntary movements, and this weakening of Adam's will had a disastrous effect. His body, and parts of his body, stopped obeying his commands, revolted against him, and the sexual parts of his body were the first to rise up in this disobedience. The famous gesture of Adam covering his genitals with a fig leaf is, according to Augustine, due not to the simple fact that Adam was ashamed of their presence but to the fact that his sexual organs were moving by themselves without his consent. Sex in erection is the image of man revolted against God. The arrogance of sex is the punishment and consequence of the arrogance of man. His uncontrolled sex is exactly the same as what he himself has been toward God—a rebel.

Why have I insisted so much on what may be nothing more than one of those exegetic fantasies of which Christian literature has been so prodigal? I think this text bears witness to the new type of relationship which Christianity established between sex and subjectivity. Augustine's conception is still dominated by the theme and form of male sexuality. But the main question is not, as it was in Artemidorus, the problem of penetration—it is the problem of erection. As a result, it is not the problem of a relationship to other people but the problem of the relationship of oneself to oneself, or, more precisely, the relationship between one's will and involuntary assertions.

The principle of autonomous movements of sexual organs is called libido by Augustine. The problem of libido, of its strength, origin, and effect, thus becomes the main issue of one's will. It is not an external obstacle to the will; it is a part, an internal component, of the will. And it is not the manifestation of petty desires. Libido is the result of one's will when it goes beyond the limits God originally set for it. As a consequence, the means of the spiritual struggle against libido do not consist, as with Plato, in turning our eyes upward and memorizing the reality we have previously known and forgotten; the spiritual struggle consists, on the contrary, in turning our eyes continuously downward or inward in order to decipher, among the movements of the soul, which ones come from the libido. The task is at first indefinite, since libido and will can never be substantially dissociated from one another. And this task is not only an issue of mastership but also a question of the diagnosis of truth and illusion. It requires a permanent hermeneutics of oneself.

In such a perspective, sexual ethics imply very strict truth obligations. These consist not only in learning the rules of a moral sexual behavior but also in constantly scrutinizing ourselves as libidinal beings. Shall we say that, after Augustine, we experience our sex in the head? Let us say at least that, in Augustine's analysis, we witness a real libidinization of sex. His moral theology is, to a certain extent, a systematization of a lot of previous speculation, but it is also an ensemble of spiritual techniques.

When one reads the ascetic and monastic literature of the fourth and fifth centuries, one cannot but be struck by the fact that these techniques are not directly concerned with the effective control of sexual behavior. There is little mention of homosexual relations, in spite of the fact that most ascetics lived in permanent and numerous communities. The techniques were mainly concerned with the stream of thoughts flowing into consciousness, disturbing by their multiplicity the necessary unity of contemplation and secretly conveying images or suggestions from Satan. The monk's task was not the philosopher's task: to acquire mastership over oneself by the definitive victory of the will. It was perpetually to control one's thoughts, examining them to see if they were pure, whether something dangerous was not hiding in or behind them, if they were not conveying something other than what primarily appeared, if they were not a form of illusion and seduction. Such data have always to be considered with suspicion; they need to be scrutinized and tested. According to Cassian, for instance, one must be toward oneself as a moneychanger, who must try the coins he receives. Real purity is not acquired when one can lie down with a young and beautiful boy without even touching him, as Socrates did with Alcibiades. A monk was really chaste when no impure image occurred in his mind, even during the night, even during dreams. The criterion of purity does not consist in keeping control of oneself even in the presence of the most desirable people; it consists in discovering the truth in myself and defeating the illusions in myself, in cutting out the images and thoughts my mind continuously produces. Hence the axis of the spiritual struggle against impurity. The main question of sexual ethics has moved from relations to people, and from the penetration model to the relation to oneself and to the erection problem: I mean to the set of internal movements that develop from the first and nearly imperceptible thought to the final but still solitary pollution. However different and eventually contradictory they were, a common effect was elicited: sexuality, subjectivity, and truth were strongly linked together. This, I think, is the religious framework in which the masturbation problem—which was nearly ignored or at least neglected by the Greeks, who considered masturbation a thing for slaves and for satyrs, but not for free citizens— appeared as one of the main issues of the sexual life.

NOTES

a   In this talk, which was given in English and first appeared in the *London Review of Books* (3:9 [21 May–5 June 1981]: 3, 5, and 6), Foucault misspoke, or was misheard, in calling the doctor "Louren." Its French translation, which we follow, corrects the error. The French editors further provide the source of the anecdote: F. Leuret, *Du traitement moral de la folie* (Paris: Baillière, 1840), pp. 197–98.

b   François de Sales, *Introduction à la vie dévotée* (Dôle: Bluzet-Guimier, 1988), bk. 3, ch. 39, pp. 431–32. The seminar to which Foucault refers here was conducted with Richard Sennett at New York University's Institute for the Humanities in November 1980. A statement by Sennett accompanies Foucault's in the *London Review*.

THE BATTLE FOR CHASTITY*

The battle for chastity is discussed in detail by John Cassian in the sixth chapter of the *Institutiones*, "Concerning the spirit of fornication," and in several of his *Conferences*: the fourth on "the lusts of the flesh and of the spirit," the fifth on "the eight principal vices," the twelfth on "chastity," and the twenty-second on "night visions." It ranks second in a list of eight battles,[1] in the shape of a fight against the spirit of fornication. As for fornication itself, it is subdivided into three categories.[2] On the face of it a very unjuridical list, if one compares it with the catalog of sins that are to be found when the medieval Church organizes the sacrament of penance on the lines of a penal code. But Cassian's specifications obviously have a different meaning.

Let us first examine the place of fornication among the other sinful tendencies.

Cassian arranges his eight sins in a particular order. He sets up pairs of vices that seem linked in some specifically close way:[3] pride and vainglory, sloth and accidie, avarice and wrath. Fornication is coupled with greed, for several reasons. They are two "natural" vices, innate

*The opening paragraph of the original text, a contribution to a 1982 volume on occidental sexualities edited by Philippe Ariès and André Béjin, is omitted in this translation. The paragraph describes the text as an extract from the third volume of *The History of Sexuality*; but the description precedes Foucault's decision to relegate discussion of the period discussed in the text to a fourth volume, *Aveux de la chair* [*Confessions of the Flesh*], which remains unpublished. The full paragraph reads: "*Ce texte est extrait du troisième volume de* l'Histoire de la sexualité. *Après avoir consulté Philippe Ariès sur l'orientation générale du présent recueil, j'ai pensé que ce texte consonait avec les autres études. Il nous semble en effet que l'idée qu'on se fait d'ordinaire d'une ethique sexuelle chrétienne est à réviser profondément; et que, d'autre part, la valeur centrale de la ques-*

and hence very difficult to cure. They are also the two vices that involve the participation of the body, not only in their growth but also in achieving their object; and finally they also have a direct causal connection— overindulgence in food and drink fuels the urge to commit fornication.[4] In addition, the spirit of fornication occupies a position of peculiar importance among the other vices, either because it is closely bound with greed, or simply by its very nature.

First, the causal chain. Cassian emphasizes the fact that the vices do not exist in isolation, even though an individual may be particularly affected by one vice or another.[5] There is a causal link that binds them all together. It begins with greed, which arises in the body and inflames the spirit of fornication; these two engender avarice, understood as an attachment to worldly wealth, which in turn leads to rivalries, quarreling, and wrath. The result is despondency and sorrow, provoking the sin of accidie and total disgust with monastic life. Such a progression implies that one will never be able to conquer a vice unless one can conquer the one on which it leans: "The defeat of the first weakens the one that depends on it; victory over the former leads to the collapse of the latter without further effort." As with the others, the greed– fornication pair, like "a huge tree whose shadow stretches afar," has to be uprooted. Hence the importance for the ascetic of fasting as a way of conquering greed and suppressing fornication. Therein lies the basis of the practice of asceticism, for it is the first link in the causal chain.

The spirit of fornication is seen as being in an odd relationship to the last vices on the list, especially pride. In fact, for Cassian, pride and vainglory do not form part of the causal chain of other vices. Far from being generated by them, they result from victory over them:[6] "carnal pride," that is, flaunting one's fasts, one's chastity, one's poverty, and so on before other people, and "spiritual pride," which makes one think that one's progress is all due to one's own merits.[7] One vice that springs from the defeat of another means a fall that is that much greater.

---

tion de la masturbation a une toute autre origine que la campagne des médecins aux XVIIIᵉ et XIXᵉ siècles" ("This text is an extract from the third volume of *The History of Sexuality*. After having discussed with Philippe Ariès the general orientation of the present collection, I thought that the text was consonant with the other studies. It indeed seems to us that the idea one ordinarily has of a Christian sexual ethics should be profoundly revised; and that, moreover, the central value of the question of masturbation has an altogether other origin from that of the doctors' campaign of the eighteenth and nineteenth centuries"). The text that appears here, translated by Anthony Forster and originally published in *Western Sexuality*, ed. P. Ariès and A. Béjin (Oxford: Basil Blackwell, 1985), has been amended.

And fornication, the most disgraceful of all the vices, the one that is most shameful, is the consequence of pride—a chastisement but also a temptation, the proof God sends to the presumptuous mortal to remind him that he is always threatened by the weakness of the flesh if the grace of God does not come to his help. "Because someone has for long exulted in the pureness of his heart and his body, it naturally follows... that in the back of his mind he rather prides himself on it...so it is a good thing for the Lord to desert him, for his own good. The pureness which has been making him so self-assured begins to worry him, and in the midst of his spiritual well-being he finds himself faltering."[8] When the soul has only itself to combat, the wheel comes full circle, the battle begins again, and the prickings of the flesh are felt anew, showing the inevitable continuance of the struggle and the threat of a perpetual recurrence.

Finally, fornication has, as compared with other vices, an ontological particularity that gives it a special ascetic importance. Like greed, it is rooted in the body and impossible to beat without chastisement. While wrath or despondency can be fought only in the mind, fornication cannot be eradicated without "mortifying the flesh, by vigils, fasts and back-breaking labor."[9] This does not exclude—on the contrary—the battle the mind has to wage against itself, since fornication may be born of thoughts, images, and memories. "When the Devil, with subtle cunning, has insinuated into our hearts the memory of a woman, beginning with our mother, our sisters, or certain pious women, we should as quickly as possible expel these memories for fear that, if we linger on them too long, the tempter may seize the opportunity to lead us unwittingly to think about other women."[10] Nevertheless, there is one fundamental difference between fornication and greed. The fight against the latter has to be carried on with a certain restraint, since one cannot give up all food: "The requirements of life have to be provided for...for fear lest the body, deprived through our own error, may lose the strength to carry out the necessary spiritual exercises."[11] This natural propensity for eating has to be kept at arm's length, treated unemotionally, but not abolished. It has its own legitimacy; to repudiate it totally, that is to say, to the point of death, would be to burden one's soul with a crime. On the other hand, there are no holds barred in the fight against the spirit of fornication; everything that can direct our steps to it must be eradicated, and no call of nature can be allowed to justify the satisfaction of a need in this domain. This is an appetite whose suppression does not lead to our bodily death, and it must be totally eradicated. Of the eight sins, fornication is the only one that is at once innate, natural, physical in origin, and needing to be as totally destroyed as the vices of the soul, such as avarice and pride. There must be severe mortification therefore, which lets us live in our bodies while releasing us from the flesh. "Depart from this flesh while living in the body."[12] It is into this region beyond nature, but in our earthly lives, that the fight against fornication leads us. It "drags us from the slough of the earth." It causes us to live in this world a life that is not of this world. Because this mortification is the harshest, it promises the most to us in this world below: "rooted in the flesh," it offers "the citizenship which the saints have the promise of possessing once they are delivered from the corruption of the flesh."[13]

Thus, one sees how fornication, though just one of the elements in the table of vices, has its own special position, heading the causal chain, and is the sin chiefly responsible for backsliding and battles, at one of the most difficult and decisive points in the struggle for an ascetic life.

In his fifth *Conference*, Cassian divides fornication into three varieties. The first consists of the "joining together of the two sexes" (*commixtio sexus utriusque*); the second takes place "without contact with the woman" (*absque femineo tactu*)—the damnable sin of Onan; the third is "conceived in the mind and the thoughts."[14] Almost the same distinction is repeated in the twelfth *Conference*: "carnal conjunction" (*carnalis commixtio*), which Cassian calls *fornicatio* in its restricted sense; next uncleanness, *immunditia*, which takes place without contact with a woman, while one is either sleeping or awake, and which is due to "the negligence of an unwatchful mind"; finally there is *libido*, which develops in "the dark corners of the soul" without "physical passion" (*sine passione corporis*).[15] These distinctions are important, for they alone help one to understand what Cassian meant by the general term *fornicatio*, to which he gives no definition elsewhere; but they are particularly important for the way he uses these three categories—in a way that differs so much from what one finds in earlier texts.

There already existed a traditional trilogy of the sins of the flesh: adultery, fornication (meaning sexual relations outside marriage), and "the corruption of children." At least these are the three categories to be found in the *Didache*: "Thou shalt not commit adultery; thou shalt not commit fornication; thou shalt not seduce young boys."[16] And these are what we find in the "Epistle of Saint Barnabas": "Do not commit fornication or adultery; do not corrupt the young."[17] We often find later that only the first two precepts are imposed, fornication covering all sexual offenses, and adultery covering those which infringe the marriage vows.[18] But, in any case, these were habitually accompanied by precepts about covetousness in thought or sight or anything that might lead one to commit a forbidden sexual act: "Refrain from covetousness, for it leads to fornication; abstain from obscene talk and brazen looks, for all this sort of thing leads to adultery."[19]

Cassian's analysis has two special features: one is that he does not deal separately with adultery, but places it with fornication in its limited sense; and the other is that he devotes attention mostly to the other two categories. Nowhere in the various texts in which he speaks of the battle for chastity does he refer to actual sexual relations. Nowhere are the various sins set out dependent on actual sexual relations—the partner with whom it was committed, his or her age, or possible degree of consanguinity. Not one of the categories that in the Middle Ages were to be built up into a great code of sins is to be found here. Doubtless, Cassian, who was addressing an audience of monks who had taken vows to renounce all sexual relations, felt he could skip these preliminaries. One notices, however, that on one very important aspect of celibacy, where Basil of Caesarea and Chrysostom had given explicit advice,[20] Cassian does make discreet allusion: "Let no one, especially when among young folk, remain alone with another, even for a short time, or withdraw with him or take him by the hand."[21] He carries on his discussion as if he is only interested in his last two categories (about what goes on without sexual relationship or physical passion), as if he was passing over fornication as a physical union of two individuals and only devoting serious attention to behavior which up until then had been severely censured only when leading up to real sexual acts.

Yet even though Cassian's analysis ignores physical sex, and its sphere of action is quite solitary and secluded, his reasoning is not purely negative. The whole essence of the fight for chastity is that it aims at a target which has nothing to do with actions or relationships; it concerns a different reality than that of a sexual connection between two individuals. A passage in the twelfth *Conference* reveals the nature of this reality: in it Cassian describes the six stages that mark the advance toward chastity. The object of the description is not to define chastity itself but to pick out the negative signs by which one can trace progress toward it—the various signs of impurity that disappear one by one—and so to get an idea of what one must contend with in the fight for chastity.

First sign of progress: When the monk awakes he is not "smitten by a carnal impulse" (*impugnatione carnali non eliditur*), that is, the mind [*âme*] is no longer troubled by physical reactions over which the will has no control.

Second stage: If "voluptuous thoughts" (*voluptariae cogitationes*) should arise in the monk's mind, he does not let it dwell on them. He can stop thinking about things that have arisen in his mind involuntarily and in spite of himself.[22]

Third stage: When a glimpse of the world outside can no longer arouse lustful feelings, and one can look upon a woman without any feeling of desire.

Fourth stage: One no longer in one's waking hours feels any, even the most innocent, movement of the flesh. Does Cassian mean that there *is* no movement of the flesh, and that therefore one has total control over one's own body? Probably not, since elsewhere he often insists on the persistence of involuntary bodily movements. The term he uses, *perferre*, signifies no doubt that such movements are not capable of affecting the mind [*âme*], which thus does not suffer from them.

Fifth stage: "If the subject of a discourse or the logical consequence of a reading involves the idea of human procreation, the mind does not allow itself to be touched by the remotest thought of sexual pleasure, but contemplates the act in a mood of calmness and purity, as a simple function, a necessary adjunct to the prolongation of the human race, and departs no more affected by the recollection of it than if it had been thinking about brickmaking or some other trade."

Finally, the last stage is reached when our sleep is not troubled by the vision of a seductive woman. Even though we may not think it a sin to be subject to such illusions, it is however a sign that some lustful feeling still lurks in the depths of our being.[23]

Amid all this description of the different symptoms of fornication, gradually fading out as one approaches the state of chastity, there is no mention of relationships with others, no acts, not even any intention of committing one. In fact, there is no fornication in the strict sense of the word. This microcosm of the solitary life lacks the two major elements on which is centered not only the sexual ethic of the philosophers of the ancient world but also that of a Christian like Clement of Alexandria (at least in Epistle 2 of his *Pedagogus*), namely, the sexual union of two individuals (*sunousia*) and the pleasure of the act (*aphrodisia*). Cassian is interested in the movements of the body and the mind [*âme*], images, feelings, memories, faces in dreams, the spontaneous movements of thoughts, the consenting (or refusing) will, waking and sleeping. And two poles are sketched out which, it must be stressed, do not coincide with the body and soul. They are, first, the involuntary pole, which consists either of physical movements or of feelings evoked by memories and images that survive from the past and ferment in the mind, besieging and enticing the will; and, second, the pole of the will itself, which accepts or repels, averts its eyes or allows itself to be ensnared, holds back or consents. On the one side, then, bodily and mental reflexes that bypass the mind [*âme*] and, becoming infected with impurity, may proceed to corruption [*pollution*], and on the other side, an internal play of thoughts. Here we find the two kinds of "fornication" as broadly defined by Cassian, to which he confines the whole of his analysis, leaving aside the question of physical sex. His theme is *immunditia*, something that catches the mind [*âme*], waking or sleeping, off its guard and can lead to pollution, without any contact with another; and the *libido*, which develops in the dark corners of the mind [*âme*]. In this connection, Cassian reminds us that *libido* has the same origin as *libet* ("it pleases").[24]

The spiritual battle and the advance toward chastity, whose six stages are described by Cassian, can thus be seen as a task of dissociation. We are now far away from the rationing of pleasure and its strict limitation to permissible actions; far away, too, from the idea of a separation as drastic as possible between mind [*âme*] and body. But what does concern us is a never-ending struggle over the movements of our thoughts (whether they extend or reflect those of our body, or whether they motivate them), over its simplest manifestations, over the factors that can activate it. The aim is that the subject should never be affected in his effort by the obscurest or the most seemingly "unwilled" presence of will. The six stages that lead to chastity represent steps toward the disinvolvement of the will. The first step is to exclude its involvement in bodily reactions; then exclude it from the imagination (not to linger on what crops up in one's mind); then exclude it from the action of the senses (cease to be conscious of bodily movements); then exclude it from figurative involvement (cease to think of things as possible objects of desire); and, finally, oneiric involvement (the desires that may be stirred by images that appear, albeit spontaneously, in dreams). This

sort of involvement, of which the willful act or the explicit will to commit an act is the most visible form, Cassian calls *concupiscence*. It is
against this that spiritual combat—and the effort at dissociation, at
disimplication that it pursues—is turned.

Here is the reason why, all through this battle against the spirit of
fornication and for chastity, the sole fundamental problem is that of
pollution—whether as something that is subservient to the will and a
possible form of self-indulgence, or as something happening spontaneously and involuntarily in sleep or dreams. So important is it that
Cassian makes the absence of erotic dreams and nocturnal pollution a
sign that one has reached the pinnacle of chastity. He often returns to
this topic: "The proof that one has achieved this state of purity will be
that no apparition will beguile us when resting or stretched out in
sleep"[25]; or again, "This is the sum of integrity and the final proof:
that we are not visited by voluptuous thoughts during sleep and that
we should be unaware of the pollutions to which we are subjected by
nature."[26] The whole of the twenty-second *Conference* is devoted to the
question of "nocturnal pollutions" and "the necessity of using all our
strength to be delivered from them." And on various occasions, Cassian
calls to mind holy characters like Serenus, who had attained such a
high degree of virtue that they were never troubled by inconveniences
of this kind.[27]

Obviously, in a rule of life where renunciation of all sexual relations was absolutely basic, it was quite logical that this topic should
assume such importance. One is reminded of the importance, in groups
inspired by Pythagorean ideas, accorded the phenomena of sleep and
dreams for what they reveal about the quality of existence, and to the
self-purification that was supposed to guarantee its serenity. Above all,
one must realize that nocturnal pollution raised problems where ritual purity was concerned, and it was precisely these problems which
prompted the twenty-second *Conference*: can one draw near to the
"holy altars" and partake of the bread and wine when one has suffered
nocturnal defilement?[28] But even if all these reasons can explain such
preoccupations among the theoreticians of monastic life, they cannot
account for the absolutely central position occupied by the question of
voluntary/involuntary pollution in the whole discussion of the battle
for chastity. Pollution was not simply the object of a stricter ban than
anything else, or harder to control. It was a yardstick [*analyseur*] of
concupiscence, in that it helped to decide—in the light of what formed

its background, initiated it, and finally unleashed it—the part played by the will in forming these images, feelings, and memories in the mind [*âme*]. The monk concentrates his whole energy on never letting his will be involved in this reaction, which goes from the body to the mind [*âme*] and from the mind [*âme*] to the body, and over which the will may have a hold, either to encourage it or halt it through mental activity. The first five stages of the advance toward chastity constitute increasingly subtle disengagements of the will from the increasingly restricted reactions that may bring on this pollution.

There remains the final stage, attainable by holiness: absence of "absolutely" involuntary pollutions during sleep. Again, Cassian points out that these pollutions are not necessarily all involuntary. Overeating and impure thoughts during the day all show that one is willing, if not intending, to have them. He makes a distinction between the type of dream that accompanies them and the images' degree of impurity. Anyone who is taken by surprise would be wrong to blame his body or sleep: "It is a sign of the corruption that festers within, and not just a product of the night. Buried in the depth of the soul, the corruption has come to the surface during sleep, revealing the hidden fever of passions with which we have become infected by glutting ourselves all day long on unhealthy emotions."[29] Finally, there is the pollution that is totally involuntary, devoid of the pleasure that implies consent, without even the slightest trace of a dream image. Doubtless this is the goal attainable by the ascetic who has practiced with sufficient rigor; the pollution is only a "residue" in which the person concerned plays no part. "We have to repress the reactions of our minds and the emotions of our bodies until the flesh can satisfy the demands of nature without giving rise to any pleasurable feelings, getting rid of the excess of our bodily humors without any unhealthy urges and without having to plunge back into the battle for our chastity."[30] Since this is a supranatural phenomenon, only a supranatural power can give us this freedom, spiritual grace. This is why nonpollution is the sign of holiness, the stamp of the highest chastity possible, a blessing one may hope for but not attain.

For his part, man must do nothing less than remain in relation to himself in a state of perpetual vigilance even as far as the least impulses that might be produced in his body or his soul are concerned. To stay awake night and day—at night for the day and in the day thinking of the night to come. "As purity and vigilance during the day dispose one to be chaste during the night, so too nocturnal vigilance replenishes the strength of the heart to observe chastity during the day."[31] This vigilance means exerting the sort of "discrimination" that lies at the heart of the self-analysis [*techniques de soi-même*] developed in active spirituality. The work of the miller sorting out his grain, the centurion picking his troops, the moneychanger who weighs coins before accepting or refusing them—this is how the monk must unceasingly treat his own thoughts, so as to identify those which may bring temptation. Such an effort will allow him to sort out his thoughts according to their origin, to distinguish them by their quality, and to separate the objects they represent from the pleasure they can evoke. This is an endless task of analysis that one must apply to oneself and, by the duty of confession, to our relations with others.[32] Neither the idea of the inseparability of chastity and "fornication" affirmed by Cassian, nor the way in which he analyzes them, nor the different elements that, according to him, inhere in them, nor the connections he establishes between them—pollution, libido, concupiscence—can be understood without reference to the techniques of self-analysis [*technologies de soi*] that characterize monastic life and the spiritual battle it traverses.

Do we find that, between Tertullian and Cassian, prohibitions have been intensified, an even greater importance attached to absolute continence, and the sexual act increasingly stigmatized? This is not the way the question should be framed.

The organization of monasticism and the dimorphism that developed between monastic and secular life brought about important changes in the problem of sexual renunciation. They brought with them the development of very complex techniques of self-analysis [*techniques de soi*]. So, in the very manner in which sex was renounced there appeared a rule of life and a mode of analysis which, in spite of obvious continuities, showed important differences with the past. With Tertullian, the state of virginity implied the external and internal posture of one who has renounced the world and has adopted the rules governing appearance, behavior, and general conduct this renunciation involves. In the mystique of virginity which developed after the thirteenth century, the rigor of this renunciation (in line with the theme, already found in Tertullian, of union with Christ) transforms the negative aspect of continence into the promise of spiritual marriage. With Cassian, who describes rather than innovates, there occurs a sort of double action, a withdrawal that also reveals hidden depths within.

This has nothing to do with the internalization of a whole list of for-hidden things, merely substituting the prohibition of the intention for that of the act itself. It is, rather, the opening up of an area (whose importance has already been stressed by the writings of Gregory of Nyssa and, especially, of Basil of Ancyra) which is that of thought, operating erratically and spontaneously, with its images, memories, and perceptions, with movements [*mouvements*] and impressions transmitted from the body to the mind [*âme*] and the mind [*âme*] to the body. This has nothing to do with a code of permitted or forbidden actions but is a whole technique for analyzing and diagnosing thought, its origins, its qualities, its dangers, its potential for temptation, and all the dark forces that can lurk behind the mask it may assume. Given the objective of expelling for good everything impure or conducive to impurity, this can only be achieved by eternal vigilance, a suspiciousness directed every moment against one's thought, an endless self-questioning to flush out any secret fornication lurking in the inmost recesses of the mind [*âme*].

In this chastity-oriented asceticism [*ascèse*] one can see a process of "subjectivation" which has nothing to do with a sexual ethic based on physical self-control. But two things stand out. This subjectivation is linked with a process of familiarization which makes the obligation to seek and state the truth about oneself an indispensable and permanent condition of this asceticism; and if there is subjectivation, it also involves an indeterminate objectivization of the self by the self—indeterminate in the sense that one must be forever extending as far as possible the range of one's thoughts, however insignificant and innocent they may appear to be. Moreover, this subjectivation, in its quest for the truth about oneself, functions through complex relations with others, and in many ways. One must rid oneself of the power of the Other, the Enemy, who hides behind seeming likenesses of oneself, and eternal warfare must be waged against this Other, which one cannot win without the help of the Almighty, who is mightier than he. Finally, confession to others, submission to their advice, and permanent obedience to one's superiors are essential in this battle.

These new modalities taken up regarding sexual ethics in monastic life, the buildup of a new relationship between the subject and the truth, and the establishment of complex relations of obedience to the other all form part of a whole whose coherence is well illustrated in Cassian's text. No new point of departure is involved. Going back in time before Christianity, one may find many of these elements in embryonic form

and sometimes fully shaped in ancient philosophy—Stoic or Neoplatonic, for instance. Moreover, Cassian himself presents in a systematic
way (how far he makes his own contribution is another question which
need not concern us here) a sum of experience which he asserts to be
that of Eastern monasticism. In any case, study of a text of this kind
shows that it hardly makes sense to talk about a "Christian sexual
ethic," still less about a "Judeo-Christian" one. So far as consideration of sexual behavior was concerned, some fairly involved thinking
went on between the Hellenistic period and Saint Augustine. Certain
important events stand out, such as the guidelines for conscience laid
down by the Stoics and the Cynics, the organization of monasticism,
and many others. On the other hand, the coming of Christianity, considered as a massive rupture with earlier moralities and the dominant
introduction of a quite different one, is barely noticeable. As Peter
Brown says, in speaking of Christianity as part of our reading of the
giant mass of antiquity, the topography of the parting of the waters is
hard to pin down.

NOTES

1   The seven others are greed, avarice, wrath, sloth, accidie, vainglory, and pride.

2   *Conferences* 5.11 and 12.2.

3   *Conferences* 5.10.

4   *Institutions* 5, and *Conferences* 5.

5   *Conferences* 5.13–14.

6   *Conferences* 5.10.

7   *Institutions* 12.2.

8   *Conferences* 12.6. For examples of lapses into pride and presumptuousness, see *Conferences* 2.13
    and especially *Institutions* 12.20–21, where offenses against humility are punished by the most
    humiliating temptation, that of a desire *contra usum naturae.*

9   *Conferences* 5.4.

10 *Institutions* 6.13.

11 Ibid., 5.8.

12 Ibid., 6.6.

13 Ibid., 6.6.

14 *Conferences* 5.11.

15 Ibid., 12.2.

16 *Didache* 2.2.

17 *Epistle of Saint Barnabas* 19.4. Earlier on, dealing with forbidden foods, the same text interprets the ban on eating hyena flesh as forbidding adultery, of hare as forbidding the seduction of children, of weasel as forbidding oral sex.

18 For instance Saint Augustine, *Sermon* 56.

19 *Didache* 3.3.

20 Basil of Caesarea, *Exhortation to Renounce the World* 5: "Eschew all dealing, all relations with young men of your own age. Avoid them as you would fire. Many, alas, are those who through mixing with them, have been consigned by the Enemy to burn eternally in hell-fire." See the precautions laid down in *The Great Precepts* (34) and *The Short Precepts* (220); see also John Chrysostom, *Adversus oppugnatores vitae monasticae*.

21 *Institutions* 2.15. Those who infringe this rule commit a grave offense and are under suspicion (*conjurationis pravique consilii*). Are these words hinting at amorous behavior or are they simply aimed at the danger of members of the same community showing particular favor to one another? Similar recommendations are to be found in *Institutions* 4.16.

22 The word used by Cassian for dwelling on such thoughts is *immorari*. Later, *delectatio morosa* has an important place in the medieval sexual ethic.

23 *Conferences* 12.7.

24 *Conferences* 5.11 and 12.2.

25 *Institutions* 6.10.

26 Ibid., 6.20.

27 *Conferences* 7.1, 12.7. Other allusions to this theme in *Institutions* 2.13.

28 *Conferences* 22.5.

29 *Institutions* 6.11.

30 Ibid., 6.22.

31 Ibid., 6.23.

32 See, in the twenty-second *Conferences* (6), the case of a consultation over a monk, who each time he was going to communion suffered a nocturnal visitation and dared not participate in the holy mysteries. The "spiritual physicians" after an interrogation and discussions diagnosed that it was the Devil who sent these visitations so as to prevent the monk from attending the desired communion. To abstain was to fall into the Devil's trap; to communicate in spite of everything was to defeat him. Once this decision had been taken, the Devil appeared no more.

PREFACE TO *THE*
HISTORY OF SEXUALITY, VOLUME TWO*

In this series of researches on sexuality, it was not my aim to reconstitute the history of sexual behavior—by studying its successive forms,
their respective models, how they spread, how they conflicted or agreed
with laws, rules, customs, or conventions. Nor did I intend to analyze
religious, moral, medical, or biological ideas about sexuality. Not that
such inquiries should be considered illegitimate, impossible, or ster-
ile; plenty of work has proved otherwise. But I wanted to confront this
very everyday notion of sexuality, step away from it, monitor [*éprouver*]
its familiar evidence, and analyze the theoretical and practical content
in which it made its appearance and with which it is still associated.

I wanted to undertake a history in which sexuality would not be conceived as a general type of behavior whose particular elements might
vary according to demographic, economic, social, or ideological conditions, any more than it would be seen as a collection of representations
(scientific, religious, moral) which, though diverse and changeable, are
joined to an invariant reality. My object was to analyze sexuality as a
historically singular form of experience. Taking this historical singularity into account does not mean overinterpreting the recent emergence
of the term *sexuality*, or taking it for granted that the word has brought
in its trail the reality to which it refers. Rather, it means an effort to

----

*The first paragraph of the French text, omitted here, reads: "This volume appears later
than I had foreseen and in a quite different form." In fact, the text does not serve as
the preface to the second volume of *The History of Sexuality*. Foucault replaced it with a
much longer version, and chose to publish it separately. It initially appeared in English
translation in *The Foucault Reader*, ed. P. Rabinow (New York: Pantheon Books, 1984),
pp. 333-39. The translation, by William Smock, is reproduced here slightly amended.

treat sexuality as the correlation of a domain of knowledge [*savoir*], a type of normativity, and a mode of relation to the self; it means trying to decipher how, in Western societies, a complex experience is constituted from and around certain forms of behavior: an experience that conjoins a field of knowledge [*connaissance*] (with its own concepts, theories, diverse disciplines), a collection of rules (which differentiate the permissible from the forbidden, natural from monstrous, normal from pathological, what is decent from what is not, and so on), and a mode of relation between the individual and himself (which enables him to recognize himself as a sexual subject amid others).

To study forms of experience in this way—in their history—is an idea that originated with an earlier project, in which I made use of the methods of existential analysis in the field of psychiatry and in the domain of "mental illness." For two reasons, not unrelated to each other, this project left me unsatisfied: its theoretical weakness in elaborating the notion of experience, and its ambiguous link with a psychiatric practice, which it simultaneously ignored and took for granted. One could deal with the first problem by referring to a general theory of the human being, and treat the second altogether differently by turning, as is so often done, to the "economic and social context"; one could choose, by doing so, to accept the resulting dilemma of a philosophical anthropology and a social history. But I wondered whether, rather than playing on this alternative, it would not be possible to consider the very historicity of forms of experience. This entailed two negative tasks: first, a "nominalist" reduction of philosophical anthropology and the notions that could rest upon it, and second, a shift of domain to the concepts and methods of the history of societies. On the positive side, the task was to bring to light the domain where the formation, development, and transformation of forms of experience can situate themselves—that is, a history of thought. By "thought," I mean what establishes, in a variety of possible forms, the play of true and false, and consequently constitutes the human being as a knowing subject [*sujet de connaissance*]; in other words, it is the basis for accepting or refusing rules, and constitutes human beings as social and juridical subjects; it is what establishes the relation with oneself and with others, and constitutes the human being as ethical subject.

"Thought," understood in this way, then, is not to be sought only in theoretical formulations such as those of philosophy or science; it can and must be analyzed in every manner of speaking, doing, or behaving in which the individual appears and acts as knowing subject [*sujet de connaissance*], as ethical or juridical subject, as subject conscious of himself and others. In this sense, thought is understood as the very form of action—as action insofar as it implies the play of true and false, the acceptance or refusal of rules, the relation to oneself and others. The study of forms of experience can thus proceed from an analysis of "practices"—discursive or not—as long as one qualifies that word to mean the different systems of action *insofar as* they are inhabited by thought as I have characterized it here.

Posing the question in this way brings into play certain altogether general principles. Singular forms of experience may perfectly well harbor universal structures; they may well not be independent of the concrete determinations of social existence. However, neither those determinations nor those structures can allow for experiences (that is, for understandings of a certain type, for rules of a certain form, for certain modes of consciousness of oneself and of others) except through thought. There is no experience that is not a way of thinking and cannot be analyzed from the viewpoint of the history of thought; this is what might be called the principle of irreducibility of thought. According to a second principle, this thought has a historicity which is proper to it. That it should have this historicity does not mean it is deprived of all universal form but, rather, that the putting into play of these universal forms is itself historical. And that this historicity should be proper to it means not that it is independent of all the other historical determinations (of an economic, social, or political order) but that it has complex relations with them, which always leave their specificity to the forms, transformations, and events of thought. This is what could be called the principle of singularity of the history of thought: there are events of thought. There is a third and final principle implied by this enterprise: an awareness that criticism—understood as analysis of the historical conditions that bear on the creation of links to truth, to rules, and to the self—does not mark out impassable boundaries or describe closed systems; it brings to light transformable singularities. These transformations could not take place except by means of a working of thought upon itself; that is the principle of the history of thought as critical activity. All of this bears upon the work and teaching I have labeled "the history of systems of thought"; it infers a double reference—to philosophy, which must be asked to explain how thought could have a history, and to history, which must be asked to produce the various forms of thought in whatever concrete forms they may assume (system of representations, institutions, practices). What is the price to philosophy of a history of thought? What is the effect, within history, of thought and the events that are proper to it? In what way do individual or collective experiences arise from singular forms of thought—that is, from what constitutes the subject in its relations to the true, to rules, to itself? It is easy to see how the reading of Nietzsche in the early fifties has given access to these kinds of questions, by breaking with the double tradition of phenomenology and Marxism.

I know this rereading is schematic: things did not really unfold so neatly, and there were many obscurities and hesitations along the way. But in *Madness and Civilization* I was trying, after all, to describe a locus of experience from the viewpoint of the history of thought, even if my usage of the word "experience" was very floating. Looking at practices of internment, on the one hand, and medical procedures, on the other, I tried to analyze the genesis, during the seventeenth and eighteenth centuries, of a system of thought as the matter of possible experiences: first, the formation of a domain of recognitions [*connaissances*] that constitute themselves as specific knowledge [*savoir*] of "mental illness"; second, the organization of a normative system built on a whole technical, administrative, juridical, and medical apparatus whose purpose was to isolate and take custody of the insane; and finally, the definition of a relation to oneself and to others as possible subjects of madness. It is also these three axes and the play between types of understanding [*savoir*], forms of normality, and modes of relation to oneself and others which seemed to me to give individual cases the status of significant experiences—cases such as those of Pierre Rivière or Alexina B.—and to assign a like importance to that permanent dramatization of family affairs which one finds in the *lettres de cachet* (whereby people committed their relatives to asylums) in the eighteenth century.

Yet the relative importance of these three axes is not always the same for all forms of experience. And, moreover, it was necessary to elaborate the analysis of each a little more precisely, starting with the problem of the formation of domains of knowledge [*savoir*]. The work was directed along two lines: first, in the "vertical" dimension, taking the example of sickness, and studying how an institutional organization for therapy, instruction, and research is related to the constitution of a

clinical medicine articulated on the development of pathological anatomy. The object was to bring out the complex causalities and reciprocal determinations affecting, on the one hand, the development of a
certain kind of medical knowledge [*savoir*] and, on the other, the transformations of an institutional field linked directly to social and political
changes. Then, once scientific knowledge [*savoir*] was endowed with
its own rules for which external determinations could not account—its
own structure as discursive practice—I tried to show what common,
but transformable, criteria—what epistemes [*épistémès*]—governed
those bodies of knowledge which, from the seventeenth to the early
nineteenth centuries, had been charged with explaining certain aspects
of human activity or existence: the wealth men produce, exchange, and
circulate; the linguistic signs they use to communicate; and the collec-
tivity of living things to which they belong.

It is the second axis—the relation to rules—that I wanted to explore
using the example of punitive practices. It was a matter not of studying the theory of penal law itself, or the evolution of such and such
penal institution, but of analyzing the formation of a certain "punitive
rationality" whose appearance might seem that much more surprising
in that it offered, as its principal means of action, a practice of imprisonment which had long been and still was criticized at the time. Instead
of seeking the explanation in a general conception of the law, or in the
evolving modes of industrial production (as Rusche and Kirchheimer
did), it seemed to me far wiser to look at the workings of power. I was
concerned not with some omnipresent power, almighty and above all
clairvoyant, diffusing itself throughout the social body in order to control it down to the tiniest detail, but with the refinement, the elaboration, and the installation since the seventeenth century of techniques
for "governing" individuals—that is, for "guiding their conduct"—in
domains as different as the school, the army, and the workshop. The
new punitive rationality must be relocated in the context of this technology, itself linked to the demographic, economic, and political changes
that accompany the development of industrial states. Accordingly, the
analysis does not revolve around the general principle of the law or the
myth of power, but concerns itself with the complex and multiple practices of a "governmentality" that presupposes, on the one hand, rational
forms, technical procedures, instrumentations through which to operate, and, on the other, strategic games that subject the power relations
they are supposed to guarantee to instability and reversal. Starting from

an analysis of these forms of "government," one can see how criminality was constituted as an object of knowledge [*savoir*], and how a certain "consciousness" of criminality could be formed (including the image that criminals might have of themselves, and the representation of criminals which the rest of us might entertain).

The project of a history of sexuality was linked to a desire on my part to analyze more closely the third of the axes that constitute any matrix of experience: the modality of relation to the self. Not that sexuality cannot and should not—like madness, sickness, or criminality—be envisaged as a locus of experience, one that includes a domain of knowledge [*savoir*], a system of rules, and a model for relations to the self. However, the relative importance of the last element recommends it as a guiding thread for the very history of this experience and its formation; my planned study of children, women, and "perverts" as sexual subjects was to have followed those lines.

I found myself confronted with a choice that was a long time in unraveling: a choice between fidelity to the chronological outline I had originally imagined, and a different line of inquiry in which the modes of relation to the self took precedence. The period when this singular form of experience, sexuality, took shape is particularly complex: the very important role played at the end of the eighteenth and in the nineteenth centuries by the formation of domains of knowledge [*savoir*] about sexuality from the points of view of biology, medicine, psychopathology, sociology, and ethnology; the determining role also played by the normative systems imposed on sexual behavior through the intermediary of education, medicine, and justice made it hard to distinguish the form and effects of the relation to the self as particular elements in the constitution of this experience. There was always the risk of reproducing, with regard to sexuality, forms of analysis focused on the organization of a domain of learning [*connaissance*], or on the techniques of control and coercion, as in my previous work on sickness or criminality. In order better to analyze the forms of relation to the self, in and of themselves, I found myself spanning eras in a way that took me farther and farther from the chronological outline I had first decided on, both in order to address myself to periods when the effect of scientific knowledges and the complexity of normative systems were less, and in order eventually to make out forms of relation to the self different from those characterizing the experience of sexuality. And that is how, little by little, I ended up placing the work's emphasis on what was to have been simply the point of departure or historical background; rather than placing myself at the threshold of the formation of the experience of sexuality, I tried to analyze the formation of a certain mode of relation to the self in the experience of the flesh. This called for a marked chronological displacement because it became obvious that I should study the period in late antiquity when the principal elements of the Christian ethic of the flesh were being formulated. And it led in turn to a rearrangement of my original plan, a considerable delay in publication, and the hazards of studying material I had barely heard of six or seven years ago. But I reflected that, after all, it was best to sacrifice a definite program to a promising line of approach. I also reminded myself that it would probably not be worth the trouble of making books if they failed to teach the author something he had not known before, if they did not lead to unforeseen places, and if they did not disperse one toward a strange and new relation with himself. The pain and pleasure of the book is to be an experience.

SELF WRITING

These pages are part of a series of studies on "the arts of oneself," that is, on the aesthetics of existence and the government of oneself and of others in Greco-Roman culture during the first two centuries of the empire.

The *Vita Antonii* of Athanasius presents the written notation of actions and thoughts as an indispensable element of the ascetic life. "Let this observation be a safeguard against sinning: let us each note and write down our actions and impulses of the soul as though we were to report them to each other; and you may rest assured that from utter shame of becoming known we shall stop sinning and entertaining sinful thoughts altogether. Who, having sinned, would not choose to lie, hoping to escape detection? Just as we would not give ourselves to lust within sight of each other, so if we were to write down our thoughts as if telling them to each other, we shall so much the more guard ourselves against foul thoughts for shame of being known. Now, then, let the written account stand for the eyes of our fellow ascetics, so that blushing at writing the same as if we were actually seen, we may never ponder evil. Molding ourselves in this way, we shall be able to bring our body into subjection, to please the Lord and to trample under foot the machinations of the Enemy."[1] Here, writing about oneself appears clearly in its relationship of complementarity with reclusion: it palliates the dangers of solitude; it offers what one has done or thought to a possible gaze; the fact of obliging oneself to write plays the role of a companion by giving rise to the fear of disapproval and to shame.

Hence, a first analogy can be put forward: what others are to the ascetic in a community, the notebook is to the recluse. But, at the same time, a second analogy is posed, one that refers to the practice of ascesis as work not just on actions but, more precisely, on thought: the constraint that the presence of others exerts in the domain of conduct, writing will exert in the domain of the inner impulses of the soul. In this sense, it has a role very close to that of confession to the director, about which John Cassian will say, in keeping with Evagrian spirituality, that it must reveal, without exception, all the impulses of the soul (*omnes cogitationes*). Finally, writing about inner impulses appears, also according to Athanasius's text, as a weapon in spiritual combat. While the Devil is a power who deceives and causes one to be deluded about oneself (fully half of the *Vita Antonii* is devoted to these ruses), writing constitutes a test and a kind of touchstone: by bringing to light the impulses of thought, it dispels the darkness where the enemy's plots are hatched. This text—one of the oldest that Christian literature has left us on the subject of spiritual writing—is far from exhausting all the meanings and forms the latter will take on later. But one can focus on several of its features that enable one to analyze retrospectively the role of writing in the philosophical cultivation of the self just before Christianity: its close link with companionship, its application to the impulses of thought, its role as a truth test. These diverse elements are found already in Seneca, Plutarch, Marcus Aurelius, but with very different values and following altogether different procedures.

No technique, no professional skill can be acquired without exercise; nor can the art of living, the *tekhnē tou biou*, be learned without an *askēsis* that should be understood as a training of the self by oneself. This was one of the traditional principles to which the Pythagoreans, the Socratics, the Cynics had long attached a great importance. It seems that, among all the forms taken by this training (which included abstinences, memorizations, self-examinations, meditations, silence, and listening to others), writing—the act of writing for oneself and for others—came, rather late, to play a considerable role. In any case, the texts from the imperial epoch relating to practices of the self placed a good deal of stress on writing. It is necessary to read, Seneca said, but also to write.[2] And Epictetus, who offered an exclusively oral teaching, nonetheless emphasizes several times the role of writing as a personal exercise: one should "meditate" (*meletan*), write (*graphein*), train oneself (*gumnazein*): "May these be my thoughts, these my studies, writing or reading, when death comes upon me."[3] Or further: "Let these thoughts be at your command [*prokheiron*] by night and day: write them, read them, talk of them, to yourself and to your neighbor... if some so-called undesirable event should befall you, the first immediate relief to you will be that it was not unexpected."[4] In these texts by Epictetus, writing appears regularly associated with "meditation," with that exercise of thought on itself that reactivates what it knows, calls to mind a principle, a rule, or an example, reflects on them, assimilates them, and in this manner prepares itself to face reality. Yet one also sees that writing is associated with the exercise of thought in two different ways. One takes the form of a linear "series": it goes from meditation to the activity of writing and from there to *gumnazein*, that is, to training and trial in a real situation—a labor of thought, a labor through writing, a labor in reality. The other is circular: the meditation precedes the notes which enable the rereading which in turn re-initiates the meditation. In any case, whatever the cycle of exercise in which it takes place, writing constitutes an essential stage in the process to which the whole *askēsis* leads: namely, the fashioning of accepted discourses, recognized as true, into rational principles of action. As an element of self-training, writing has, to use an expression that one finds in Plutarch, an *ethopoietic* function: it is an agent of the transformation of truth into *ēthos*.

This ethopoietic writing, such as it appears through the documents of the first and the second centuries, seems to have lodged itself outside of two forms that were already well known and used for other purposes: the *hupomnēmata* and the *correspondence*.

THE *HUPOMNĒMATA*

Hupomnēmata, in the technical sense, could be account books, public registers, or individual notebooks serving as memory aids. Their use as books of life, as guides for conduct, seems to have become a common thing for a whole cultivated public. One wrote down quotes in them, extracts from books, examples, and actions that one had witnessed or read about, reflections or reasonings that one had heard or that had come to mind. They constituted a material record of things read, heard, or thought, thus offering them up as a kind of accumulated treasure for subsequent rereading and meditation. They also formed a raw material for the drafting of more systematic treatises, in which one presented arguments and means for struggling against some weakness (such as anger, envy, gossip, flattery) or for overcoming some difficult circumstance (a grief, an exile, ruin, disgrace). Thus, when Fundamus requests advice for struggling against the agitations of the soul, Plutarch at that moment does not really have the time to compose a treatise in the proper form, so he will send him, in their present state, the *hupomnēmata* he had written himself on the theme of the tranquility of the soul; at least this is how he introduces the text of the *Peri euthumias*.[5] Feigned modesty? Doubtless this was a way of excusing the somewhat disjointed character of the text, but the gesture must also be seen as an indication of what these notebooks were—and of the use to make of the treatise itself, which kept a little of its original form.

These *hupomnēmata* should not be thought of simply as a memory support, which might be consulted from time to time, as occasion arose; they are not meant to be substituted for a recollection that may fail. They constitute, rather, a material and a framework for exercises to be carried out frequently: reading, rereading, meditating, conversing with oneself and with others. And this was in order to have them, according to the expression that recurs often, *prokheiron, ad manum, in promptu.* "Near at hand," then, not just in the sense that one would be able to recall them to consciousness, but that one should be able to use them, whenever the need was felt, in action. It is a matter of constituting a *logos bioēthikos* for oneself, an equipment of helpful discourses, capable—as Plutarch says—of elevating the voice and silencing the passions like a master who with one word hushes the growling of dogs.[6] And for that they must not simply be placed in a sort of memory cabinet but deeply lodged in the soul, "planted in it," says Seneca, and they must form part of ourselves: in short, the soul must make them not merely its own but itself. The writing of the *hupomnēmata* is an important relay in this subjectivation of discourse.

However personal they may be, these *hupomnēmata* ought not to be understood as intimate journals or as those accounts of spiritual experience (temptations, struggles, downfalls, and victories) that will be found in later Christian literature. They do not constitute a "narrative of oneself"; they do not have the aim of bringing to the light of day the *arcana conscientiae*, the oral or written confession of which has a purificatory value. The movement they seek to bring about is the reverse of that: the intent is not to pursue the unspeakable, nor to reveal the hidden, nor to say the unsaid, but on the contrary to capture the already-said, to collect what one has managed to hear or read, and for a purpose that is nothing less than the shaping of the self.

The *hupomnēmata* need to be resituated in the context of a tension that was very pronounced at the time. Inside a culture strongly stamped by traditionality, by the recognized value of the already-said, by the recurrence of discourse, by "citational" practice under the seal of antiquity and authority, there developed an ethic quite explicitly oriented by concern for the self toward objectives defined as: withdrawing into oneself, getting in touch with oneself, living with oneself, relying on oneself, benefiting from and enjoying oneself. Such is the aim of the *hupomnēmata*: to make one's recollection of the fragmentary *logos*, transmitted through teaching, listening, or reading, a means of establishing a relationship of oneself with oneself, a relationship as adequate and accomplished as possible. For us, there is something paradoxical in all this: how could one be brought together with oneself with the help of a timeless discourse accepted almost everywhere? In actual fact, if the writing of *hupomnēmata* can contribute to the formation of the self through these scattered *logoi*, this is for three main reasons: the limiting effects of the coupling of writing with reading, the regular practice of the disparate that determines choices, and the appropriation which that practice brings about.

1. Seneca stresses the point: the practice of the self involves reading, for one could not draw everything from one's own stock or arm oneself by oneself with the principles of reason that are indispensable for self-conduct: guide or example, the help of others is necessary. But reading and writing must not be dissociated; one ought to "have alternate recourse" to these two pursuits and "blend one with the other." If too much writing is exhausting (Seneca is thinking of the demands of style), excessive reading has a scattering effect: "In reading of many books is distraction."[7] By going constantly from book to book, without ever stopping, without returning to the hive now and then with one's supply of nectar—hence without taking notes or constituting a treasure store of reading—one is liable to retain nothing, to spread oneself across different thoughts, and to forget oneself. Writing, as a way of gathering in the reading that was done and of collecting one's thoughts about it, is an exercise of reason that counters the great deficiency of *stultitia*, which endless reading may favor. *Stultitia* is defined by mental agitation, distraction, change of opinions and wishes, and con-

sequently weakness in the face of all the events that may occur; it is also characterized by the fact that it turns the mind toward the future, makes it interested in novel ideas, and prevents it from providing a fixed point for itself in the possession of an acquired truth.[8] The writing of *hupomnēmata* resists this scattering by fixing acquired elements, and by constituting a share of the past, as it were, toward which it is always possible to turn back, to withdraw. This practice can be connected to a very general theme of the period; in any case, it is common to the moral philosophy of the Stoics and that of the Epicureans—the refusal of a mental attitude turned toward the future (which, due to its uncertainty, causes anxiety and agitation of the soul) and the positive value given to the possession of a past that one can enjoy to the full and without disturbance. The *hupomnēmata* contribute one of the means by which one detaches the soul from concern for the future and redirects it toward contemplation of the past.

2. Yet while it enables one to counteract dispersal, the writing of the *hupomnēmata* is also (and must remain) a regular and deliberate practice of the disparate. It is a selecting of heterogeneous elements. In this, it contrasts with the work of the grammarian, who tries to get to know an entire work or all the works of an author; it also conflicts with the teaching of professional philosophers who subscribe to the doctrinal unity of a school. It does not matter, says Epictetus, whether one has read all of Zeno or Chrysippus; it makes little difference whether one has grasped exactly what they meant to say, or whether one is able to reconstruct their whole argument.[9] The notebook is governed by two principles, which one might call "the local truth of the precept" and "its circumstantial use value." Seneca selects what he will note down for himself and his correspondents from one of the philosophers of his own sect, but also from Democritus and Epicurus.[10] The essential requirement is that he be able to consider the selected sentence as a maxim that is true in what it asserts, suitable in what it prescribes, and useful in terms of one's circumstances. Writing as a personal exercise done by and for oneself is an art of disparate truth—or, more exactly, a purposeful way of combining the traditional authority of the already-said with the singularity of the truth that is affirmed therein and the particularity of the circumstances that determine its use. "So you should always read standard authors; and when you crave a change, fall back upon those whom you read before. Each day acquire something that will fortify you against poverty, against death, indeed against other

misfortunes as well; and after you have run over many thoughts, select
one to be thoroughly digested that day. This is my own custom; from
the many things which I have read, I claim some part for myself. The
thought for today is one which I discovered in Epicurus; for I am wont
to cross over even to the enemy's camp,—not as a deserter, but as a
scout [*tanquam explorator*]."[11]

3. This deliberate heterogeneity does not rule out unification. But the
latter is not implemented in the art of composing an ensemble; it must
be established in the writer himself, as a result of the *hupomnēmata*,
of their construction (and hence in the very act of writing) and of their
consultation (and hence in their reading and their rereading). Two
processes can be distinguished. On the one hand, it is a matter of uni-
fying these heterogeneous fragments through their subjectivation in the
exercise of personal writing. Seneca compares this unification, according to quite traditional metaphors, with the bee's honey gathering, or
the digestion of food, or the adding of numbers forming a sum: "We
should see to it that whatever we have absorbed should not be allowed
to remain unchanged, or it will be no part of us. We must digest it;
otherwise it will merely enter the memory and not the reasoning power
[*in memoriam non in ingenium*]. Let us loyally welcome such foods and
make them our own, so that something that is one may be formed out
of many elements, just as one number is formed of several elements."[12]
The role of writing is to constitute, along with all that reading has constituted, a "body" (*quicquid lectione collectum est, stilus redigat in corpus*). And this body should be understood not as a body of doctrine but,
rather—following an often-evoked metaphor of digestion—as the very
body of the one who, by transcribing his readings, has appropriated
them and made their truth his own: writing transforms the thing seen
or heard "into tissue and blood" (*in vires et in sanguinem*). It becomes
a principle of rational action in the writer himself.

Yet, conversely, the writer constitutes his own identity through this
recollection of things said. In this same Letter 84—which constitutes
a kind of short treatise on the relations between reading and writing—
Seneca dwells for a moment on the ethical problem of resemblance,
of faithfulness and originality. One should not, he explains, reshape
what one retains from an author in such a way that the latter might be
recognized; the idea is not to constitute, in the notes that one takes and
in the way one restores what one has read through writing, a series of
"portraits," recognizable but "lifeless" (Seneca is thinking here of those

portrait galleries by which one certified his birth, asserted his status, and showed his identity through reference to others). It is one's own soul that must be constituted in what one writes; but, just as a man bears his natural resemblance to his ancestors on his face, so it is good that one can perceive the filiation of thoughts that are engraved in his soul. Through the interplay of selected readings and assimilative writing, one should be able to form an identity through which a whole spiritual genealogy can be read. In a chorus there are tenor, bass, and baritone voices, men's and women's tones: "The voices of the individual singers are hidden; what we hear is the voices of all together...I would have my mind of such a quality as this; it should be equipped with many arts, many precepts, and patterns of conduct taken from many epochs of history; but all should blend harmoniously into one."[13]

CORRESPONDENCE

Notebooks, which in themselves constitute personal writing exercises, can serve as raw material for texts that one sends to others. In return, the missive, by definition a text meant for others, also provides occasion for a personal exercise. For, as Seneca points out, when one writes one reads what one writes, just as in saying something one hears oneself saying it. The letter one writes acts, through the very action of writing, upon the one who addresses it, just as it acts through reading and rereading on the one who receives it. In this dual function, correspondence is very close to the *hupomnēmata*, and its form is often very similar. Epicurean literature furnishes examples of this. The text known as the "Letter to Pythocles" begins by acknowledging receipt of a letter in which the student has expressed his affection for the teacher and has made an effort to "recall the [Epicurean] arguments" enabling one to attain happiness; the author of the reply gives his endorsement: the attempt was not bad; and he sends in return a text—a summary of Epicurus's *Peri phuseōs*—that should serve Pythocles as material for memorization and as a support for his meditation.[14]

Seneca's letters show an activity of direction brought to bear, by a man who is aged and already retired, on another who still occupies important public offices. But in these letters, Seneca does not just give him advice and comment on a few great principles of conduct for his benefit. Through these written lessons, Seneca continues to exercise himself, according to two principles that he often invokes: it is necessary to train oneself all one's life, and one always needs the help of others in the soul's labor upon itself. The advice he gives in Letter 7 constitutes a description of his own relations with Lucilius. There he characterizes the way in which he occupies his retirement with the two-fold work he carries out at the same time on his correspondent and on himself: withdrawing into oneself as much as possible; attaching one-self to those capable of having a beneficial effect on oneself; opening one's door to those whom one hopes to make better—"The process is mutual; for men learn while they teach."[15]

The letter one sends in order to help one's correspondent—advise him, exhort him, admonish him, console him—constitutes for the writer a kind of training: something like soldiers in peacetime practicing the manual of arms, the opinions that one gives to others in a pressing sit-uation are a way of preparing oneself for a similar eventuality. For example, Letter 99 to Lucilius: it is in itself the copy of another mis-sive that Seneca had sent to Marullus, whose son had died some time before.[16] The text belongs to the "consolation" genre: it offers the cor-respondent the "logical" arms with which to fight sorrow. The inter-vention is belated, since Marullus, "shaken by the blow," had a moment of weakness and "lapsed from his true self"; so, in that regard, the let-ter has an admonishing role. Yet for Lucilius, to whom it is also sent, and for Seneca who writes it, it functions as a principle of reactiva-tion—a reactivation of all the reasons that make it possible to overcome grief, to persuade oneself that death is not a misfortune (neither that of others nor one's own). And, with the help of what is reading for the one, writing for the other, Lucilius and Seneca will have increased their readiness for the case in which this type of event befalls them. The *consolatio* that should assist and correct Marullus is at the same time a useful *praemeditatio* for Lucilius and Seneca. The writing that aids the addressee arms the writer—and possibly the third parties who read it.

Yet it also happens that the soul service rendered by the writer to his correspondent is handed back to him in the form of "return advice"; as the person being directed progresses, he becomes more capable, in his turn, of giving opinions, exhortations, words of comfort to the one who has undertaken to help him. The direction does not remain one-way for long; it serves as a context for exchanges that help it become more egalitarian. Letter 34 already signals this movement, starting from a situation in which Seneca could nonetheless tell his correspondent: "I claim you for myself...I exhorted you, I applied the goad and did not permit you to march lazily, but roused you continually. And now I do the same; but by this time I am now cheering on one who is in the race and so in turn cheers me on."[17] And in the following letter, he evokes the reward for perfect friendship, in which each of the two will be for the other the continuous support, the inexhaustible help, that will be mentioned in Letter 109: "Skilled wrestlers are kept up to the mark by practice; a musician is stirred to action by one of equal proficiency. The wise man also needs to have his virtues kept in action; and as he prompts himself to do things, so he is prompted by another wise man."[18]

Yet despite all these points in common, correspondence should not be regarded simply as an extension of the practice of *hupomnēmata*. It is something more than a training of oneself by means of writing, through the advice and opinions one gives to the other: it also constitutes a certain way of manifesting oneself to oneself and to others. The letter makes the writer "present" to the one to whom he addresses it. And present not simply through the information he gives concerning his life, his activities, his successes and failures, his good luck or misfortunes; rather, present with a kind of immediate, almost physical presence. "I thank you for writing to me so often; for you are revealing yourself to me [*te mihi ostendis*] in the only way you can. I never receive a letter from you without being in your company forthwith. If the pictures of our absent friends are pleasing to us...how much more pleasant is a letter, which brings us real traces, real evidence of an absent friend! For that which is sweetest when we meet face to face is afforded by the impress of a friend's hand upon his letter—recognition."[19]

To write is thus to "show oneself," to project oneself into view, to make one's own face appear in the other's presence. And by this it should be understood that the letter is both a gaze that one focuses on the addressee (through the missive he receives, he feels looked at) and a way of offering oneself to his gaze by what one tells him about oneself. In a sense, the letter sets up a face-to-face meeting. Moreover Demetrius, explaining in *De elocutione* what the epistolary style should be, stressed that it could only be a "simple" style, free in its composition, spare in its choice of words, since in it each one should reveal his soul.[20] The reciprocity that correspondence establishes is not simply that of counsel and aid; it is the reciprocity of the gaze and the examination. The letter that, as an exercise, works toward the subjectivation of true discourse, its assimilation and its transformation as a "personal asset," also constitutes, at the same time, an objectification of the soul. It is noteworthy that Seneca, commencing a letter in which he must lay out his daily life to Lucilius, recalls the moral maxim that "we should live as if we lived in plain sight of all men,"[21] and the philosophical principle that nothing of ourselves is concealed from god who is always present to our souls. Through the missive, one opens oneself to the gaze of others and puts the correspondent in the place of the inner god. It is a way of giving ourselves to that gaze about which we must tell ourselves that it is plunging into the depths of our heart (*in pectis intimum introspicere*) at the moment we are thinking.

The work the letter carries out on the recipient, but is also brought to bear on the writer by the very letter he sends, thus involves an "introspection"; but the latter is to be understood not so much as a decipherment of the self by the self as an opening one gives the other onto oneself. Still, we are left with a phenomenon that may be a little surprising, but which is full of meaning for anyone wishing to write a history of the cultivation of the self: the first historical developments of the narrative of the self are not to be sought in the direction of the "personal notebooks," the *hupomnēmata*, whose role is to enable the formation of the self out of the collected discourse of others; they can be found, on the other hand, in the correspondence with others and the exchange of soul service. And it is a fact that in the correspondence of Seneca with Lucilius, of Marcus Aurelius with Fronto, and in certain of Pliny's letters, one sees a narrative of the self develop that is very different from the one that could be found generally in Cicero's letters to his acquaintances: the latter involved accounting for oneself as a subject of action (or of deliberation for action) in connection with friends and enemies, fortunate and unfortunate events. In Seneca and Marcus Aurelius, occasionally in Pliny as well, the narrative of the self is the account of one's relation to oneself; there one sees two elements stand out clearly, two strategic points that will later become the privileged objects of what could be called the writing of the relation to the self: the interferences of soul and body (impressions rather than actions), and leisure activity (rather than external events); the body and the days.

1. Health reports traditionally are part of the correspondence. But they gradually increased in scope to include detailed description of the bodily sensations, the impressions of malaise, the various disorders one might have experienced. Sometimes one seeks to introduce advice on

regimen that one judges useful to one's correspondent.[22] Sometimes, too, it is a question of recalling the effects of the body on the soul, the reciprocal action of the latter, or the healing of the former resulting from the care given to the latter. For example, the long and important Letter 78 to Lucilius: it is devoted for the most part to the problem of the "good use" of illnesses and suffering; but it opens with the recollection of a grave illness that Seneca had suffered in his youth, which was accompanied by a moral crisis. Seneca relates that he also experienced, many years before, the "catarrh," the "short attacks of fever" Lucilius complains of: "I scorned it in its early stages. For when I was still young, I could put up with hardships and show a bold front to illness. But I finally succumbed, and arrived at such a state that I could do nothing but snuffle, reduced as I was to the extremity of thinness. I often entertained the impulse of ending my life then and there; but the thought of my kind old father kept me back." And what cured him were the remedies of the soul. Among them, the most important were his friends, who "helped me greatly towards good health; I used to be comforted by their cheering words, by the hours they spent at my bedside, and by their conversation."[23] It also happens that the letters retrace the movement that has led from a subjective impression to an exercise of thought. Witness that meditation walk recounted by Seneca: "I found it necessary to give my body a shaking up, in order that the bile which had gathered in my throat, if that was the trouble, might be shaken out, or, if the very breath [in my lungs] had become, for some reason, too thick, that the jolting, which I have felt was a good thing for me, might make it thinner. So I insisted on being carried longer than usual, along an attractive beach, which bends between Cumae and Servilius Vatia's country house, shut in by the sea on one side and the lake on the other, just like a narrow path. It was packed under foot, because of a recent storm.... As my habit is, I began to look about for something there that might be of service to me, when my eyes fell upon the villa which had once belonged to Vatia."[24] And Seneca tells Lucilius what formed his meditation on retirement—solitude and friendship.

2. The letter is also a way of presenting oneself to one's correspondent in the unfolding of everyday life. To recount one's day—not because of the importance of the events that may have marked it, but precisely even though there was nothing about it apart from its being like all the others, testifying in this way not to the importance of an activity but to the quality of a mode of being—forms part of the epistolary practice:

Lucilius finds it natural to ask Seneca to "give [him] an account of each separate day, and of the whole day too." And Seneca accepts this obligation all the more willingly as it commits him to living under the gaze of others without having anything to conceal: "I shall therefore do as you bid, and shall gladly inform you by letter what I am doing, and in what sequence. I shall keep watching myself continually, and—a most useful habit—shall review each day." Indeed, Seneca evokes this specific day that has gone by, which is at the same time the most ordinary of all. Its value is owing to the very fact that nothing has happened which might have diverted him from the only thing that is important for him: to attend to himself. "Today has been unbroken; no one has filched the slightest part of it from me." A little physical training, a bit of running with a pet slave, a bath in water that is barely lukewarm, a simple snack of bread, a very short nap. But the main part of the day—and this is what takes up the longest part of the letter—is devoted to meditating on the theme suggested by a Sophistic syllogism of Zeno's, concerning drunkenness.[25]

When the missive becomes an account of an ordinary day, a day to oneself, one sees that it relates closely to a practice that Seneca discreetly alludes to, moreover, at the beginning of Letter 83, where he evokes the especially useful habit of "reviewing one's day": this is the self-examination whose form he had described in a passage of the *De Ira*.[26] This practice—familiar in different philosophical currents: Pythagorean, Epicurean, Stoic—seems to have been primarily a mental exercise tied to memorization: it was a question of both constituting oneself as an "inspector of oneself," and hence of gauging the common faults, and of reactivating the rules of behavior that one must always bear in mind. Nothing indicates that this "review of the day" took the form of a written text. It seems therefore that it was in the epistolary relation—and, consequently, in order to place oneself under the other's gaze—that the examination of conscience was formulated as a written account of oneself: an account of the everyday banality, an account of correct or incorrect actions, of the regimen observed, of the physical or mental exercises in which one engaged. One finds a notable example of this conjunction of epistolary practice with self-examination in a letter from Marcus Aurelius to Fronto. It was written during one of those stays in the country which were highly recommended as moments of detachment from public activities, as health treatments, and as occasions for attending to oneself. In this text, one finds the two combined themes of the peasant life—healthy because it was natural—and the life of leisure given over to conversation, reading, and meditation. At the same time, a whole set of meticulous notations on the body, health, physical sensations, regimen, and feelings shows the extreme vigilance of an attention that is intensely focused on oneself. "We are well. I slept somewhat late owing to my slight cold, which seems now to have subsided. So from five A.M. till nine I spent the time partly in reading some of Cato's *Agriculture* and partly in writing not such wretched stuff, by heaven, as yesterday. Then, after paying my respects to my father, I relieved my throat, I will not say by gargling—though the word *gargarisso* is I believe, found in Novius and elsewhere—but by swallowing honey water as far as the gullet and ejecting it again. After easing my throat I went off to my father and attended him at a sacrifice. Then we went to luncheon. What do you think I ate? A wee bit of bread, though I saw others devouring beans, onions, and herrings full of roe. We then worked hard at grape-gathering, and had a good sweat, and were merry.... After six o'clock we came home.

"I did but little work and that to no purpose. Then I had a long chat with my little mother as she sat on the bed.... Whilst we were chattering in this way and disputing which of us two loved the one or other of you two the better, the gong sounded, an intimation that my father had gone to his bath. So we had supper after we had bathed in the oil-press room; I do not mean bathed in the oil-press room, but when we had bathed, had supper there, and we enjoyed hearing the yokels chaffing one another. After coming back, before I turn over and snore, I get my task done [*meum penso explico*] and give my dearest of masters an account of the day's doings [*diei rationem meo suavissimo magistro reddo*] and if I could miss him more, I would not grudge wasting away a little more."[27]

The last lines of the letter clearly show how it is linked to the practice of self-examination: the day ends, just before sleep, with a kind of reading of the day that has passed; one rolls out the scroll on which the day's activities are inscribed, and it is this imaginary book of memory that is reproduced the next day in the letter addressed to the one who is both teacher and friend. The letter to Fronto recopies, as it were, the examination carried out the evening before by reading the mental book of conscience.

It is clear that one is still very far from that book of spiritual combat to which Athanasius refers a few centuries later, in the *Life of Saint*

Antony. But one can also measure the extent to which this procedure of self-narration in the daily run of life, with scrupulous attention to what occurs in the body and in the soul, is different from both Ciceronian correspondence and the practice of *hupomnēmata*, a collection of things read and heard, and a support for exercises of thought. In this case—that of the *hupomnēmata*—it was a matter of constituting oneself as a subject of rational action through the appropriation, the unification, and the subjectivation of a fragmentary and selected already-said; in the case of the monastic notation of spiritual experiences, it will be a matter of dislodging the most hidden impulses from the inner recesses of the soul, thus enabling oneself to break free of them. In the case of the epistolary account of oneself, it is a matter of bringing into congruence the gaze of the other and that gaze which one aims at oneself when one measures one's everyday actions according to the rules of a technique of living.

NOTES

1 Saint Athanasius, *Vita Antonii: Vie et conduite de notre Saint-Père Antoine, écrite et adressée aux moines habitant en pays étranger, par notre Saint-Père Athanase, évêque d'Alexandrie,* trans. B. Lavaud (repub. Paris: Cerf, 1989), pp. 69-70 [*The Life of Saint Antony,* trans. Robert T. Meyer (Westminster, Md.: Newman, 1950), §55, pp. 67-68].

2 Seneca, *Lettres à Lucilius,* trans. H. Nublot (Paris: Belles Lettres, 1945-64), vol. 3 (1957), bk. 11, let. 84, §1, p. 121 [*Ad Lucilium Epistulae Morales, with an English translation by Richard M. Gummere* (Cambridge, Mass.: Harvard University Press, 1961), vol. 2, lct. 84, p. 277].

3 Epictetus, *Entretiens,* trans. J. Souilhé (Paris: Belles Lettres, 1963), vol. 3, bk. 3, ch. 5: "A ceux qui quittent l'école pour raisons de santé," §11, p. 23 [*The Discourses and Manual,* trans. P. E. Matheson (Oxford: Oxford University Press, 1916), vol. 2, bk. 3: "Against those who make illness an excuse for leaving the lecture-room," p. 20].

4 Ibid., bk. 3, ch. 24: "Qu'il ne faut pas s'émouvoir pour ce qui ne depend pas de nous," §103, p. 109 [ch. 24: "That We Ought Not Spend Our Feelings on Things Beyond Our Power," p. 99].

5 Plutarch, *De Tranquillitate,* 464e.

6 Ibid., 465c.

7 Seneca, *Lettres,* vol. 1 (1945), bk. 1, let. 2, §3, p. 6 [vol. 1, let. 2, §3, p. 7].

8 Ibid., vol. 2 (1947), bk. 5, let. 52, §§1-2, pp. 41-42 [vol. 1, let. 52, p. 345].

9 Epictetus, *Entretiens,* vol. 2, bk. 1, ch. 17: "De la Nécessité de la logique," §§11-14, p. 65 [vol. 1, bk. 1, ch. 17, p. 95: "That the Processes of Logic Are Necessary"].

10 Seneca, *Lettres,* vol. 1 (1945), bk. 1, lets. 2, §5, p. 6; 3, §6, p. 9; 4, §10, p. 12; 7, §11, pp. 21-22; 8, §§7-8, p. 24, etc. [vol. 1, lets. 2, §5, p. 9; 2, §6, p. 13; 4, §10, p. 19; 7, §11, pp. 35-37; 8, §§7-9, p. 41].

11 Ibid., let. 2, §§4-5, p. 6 [vol. 1, let. 2, §§4-5, p. 9].

12 Ibid., vol. 3 (1957), bk. 11, let. 84, §§6–7, p. 123 [let. 84, §§6–7, p. 281].

13 Ibid., §§9–10, p. 124 [§§9–10, pp. 281–83].

14 *Lettre à Pythocles*, trans. A. Ernout, in Lucretius, *De Rerum natura: Commentaire par Alfred Ernout et Léon Robin* (Paris: Belles Lettres, 1925), vol. 1, §§84–85, p. 87 ["Letter to Pythocles," in *Epicurus: The Extant Remains*, trans. Cyril Bailey (Oxford: Oxford University Press, 1926), p. 57].

15 Seneca, *Lettres*, vol. 1 (1945), bk. 1, let. 7, §8, p. 21 [vol. 1, let. 7, §8, p. 35].

16 Ibid., vol. 4 (1962), bk. 16, let. 99, pp. 125–34 [vol. 3, let. 99, pp. 129–49].

17 Ibid., vol. 1 (1945), bk. 4, let. 34, §2, p. 190 [vol. 1, let. 34, §2, p. 241].

18 Ibid., vol. 4 (1962), bk. 18, let. 109, §2, p. 190 [vol. 3, let. 109, §2, p. 255].

19 Ibid., vol. 1 (1945), bk. 4, let. 40, §1, p. 161 [vol. 1, let. 40, §1, pp. 263–65].

20 Demetrius of Phaleron, *De Elocutione* 4.§§223–25.

21 Seneca, *Lettres*, vol. 3 (1957), bk. 10, let. 83, §1, p. 110 [vol. 2, let. 84, §1, p. 259].

22 Pliny, The Younger, *Lettres*, bk. 3, let. 1, trans. A.-M. Guillemin (Paris: Belles Lettres, 1927), vol. 1, pp. 97–100 [Pliny, *Letters and Panegyrecus*, trans. Betty Radice (Cambridge, Mass.: Harvard University Press, 1969), vol. 1, bk. 3, §1, pp. 159–63].

23 Seneca, *Lettres*, vol. 3 (1957), bk. 9, let. 78, §§1–4, pp. 71–72 [vol. 2, let. 78, §§1–4, pp. 181–83].

24 Ibid., vol. 2 (1947), bk. 6, let. 55, §§2–3, pp. 56–57, or also let. 57, §§2–3, p. 67 [vol. 1, let. 55, §§2–3, pp. 365–67, or also let. 57, §§2–3, pp. 383–85].

25 Ibid., vol. 3 (1957), bk. 10, let. 83, §§2–3, pp. 110–11 [vol. 2, let. 83, §§2–3, pp. 259–61].

26 Seneca, *De Ira: De la Colère*, trans. A. Bourgery, let. 36, §§1–2, in *Dialogues* (Paris: Belles Lettres, 1922), vol. 1, pp. 102–103 [let. 36, §§1–2, in *Moral Essays*, trans. John W. Basore (Cambridge, Mass.: Harvard University Press, 1958), vol. 1, pp. 339–41].

27 Marcus Aurelius, *Lettres*, bk. 4, let. 6, trans. A. Cassan (Paris: Levavasseur, 1830), pp. 249–51 [in *The Correspondence of Marcus Cornelius Fronto*, trans. C. R. Haines (Cambridge, Mass.: Harvard University Press, 1982), vol. 1, p. 183].

I

Technologies of the Self

When I began to study the rules, duties, and prohibitions of sexuality, the interdictions and restrictions associated with it, I was concerned not simply with the acts that were permitted and forbidden but with the feelings represented, the thoughts, the desires one might experience, the inclination to seek within the self any hidden feeling, any movement of the soul, any desire disguised under illusory forms. There is a very significant difference between interdictions about sexuality and other forms of interdiction. Unlike other interdictions, sexual interdictions are constantly connected with the obligation to tell the truth about oneself.

Two facts may be raised against me: first, that confession played an important part in penal and religious institutions for all offenses, not only in sex. But the task of analyzing one's sexual desire is always more important than analyzing any other kind of sin.

I am also aware of the second objection: that sexual behavior more than any other was submitted to very strict rules of secrecy, decency, and modesty so that sexuality is related in a strange and complex way both to verbal prohibition and to the obligation to tell the truth, of hiding what one does and of deciphering who one is.

---

*This text derives from a seminar Foucault gave at the University of Vermont in October 1982. It appears here amended for style and clarity; it has been supplemented with notes to correspond to the text in *Dits et écrits*.

The association of a prohibition and a strong injunction to speak is a constant feature of our culture. The theme of the renunciation of the flesh was linked to the confession of the monk to the abbot, to the monk confiding to the abbot everything that was on his mind.

I conceived of a rather odd project: not the study of the evolution of sexual behavior but of the historical study of the link between the obligation to tell the truth and the prohibitions weighing on sexuality. I asked: How had the subject been compelled to decipher himself in regard to what was forbidden? It is a question that interrogates the relation between asceticism and truth.

Max Weber posed the question: If one wants to behave rationally and regulate one's action according to true principles, what part of one's self should one renounce? What is the ascetic price of reason? To what kind of asceticism should one submit? I posed the opposite question: How have certain kinds of interdictions required the price of certain kinds of knowledge about oneself? What must one know about oneself in order to be willing to renounce anything?

Thus, I arrived at the hermeneutics of technologies of the self in pagan and early Christian practice. I encountered certain difficulties in this study because these practices are not well known. First, Christianity has always been more interested in the history of its beliefs than in the history of real practices. Second, such a hermeneutics was never organized into a body of doctrine like textual hermeneutics. Third, the hermeneutics of the self has been confused with theologies of the soul—concupiscence, sin, and the fall from grace. Fourth, a hermeneutics of the self has been diffused across Western culture through numerous channels and integrated with various types of attitudes and experience, so that it is difficult to isolate and separate it from our own spontaneous experiences.

Context of Study

My objective for more than twenty-five years has been to sketch out a history of the different ways in our culture that humans develop knowledge about themselves: economics, biology, psychiatry, medicine, and penology. The main point is not to accept this knowledge at face value but to analyze these so-called sciences as very specific "truth games" related to specific techniques that huamn beings use to understand themselves.

As a context, we must understand that there are four major types of these "technologies," each a matrix of practical reason: (1) technologies of production, which permit us to produce, transform, or manipulate things; (2) technologies of sign systems, which permit us to use signs, meanings, symbols, or signification; (3) technologies of power, which determine the conduct of individuals and submit them to certain ends or domination, an objectivizing of the subject; (4) technologies of the self, which permit individuals to effect by their own means, or with the help of others, a certain number of operations on their own bodies and souls, thoughts, conduct, and way of being, so as to transform themselves in order to attain a certain state of happiness, purity, wisdom, perfection, or immortality.

These four types of technologies hardly ever function separately, although each one of them is associated with a certain type of domination. Each implies certain modes of training and modification of individuals, not only in the obvious sense of acquiring certain skills but also in the sense of acquiring certain attitudes. I wanted to show both their specific nature and their constant interaction. For instance, the relation between manipulating things and domination appears clearly in Karl Marx's *Capital*, where every technique of production requires modification of individual conduct—not only skills but also attitudes.

Usually, the first two technologies are used in the study of the sciences and linguistics. It is the last two, the technologies of domination and self, which have most kept my attention. I have attempted a history of the organization of knowledge with respect to both domination and the self. For example, I studied madness not in terms of the criteria of formal sciences but to show what type of management of individuals inside and outside of asylums was made possible by this strange discourse. This encounter between the technologies of domination of others and those of the self I call "governmentality."

Perhaps I've insisted too much on the technology of domination and power. I am more and more interested in the interaction between oneself and others, and in the technologies of individual domination, in the mode of action that an individual exercises upon himself by means of the technologies of the self.

The Development of Technologies of the Self

I wish to sketch out the evolution of the hermeneutics of the self in two different contexts that are historically contiguous: (1) Greco-Roman phi-

losophy in the first two centuries A.D. of the early Roman Empire, and
(2) Christian spirituality and the monastic principles developed in the
fourth and fifth centuries of the late Roman Empire.

Moreover, I wish to take up the subject not only in theory but in relation to a set of practices in late antiquity. Among the Greeks, these
practices took the form of a precept: *epimeleisthai sautou,* "to take care
of yourself," to take "care of the self," "to be concerned, to take care
of yourself."

The precept of the "care of the self" [*souci de soi*] was, for the Greeks,
one of the main principles of cities, one of the main rules for social
and personal conduct and for the art of life. For us now, this notion is
rather obscure and faded. When one is asked "What is the most important moral principle in ancient philosophy?" the immediate answer is
not "Take care of oneself" but the Delphic principle, *gnōthi seauton*
("Know yourself").

Without doubt, our philosophical tradition has overemphasized the
latter and forgotten the former. The Delphic principle was not an abstract one concerning life; it was technical advice, a rule to be observed
for the consultation of the oracle. "Know yourself" meant "Do not suppose yourself to be a god." Other commentators suggest that it meant
"Be aware of what you really ask when you come to consult the oracle."

In Greek and Roman texts, the injunction of having to know oneself was always associated with the other principle of the care of the
self, and it was that need to care for oneself that brought the Delphic
maxim into operation. It is implicit in all Greek and Roman culture
and has been explicit since Plato's *Alcibiades I.*[1] In the Socratic dialogues, in Xenophon, Hippocrates, and in the Neoplatonist tradition
from Albinus on, one had to be concerned with oneself. One had to
occupy oneself with oneself before the Delphic principle was brought
into action. There was a subordination of the second principle to the
former. I have three or four examples of this.

In Plato's *Apology,* 29e, Socrates presents himself before his judges
as a master of *epimeleia heautou.*[2] You "preoccupy yourselves without
shame in acquiring wealth and reputation and honors," he tells them,
but you do not concern yourselves with yourselves, that is, with "wisdom, truth and the perfection of the soul." He, on the other hand,
watches over the citizens to make sure they concern themselves with
themselves.

Socrates says three important things with regard to his invitation to

others to occupy themselves with themselves: (1) His mission was conferred on him by the gods, and he won't abandon it except with his
last breath. (2) For this task he demands no reward; he is disinterested; he performs it out of benevolence. (3) His mission is useful for
the city—more useful than the Athenians' military victory at Olympia—
because, in teaching people to occupy themselves with themselves, he
teaches them to occupy themselves with the city.

Eight centuries later, one finds the same notion and the same phrase
in Gregory of Nyssa's treatise, *On Virginity*, but with an entirely different meaning. Gregory did not mean the movement by which one
takes care of oneself and the city; he meant the movement by which
one renounces the world and marriage as well as detaches oneself from
the flesh and, with virginity of heart and body, recovers the immortality of which one has been deprived. In commenting on the parable of
the drachma (Luke 15.8–10), Gregory exhorts man to light his lamp
and turn the house over and search, until gleaming in the shadow he
sees the drachma within. In order to recover the efficacy that God has
printed on the human soul and the body has tarnished, man must take
care of himself and search every corner of his soul.[3]

We see that Christian asceticism and ancient philosophy are placed
under the same sign: that of the care of the self. The obligation to know
oneself is one of the central elements of Christian asceticism. Between
these two extremes—Socrates and Gregory of Nyssa—taking care of
oneself constituted not only a principle but also a constant practice.

I have two more examples. The first Epicurean text to serve as a
manual of morals was the *Letter to Menoeceus*.[4] Epicurus writes that
it is never too early, never too late, to occupy oneself with one's soul.
One should philosophize when one is young and also when one is old.
It is a task to be carried on throughout life. Precepts governing everyday life are organized around the care of the self in order to help every
member of the group with the common task of salvation.

Another example comes from an Alexandrian text, *On the Contemplative Life*, by Philo of Alexandria. He describes an obscure, enigmatic
group on the periphery of Hellenistic and Hebraic culture called the
Therapeutae, marked by its religiosity. It is an austere community,
devoted to reading, to healing meditation, to individual and collective
prayer, and to meeting for a spiritual banquet (*agapē*, "feast"). These
practices stem from the principal task, the care of the self.[5]

This is the point of departure for a possible analysis of the care of the self in ancient culture. I would like to analyze the relation between the care of the self and knowledge of the self, the relation found in Greco-Roman and Christian traditions between the preoccupation an individual has with himself and the too-well-known principle "Know yourself." Just as there are different forms of care, there are different forms of self.

Summary

There are several reasons why "Know yourself" has obscured "Take care of yourself." First, there has been a profound transformation in the moral principles of Western society. We find it difficult to base rigorous morality and austere principles on the precept that we should give more care to ourselves than to anything else in the world. We are more inclined to see taking care of ourselves as an immorality, as a means of escape from all possible rules. We inherit the tradition of Christian morality which makes self-renunciation the condition for salvation. To know oneself was, paradoxically, a means of self-renunciation.

We also inherit a secular tradition that sees in external law the basis for morality. How then can respect for the self be the basis for morality? We are the inheritors of a social morality that seeks the rules for acceptable behavior in relations with others. Since the sixteenth century, criticism of established morality has been undertaken in the name of the importance of recognizing and knowing the self. Therefore, it is difficult to see the care of the self as compatible with morality. "Know thyself" has obscured "Take care of yourself" because our morality, a morality of asceticism, insists that the self is that which one can reject.

The second reason is that, in theoretical philosophy from Descartes to Husserl, knowledge of the self (the thinking subject) takes on an ever-increasing importance as the first step in the theory of knowledge.

To summarize: There has been an inversion in the hierarchy of the two principles of antiquity, "Take care of yourself" and "Know yourself." In Greco-Roman culture, knowledge of oneself appeared as the consequence of the care of the self. In the modern world, knowledge of oneself constitutes the fundamental principle.

II

The first philosophical elaboration of the concern with taking care of oneself that I wish to consider is found in Plato's *Alcibiades I*. The date of its writing is uncertain, and it may be a spurious Platonic dialogue. It is not my intention to study dates but to point out the principal features of the care of the self which is the center of the dialogue.

The Neoplatonists in the third or fourth century A.D. show the significance given to this dialogue and the importance it assumed in the classical tradition. They wanted to transform Plato's dialogues into a pedagogical tool, to make them the matrix for encyclopedic knowledge. They considered *Alcibiades* to be the first dialogue of Plato—the first to be read, the first to be studied. It was the *arkhē.* In the second century, Albinus said that every gifted young man who wanted to stand apart from politics and practice virtue should study the *Alcibiades.*[6] It provided the point of departure and a program for all Platonic philosophy. "Taking care of oneself" is its first principle. I would like to analyze the care of self in the *Alcibiades I* in terms of three aspects.

1. How is this question introduced into the dialogue? What are the reasons Alcibiades and Socrates are brought to the notion of the care of the self?

Alcibiades is about to begin his public and political life. He wishes to speak before the people and be all-powerful in the city. He is not satisfied with his traditional status, with the privileges of his birth and heritage. He wishes to gain personal power over all others both inside and outside the city. At this point of intersection and transformation, Socrates intervenes and declares his love for Alcibiades. Alcibiades can no longer be the beloved; he must become a lover. He must become active in the political and the love game. Thus, there is a dialectic between political and erotic discourse. Alcibiades makes his transition in specific ways in both politics and love.

An ambivalence is evident in Alcibiades' political and erotic vocabulary. During his adolescence, Alcibiades was desirable and had many admirers, but now that his beard is growing, his suitors are disappearing. Earlier, he had rejected them all in the bloom of his beauty because he wanted to be dominant, not dominated. He refused to let himself be dominated in youth, but now he wants to dominate others. This is the moment Socrates appears, and he succeeds where the others have failed: he will make Alcibiades submit, but in a different sense. They make a pact—Alcibiades will submit to his lover, Socrates, not in a physical but in a spiritual sense. The intersection of political ambition and philosophical love is "the care of the self."

2. In such a relationship, why should Alcibiades be concerned with

himself, and why is Socrates preoccupied with that concern of Alcibiades? Socrates asks Alcibiades about his personal capacities and the nature of his ambition. Does he know the meaning of the rule of law, of justice or concord? Alcibiades clearly knows nothing. Socrates calls upon him to compare his education with that of the Persian and Spartan kings, his rivals. Spartan and Persian princes have teachers in wisdom, justice, temperance, and courage. By comparison, Alcibiades' education is like that of an old, ignorant slave: he doesn't know these things, so he can't apply himself to knowledge. But, says Socrates, it is not too late. To help him gain the upper hand—to acquire *tekhnē*—Alcibiades must apply himself, he must take care of himself. But Alcibiades does not know to what he must apply himself. What is this knowledge he seeks? He is embarrassed and confused. Socrates calls upon him not to lose heart.

In 127d of the *Alcibiades* we find the first appearance of the phrase *epimeleisthai sautou*. Concern for self always refers to an active political and erotic state. *Epimeleisthai* expresses something much more serious than the simple fact of paying attention. It involves various things: taking pains with one's holdings and one's health. It is always a real activity and not just an attitude. It is used in reference to the activity of a farmer tending his fields, his cattle, and his house, or to the job of the king in taking care of his city and citizens, or to the worship of ancestors or gods, or as a medical term to signify the fact of caring. It is highly significant that the concern for self in *Alcibiades I* is directly related to a defective pedagogy, one that concerns political ambition and a specific moment of life.

3. The rest of the text is devoted to an analysis of this notion of *epimeleisthai*, "taking pains with oneself." It is divided into two questions: What is this self of which one has to take care, and of what does that care consist?

First, what is the self (129b)? *Self* is a reflexive pronoun, and it has two meanings. *Auto* means "the same," but it also conveys the notion of identity. The latter meaning shifts the question from "What is this self?" to "Departing from what ground shall I find my identity?" Alcibiades tries to find the self in a dialectical movement. When you take care of the body, you do not take care of the self. The self is not clothing, tools, or possessions; it is to be found in the principle that uses these tools, a principle not of the body but of the soul. You have to worry about your soul—that is the principal activity of caring for yourself. The care of the self is the care of the activity and not the care of the soul-as-substance.

The second question is: How must we take care of this principle of activity, the soul? Of what does this care consist? One must know of what the soul consists. The soul cannot know itself except by looking at itself in a similar element, a mirror. Thus, it must contemplate the divine element. In this divine contemplation, the soul will be able to discover rules to serve as a basis for just behavior and political action. The effort of the soul to know itself is the principle on which just political action can be founded, and Alcibiades will be a good politician insofar as he contemplates his soul in the divine element.

Often the discussion gravitates around and is phrased in terms of the Delphic principle "Know yourself." To take care of oneself consists of knowing oneself. Knowing oneself becomes the object of the quest of concern for self. Being occupied with oneself and political activities are linked. The dialogue ends when Alcibiades knows he must take care of himself by examining his soul.

This text, one of Plato's first, illuminates the historical background of the precept "taking care of oneself" and sets out four main problems that endure throughout antiquity, although the solutions offered often differ from those in Plato's *Alcibiades*.

First, there is the problem of the relation between the care of the self and political activity. In the later Hellenistic and imperial periods, the question is presented in an alternative way: When is it better to turn away from political activity to concern oneself with oneself?

Second, there is the problem of the relationship between the care of the self and pedagogy. For Socrates, occupying oneself with oneself is the duty of a young man, but later in the Hellenistic period it is seen as the permanent duty of one's whole life.

Third, there is the problem of the relationship between the care of the self and the knowledge of oneself. Plato gave priority to the Delphic maxim "Know yourself." The privileged position of "Know yourself" is characteristic of all Platonists. Later, in the Hellenistic and Greco-Roman periods, this is reversed: the accent was not on the knowledge of self but on the concern with oneself. The latter was given an autonomy and even a preeminence as a philosophical issue.

Fourth, there is the problem of the relationship between the care of self and philosophical love, or the relation to a master.

In the Hellenistic and imperial periods, the Socratic notion of "the care of the self" became a common, universal philosophical theme.

"Care of the self" was accepted by Epicurus and his followers, by the Cynics, and by such Stoics as Seneca, Rufus, and Galen. The Pythagoreans gave attention to the notion of an ordered life in common. This theme of the care of the self was not abstract advice but a widespread activity, a network of obligations and services to the soul. Following Epicurus himself, the Epicureans believed that it is never too late to occupy oneself with oneself. The Stoics say you must attend to the self, "retire into the self and stay there." Lucian parodied the notion.[7] It was an extremely widespread activity, and it brought about competition between the rhetoricians and those who turned toward themselves, particularly over the question of the role of the master.

There were charlatans, of course, but certain individuals took it seriously. It was generally acknowledged that it was good to be reflective, at least briefly. Pliny advises a friend to set aside a few moments a day, or several weeks or months, for a retreat into himself. This was an active leisure—to study, to read, to prepare for misfortune or death. It was a meditation and a preparation.

Writing was also important in the culture of the care of the self. One of the tasks that defines the care of the self is that of taking notes on oneself to be reread, writing treatises and letters to friends to help them, and keeping notebooks in order to reactivate for oneself the truths one needed. Seneca's letters are an example of this self-exercise.

In traditional political life, oral culture was largely dominant, and therefore rhetoric was important. Yet the development of the administrative structures and the bureaucracy of the imperial period increased the amount and role of writing in the political sphere. In Plato's writings, dialogue gave way to the literary pseudodialogue. By the Hellenistic age, though, writing prevailed, and real dialectic passed to correspondence. Taking care of oneself became linked to constant writing activity. The self is something to write about, a theme or object (subject) of writing activity. That is not a modern trait born of the Reformation or of Romanticism; it is one of the most ancient Western traditions. It was well established and deeply rooted when Augustine started his *Confessions*.[8]

The new care of the self involved a new experience of self. The new form of the experience of the self is to be seen in the first and second centuries, when introspection becomes more and more detailed. A relation developed between writing and vigilance. Attention was paid to nuances of life, mood, and reading, and the experience of self was intensified and widened by virtue of this act of writing. A whole field of experience opened which earlier was absent.

One can compare Cicero to the later Seneca or Marcus Aurelius. We see, for example, Seneca's and Marcus's meticulous concern with the details of daily life, with the movements of the spirit, with self-analysis. Everything in the imperial period is present in Marcus Aurelius's letter of 144–45 A.D. to Fronto:

Hail, my sweetest of masters.

We are well. I slept somewhat late owing to my slight cold, which seems now to have subsided. So from five A.M. till nine I spent the time partly in reading some of Cato's *Agriculture* and partly in writing not quite such wretched stuff, by heavens, as yesterday. Then, after paying my respects to my father, I relieved my throat, I will not say by gargling—though the word *gargarisso* is, I believe, found in Novius and elsewhere —but by swallowing honey water as far as the gullet and ejecting it again. After easing my throat I went off to my father and attended him at a sacrifice. Then we went to luncheon. What do you think I ate? A wee bit of bread, though I saw others devouring beans, onions, and herrings full of roe. We then worked hard at grape-gathering, and had a good sweat, and were merry and, as the poet says, "still left some clusters hanging high as gleanings of the vintage." After six o'clock we came home.

I did but little work and that to no purpose. Then I had a long chat with my little mother as she sat on the bed. My talk was this: "What do you think my Fronto is now doing?" Then she: "And what do you think my Gratia is doing?" Then I: "And what do you think our little sparrow, the wee Gratia, is doing?" Whilst we were chattering in this way and disputing which of us two loved the one or other of you two the better, the gong sounded, an intimation that my father had gone to his bath. So we had supper after we had bathed in the oil-press room; I do not mean bathed in the oil-press room, but when we had bathed, had supper there, and we enjoyed hearing the yokels chaffing one another. After coming back, before I turn over and snore, I get my task done and give my dearest of masters an account of the day's doings, and if I could miss him more, I would not grudge wasting away a little more. Farewell, my Fronto, wherever you are, most honey-sweet, my love, my delight. How is it between you and me? I love you and you are away.[9]

This letter presents a description of everyday life. All the details of taking care of oneself are here, all the unimportant things he has done.

Cicero tells only important things, but in Aurelius's letter these details are important because they are you—what you thought, what you felt.

The relation between the body and the soul is interesting too. For the Stoics, the body was not so important, but Marcus Aurelius speaks of himself, his health, what he has eaten, his sore throat. That is quite characteristic of the ambiguity about the body in this cultivation of the self. Theoretically, the cultivation of the self is soul-oriented, but all the concerns of the body take on a considerable importance. In Pliny and Seneca, hypochondria is an essential trait. They retreat to a house in the countryside. They have intellectual activities but rural activities as well. They eat and participate in the activities of peasants. The importance of the rural retreat in this letter is that nature helps put one in contact with oneself.

There is also a love relationship between Aurelius and Fronto, one between a twenty-four-year-old and a forty-year-old man. *Ars erotica* is a theme of discussion. Homosexual love was important in this period and carried over into Christian monasticism.

Finally, in the last lines, there is an allusion to the examination of conscience at the end of the day. Aurelius goes to bed and looks in the notebook to see what he was going to do and how it corresponds to what he did. The letter is the transcription of that examination of conscience. It stresses what the individual did, not what he thought. That is the difference between practice in the Hellenistic and imperial periods and later monastic practice. In Seneca, too, there are only deeds, not thoughts; but it does prefigure Christian confession.

This genre of epistles shows a side apart from the philosophy of the era. The examination of conscience begins with this letter-writing. Diary-writing comes later. It dates from the Christian era and focuses on the notion of the struggle of the soul.

III

In my discussion of Plato's *Alcibiades*, I have isolated three major themes: (1) the relation between care of the self and care for the political life; (2) the relation between the care of the self and defective education; and (3) the relation between the care of the self and knowing oneself. Whereas we saw in the *Alcibiades* the close relation between "Take care of yourself" and "Know yourself," taking care of yourself eventually was absorbed in knowing yourself.

We can see these three themes in Plato, also in the Hellenistic period, and four to five centuries later in Seneca, Plutarch, Epictetus, and the like. If the problems are the same, the solutions and themes are quite different and, in some cases, the opposite of the Platonic meanings.

First, to be concerned with self in the Hellenistic and Roman periods is not exclusively a preparation for political life. Care of the self has become a universal principle. One must leave politics to take better care of the self.

Second, the concern with oneself is not just obligatory for young people concerned with their education; it is a way of living for everybody throughout their lives.

Third, even if self-knowledge plays an important role in the care of the self, it involves other relationships as well.

I want to discuss briefly the first two points: the universality of the care of the self independent of political life, and the care of the self throughout one's life.

1. A medical model was substituted for Plato's pedagogical model. The care of the self isn't another kind of pedagogy; it has to become permanent medical care. Permanent medical care is one of the central features of the care of the self. One must become the doctor of oneself.

2. Since we have to take care throughout life, the objective is no longer to get prepared for adult life, or for another life, but to get prepared for a certain complete achievement of life. This achievement is complete at the moment just prior to death. This notion of a happy proximity to death—of old age as completion—is an inversion of the traditional Greek values on youth.

3. Lastly, we have the various practices to which cultivation of self has given rise and the relation of self-knowledge to these.

In *Alcibiades I*, the soul had a mirror relation to itself, which relates to the concept of memory and justifies dialogue as a method of discovering truth in the soul. Yet from the time of Plato to the Hellenistic age, the relationship between care of the self and knowledge of the self changed. We may note two perspectives.

In the philosophical movements of Stoicism in the imperial period, there is a different conception of truth and memory, and another method of examining the self. First, we see the disappearance of dialogue and the increasing importance of a new pedagogical relationship—a new pedagogical game where the master-teacher speaks and does not ask questions, and the disciple does not answer but must listen and keep silent. A cultivation of silence becomes more and more important. In Pythagorean cultivation, disciples kept silent for five years as a pedagogical rule. They did not ask questions or speak up during the lesson, but they developed the art of listening. This is the positive condition for acquiring truth. The tradition is picked up during the imperial period, where we see the beginning of the cultivation of silence and the art of listening rather than the cultivation of dialogue as in Plato.

To learn the art of listening, we have to read Plutarch's treatise on the art of listening to lectures, *Peri tou akouein*.[10] At the beginning of this treatise, Plutarch says that, following schooling, we must learn to listen to *logos* throughout our adult life. The art of listening is crucial so that you can tell what is true and what is dissimulation, what is rhetorical truth and what is falsehood in the discourse of the rhetoricians. Listening is linked to the fact that the disciple is not under the control of the masters but must listen to *logos*. One keeps silent at the lecture; one thinks about it afterward. This is the art of listening to the voice of the master and the voice of reason in the self.

The advice may seem banal, but I think it is important. In his treatise *On the Contemplative Life*, Philo of Alexandria describes banquets of silence, not debauched banquets with wine, boys, revelry, and dialogue. There is instead a teacher who gives a monologue on the interpretation of the Bible and a very precise indication of the way people must listen.[11] For example, they must always assume the same posture when listening. The morphology of this notion is an interesting theme in monasticism and pedagogy henceforth.

In Plato, the themes of contemplation of self and care of self are related dialectically through dialogue. Now in the imperial period, we have the theories of, on one side, the obligation of listening to the truth and, on the other side, of looking and listening to the self for the truth within. The difference between the one era and the other is one of the great signs of the disappearance of the dialectical structure.

What was an examination of conscience in this culture, and how does one look at oneself? For the Pythagoreans, the examination of conscience had to do with purification. Since sleep was related to death as a kind of encounter with the gods, one had to purify oneself before going to sleep. Remembering the dead was an exercise for the memory. But in the Hellenistic and the early imperial periods, you see this practice acquiring new values and signification. There are several relevant texts: Seneca's *De Ira* and *De Tranquillitae*,[12] and the beginning of Marcus Aurelius's fourth book of *Meditations*.[13]

Seneca's *De Ira* (Book Three) contains some traces of the old tradition.[14] He describes an examination of conscience. The same thing was recommended by the Epicureans, and the practice was rooted in the Pythagorean tradition. The goal was the purification of the conscience using a mnemonic device. Do good things, have a good examination of the self, and a good sleep follows together with good dreams, which is contact with the gods.

Seneca seems to use juridical language, and it seems that the self is both the judge and the accused. Seneca is the judge and prosecutos the self so that the examination is a kind of trial. Yet if you look closer, it is rather different from a court: Seneca uses terms related not to juridical but to administrative practices, as when a comptroller looks at the books or when a building inspector examines a building. Self-examination is taking stock. Faults are simply good intentions left undone. The rule is a means of doing something correctly, not judging what has happened in the past. Later, Christian confession will look for bad intentions.

It is this administrative view of his own life much more than the juridical model that is important. Seneca is not a judge who has to punish but a stock-taking administrator. He is a permanent administrator of himself, not a judge of his past. He sees that everything has been done correctly following the rule but not the law. It is not real faults for which he reproaches himself but, rather, his lack of success. His errors are of strategy, not of moral character. He wants to make adjustments between what he wanted to do and what he had done, and to reactivate the rules of conduct, not excavate his guilt. In Christian confession, the penitent is obliged to memorize laws but does so in order to discover his sins.

For Seneca, the problem is not that of discovering truth in the subject but of remembering truth, recovering a truth that has been forgotten. Second, the subject does not forget himself, his nature, origin, or his supernatural affinity, but the rules of conduct, what he ought to have done. Third, the recollection of errors committed in the day measures the distinction between what has been done and what should have been done. Fourth, the subject is not the operating ground for the process of deciphering but the point where rules of conduct come together in memory. The subject constitutes the intersection between acts that have to be regulated and rules for what ought to be done. This is quite dif-

ferent from the Platonic conception and from the Christian conception
of conscience.

The Stoics spiritualized the notion of *anakhōrēsis*, the retreat of an
army, the hiding of an escaped slave from his master, or the retreat
into the country away from the towns, as in Marcus Aurelius's country
retreat. A retreat into the country becomes a spiritual retreat into oneself. It is a general attitude and also a precise act every day; you retire
into the self to discover—but not to discover faults and deep feelings,
only to remember rules of action, the main laws of behavior. It is a
mnemotechnical formula.

IV

I have spoken of three Stoic technologies of the self: letters to friends
and disclosure of self; examination of self and conscience, including a
review of what was done, of what should have been done, and comparison of the two. Now I want to consider the third Stoic technique,
askēsis, not a disclosure of the secret self but a remembering.

For Plato, one must discover the truth that is within one. For the
Stoics, truth is not in oneself but in the *logoi*, the teachings of the masters. One memorizes what one has heard, converting the statement one
hears into rules of conduct. The subjectivation of truth is the aim of
these techniques. During the imperial period, one could not assimilate
ethical principles without a theoretical framework such as science, as
for example in Lucretius's *De Rerum natura*.[15] There are structural
questions underlying the practice of the examination of the self every
night. I want to underscore the fact that in Stoicism it is not the deciphering of the self, not the means to disclose secrecy, which is important; it is the memory of what one has done and what one has had to do.

In Christianity, asceticism always refers to a certain renunciation of
the self and of reality because most of the time the self is a part of that
reality that must be renounced in order to gain access to another level
of reality. This move to attain the renunciation of the self distinguishes
Christian asceticism.

In the philosophical tradition inaugurated by Stoicism, *askēsis* means
not renunciation but the progressive consideration of self, or mastery
over oneself, obtained not through the renunciation of reality but
through the acquisition and assimilation of truth. It has as its final
aim not preparation for another reality but access to the reality of this

world. The Greek word for this is *paraskeuazō* ("to get prepared"). It is a set of practices by which one can acquire, assimilate, and transform truth into a permanent principle of action. *Alētheia* becomes *ēthos*. It is a process of the intensification of subjectivity.

What are the principal features of *askēsis*? They include exercises in which the subject puts himself in a situation in which he can verify whether he can confront events and use the discourses with which he is armed. It is a question of testing the preparation. Is this truth assimilated enough to become ethics so that we can behave as we must when an event presents itself?

The Greeks characterized the two poles of those exercises by the terms *melete* and *gymnasia*. *Melete* means "meditation," according to the Latin translation, *meditatio*. It has the same root as *epimeleisthai*. It is a rather vague term, a technical term borrowed from rhetoric. *Melete* is the work one undertakes in order to prepare a discourse or an improvisation by thinking over useful terms and arguments. It is a matter of anticipating the real situation through dialogue in one's thoughts. The philosophical meditation is this kind of meditation: it is composed of memorizing responses and reactivating those memories by placing oneself in a situation where one can imagine how one would react. One judges the reasoning one should use in an imaginary exercise ("Let us suppose...") in order to test an action or event (for example, "How would I react?"). Imagining the articulation of possible events to test how one would react—that is meditation.

The most famous exercise of meditation is the *praemeditatio malorum* as practiced by the Stoics. It is an ethical, imaginary experience. In appearance, it is a rather dark and pessimistic vision of the future. You can compare it to what Husserl says about eidetic reduction.

The Stoics developed three eidetic reductions of future misfortune. First, it is not a question of imagining the future as it is likely to turn out but to imagine the worst that can happen, even if there is little chance that it will turn out that way—the worst as certainty, as actualizing what could happen, not as calculation of probability. Second, one should not envisage things as possibly taking place in the distant future but as already actual and in the process of taking place. For example, imagining not that one might be exiled but rather that one is already exiled, subjected to torture, and dying. Third, one does this not in order to experience inarticulate sufferings but in order to convince oneself that they are not real ills. The reduction of all that is possible, of all the duration and of all the misfortunes, reveals not something bad but what we must accept. It consists of having at the same time the future and the present event. The Epicureans were hostile to it because they thought it was useless: they thought it was better to recollect and memorize past pleasures in order to derive pleasure from present events.

At the opposite pole is *gymnasia* ("to train oneself"). While *meditatio* is an imaginary experience that trains thought, *gymnasia* is training in a real situation, even if it has been artificially induced. There is a long tradition behind this: sexual abstinence, physical privation, and other rituals of purification.

Those practices of abstinence have other meanings than purification or witnessing demonic force, as in Pythagoras and Socrates. In the culture of the Stoics, their function is to establish and test the independence of the individual with regard to the external world. For example, in Plutarch's *On the Daemon of Socrates*, one gives oneself over to very hard sporting activities. Or one tempts oneself by placing oneself in front of many tantalizing dishes and then renouncing them; then one calls his slaves and gives them the dishes, and takes the meal prepared for the slaves.[16] Another example is Seneca's Letter 18 to Lucilius: he prepares for a great feast day by acts of mortification of the flesh in order to convince himself that poverty is not an evil, and that he can endure it.[17]

Between these poles of training in thought and training in reality, *meletē* and *gymnasia*, there are a whole series of intermediate possibilities. Epictetus provides the best example of the middle ground between these poles. He wants to watch perpetually over representations, a technique that will find its apogee in Freud. There are two metaphors important from his point of view: the night watchman, who will not admit anyone into town if that person cannot prove who he is (we must be "watchmen" over the flux of thought),[18] and the moneychanger, who verifies the authenticity of currency, looks at it, weighs and assures himself of its worth. We have to be moneychangers of our own representations, of our thoughts, vigilantly testing them, verifying them, their metal, weight, effigy.[19]

The same metaphor of the moneychanger is found in the Stoics and in early Christian literature, but with different meanings. When Epictetus says you must be a moneychanger, he means as soon as an idea comes to mind you have to think of the rules you must apply to evaluate it. For Cassian, being a moneychanger and looking at your thoughts means something very different: it means you must try to decipher if, at the root of the movement that brings you the representations, there is or is not concupiscence or desire—if your innocent thought has evil origins; if you have something underlying which is the great Seducer, which is perhaps hidden, the money of your thought.[20]

In Epictetus there are two exercises—sophistical and ethical. The first are exercises borrowed from school, question-and-answer games. This must be an ethical game; that is, it must teach a moral lesson.[21] The second are ambulatory exercises. In the morning you go for a walk, and you test your reactions to that walk. The purpose of both exercises is control of representations, not the deciphering of truth. They are reminders about conforming to the rules in the face of adversity. A pre-Freudian machine of censorship is described word for word in the tests of Epictetus and Cassian. For Epictetus, the control of representations means not deciphering but recalling principles of acting, and thus seeing, through self-examination, if they govern one's life. It is a kind of permanent self-examination. One must be one's own censor. The meditation on death is the culmination of all these exercises.

In addition to letters, examination, and *askēsis*, we must now evoke a fourth technique in the examination of the self, the interpretation of dreams. It was to have an important destiny in the nineteenth century, but it occupied a relatively marginal position in the ancient world. Philosophers had an ambivalent attitude toward the interpretation of dreams. Most Stoics are critical and skeptical about such interpretation; but there is still the popular and general practice of it. There were experts who were able to interpret dreams, including Pythagoras and some of the Stoics, and some experts who wrote books to teach people to interpret their own dreams. There were huge amounts of literature on how to do it, but the only surviving dream manual is *The Interpretation of Dreams* by Artemidorus (second century A.D.).[22] Dream interpretation was important because, in antiquity, the meaning of a dream was an announcement of a future event.

I should mention two other documents dealing with the importance of dream interpretation for everyday life. The first is by Synesius of Cyrene in the fourth century A.D.[23] He was well known and cultivated. Even though he was not a Christian, he asked to be a bishop. His remarks on dreams are interesting, for public divination was forbidden in order to spare the emperor bad news. Therefore, one had to interpret one's own dreams; one had to be a self-interpreter. To do it, one had to remember not only one's own dreams but the events before and after. One had to record what happened every day, both the life of the day and the life of the night.

Aelius Aristides' *Sacred Discourses*,[24] written in the second century, records his dreams and explains how to interpret them. He believed that in the interpretation of dreams we receive advice from the gods about remedies for illness. With this work, we are at the crossing point of two kinds of discourses. It is not the writing of the self's daily activities that is the matrix of the *Sacred Discourses* but the ritual inscription of praises to the gods that have healed you.

V

I wish to examine the scheme of one of the main techniques of the self in early Christianity and what it was as a truth game. To do so, I must look at the transition from pagan to Christian culture, in which it is possible to see clear-cut continuities and discontinuities.

Christianity belongs to the salvation religions. It is one of those religions which is supposed to lead the individual from one reality to another, from death to life, from time to eternity. In order to achieve that, Christianity imposed a set of conditions and rules of behavior for a certain transformation of the self.

Christianity is not only a salvation religion, it is a confessional religion; it imposes very strict obligations of truth, dogma, and canon, more so than do the pagan religions. Truth obligations to believe this or that were and are still very numerous. The duty to accept a set of obligations, to hold certain books as permanent truth, to accept authoritarian decisions in matters of truth, not only to believe certain things but to show that one believes, and to accept institutional authority are all characteristic of Christianity.

Christianity requires another form of truth obligation different from faith. Each person has the duty to know who he is, that is, to try to know what is happening inside him, to acknowledge faults, to recognize temptations, to locate desires; and everyone is obliged to disclose these things either to God or to others in the community and, hence, to bear public or private witness against oneself. The truth obligations of faith and the self are linked together. This link permits a purification of the soul impossible without self-knowledge.

It is not the same in the Catholic as in the Reform tradition. But the main features of both are an ensemble of truth obligations dealing with faith, books, dogma, and one dealing with truth, heart, and soul. Access to truth cannot be conceived of without purity of the soul. Purity of the soul is the consequence of self-knowledge and a condition for understanding the text: *quis facit veritatem* (to make truth in oneself, to get access to the light), in Augustine.

I would like to analyze the ways by which, in order to get access to the light, the Church conceived of illumination: the disclosure of the self. The sacrament of penance and the confession of sins are rather late innovations. Christians of the first centuries had different forms for discovering and deciphering truth about themselves. One of the two main forms of these discourses can be characterized by the word *exomologēsis*, or "recognition of fact." Even the Latin fathers used this Greek term with no exact translation. For Christians, it meant to recognize publicly the truth of their faith or to recognize publicly that they were Christians.

The word also had a penitential meaning. When a sinner seeks penance, he must visit the bishop and ask for it. In early Christianity, penitence was not an act or a ritual but a status imposed on somebody who had committed very serious sins.

Exomologesis was a ritual of recognizing oneself as a sinner and penitent. It had several characteristics. First, you were a penitent for four to ten years, and this status affected your life. There was fasting, and there were rules about clothing and prohibitions about sex; the individual was marked so he could not live the same life as others. Even after his reconciliation, he suffered from a number of prohibitions; for example, he could not marry or become a priest.

Within this status you find the obligation of exomologesis. The sinner seeks his penance. He visits the bishop and asks the bishop to impose on him the status of a penitent. He must explain why he wants the status, and he must explain his faults. This was not a confession; it was a condition of the status. Later, in the medieval period, exomologesis became a ritual that took place at the end of the period of penance, just before reconciliation. This ceremony placed him among the other Christians. Of this recognition ceremony, Tertullian says that wearing a hair shirt and ashes, wretchedly dressed, the sinner stands humbled before the church. Then he prostrates himself and kisses the brethren's knees.[25] Exomologesis is not a verbal behavior but the dramatic recognition of one's status as a penitent. Much later, in the *Epistles* of Jerome, there is a description of the penitence of Fabiola, a Roman lady.[26] During these days, Fabiola was in the ranks of penitents. People wept with her, lending drama to her public chastisement.

Recognition also designates the entire process that the penitent experiences in this status over the years. He is the aggregate of manifested penitential behavior, of self-punishment as well as of self-revelation. The acts by which he punishes himself are indistinguishable from the acts by which he reveals himself: self-punishment and the voluntary expression of the self are bound together. This link is evident in many writings; Cyprian, for example, talks of exhibitions of shame and modesty. Penance is not nominal but theatrical.[27]

To prove suffering, to show shame, to make visible humility and exhibit modesty—these are the main features of punishment. Penitence in early Christianity is a way of life acted out at all times by accepting the obligation to disclose oneself. It must be visibly represented and accompanied by others who recognize the ritual. This approach endured until the fifteenth and sixteenth centuries.

Tertullian uses the term *publicatio sui* to characterize exomologesis. *Publicatio sui* is related to Seneca's daily self-examination, which was, however, completely private. For Seneca, exomologesis or *publicatio sui* does not imply verbal analysis of deeds or thoughts; it is only a somatic and symbolic expression. What was private for the Stoics was public for the Christians.

What were its functions? First, this publication was a way to rub out sin and to restore the purity acquired by baptism. Second, it was also to show a sinner as he is. That is the paradox at the heart of exomologesis: it rubs out the sin and yet reveals the sinner. The greater part of the act of penitence was not in telling the truth of sin but in showing the true sinful being of the sinner; it was not a way for the sinner to explain his sins but a way to present himself as a sinner.

Why should showing forth efface the sins? Exposé is the heart of exomologesis. In the Christianity of the first centuries, Christian authors had recourse to three models to explain the relation between the paradox of rubbing out sins and disclosing oneself.

The first is the medical model: one must show one's wounds in order to be cured. Another model, which was less frequent, was the tribunal model of judgment: one always appeases one's judge by confessing faults. The sinner plays devil's advocate, as will the devil on the Day of Judgment.

The most important model used to explain exomologesis was the model of death, of torture, or of martyrdom. The theories and practices of penance were elaborated around the problem of the man who prefers to die rather than to compromise or abandon the faith; the way the martyr faces death is the model for the penitent. For the relapsed to be reintegrated into the Church, he must expose himself voluntarily to ritual martyrdom. Penance is the affect of change, of rupture with self, past, and world. It is a way to show that you are able to renounce life and self, to show that you can face and accept death. Penitence of sin does not have as its target the establishing of an identity but, instead, serves to mark the refusal of the self, the breaking away from self· *ego non sum, ego*. This formula is at the heart of *publicatio sui*. It represents a break with one's past identity. These ostentatious gestures have the function of showing the truth of the state of being of the sinner. Self-revelation is at the same time self-destruction.

The difference between the Stoic and Christian traditions is that in the Stoic tradition examination of self, judgment, and discipline show the way to self-knowledge by superimposing truth about self through memory, that is, by memorizing the rules. In exomologesis, the penitent superimposes truth about self by violent rupture and dissociation. It is important to emphasize that this exomologesis is not verbal. It is symbolic, ritual, and theatrical.

VI

During the fourth century, we find a very different technology for the disclosure of the self, *exagoreusis*, much less famous than exomologesis but more important. This one is reminiscent of the verbalizing exercises in relation to a teacher-master of the pagan philosophical schools. We can see the transfer of several Stoic techniques of the self to Christian spiritual techniques.

At least one example of self-examination, proposed by Chrysostom, was exactly the same form and the same administrative character as that described by Seneca in *De Ira*. In the morning, we must take account of our expenses, and in the evening we must ask ourselves to render account of our conduct of ourselves, to examine what is to our advantage and what is prejudicial against us, with prayers instead of indiscreet words.[28] That is exactly the Senecan style of self-examination. It is also important to note that this self-examination is rare in Christian literature.

The well-developed and elaborated practice of the self-examination in monastic Christianity is different from the Senecan self-examination and very different from Chrysostom and from exomologesis. This new kind of practice must be understood from the viewpoint of two principles of Christian spirituality: obedience and contemplation.

In Seneca, the relationship of the disciple with the master was important, but it was instrumental and professional. It was founded on the capacity of the master to lead the disciple to a happy and autonomous life through good advice. The relationship would end when the disciple gained access to that life.

For a long series of reasons, obedience has a very different character in monastic life. It differs from the Greco-Roman type of relation to the master in the sense that obedience is not based just upon a need for self-improvement but must bear on all aspects of a monk's life. There is no element in the life of the monk which may escape from this fundamental and permanent relation of total obedience to the master. Cassian repeats an old principle from the oriental tradition: "Everything the monk does without permission of his master constitutes a theft."[29] Here, obedience is complete control of behavior by the master, not a final autonomous state. It is a sacrifice of the self, of the subject's own will. This is the new technology of the self.

The monk must have the permission of his director to do anything, even die. Everything he does without permission is stealing; there is not a single moment when the monk can be autonomous. Even when he becomes a director himself, he must retain the spirit of obedience. He must keep the spirit of obedience as a permanent sacrifice of the complete control of behavior by the master. The self must constitute itself through obedience.

The second feature of monastic life is that contemplation is considered the supreme good. It is the obligation of the monk to turn his thoughts continuously to that point which is God and to make sure that his heart is pure enough to see God. The goal is permanent contemplation of God.

This new technology of the self, which developed from obedience and contemplation in the monastery, presents some peculiar characteristics. Cassian gives a rather clear exposition of this technology of the self, a principle of self-examination which he borrowed from the Syrian and Egyptian monastic traditions.

This technology of self-examination of oriental origins, dominated by obedience and contemplation, is much more concerned with thought than with action. Seneca had placed his stress on action. With Cassian, the object is not past actions of the day—it is the present thoughts. Since the monk must continuously turn his thoughts toward God, he must scrutinize the actual course of this thought. This scrutiny thus has as its object the permanent discrimination between thoughts which lead toward God and those which don't. This continual concern with the present is different from the Senecan memorization of deeds and their correspondence with rules. It is what the Greeks referred to with a pejorative word: *logismoi*, "cogitations, reasoning, calculating thought." There is an etymology of *logismoi* in Cassian, but I do not know if it is sound: as *agitationes*. The spirit is *polukinetos*, "perpetually moving."[30] In Cassian, perpetual mobility of spirit is the spirit's weakness. It distracts one from contemplation of God.[31]

The scrutiny of conscience consists of trying to immobilize consciousness, to eliminate movements of the spirit which divert one from God. That means we must examine any thought that presents itself to consciousness to see the relation between act and thought, truth and reality, to see if there is anything in this thought which will move our spirit, provoke our desire, turn our spirit away from God. The scrutiny is based on the idea of a secret concupiscence.

There are three major types of self-examination: (1) self-examination with respect to thoughts in correspondence to reality (Cartesian); (2) self-examination with respect to the way our thoughts relate to rules (Senecan); (3) the examination of self with respect to the relation between the hidden thought and an inner impurity. At this moment begins the Christian hermeneutics of the self with its deciphering of inner thoughts. It implies that there is something hidden in ourselves and that we are always in a self-illusion that hides the secret.

In order to make this kind of scrutiny, Cassian says we must care for ourselves, to attest to our thoughts directly. He gives three analogies. First is the analogy of the mill.[32] Thoughts are like grains, and consciousness is the mill store: it is our role as the miller to sort out among the grains those which are bad and those which can be admitted to the mill store to give the good flour and good bread of our salvation.

Second, Cassian makes military analogies.[33] He uses an analogy of the officer who orders the good soldiers to march to the right, the bad to the left. We must act like officers who divide soldiers into two files, the good and the bad.

Third, he uses the analogy of a moneychanger.[34] Conscience is the moneychanger of the self. It must examine coins, their effigy, their metal, where they came from. It must weigh them to see if they have been ill used. As there is the image of the emperor on money, so must the image of God be on our thoughts. We must verify the quality of the thought: This effigy of God, is it real? What is its degree of purity? Is it mixed with desire or concupiscence? Thus, we find the same image as in Seneca, but with a different meaning.

Since we have as our role to be a permanent moneychanger of ourselves, how is it possible to make this discrimination and recognize if a thought is of good quality? How can this "discrimination" actively be done? There is only one way: to tell all thoughts to our director, to be obedient to our master in all things, to engage in the permanent verbalization of all our thoughts. In Cassian, self-examination is subordinated to obedience and the permanent verbalization of thoughts. Neither is true of Stoicism. By telling himself not only his thoughts but also the smallest movements of consciousness, his intentions, the monk stands in a hermeneutic relation not only to the master but to himself. This verbalization is the touchstone or the money of thought.

Why is confession able to assume this hermeneutic role? How can we be the hermeneuts of ourselves in speaking and transcribing all of our thoughts? Confession permits the master to know because of his greater experience and wisdom and therefore to give better advice. Even if the master, in his role as a discriminating power, does not say anything, the fact that the thought has been expressed will have an effect of discrimination.

Cassian gives an example of the monk who stole bread. At first he cannot tell. The difference between good and evil thoughts is that evil thoughts cannot be expressed without difficulty, for evil is hidden and unstated. Because evil thoughts cannot be expressed without difficulty and shame, the cosmological difference between light and dark, between verbalization and sin, secrecy and silence, between God and the Devil, may not emerge. Then the monk prostrates himself and confesses. Only when he confesses verbally does the Devil go out of him. The verbal expression is the crucial moment.[35] Confession is a mark of truth. This idea of the permanent verbal is only an ideal: it is never completely possible. But the price of the permanent verbal was to make everything that could not be expressed into a sin.

In conclusion, in the Christianity of the first centuries, there are two main forms of disclosing self, of showing the truth about oneself. The first is exomologesis, or a dramatic expression of the situation of the penitent as sinner which makes manifest his status as sinner. The second is what was called in the spiritual literature exagoreusis. This is an analytical and continual verbalization of thoughts carried on in the relation of complete obedience to someone else; this relation is modeled on the renunciation of one's own will and of one's own self.

There is a great difference between exomologesis and exagoreusis; yet we have to underscore the fact that there is one important element in common: you cannot disclose without renouncing. In exomologesis, the sinner must "kill" himself through ascetic macerations. Whether through martyrdom or through obedience to a master, disclosure of self is the renunciation of one's own self. In exagoreusis, on the other hand, you show that, in permanently verbalizing your thoughts and permanently obeying the master, you are renouncing your will and yourself. This practice continues from the beginning of Christianity to the seventeenth century. The inauguration of penance in the thirteenth century is an important step in its rise.

This theme of self-renunciation is very important. Throughout Christianity there is a correlation between disclosure of the self, dramatic or verbalized, and the renunciation of self. My hypothesis, from looking at these two techniques, is that it is the second one, verbalization, that becomes the more important. From the eighteenth century to the present, the techniques of verbalization have been reinserted in a different context by the so-called human sciences in order to use them without renunciation of the self but to constitute, positively, a new self. To use these techniques without renouncing oneself constitutes a decisive break.

NOTES

1 Plato, *Alcibiade*, trans. M. Croiset (Paris: Belles Lettres, 1925) [Plato, *Alcibiades*, trans. W. R. M. Lamb, in *Plato* (Cambridge, Mass.: Harvard, 1967), vol. 12].

2 Plato, *Apologie de Socrate*, trans. M. Croiset (Paris: Belles Lettres, 1925), p. 157 [*Socrates' Defense (Apology)*, trans. H. Tredennick, in *Plato: The Collected Dialogues*, eds. E. Hamilton and H. Cairns (Princeton: Princeton University, 1961), p. 16].

3 Gregory of Nyssa, *Traité de la virginité*, trans. M. Aubineau (Paris: Cerf, 1966), ch. 13, §3, pp. 411–17 [*Treatise on Virginity*, trans. V. W. Callahan, in *Saint Gregory of Nyssa: Ascetical Works* (Washington, D.C.: Catholic University of America Press, 1966), p. 46–48].

4 Epicurus, *Lettre à Ménécée*, in *Lettres et Maximes*, trans. M. Conche (Villiers-sur-Mer: Mégare, 1977), pp. 215–27 [*Letter to Menoeceus*, in *The Philosophy of Epicurus*, trans. and ed. G. K. Strodach (Evanston, Ill.: Northwestern University, 1963), pp. 122–35].

5   Philo of Alexandria, *La Vie contemplative*, trans. P. Miquel (Paris: Cerf, 1963), §36, p. 105 [*The Contemplative Life*, in *Philo of Alexandria*, trans. D. Winston (New York: Paulist Press, 1981), pp. 42–43].

6   Albinus, *Prologos*, §5 (cited in A. S. Festugière, *Etudes de philosophie grecque* [Paris: Vrin, 1971], p. 536).

7   Lucian, *Hermotine Works*, trans. K. Kiburn (Cambridge, Mass.: Harvard, 1959), vol. 4, p. 65.

8   Augustine composes his *Confessions* between 397 and 401. In *Oeuvres complètes*, trans. G. Bouissou and E. Tréhorel (Paris: Desclée de Brouwer, 1962), vols. 13–14 [Saint Augustine, *Confessions*, trans. R. S. Pine-Coffin (London: Penguin, 1961)].

9   Marcus Aurelius, *Lettres à Fronton*, in *Pensées*, trans. A. Cassan (Paris: Charpentier et Fasquelle, n.d.), let. 29, pp. 391–93 [*Letter to Fronto*, in *The Correspondence of Marcus Cornelius Fronto*, ed. and trans. C. R. Haines (New York: G. Putnam's Sons, 1919), pp. 181–83].

10 Plutarch, *Comment écouter*, in *Oeuvres Complètes*, trans. R. Klaerr, A. Philippon, and J. Sirinelli (Paris: Belles Lettres, 1989), vol. 1, 2d part, ch. 3, pp. 39–40 [*Concerning Hearing*, in *The Complete Works of Plutarch*, ed. W. Lloyd Bevan (New York: Thomas Y. Crowell, 1909), vol. 2, p. 393].

11 Philo of Alexandria, *La Vie contemplative*, p. 77 [*The Contemplative Life*, p. 47].

12 Seneca, *De Ira* (*De la colère*), trans. A. Bourgery, in *Dialogues* (Paris: Belles Lettres, 1922) [*On Anger*, trans. J. W. Basore, in *Seneca: Moral Essays* (New York: G. Putnam's Sons, 1928)]; *De la tranquillité de l'âme*, trans. R. Waltz, in *Dialogues*, vol. 4, bk. 6, §§1–8, pp. 84–86 [*De Tranquillitate Animi*, in *Seneca: Four Dialogues*, ed. and trans. C. D. N. Costa (Warminster, Eng.: Aris and Phillips Ltd., 1994), pp. 54–56].

13 Marcus Aurelius Antoninus, *Pensées*, trans. A. Trannoy (Paris: Belles Lettres, 1925), bk. 4, §3, pp. 27–29 [*To Himself*, in *The Communings with Himself of Marcus Aurelius Antoninus, Emperor of Rome*, trans. C. R. Haines (New York: G. Putnam's Sons, 1930), bk. 4, §3, pp. 67–71].

14 Seneca, *De Ira* (*De la colère*), bk. 3, §36, pp. 102–103 [*On Anger*, pp. 339–41].

15 Lucretius, *De la nature des choses*, trans. A. Ernout, 5th ed. (Paris: Belles Lettres, 1984–85) [*On the Nature of Things*, ed. and trans. A. M. Esolen (Baltimore: Johns Hopkins, 1995)].

16 Plutarch, *Le Démon de Socrate*, trans. J. Hani, in *Oeuvres Complètes*, vol. 8 (1980), §585a, p. 95 [*A Discourse Concerning the Demon of Socrates*, in *The Complete Works of Plutarch*, vol. 1, pp. 643–44].

17 Seneca, *Lettres à Lucilius*, trans. H. Noblot (Paris: Belles Lettres, 1945), let. 18, §§1–8, pp. 71–76 [*Ad Lucilium Epistulae Morales*, trans. R. M. Gummere (New York: G. Putnam's Sons, 1917), vol. 1, let. 18, §§1–8, pp. 116–21].

18 Epictetus, *Entretiens*, trans. J. Souilhé (Paris: Belles Lettres, 1963), bk. 3, ch. 12, §15, p. 45 [*The Discourses of Epictetus*, trans. and ed. G. Lond (New York: A. L. Burt, n.d.), bk. 3, ch. 12, pp. 252–54].

19 Epictetus, *Entretiens*, pp. 76–77 [*The Discourses of Epictetus*, bk. 3, ch. 22, pp. 283–85].

20 John Cassian, *Première conférence de l'abbé Moïse*, in *Conférences*, trans. Dom E. Pichery (Paris: Cerf, 1955), vol. 1, ch. 20, pp. 101–105 ["The Goal or Objective of the Monk," in *Conferences*, trans. C. Luibheid (New York: Paulist Press, 1985), pp. 54–57].

21 Epictetus, *Entretiens*, pp. 32–33 [*The Discourses of Epictetus*, bk. 3, ch. 8, pp. 243–44].

22 Artemidorus, *La Clef des songes: Onirocriticon*, trans. A. J. Festugière (Paris: Vrin, 1975) [*The Interpretation of Dreams*, trans. R. J. White (Park Ridge, N.J.: Noyes, 1975)].

23 Synesius of Cyrene, *Sur les rêves*, in *Oeuvres*, trans. H. Druon (Paris: Hachette, 1878), pp. 346-76 [*Concerning Dreams*, in *The Essays and Hymns of Synesius of Cyrene*, trans. and ed. A. Fitzgerald (Oxford: Oxford University, 1930), vol. 2, pp. 326-59].

24 Aelius Aristides, *Discours sacrés*, trans. A. J. Festugière (Paris: Macula, 1986) [see C. A. Behr, *Aelius Aristides and the Sacred Tales* (Amsterdam: A. M. Hakkert, 1968)].

25 Tertullian, *Le Pénitence*, trans. C. Munier (Paris: Cerf, 1984), ch. 9, p. 181 [*On Penitence*, in Tertullian: *Treatises on Penance*, trans. W. P. Le Saint (Westminster, Md.: Newman, 1959), pp. 28-33].

26 Saint Jerome *Corréspondance*, trans. J. Labourt (Paris: Belles Lettres, 1954), vol. 4, let. 78, pp. 42-44.

27 Cyprian of Carthage, *De ceux qui ont failli*, in *Textes*, trans. D. Gorce (Namur: Soleil levant, 1958), pp. 89-92 [*The Lapsed*, in *Saint Cyprian: Treatises*, trans. and ed. R. J. Deferrari (New York: Fathers of the Church, Inc., 1961), pp. 81-86].

28 John Chrysostom, *Homélie*: "Qu'il est dangereux pour l'orateur et l'auditeur de parler pour plaire, qu'il est de la plus grande utilité comme de la plus rigoureuse justice d'accuser ses pechés" [Just as it is dangerous for the speaker and auditor to speak in order to please, so it is of the greatest utility and the most rigorous justice to denounce his sins], in *Oeuvres Complètes*, trans. M. Jeannin (Nancy: Thomas et Pieron, 1864), vol. 3, p. 401.

29 Cassian, *Institutions cénobitiques*, trans. J. A. Guy (Paris: Cerf, 1965), bk. 4, chs. 10-12, pp. 133-37; chs. 23-32, pp. 153-71.

30 Cassian, *Première Conférences de l'abbé Serenus*, "De la mobilité de l'âme et des esprits du mal," in *Conférences*, trans. Dom E. Pichery (Paris: Cerf, 1955), p. 248.

31 Cassian, *Première Conférence de l'abbé Nesterus*, in *Conférences*, vol. 2 (1958), pp. 199-201.

32 Cassian, *Première Conférence de l'abbé Moïse*, in *Conférences*, p. 99 ["The Goal or Objective of the Monk," in *Conferences*, p. 52].

33 Cassian, *Première Conférence de l'abbé Serenus*, in *Conférences*, pp. 249-52.

34 Cassian, *Première Conférence de l'abbé Moïse*, in *Conférences*, pp. 101-107 ["The Goal or Objective of the Monk," in *Conferences*, pp. 54-57].

35 Cassian, *Deuxième Conférence de l'abbé Moïse*, in *Conférences*, pp. 121-23 ["On Discernment," in *Conferences*, p. 52].

ON THE GENEALOGY OF ETHICS:
AN OVERVIEW OF WORK IN PROGRESS*

HISTORY OF THE PROJECT

Q. The first volume of *The History of Sexuality* was published in 1976, and none has appeared since. Do you still think that understanding sexuality is central for understanding who we are?

M.F. I must confess that I am much more interested in problems about techniques of the self and things like that than sex...sex is boring.

Q. It sounds like the Greeks were not too interested either.

M.F. No, they were not much interested in sex. It was not a great issue. Compare, for instance, what they say about the place of food and diet. I think it is very, very interesting to see the move, the very slow move, from the privileging of food, which was overwhelming in Greece, to interest in sex. Food was still much more important during the early Christian days than sex. For instance, in the rules for monks, the problem was food, food, food. Then you can see a very slow shift during the Middle Ages, when they were in a kind of equilibrium...and after the seventeenth century it was sex.

Q. Yet Volume Two of *The History of Sexuality*, *L'Usage des plaisirs* [*The Uses of Pleasure*], is concerned almost exclusively with, not to put too fine a point on it, sex.

---

*The following is the result of a series of working sessions with Michel Foucault conducted by Paul Rabinow and Hubert Dreyfus at Berkeley in April 1983. Although we have retained the interview form, the material was jointly reedited. Foucault generously allowed the interviewers to publish these preliminary formulations, which were the product of oral interviews and free conversations in English and therefore lack the precision and supporting scholarship found in Foucault's written texts.

M.F. Yes. One of the numerous reasons I had so much trouble with that book was that I first wrote a book about sex, which I put aside. Then I wrote a book about the self and the techniques of the self; sex disappeared, and for the third time I was obliged to rewrite a book in which I tried to keep the equilibrium between one and the other.

You see, what I wanted to do in Volume Two of *The History of Sexuality* was to show that you have nearly the same restrictive, the same prohibitive code in the fourth century B.C. and in the moralists and doctors at the beginning of the empire. But I think that the way they integrate those prohibitions in relation to oneself is completely different. I don't think one can find any normalization in, for instance, the Stoic ethics. The reason is, I think, that the principal aim, the principal target of this kind of ethics, was an aesthetic one. First, this kind of ethics was only a problem of personal choice. Second, it was reserved for a few people in the population; it was not a question of giving a pattern of behavior for everybody. It was a personal choice for a small elite. The reason for making this choice was the will to live a beautiful life, and to leave to others memories of a beautiful existence. I don't think that we can say that this kind of ethics was an attempt to normalize the population.

The continuity of the themes of this ethics is something very striking, but I think that behind, below this continuity, there were some changes, which I have tried to acknowledge.

Q. So the equilibrium in your work has shifted from sex to techniques of the self?

M.F. I wondered what the technology of the self before Christianity was, or where the Christian technology of the self came from, and what kind of sexual ethics was characteristic of the ancient culture. And then I was obliged after I finished *Les Aveux de la chair* ["Confessions of the Flesh," as yet unpublished], the book about Christianity, to reexamine what I said in the introduction to *L'Usage des plaisirs* about the supposed pagan ethics, because what I had said about pagan ethics were only clichés borrowed from secondary texts. And then I discovered, first, that this pagan ethics was not at all liberal, tolerant, and so on, as it was supposed to be; second, that most of the themes of Christian austerity were very clearly present nearly from the beginning, but that also in pagan culture the main problem was not the rules for austerity but much more the techniques of the self.

Reading Seneca, Plutarch, and all those people, I discovered that there were a very great number of problems or themes about the self, the ethics of the self, the technology of the self, and I had the idea of writing a book composed of a set of separate studies, papers about such and such aspects of ancient, pagan technologies of the self.

Q. What is the title?

M.F. *Le Souci de soi* [*The Care of the Self*]. So in the series about sexuality: the first one is *L'Usage des plaisirs*, and in this book there is a chapter about the technology of the self, since I think it's not possible to understand clearly what Greek sexual ethics was without relating it to this technology of the self. Then, a second volume in the same sex series, *Les Aveux de la chair*, deals with Christian technologies of the self. And then, *Le Souci de soi*, a book separate from the sex series, is composed of different papers about the self—for instance, a commentary on Plato's *Alcibiades* in which you find the first elaboration of the notion of *epimeleia heautou*, "care of the self," about the role of reading and writing in constituting the self, maybe the problem of the medical experience of the self, and so on....

Q. And what will come next? Will there be more on the Christians when you finish these three?

M.F. Well, I am going to take care of myself!... I have more than a draft of a book about sexual ethics in the sixteenth century, in which also the problem of the techniques of the self, self-examination, the cure of souls, is very important, both in the Protestant and Catholic churches.

What strikes me is that in Greek ethics people were concerned with their moral conduct, their ethics, their relations to themselves and to others much more than with religious problems. For instance, what happens to us after death? What are the gods? Do they intervene or not?—these are very, very unimportant problems for them, and they are not directly related to ethics, to conduct. The second thing is that ethics was not related to any social—or at least to any legal—institutional system. For instance, the laws against sexual misbehavior were very few and not very compelling. The third thing is that what they were worried about, their theme was to constitute a kind of ethics which was an aesthetics of existence.

Well, I wonder if our problem nowadays is not, in a way, similar to this one, since most of us no longer believe that ethics is founded in religion, nor do we want a legal system to intervene in our moral, personal, private life. Recent liberation movements suffer from the fact that they cannot find any principle on which to base the elaboration of a new ethics. They need an ethics, but they cannot find any other ethics than an ethics founded on so-called scientific knowledge of what the self is, what desire is, what the unconscious is, and so on. I am struck by this similarity of problems.

Q. Do you think that the Greeks offer an attractive and plausible alternative?

M.F. No! I am not looking for an alternative; you can't find the solution of a problem in the solution of another problem raised at another moment by other people. You see, what I want to do is not the history of solutions—and that's the reason why I don't accept the word *alternative*. I would like to do the genealogy of problems, of *problématiques*. My point is not that everything is bad, but that everything is dangerous, which is not exactly the same as bad. If everything is dangerous, then we always have something to do. So my position leads not to apathy but to a hyper- and pessimistic activism.

I think that the ethico-political choice we have to make every day is to determine which is the main danger. Take as an example Robert Castel's analysis of the history of the antipsychiatry movement [*La Gestion des risques*]. I agree completely with what Castel says, but that does not mean, as some people suppose, that the mental hospitals were better than antipsychiatry; that does not mean that we were not right to criticize those mental hospitals. I think it was good to do that, because *they* were the danger. And now it's quite clear that the danger has changed. For instance, in Italy they have closed all the mental hospitals, and there are more free clinics, and so on—and they have new problems.

Q. Isn't it logical, given these concerns, that you should be writing a genealogy of bio-power?

M.F. I have no time for that now, but it could be done. In fact, I have to do it.

WHY THE ANCIENT WORLD WAS NOT A GOLDEN AGE, BUT WHAT WE CAN LEARN FROM IT ANYWAY

Q. So Greek life may not have been altogether perfect; still, it seems an attractive alternative to endless Christian self-analysis.

M.F. The Greek ethics were linked to a purely virile society with slaves, in which the women were underdogs whose pleasure had no importance, whose sexual life had only to be oriented toward, determined by, their status as wives, and so on.

Q. So the women were dominated, but surely homosexual love was better than now?

M.F. It might look that way. Since there is an important and large literature about loving boys in Greek culture, some historians say, "Well, that's the proof that they loved boys." But I say that proves that loving boys was a problem. Because if there were no problem, they would speak of this kind of love in the same terms as love between men and women. The problem was that they couldn't accept that a young boy who was supposed to become a free citizen could be dominated and used as an object for someone's pleasure. A woman, a slave, could be passive: such was their nature, their status. All this reflection, philosophizing about the love of boys—with always the same conclusion: please, don't treat a boy as a woman—is proof that they could not integrate this real practice in the framework of their social selves.

You can see through a reading of Plutarch how they couldn't even imagine reciprocity of pleasure between a boy and a man. If Plutarch finds problems in loving boys, it is not at all in the sense that loving boys was antinatural or something like that. He says, "It's not possible that there could be any reciprocity in the physical relations between a boy and a man."

Q. There seems to be an aspect of Greek culture that we are told about in Aristotle, that you don't talk about, but that seems very important—friendship. In classical literature, friendship is the locus of mutual recognition. It's not traditionally seen as the highest virtue, but both in Aristotle and in Cicero, you could read it as really being the highest virtue because it's selfless and enduring, it's not easily bought, it doesn't deny the utility and pleasure of the world, but yet it seeks something more.

M.F. But don't forget *L'Usage des plaisirs* is a book about sexual ethics; it's not a book about love, or about friendship, or about reciprocity. And it's very significant that when Plato tries to integrate love for boys and friendship, he is obliged to put aside sexual relations. Friendship is reciprocal, and sexual relations are not reciprocal: in sexual relations, you can penetrate or you are penetrated. I agree completely with what you say about friendship, but I think it confirms what I say about Greek sexual ethics: if you have friendship, it is difficult to have sexual relations. If you look at Plato, reciprocity is very important in a friendship, but you can't find it on the physical level; one of the reasons why they needed a philosophical elaboration in order to justify this kind of love was that they could not accept a physical reciprocity. You find in Xenophon, in the *Banquet*, Socrates saying that between a man and a boy it is obvious that the boy is only the spectator of the man's pleasure. What they say about this beautiful love of boys implies that the pleasure of the boy was not to be taken into account; moreover, that it was dishonorable for the boy to feel any kind of physical pleasure in a relation with a man.

What I want to ask is: Are we able to have an ethics of acts and their pleasures which would be able to take into account the pleasure of the other? Is the pleasure of the other something that can be integrated in our pleasure, without reference either to law, to marriage, to I don't know what?

Q. It looks like nonreciprocity was a problem for the Greeks all right, but it seems to be the kind of problem that one could straighten out. Why does sex have to be virile? Why couldn't women's pleasure and boys' pleasure be taken account of without any big change to the general framework? Or is it that it's not just a little problem, because if you try to bring in the pleasure of the other, the whole hierarchical, ethical system would break down?

M.F. That's right. The Greek ethics of pleasure is linked to a virile society, to dissymmetry, exclusion of the other, an obsession with penetration, and a kind of threat of being dispossessed of your own energy, and so on. All that is quite disgusting!

Q. OK, granted that sexual relations were both nonreciprocal and a cause of worry for the Greeks, at least pleasure itself seems unproblematic for them.

M.F. Well, in *L'Usage des plaisirs* I try to show, for instance, that there is a growing tension between pleasure and health. When you take the physicians and all the concern with diet, you see first that the main themes are very similar during several centuries. But the idea that sex has its dangers is much stronger in the second century A.D. than in the fourth century B.C. I think that you can show that, for Hippocrates, the sexual act was already dangerous, so you had to be very careful with it and not have sex all the time, only in certain seasons and so on. But in the first and second centuries it seems that, for a physician, the sexual act is much closer to *pathos*. And I think the main shift is this one: that in the fourth century B.C., the sexual act was an activity, and for the Christians it is a passivity. You have a very interesting analysis by Augustine which is, I think, quite typical concerning the problem of erection. The erection was, for the Greek of the fourth century, the sign of activity, the main activity. But since, for Augustine and the Christians, the erection is not something voluntary, it is a sign of a passivity—it is a punishment for the first sin.

Q. So the Greeks were more concerned with health than with pleasure?

M.F. Yes, about what the Greeks had to eat in order to be in good health, we have thousands of pages. And there are comparatively few things about what to do when you have sex with someone. Concerning food, it was the relation between the climate, the seasons, the humidity or dryness of the air and the dryness of the food, and so on. There are very few things about the way they had to cook it; much more about these qualities. It's not a cooking art; it's a matter of choosing.

Q. So, despite the German Hellenists, classical Greece was not a golden age. Yet surely we can learn something from it?

M.F. I think there is no exemplary value in a period that is not our period...it is not anything to get back to. But we do have an example of an ethical experience which implied a very strong connection between pleasure and desire. If we compare that to our experience now, where everybody—the philosopher or the psychoanalyst—explains that what is important is desire, and pleasure is nothing at all, we can wonder whether this disconnection wasn't a historical event, one that was not at all necessary, not linked to human nature, or to any anthropological necessity.

Q. But you already illustrated that in *The History of Sexuality* by contrasting our science of sexuality with the oriental *ars erotica*.

M.F. One of the numerous points where I was wrong in that book was what I said about this *ars erotica*. I should have opposed our science of sex to a contrasting practice in our own culture. The Greeks and Romans did not have any *ars erotica* to be compared with the Chinese *ars erotica* (or at least it was not something very important in their culture). They had a *tekhnē tou biou* in which the economy of pleasure played a very large role. In this "art of life," the notion of exercising a perfect mastery over oneself soon became the main issue. And the Christian hermeneutics of the self constituted a new elaboration of this *tekhnē*.

Q. But, after all you have told us about nonreciprocity and obsession with health, what can we learn from this third possibility?

M.F. What I want to show is that the general Greek problem was not the *tekhnē* of the self, it was the *tekhnē* of life, the *tekhnē tou biou*, how to live. It's quite clear from Socrates to Seneca or Pliny, for instance, that they didn't worry about the afterlife, what happened after death, or whether God exists or not. That was not really a great problem for them; the problem was: Which *tekhnē* do I have to use in order to live well as I ought to live? And I think that one of the main evolutions in ancient culture has been that this *tekhnē tou biou* became more and more a *tekhnē* of the self. A Greek citizen of the fifth or fourth century would have felt that his *tekhnē* for life was to take care of the city, of his companions. But for Seneca, for instance, the problem is to take care of himself.

With Plato's *Alcibiades*, it's very clear: you have to take care of yourself because you have to rule the city. But taking care of yourself for its own sake starts with the Epicureans—it becomes something very general with Seneca, Pliny, and so on: everybody has to take care of himself. Greek ethics is centered on a problem of personal choice, of the aesthetics of existence.

The idea of the *bios* as a material for an aesthetic piece of art is something that fascinates me. The idea also that ethics can be a very strong structure of existence, without any relation with the juridical per se, with an authoritarian system, with a disciplinary structure. All that is very interesting.

Q. How, then, did the Greeks deal with deviance?

M.F. The great difference in sexual ethics for the Greeks was not between people who prefer women or boys or have sex in this way or another, but was a question of quantity and of activity and passivity. Are you a slave of your own desires or their master?

Q. What about someone who had sex so much he damaged his health?

M.F. That's hubris, that's excess. The problem is not one of deviancy but of excess or moderation.

Q. What did they do with these people?

M.F. They were considered ugly; they had a bad reputation.

Q. They didn't try to cure or reform such people?

M.F. There were exercises in order to make one master of oneself. For Epictetus, you had to be able to look at a beautiful girl or a beautiful boy without having any desire for her or him. You have to master yourself completely.

Sexual austerity in Greek society was a trend or movement, a philosophical movement coming from very cultivated people in order to give to their life much more intensity, much more beauty. In a way, it's the same in the twentieth century when people, in order to get a more beautiful life, tried to get rid of all the sexual repression of their society, of their childhood. Gide in Greece would have been an austere philosopher.

Q. In the name of a beautiful life they were austere, and now in the name of psychological science we seek self-fulfillment.

M.F. Exactly. My idea is that it's not at all necessary to relate ethical problems to scientific knowledge. Among the cultural inventions of mankind there is a treasury of devices, techniques, ideas, procedures, and so on, that cannot exactly be reactivated but at least constitute, or help to constitute, a certain point of view which can be very useful as a tool for analyzing what's going on now—and to change it.

We don't have to choose between our world and the Greek world. But since we can see very well that some of the main principles of our ethics have been related at a certain moment to an aesthetics of existence, I think that this kind of historical analysis can be useful. For centuries we have been convinced that between our ethics, our personal ethics, our everyday life, and the great political and social and economic structures, there were analytical relations, and that we couldn't change anything, for instance, in our sex life or our family life, without ruining our economy, our democracy, and so on. I think we have to get rid of this idea of an analytical or necessary link between ethics and other social or economic or political structures.

Q. So what kind of ethics can we build now, when we know that between ethics and other structures there are only historical coagulations and not a necessary relation?

M.F. What strikes me is the fact that, in our society, art has become something that is related only to objects and not to individuals or to life. That art is something which is specialized or done by experts who are artists. But couldn't everyone's life become a work of art? Why should the lamp or the house be an art object but not our life?

Q. Of course, that kind of project is very common in places like Berkeley where people think that everything from the way they eat breakfast, to the way they have sex, to the way they spend their day, should itself be perfected.

M.F. But I am afraid in most of those cases, most of the people think if they do what they do, if they live as they live, the reason is that they know the truth about desire, life, nature, body, and so on.

Q. But if one is to create oneself without recourse to knowledge or universal rules, how does your view differ from Sartrean existentialism?

M.F. I think that from the theoretical point of view, Sartre avoids the idea of the self as something that is given to us, but through the moral notion of authenticity, he turns back to the idea that we have to be ourselves—to be truly our true self. I think that the only acceptable practical consequence of what Sartre has said is to link his theoretical insight to the practice of creativity—and not that of authenticity. From the idea that the self is not given to us, I think that there is only one practical consequence: we have to create ourselves as a work of art. In his analyses of Baudelaire, Flaubert, and so on, it is interesting to see that Sartre refers the work of creation to a certain relation to oneself— the author to himself—which has the form of authenticity or inauthenticity. I would like to say exactly the contrary: we should not have to refer the creative activity of somebody to the kind of relation he has to himself, but should relate the kind of relation one has to oneself to a creative activity.

Q. That sounds like Nietzsche's observation in *The Gay Science* that one should create one's life by giving style to it through long practice and daily work [no. 290].

M.F. Yes. My view is much closer to Nietzsche's than to Sartre's.

THE STRUCTURE OF
GENEALOGICAL INTERPRETATION

Q. How do the next two books after *The History of Sexuality*, Volume One, *L'Usage des plaisirs* and *Les Aveux de la chair*, fit into the structure of your genealogy project?

M.F. Three domains of genealogy are possible. First, a historical ontology of ourselves in relation to truth through which we constitute ourselves as subjects of knowledge; second, a historical ontology of ourselves in relation to a field of power through which we constitute ourselves as subjects acting on others; third, a historical ontology in relation to ethics through which we constitute ourselves as moral agents.

So, three axes are possible for genealogy. All three were present, albeit in a somewhat confused fashion, in *Madness and Civilization*. The truth axis was studied in *The Birth of the Clinic* and *The Order of*

Things. The power axis was studied in *Discipline and Punish*, and the ethical axis in *The History of Sexuality.*

The general framework of the book about sex is a history of morals. I think, in general, we have to distinguish, where the history of morals is concerned, acts and moral code. The acts [*conduites*] are the real behavior of people in relation to the moral code [*prescriptions*] imposed on them. I think we have to distinguish between the code that determines which acts are permitted or forbidden and the code that determines the positive or negative value of the different possible behaviors—you're not allowed to have sex with anyone but your wife, that's an element of the code. And there is another side to the moral prescriptions, which most of the time is not isolated as such but is, I think, very important: the kind of relationship you ought to have with yourself, *rapport à soi*, which I call ethics, and which determines how the individual is supposed to constitute himself as a moral subject of his own actions.

This relationship to oneself has four major aspects. The first aspect answers the question: Which is the aspect or the part of myself or my behavior which is concerned with moral conduct? For instance, you can say, in general, that in our society the main field of morality, the part of ourselves which is most relevant for morality, is our feelings. (You can have a girl in the street or anywhere, if you have very good feelings toward your wife.) Well, it's quite clear that from the Kantian point of view, intention is much more important than feelings. And from the Christian point of view, it is desire—well, we could discuss that, because in the Middle Ages it was not the same as the seventeenth century....

Q. But, roughly, for the Christians it was desire, for Kant it was intentions, and for us now it's feelings?

M.F. Well, you can say something like that. It's not always the same part of ourselves, or of our behavior, which is relevant for ethical judgment. That's the aspect I call the ethical substance [*substance éthique*].

Q. The ethical substance is like the material that's going to be worked over by ethics?

M.F. Yes, that's it. And, for instance, when I describe the *aphrodisia* in *L'Usage des plaisirs*, it is to show that the part of sexual behavior which is relevant in Greek ethics is something different from concupiscence, from flesh. For the Greeks, the ethical substance was acts linked to pleasure and desire in their unity. And it is very different from flesh, Christian flesh. Sexuality is a third kind of ethical substance.

Q. What is the difference ethically between flesh and sexuality?

M.F. I cannot answer because all that can only be analyzed through a precise inquiry. Before I studied Greek or Greco-Roman ethics, I couldn't answer the question: What exactly is the ethical substance of Greco-Roman ethics? Now I think that I know, through the analysis of what they mean by *aphrodisia*, what the Greek ethical substance was.

For the Greeks, when a philosopher was in love with a boy, but did not touch him, his behavior was valued. The problem was: Does he touch the boy or not? That's the ethical substance: the act linked with pleasure and desire. For Augustine, it's very clear that when he remembers his relationship to his young friend when he was eighteen years old, what bothers him is what exactly was the kind of desire he had for him. So you see that the ethical substance has changed.

The second aspect is what I call the mode of subjectivation [*mode d'assujettissement*], that is, the way in which people are invited or incited to recognize their moral obligations. Is it, for instance, divine law that has been revealed in a text? Is it natural law, a cosmological order, in each case the same for every living being? Is it a rational rule? Is it the attempt to give your existence the most beautiful form possible?

Q. When you say "rational," do you mean scientific?

M.F. No, Kantian, universal. You can see, for instance, in the Stoics, how they move slowly from an idea of an aesthetics of existence to the idea that we must do such and such things because we are rational beings—as members of the human community, we must do them. For example, you find in Isocrates a very interesting discourse, which is supposed to be held with Nicocles, who was the ruler of Cyprus. There he explains why he has always been faithful to his wife: "Because I am the king, and because as somebody who commands others, who rules others, I have to show that I am able to rule myself." And you can see that this rule of faithfulness has nothing to do with the universal and Stoic formulation: "I have to be faithful to my wife because I am a human and rational being." In the former case, it is because I am the king! And you can see that the way the same rule is accepted by Nicocles and by a Stoic is quite different. And that's what I call the *mode d'assujettissement*, the second aspect of ethics.

Q. When the king says, "because I am the king," is that a form of the beautiful life?

M.F. Both aesthetic and political, which were directly linked. Because if I want people to accept me as a king, I must have a kind of glory which will survive me, and this glory cannot be dissociated from aesthetic value. So political power, glory, immortality, and beauty are all linked at a certain moment. That's the *mode d'assujettissement*, the second aspect of ethics.

The third one is: What are the means by which we can change ourselves in order to become ethical subjects?

Q. How we work on this ethical substance?

M.F. Yes. What are we to do, either to moderate our acts, or to decipher what we are, or to eradicate our desires, or to use our sexual desire in order to obtain certain aims such as having children, and so on—all this elaboration of ourselves in order to behave ethically? In order to be faithful to your wife, you can do different things to the self. That's the third aspect, which I call the self-forming activity [*pratique de soi*] or *l'ascétisme—asceticism* in a very broad sense.

The fourth aspect is: Which is the kind of being to which we aspire when we behave in a moral way? For instance, shall we become pure, or immortal, or free, or masters of ourselves, and so on? So that's what I call the telos [*téléologie*]. In what we call morals, there is the effective behavior of people, there are the codes, and there is this kind of relationship to oneself with the above four aspects.

Q. Which are all independent?

M.F. There are both relationships between them and a certain kind of independence. For instance, you can very well understand why, if the goal is an absolute purity of being, then the type of techniques of self-forming activity, the techniques of asceticism you are to use, are not exactly the same as when you try to be master of your own behavior. In the first place, you are inclined to a kind of deciphering technique, or purification technique.

Now, if we apply this general framework to pagan or early Christian ethics, what would we say? First, if we take the code—what is forbidden and what is not—you see that, at least in the philosophical code of behavior, you find three main prohibitions or prescriptions. One about the body—that is, you have to be very careful with your sexual behavior since it is very costly, so do it as infrequently as possible. The second is: When you are married, please don't have sex with anybody else but your wife. And with boys—please don't touch boys. And you find this in Plato, in Isocrates, in Hippocrates, in late Stoics, and so on—and you find it also in Christianity, and even in our own society. So I think you can say that the codes in themselves didn't change a great deal. Some of those interdictions changed; some of the prohibitions are much stricter and much more rigorous in Christianity than in the Greek period. But the themes are the same. So I think that the great changes that occurred between Greek society, Greek ethics, Greek morality, and how the Christians viewed themselves are not in the code but in what I call the "ethics," which is the relation to oneself. In *L'Usage des plaisirs*, I analyze those four aspects of the relation to oneself, through the three austerity themes of the code: health, wives or women, and boys.

Q. Would it be fair to say that you're not doing the genealogy of morals because you think the moral codes are relatively stable, but that what you're doing is a genealogy of ethics?

M.F. Yes, I'm writing a genealogy of ethics. The genealogy of the subject as a subject of ethical actions, or the genealogy of desire as an ethical problem. So, if we take ethics in classical Greek philosophy or medicine, what is the ethical substance? It is the *aphrodisia*, which are at the same time acts, desire, and pleasure. What is the *mode d'assujettissement*? It is that we have to build our existence as a beautiful existence; it is an aesthetic mode. You see, what I tried to show is that nobody is obliged in classical ethics to behave in such a way as to be truthful to their wives, to not touch boys, and so on. But if they want to have a beautiful existence, if they want to have a good reputation, if they want to be able to rule others, they have to do this. So they accept those obligations in a conscious way for the beauty or glory of existence. The choice, the aesthetic choice or the political choice, for which they decide to accept this kind of existence—that's the *mode d'assujettissement*. It's a choice, it's a personal choice.

In late Stoicism, when they start saying, "Well, you are obliged to do that because you are a human being," something changes. It's not a problem of choice; you have to do it because you are a rational being. The *mode d'assujettissement* is changing.

In Christianity, what is very interesting is that the sexual rules for behavior were, of course, justified through religion. The institutions by which they were imposed were religious institutions. But the form of the obligation was a legal form. There was a kind of the internal juridification of religious law inside Christianity. For instance, all the casuistic practice was typically a juridical practice.

Q. After the Enlightenment, though, when the religious drops out, is the juridical what's left?

M.F. Yes, after the eighteenth century, the religious framework of those rules disappears in part, and then between a medical or scientific approach and a juridical framework there was competition, with no resolution.

Q. Could you sum this up?

M.F. Well, the *substance éthique* for the Greeks was the *aphrodisia*; the *mode d'assujettissement* was a politico-aesthetic choice; the *form d'ascèse* was the *tekhnē* that was used—and there we find, for example, the *tekhnē* about the body, or economics as the rules by which you define your role as husband, or the erotic as a kind of asceticism toward oneself in loving boys, and so on—and the *téléologie* was the mastery of oneself. So that's the situation I describe in the two first parts of *L'Usage des plaisirs*.

Then there is a shift within this ethics. The reason for the shift is the change of the role of men within society, both in their homes toward their wives and also in the political field, since the city disappears. So, for those reasons, the way they can recognize themselves as subjects of political, economic behavior changes. We can say roughly that along with these sociological changes something is changing also in classical ethics—that is, in the elaboration of the relationship to oneself. But I think that the change doesn't affect the ethical substance: it is still *aphrodisia*. There are some changes in the *mode d'assujettissement*, for instance, when the Stoics recognize themselves as universal beings. And there are also very important changes in the *asceticism*, the kind of techniques you use in order to recognize, to constitute yourself as a subject of ethics. And also a change in the goal. I think that the difference is that in the classical perspective, to be master of oneself meant, first, taking into account only oneself and not the other, because to be master of oneself meant that you were able to rule others. So the mastery of oneself was directly related to a dissymmetrical relation to others. You should be master of yourself in a sense of activity, dissymmetry, and nonreciprocity.

Later on, due to the changes in marriage, society, and so on, mastery of oneself is something that is not primarily related to power over others: you have to be master of yourself not only in order to rule others, as it was in the case of Alcibiades or Nicocles, but you have to be master of yourself because you are a rational being. And in this mastery of yourself, you are related to other people, who are also masters of themselves. And this new kind of relation to the other is much less nonreciprocal than before.

So those are the changes, and I try to show those changes in the three last chapters, the fourth part of *L'Usage des plaisirs*. I take the same themes—the body, wives or women, and boys—and I show that these same three austerity themes are linked to a partially new ethics. I say "partially" because some of the parts of this ethics do not change: for instance, the *aphrodisia*. On the other hand, others do: for instance, the techniques. According to Xenophon, the way to become a good husband is to know exactly what your role is inside your home or outside, what kind of authority you have to exercise on your wife, what are your expectations of your wife's behavior, and so on. All this calculation gives you the rules for behavior, and defines the way you have to be toward yourself. But for Epictetus, or for Seneca, for instance, in order to be really master of yourself, you don't have to know what your role in society or in your home is, but you do have to do some exercises like depriving yourself of eating for two or three days, in order to be sure that you can control yourself. If one day you are in prison, you won't suffer from being deprived of food, and so on. And you have to do that for all the pleasures—that's a kind of asceticism you can't find in Plato or Socrates or Aristotle.

There is no complete and identical relation between the techniques and the *telē*. You can find the same techniques in different *telē*, but there are privileged relations, some privileged techniques related to each telos.

In the Christian book—I mean the book about Christianity!—I try to show that all this ethics has changed. Because the telos has changed: the telos is immortality, purity, and so on. The asceticism has changed, because now self-examination takes the form of self-deciphering. The *mode d'assujettissement* is now divine law. And I think that even the ethical substance has changed, because it is not *aphrodisia*, but desire, concupiscence, flesh, and so on.

Q. It seems, then, that we have a grid of intelligibility for desire as an ethical problem?

M.F. Yes, we now have this scheme. If, by sexual behavior, we understand the three poles—acts, pleasure, and desire—we have the Greek "formula," which is the same at the first and at the second stage. In this Greek formula what is underscored is "acts," with pleasure and desire as subsidiary: <u>acte</u>—*plaisir*—[*désir*]. I have put desire in brackets because I think that in the Stoic ethics you start a kind of elision of desire; desire begins to be condemned.

The Chinese "formula" would be *plaisir—désir—[acte]*. Acts are put aside because you have to restrain acts in order to get the maximum duration and intensity of pleasure.

The Christian "formula" puts an accent on desire and tries to eradicate it. Acts have to become something neutral; you have to act only to produce children or to fulfill your conjugal duty. And pleasure is both practically and theoretically excluded: *[désir]—acte—[plaisir]*. Desire is practically excluded—you have to eradicate your desire—but theoretically very important.

And I could say that the modern "formula" is desire, which is theoretically underlined and practically accepted, since you have to liberate your own desire. Acts are not very important, and pleasure—nobody knows what it is!

FROM THE CLASSICAL
SELF TO THE MODERN SUBJECT

Q. What is the care of the self which you have decided to treat separately in *Le Souci de soi*?

M.F. What interests me in the Hellenistic culture, in the Greco-Roman culture, starting from about the third century B.C. and continuing until the second or third century after Christ, is a precept for which the Greeks had a specific word, *epimeleia heautou*, which means taking care of one's self. It does not mean simply being interested in oneself, nor does it mean having a certain tendency to self-attachment or self-fascination. *Epimeleia heautou* is a very powerful word in Greek which means "working on" or "being concerned with" something. For example, Xenophon used *epimeleia heautou* to describe agricultural management. The responsibility of a monarch for his fellow citizens was also *epimeleia heautou*. That which a doctor does in the course of caring for a patient is *epimeleia heautou*. It is therefore a very powerful word; it describes a sort of work, an activity; it implies attention, knowledge, technique.

Q. But isn't the application of knowledge and technology to the self a modern invention?

M.F. Knowledge played a different role in the classical care of the self. There are very interesting things to analyze about relations between scientific knowledge and the *epimeleia heautou*. The one who cared for himself had to choose among all the things that you can know through scientific knowledge only those kinds of things which were relative to him and important to life.

Q. So theoretical understanding, scientific understanding, was secondary to, and guided by, ethical and aesthetic concerns?

M.F. Their problem and their discussion concerned what limited sorts of knowledge were useful for *epimeleia*. For instance, for the Epicureans, the general knowledge of what is the world, of what is the necessity of the world, the relation between world, necessity, and the gods—all that was very important for the care of the self. Because it was first a matter of meditation: if you were able exactly to understand the necessity of the world, then you could master passions in a much better way, and so on. So, for the Epicureans, there was a kind of adequation between all possible knowledge and the care of the self. The reason that one had to become familiar with physics or cosmology was that one had to take care of the self. For the Stoics, the true self is defined only by what I can be master of.

Q. So knowledge is subordinated to the practical end of mastery?

M.F. Epictetus is very clear on that. He gives as an exercise to walk every morning in the streets looking, watching. And if you meet a consular figure you say, "Is the consul something I can master?" No, so I have nothing to do. If I meet a beautiful girl or beautiful boy, is their beauty, their desirability, something that depends on me, and so on? For the Christians, things are quite different; for Christians, the possibility that Satan can get inside your soul and give you thoughts you cannot recognize as satanic, but might interpret as coming from God, leads to uncertainty about what is going on inside your soul. You are unable to know what the real root of your desire is, at least without hermeneutic work.

Q. So, to what extent did the Christians develop new techniques of self-mastery?

M.F. What interests me about the classical concept of care of the self is that we see here the birth and development of a certain number of ascetic themes ordinarily attributed to Christianity. Christianity is usually given credit for replacing the generally tolerant Greco-Roman lifestyle with an austere lifestyle marked by a series of renunciations, interdictions, or prohibitions. Now, we can see that in this activity of the self on itself, the ancients developed a whole series of austerity practices that the Christians later directly borrowed from them. So we see that this activity became linked to a certain sexual austerity that was subsumed directly into the Christian ethic. We are not talking about a moral rupture between tolerant antiquity and austere Christianity.

Q. In the name of what does one choose to impose this lifestyle upon oneself?

M.F. In antiquity, this work on the self with its attendant austerity is not imposed on the individual by means of civil law or religious obligation, but is a choice about existence made by the individual. People decide for themselves whether or not to care for themselves.

I don't think it is to attain eternal life after death, because they were not particularly concerned with that. Rather, they acted so as to give to their life certain values (reproduce certain examples, leave behind them an exalted reputation, give the maximum possible brilliance to their lives). It was a question of making one's life into an object for a sort of knowledge, for a *tekhnē*—for an art.

We have hardly any remnant of the idea in our society that the principal work of art which one must take care of, the main area to which one must apply aesthetic values, is oneself, one's life, one's existence. We find this in the Renaissance, but in a slightly academic form, and yet again in nineteenth-century dandyism, but those were only episodes.

Q. But isn't the Greek concern with the self just an early version of our self-absorption, which many consider a central problem in our society?

M.F. You have a certain number of themes—and I don't say that you have to reutilize them in this way—which indicate to you that in a culture to which we owe a certain number of our most important constant moral elements, there was a practice of the self, a conception of the self, very different from our present culture of the self. In the Californian cult of the self, one is supposed to discover one's true self, to separate it from that which might obscure or alienate it, to decipher its truth thanks to psychological or psychoanalytic science, which is supposed to be able to tell you what your true self is. Therefore, not only do I not identify this ancient culture of the self with what you might call the Californian cult of the self, I think they are diametrically opposed.

What happened in between is precisely an overtuning of the classical culture of the self. This took place when Christianity substituted the idea of a self that one had to renounce, because clinging to the self was opposed to God's will, for the idea of a self that had to be created as a work of art.

Q. We know that one of the studies for *Le Souci de soi* concerns the role of writing in the formation of the self. How is the question of the relation of writing and the self posed by Plato?

M.F. First, to bring out a certain number of historical facts that are often glossed over when posing this problem of writing, we must look into the famous question of the *hupomnēmata*. Current interpreters see in the critique of the *hupomnēmata* in the *Phaedrus* a critique of writing as a material support for memory. Now, in fact, *hupomnēmata* has a very precise meaning: it is a copybook, a notebook. Precisely this type of notebook was coming into vogue in Plato's time for personal and administrative use. This new technology was as disrupting as the introduction of the computer into private life today. It seems to me the question of writing and the self must be posed in terms of the technical and material framework in which it arose.

Second, there are problems of interpretation concerning the famous critique of writing as opposed to the culture of memory in the *Phaedrus*. If you read the *Phaedrus*, you will see that this passage is secondary with respect to another one, which is fundamental and in line with the theme that runs throughout the end of the text. It does not matter whether a text is written or oral—the problem is whether or not the discourse in question gives access to truth. Thus, the written/oral question is altogether secondary with respect to the question of truth.

Third, what seems remarkable to me is that these new instruments were immediately used for the constitution of a permanent relationship to oneself—one must manage oneself as a governor manages the governed, as a head of an enterprise manages his enterprise, a head of household manages his household. This new idea that virtue consists essentially in perfectly governing oneself, that is, in exercising upon oneself as exact a mastery as that of a sovereign against whom there would no longer be revolts, is something very important that we will find, for centuries—practically until Christianity. So, if you will, the point at which the question of the *hupomnēmata* and the culture of the self come together in a remarkable fashion is the point at which the culture of the self takes as its goal the perfect government of the self—a sort of permanent political relationship between self and self. The ancients carried on this politics of themselves with these notebooks just as governments and those who manage enterprises administered by keeping registers. This is how writing seems to me to be linked to the problem of the culture of the self.

Q. Can you tell us more about the *hupomnēmata*?

M.F. In the technical sense, the *hupomnēmata* could be account books, public registers, individual notebooks serving as memoranda. Their use as books of life, guides for conduct, seems to have become a current thing among a whole cultivated public. Into them one entered quotations, fragments of works, examples, and actions to which one had been witness or of which one had read the account, reflections or reasonings one had heard or had come to mind. They constituted a material memory of things read, heard, or thought, thus offering these as an accumulated treasure for rereading and later meditation. They also formed a raw material for the writing of more systematic treatises in which were given arguments and means by which to struggle against some defect (such as anger, envy, gossip, flattery) or to overcome some difficult circumstance (a mourning, an exile, downfall, disgrace).

Q. But how does writing connect up with ethics and the self?

M.F. No technique, no professional skill can be acquired without exercise; neither can one learn the art of living, the *tekhnē tou biou*, without an *askēsis* which must be taken as a training of oneself by oneself: this was one of the traditional principles to which the Pythagoreans, the Socratics, the Cynics had for a long time attributed great importance. Among all the forms this training took (which included abstinences, memorizations, examinations of conscience, meditations, silence, and listening to others), it seems that writing—the fact of writing for oneself and for others—came quite late to play a sizable role.

Q. What specific role did the notebooks play when they finally became influential in late antiquity?

M.F. As personal as they were, the *hupomnēmata* must nevertheless not be taken for intimate diaries or for those accounts of spiritual experience (temptations, struggles, falls, and victories) which can be found in later Christian literature. They do not constitute an "account of oneself"; their objective is not to bring the *arcana conscientiae* to light, the confession of which—be it oral or written—has a purifying value. The movement that they seek to effect is the inverse of this last one: the point is not to pursue the indescribable, not to reveal the hidden, not to say the nonsaid, but, on the contrary, to collect the already-said, to reassemble that which one could hear or read, and this to an end which is nothing less than the constitution of oneself.

The *hupomnēmata* are to be resituated in the context of a very sensitive tension of that period. Within a culture very affected by traditionality, by the recognized value of the already-said, by the recurrence of discourse, by the "citational" practice under the seal of age and authority, an ethic was developing that was very explicitly oriented to the care of oneself, toward definite objectives such as retiring into oneself, reaching oneself, living with oneself, being sufficient to oneself, profiting by and enjoying oneself. Such is the objective of the *hupomnēmata*: to make of the recollection of the fragmentary *logos* transmitted by teaching, listening, or reading a means to establish as adequate and as perfect a relationship of oneself to oneself as possible.

Q. Before we turn to the role of these notebooks in early Christianity, could you tell us something about how Greco-Roman austerity differs from Christian austerity?

M.F. One thing that has been very important is that in Stoic ethics the question of purity was nearly nonexistent or, rather, marginal. It was important in Pythagorean circles and also in the Neoplatonic schools and became more and more important through their influence and also through religious influences. At a certain moment, the problem of an aesthetics of existence is covered over by the problem of purity, which is something else, and requires another kind of technique. In Christian asceticism, the question of purity becomes more and more important; the reason why you have to take control of yourself is to keep yourself pure. The problem of virginity, this model of feminine integrity, becomes much more important in Christianity. The theme of virginity has nearly nothing to do with sexual ethics in Greco-Roman asceticism; there the problem is a problem of self-domination. It was a virile model of self-domination, and a woman who was temperate was as virile to herself as a man. The paradigm of sexual self-restraint becomes a feminine paradigm through the theme of purity and virginity, based on the model of physical integrity. Physical integrity rather than self-regulation became important. So the problem of ethics as an aesthetics of existence is covered over by the problem of purification.

This new Christian self had to be constantly examined because in this self were lodged concupiscence and desires of the flesh. From that moment on, the self was no longer something to be made but something to be renounced and deciphered. Consequently, between paganism and Christianity, the opposition is not between tolerance and austerity but between a form of austerity linked to an aesthetics of existence and other forms of austerity linked to the necessity of renouncing the self and deciphering its truth.

Q. So Nietzsche, then, must be wrong, in *The Genealogy of Morals,*

when he credits Christian asceticism for making us the kind of crea-
tures that can make promises?

M.F. Yes, I think he has given mistaken credit to Christianity, given
what we know about the evolution of pagan ethics from the fourth century B.C. to the fourth century after.

Q. How was the role of the notebooks transformed when the technique of using them to relate oneself to oneself was taken over by the
Christians?

M.F. One important change is that the writing down of inner movements appears, according to Athanasius's text on the life of Saint
Anthony, as an arm in spiritual combat: while the demon is a force
that deceives and makes one be deceived about oneself (one great half
of the *Vita Antonii* is devoted to these ploys), writing constitutes a
test and something like a touchstone: in bringing to light the movements of thought, it dissipates the inner shadow where the enemy's
plots are woven.

Q. How could such a radical transformation take place?

M.F. There is indeed a dramatic change between the *hupomnēmata*
evoked by Xenophon, where it was only a question of remembering
the elements of a diet, and the description of the nocturnal temptations
of Saint Anthony. An interesting place to look for a transitional set of
techniques seems to be the description of dreams. Almost from the
beginning, one had to have a notebook beside one's bed upon which
to write one's dreams in order either to interpret them oneself the next
morning or to show them to someone who would interpret them. By
means of this nightly description, an important step is taken toward the
description of the self.

Q. But surely the idea that the contemplation of the self allows the
self to dissipate shadows and arrive at truth is already present in Plato?

M.F. Yes, but this is an ontological and not a psychological form of
contemplation. This ontological knowledge of the self takes shape, at
least in certain texts and in particular in the *Alcibiades*, in the form of
the contemplation of the soul by itself in terms of the famous metaphor of the eye. Plato asks, "How can the eye see itself?" The answer
is apparently very simple, but in fact it is very complicated. For Plato,
one cannot simply look at oneself in a mirror; one has to look into
another eye, that is, one *in* oneself, however in oneself in the shape of
the eye of the other. And there, in the other pupil, one will see oneself: the pupil serves as a mirror. And, in the same manner, the soul

contemplating itself in another soul (or in the divine element of the other soul), which is like its pupil, will recognize its divine element.

You see that this idea that one must know oneself—that is, gain ontological knowledge of the soul's mode of being—is independent of what one could call an exercise of the self upon the self. When grasping the mode of being of your soul, there is no need to ask yourself what you have done, what you are thinking, what the movements of your ideas or your representations are, to what you are attached. That's why you can perform this technique of contemplation using as your object the soul of an other. Plato never speaks of the examination of conscience—never!

Q. It is a commonplace in literary studies that Montaigne was the first great autobiographer, yet you seem to trace writing about the self to much earlier sources.

M.F. It seems to me that in the religious crisis of the sixteenth century—the great rejection of the Catholic confessional practices—new modes of relationship to the self were being developed. We can see the reactivation of a certain number of ancient Stoic practices. The notion, for example, of proofs of oneself seems to me thematically close to what we find among the Stoics, where the experience of the self is not a discovering of a truth hidden inside the self but an attempt to determine what one can and cannot do with one's available freedom. Among both the Catholics and Protestants, the reactivation of these ancient techniques in the form of Christian spiritual practices is quite marked.

Let me take as an example the walking exercise recommended by Epictetus. Each morning, while taking a walk in the city, one should try to determine with respect to each thing (a public official or an attractive woman), one's motives, whether one is impressed by or drawn to it, or whether one has sufficient self-mastery so as to be indifferent.

In Christianity one has the same sort of exercises, but they serve to test one's dependence on God. I remember having found in a seventeenth-century text an exercise reminiscent of Epictetus, where a young seminarist, when he is walking, does certain exercises that show in what way each thing shows his dependence vis-à-vis God—which permit him to decipher the presence of divine providence. These two walks correspond to the extent that you have a case with Epictetus of a walk during which the individual assures himself of his own sovereignty over himself and shows that he is dependent on nothing, while in the Christian case the seminarist walks and before each thing he sees, says,

"Oh, how God's goodness is great! He who made this, holds all things in his power, and me, in particular"—thus reminding himself that he is nothing.

Q. So discourse plays an important role but always serves other practices, even in the constitution of the self.

M.F. It seems to me, that all the so-called literature of the self—private diaries, narratives of the self, and so on—cannot be understood unless it is put into the general and very rich framework of these practices of the self. People have been writing about themselves for two thousand years, but not in the same way. I have the impression—I may be wrong—that there is a certain tendency to present the relationship between writing and the narrative of the self as a phenomenon particular to European modernity. Now, I would not deny it is modern, but it was also one of the first uses of writing.

So it is not enough to say that the subject is constituted in a symbolic system. It is not just in the play of symbols that the subject is constituted. It is constituted in real practices—historically analyzable practices. There is a technology of the constitution of the self which cuts across symbolic systems while using them.

Q. If self-analysis is a cultural invention, why does it seem so natural and pleasurable to us?

M.F. It may have been an extremely painful exercise at first and required many cultural valorizations before ending up transformed into a positive activity. Techniques of the self, I believe, can be found in all cultures in different forms. Just as it is necessary to study and compare the different techniques of the production of objects and the direction of men by men through government, one must also question techniques of the self. What makes the analysis of the techniques of the self difficult is two things. First, the techniques of the self do not require the same material apparatus as the production of objects; therefore they are often invisible techniques. Second, they are frequently linked to the techniques for the direction of others. For example, if we take educational institutions, we realize that one is managing others and teaching them to manage themselves.

Q. Let's move on to the history of the modern subject. To begin with, was the classical culture of the self completely lost, or was it, rather, incorporated and transformed by Christian techniques?

M.F. I do not think that the culture of the self disappeared or was covered up. You find many elements that have simply been integrated, displaced, reutilized in Christianity. From the moment that the culture of the self was taken up by Christianity, it was, in a way, put to work for the exercise of a pastoral power to the extent that the *epimeleia heautou* became, essentially, *epimeleia tōn allōn*—the care of others—which was the pastor's job. But insofar as individual salvation is channeled—to a certain extent, at least—through a pastoral institution that has the care of souls as its object, the classical care of the self disappeared, that is, was integrated and lost a large part of its autonomy.

What is interesting is that during the Renaissance you see a whole series of religious groups (whose existence is, moreover, already attested to in the Middle Ages) that resist this pastoral power and claim the right to make their own statutes for themselves. According to these groups, the individual should take care of his own salvation independently of the ecclesiastical institution and of the ecclesiastical pastorate. We can see, therefore, a reappearance, up to a certain point, not of the culture of the self, which had never disappeared, but a reaffirmation of its autonomy.

In the Renaissance, you also see—and here I refer to Burckhardt's text on the famous aesthetics of existence—the hero as his own work of art. The idea that from one's own life one can make a work of art is an idea that was undoubtedly foreign to the Middle Ages, and reappears at the moment of the Renaissance.

Q. So far you have been treating various degrees of appropriation of ancient techniques of self-mastery. In your own writing, you always show a big break between the Renaissance and the classical age. Was there an equally significant change in the way self-mastery was related to other social practices?

M.F. That is very interesting, but I won't answer you immediately. Let us start by saying that the relationship between Montaigne, Pascal, and Descartes could be rethought in terms of this question. First, Pascal was still in a tradition in which practices of the self, the practice of asceticism, were tied up with the knowledge of the world. Second, we must not forget that Descartes wrote "meditations"—and meditations are a practice of the self. But the extraordinary thing in Descartes's texts is that he succeeded in substituting a subject as founder of practices of knowledge for a subject constituted through practices of the self.

This is very important. Even if it is true that Greek philosophy founded rationality, it always held that a subject could not have access to the truth if he did not first operate upon himself a certain work that

would make him susceptible to knowing the truth—a work of purifica
tion, conversion of the soul by contemplation of the soul itself. You also
have the theme of the Stoic exercise by which a subject first ensures
his autonomy and independence—and he ensures it in a rather complex relationship to the knowledge of the world, since it is this knowledge which allows him to ensure his independence, and it is only once
he has ensured it that he is able to recognize the order of the world as
it stands. In European culture up to the sixteenth century, the problem
remains: What is the work I must effect upon myself so as to be capable and worthy of acceding to the truth? To put it another way: truth
always has a price; no access to truth without ascesis. In Western culture up to the sixteenth century, asceticism and access to truth are
always more or less obscurely linked.

Descartes, I think, broke with this when he said, "To accede to truth,
it suffices that I be *any* subject that can see what is evident." Evidence
is substituted for ascesis at the point where the relationship to the self
intersects the relationship to others and the world. The relationship to
the self no longer needs to be ascetic to get into relation to the truth.
It suffices that the relationship to the self reveals to me the obvious
truth of what I see for me to apprehend the truth definitively. Thus,
I can be immoral and know the truth. I believe this is an idea that,
more or less explicitly, was rejected by all previous culture. Before
Descartes, one could not be impure, immoral, and know the truth.
With Descartes, direct evidence is enough. After Descartes, we have a
nonascetic subject of knowledge. This change makes possible the insti-
tutionalization of modern science.

I am obviously schematizing a very long history, which is, however,
fundamental. After Descartes, we have a subject of knowledge which
poses for Kant the problem of knowing the relationship between the
subject of ethics and that of knowledge. There was much debate in the
Enlightenment as to whether these two subjects were completely different or not. Kant's solution was to find a universal subject that, to the
extent it was universal, could be the subject of knowledge, but which
demanded, nonetheless, an ethical attitude—precisely the relationship
to the self which Kant proposes in *The Critique of Practical Reason.*

Q. You mean that once Descartes had cut scientific rationality loose
from ethics, Kant reintroduced ethics as an applied form of procedural
rationality?

M.F. Right. Kant says, "I must recognize myself as universal subject, that is, I must constitute myself in each of my actions as a universal subject by conforming to universal rules." The old questions were reinterpreted: How can I constitute myself as a subject of ethics? Recognize myself as such? Are ascetic exercises needed? Or simply this Kantian relationship to the universal which makes me ethical by conformity to practical reason? Thus Kant introduces one more way in our tradition whereby the self is not merely given but is constituted in relationship to itself as subject.

THE ETHICS OF THE CONCERN OF
THE SELF AS A PRACTICE OF FREEDOM*

Q. First of all, I would like to ask what is the focus of your current thinking. Having followed the latest developments in your thought, particularly your lectures at the Collège de France in 1981–82 on the hermeneutics of the subject, I would like to know if your current philosophical approach is still determined by the poles of subjectivity and truth.

M.F. In actual fact, I have always been interested in this problem, even if I framed it somewhat differently. I have tried to find out how the human subject fits into certain games of truth, whether they were truth games that take the form of a science or refer to a scientific model, or truth games such as those one may encounter in institutions or practices of control. This is the theme of my book *The Order of Things*, in which I attempted to see how, in scientific discourses, the human subject defines itself as a speaking, living, working individual. In my courses at the Collège de France, I brought out this problematic in its generality.

Q. Isn't there a "break" between your former problematic and that of subjectivity/truth, particularly starting with the concept of the "care of the self"?

M.F. Up to that point I had conceived the problem of the relationship between the subject and games of truth in terms either of coer-

*This interview was conducted by H. Becker, R. Fornet-Betancourt, and A. Gomez-Müller on January 20, 1984. It appeared in *Concordia: Revista internacional de filosophia* 6 (July–December 1984), pp. 96–116. The translation, by P. Aranov and D. McGrawth, has been amended and the footnotes of the French text added.

cive practices—such as those of psychiatry and the prison system—or of theoretical or scientific games—such as the analysis of wealth, of language, and of living beings. In my lectures at the Collège de France, I tried to grasp it in terms of what may be called a practice of the self; although this phenomenon has not been studied very much, I believe it has been fairly important in our societies ever since the Greco-Roman period. In the Greek and Roman civilizations, such practices of the self were much more important and especially more autonomous than they were later, after they were taken over to a certain extent by religious, pedagogical, medical, or psychiatric institutions.

Q. Thus there has been a sort of shift: these games of truth no longer involve a coercive practice, but a practice of self-formation of the subject.

M.F. That's right. It is what one could call an ascetic practice, taking asceticism in a very general sense—in other words, not in the sense of a morality of renunciation but as an exercise of the self on the self by which one attempts to develop and transform oneself, and to attain to a certain mode of being. Here I am taking asceticism in a more general sense than that attributed to it by Max Weber, for example, but along the same lines.

Q. A work of the self on the self that may be understood as a certain liberation, as a process of liberation?

M.F. I would be more careful on that score. I have always been somewhat suspicious of the notion of liberation, because if it is not treated with precautions and within certain limits, one runs the risk of falling back on the idea that there exists a human nature or base that, as a consequence of certain historical, economic, and social processes, has been concealed, alienated, or imprisoned in and by mechanisms of repression. According to this hypothesis, all that is required is to break these repressive deadlocks and man will be reconciled with himself, rediscover his nature or regain contact with his origin, and reestablish a full and positive relationship with himself. I think this idea should not be accepted without scrutiny. I am not trying to say that liberation as such, or this or that form of liberation, does not exist: when a colonized people attempts to liberate itself from its colonizers, this is indeed a practice of liberation in the strict sense. But we know very well, and moreover in this specific case, that this practice of liberation is not in itself sufficient to define the practices of freedom that will still be needed if this people, this society, and these individuals are to be able to define admissible and acceptable forms of existence or political society. This is why I emphasize practices of freedom over processes of liberation; again, the latter indeed have their place, but they do not seem to me to be capable by themselves of defining all the practical forms of freedom. This is precisely the problem I encountered with regard to sexuality: does it make any sense to say, "Let's liberate our sexuality"? Isn't the problem rather that of defining the practices of freedom by which one could define what is sexual pleasure and erotic, amorous and passionate relationships with others? This ethical problem of the definition of practices of freedom, it seems to me, is much more important than the rather repetitive affirmation that sexuality or desire must be liberated.

Q. But doesn't the exercise of practices of freedom require a certain degree of liberation?

M.F. Yes, absolutely. And this is where we must introduce the concept of domination. The analyses I am trying to make bear essentially on relations of power. By this I mean something different from states of domination. Power relations are extremely widespread in human relationships. Now, this means not that political power is everywhere, but that there is in human relationships a whole range of power relations that may come into play among individuals, within families, in pedagogical relationships, political life, and so on. The analysis of power relations is an extremely complex area; one sometimes encounters what may be called situations or states of domination in which the power relations, instead of being mobile, allowing the various participants to adopt strategies modifying them, remain blocked, frozen. When an individual or social group succeeds in blocking a field of power relations, immobilizing them and preventing any reversibility of movement by economic, political, or military means, one is faced with what may be called a state of domination. In such a state, it is certain that practices of freedom do not exist or exist only unilaterally or are extremely constrained and limited. Thus, I agree with you that liberation is sometimes the political or historical condition for a practice of freedom. Taking sexuality as an example, it is clear that a number of liberations were required vis-à-vis male power, that liberation was necessary from an oppressive morality concerning heterosexuality as well as homosexuality. But this liberation does not give rise to the happy human being imbued with a sexuality to which the subject could achieve a complete and satisfying relationship. Liberation paves the way for new power relationships, which must be controlled by practices of freedom.

Q. Can't liberation itself be a mode or form of practice of the freedom?

M.F. Yes, in some cases. You have situations where liberation and the struggle for liberation are indispensable for the practice of freedom. With respect to sexuality, for example—and I am not indulging in polemics, because I don't like polemics, I think they are usually futile—there is a Reichian model derived from a certain reading of Freud. Now, in Reich's view the problem was entirely one of liberation. To put it somewhat schematically, according to him there is desire, drive, prohibition, repression, internalization, and it is by getting rid of these prohibitions, in other words, by liberating oneself, that the problem gets resolved. I think—and I know I am vastly oversimplifying much more interesting and refined positions of many authors—this completely misses the ethical problem of the practice of freedom: How can one practice freedom? With regard to sexuality, it is obvious that it is by liberating our desire that we will learn to conduct ourselves ethically in pleasure relationships with others.

Q. You say that freedom must be practiced ethically...

M.F. Yes, for what is ethics, if not the practice of freedom, the conscious [*réfléchie*] practice of freedom?

Q. In other words, you understand freedom as a reality that is already ethical in itself.

M.F. Freedom is the ontological condition of ethics. But ethics is the considered form that freedom takes when it is informed by reflection.

Q. Ethics is what is achieved in the search for or the care of the self?

M.F. In the Greco-Roman world, the care of the self was the mode in which individual freedom—or civic liberty, up to a point—was reflected [*se réfléchie*] as an ethics. If you take a whole series of texts going from the first Platonic dialogues up to the major texts of late Stoicism—Epictetus, Marcus Aurelius, and so on—you will see that the theme of the care of the self thoroughly permeated moral reflection. It is interesting to see that, in our societies on the other hand, at a time that is very difficult to pinpoint, the care of the self became somewhat suspect. Starting at a certain point, being concerned with oneself was readily denounced as a form of self-love, a form of selfishness or self-interest in contradiction with the interest to be shown in others or the self-sacrifice required. All this happened during Christianity; however, I am not simply saying that Christianity is responsible for it. The question is much more complex, for, with Christianity, achieving one's salvation is also a way of caring for oneself. But in Christianity, salvation is attained through the renunciation of self. There is a paradox in the care of the self in Christianity—but that is another problem. To come back to the question you were talking about, I believe that among the Greeks and Romans—especially the Greeks—concern with the self and care of the self were required for right conduct and the proper practice of freedom, in order to know oneself [*se connaître*]—the familiar aspect of the *gnōthi seauton*—as well as to form oneself, to surpass oneself, to master the appetites that threaten to overwhelm one. Individual freedom was very important for the Greeks—contrary to the commonplace derived more or less from Hegel that sees it as being of no importance when placed against the imposing totality of the city. Not to be a slave (of another city, of the people around you, of those governing you, of your own passions) was an absolutely fundamental theme. The concern with freedom was an essential and permanent problem for eight full centuries of ancient culture. What we have here is an entire ethics revolving around the care of the self; this is what gives ancient ethics its particular form. I am not saying that ethics is synonymous with the care of the self, but that, in antiquity, ethics as the conscious practice of freedom has revolved around this fundamental imperative: "Take care of yourself" [*souci-toi de toi-même*].

Q. An imperative that implies the assimilation of the *logoi*, truths.

M.F. Certainly. Taking care of oneself requires knowing [*connaître*] oneself. Care of the self is, of course, knowledge [*connaissance*] of the self—this is the Socratic-Platonic aspect—but also knowledge of a number of rules of acceptable conduct or of principles that are both truths and prescriptions. To take care of the self is to equip oneself with these truths: this is where ethics is linked to the game of truth.

Q. You are saying that it involves making this truth that is learned, memorized, and progressively applied into a quasi subject that reigns supreme in yourself. What is the status of this quasi subject?

M.F. In the Platonic current of thought, at least at the end of the *Alcibiades*, the problem for the subject or the individual soul is to turn its gaze upon itself, to recognize itself in what it is and, recognizing itself in what it is, to recall the truths that issue from it and that it has been able to contemplate;[1] on the other hand, in the current of thinking we can broadly call Stoicism, the problem is to learn through the teaching of a number of truths and doctrines, some of which are fun-

damental principles while others are rules of conduct. You must proceed in such a way that these principles tell you in each situation and,
as it were, spontaneously, how to conduct yourself. It is here that one
encounters a metaphor that comes not from the Stoics but from Plutarch: "You must learn the principles in such a constant way that whenever your desires, appetites, and fears awake like barking dogs, the
logos will speak like the voice of the master who silences his dogs with
a single cry."[2] Here we have the idea of a *logos* functioning, as it were,
without any intervention on your part; you have become the *logos*, or
the *logos* has become you.

Q. I would like to come back to the question of the relationship between freedom and ethics. When you say that ethics is the reflective
part [*la partie réfléchie*] of freedom, does that mean that freedom can
become aware of itself as ethical practice? Is it first and always a freedom that is, so to speak, "moralized," or must one work on oneself to
discover the ethical dimension of freedom?

M.F. The Greeks problematized their freedom, and the freedom of
the individual, as an ethical problem. But ethical in the sense in which
the Greeks understood it: *ēthos* was a way of being and of behavior. It
was a mode of being for the subject, along with a certain way of acting, a way visible to others. A person's *ēthos* was evident in his clothing, appearance, gait, in the calm with which he responded to every
event, and so on. For the Greeks, this was the concrete form of freedom; this was the way they problematized their freedom. A man pos-
sessed of a splendid *ēthos*, who could be admired and put forward as
an example, was someone who practiced freedom in a certain way. I
don't think that a shift is needed for freedom to be conceived as *ēthos*;
it is immediately problematized as *ēthos*. But extensive work by the
self on the self is required for this practice of freedom to take shape
in an *ēthos* that is good, beautiful, honorable, estimable, memorable,
and exemplary.

Q. Is this where you situate the analysis of power?

M.F. I think that insofar as freedom for the Greeks signifies nonslavery—which is quite a different definition of freedom from our
own—the problem is already entirely political. It is political in that
nonslavery to others is a condition: a slave has no ethics. Freedom is
thus inherently political. And it also has a political model insofar as
being free means not being a slave to oneself and one's appetites,
which means that with respect to oneself one establishes a certain

relationship of domination, of mastery, which was called *arkhē*, or power, command.

Q. As you have stated, care of the self is in a certain sense care for others. In this sense, the care of the self is also always ethical, and ethical in itself.

M.F. What makes it ethical for the Greeks is not that it is care for others. The care of the self is ethical in itself; but it implies complex relationships with others insofar as this *ēthos* of freedom is also a way of caring for others. This is why it is important for a free man who conducts himself as he should to be able to govern his wife, his children, his household; it is also the art of governing. *Ethos* also implies a relationship with others, insofar as the care of the self enables one to occupy his rightful position in the city, the community, or interpersonal relationships, whether as a magistrate or a friend. And the care of the self also implies a relationship with the other insofar as proper care of the self requires listening to the lessons of a master. One needs a guide, a counselor, a friend, someone who will be truthful with you. Thus, the problem of relationships with others is present throughout the development of the care of the self.

Q. The care of the self always aims for the well-being of others; it aims to manage the space of power that exists in all relationships, but to manage it in a nonauthoritarian manner. What role could a philosopher play in this context, as a person who is concerned with care for others?

M.F. Let's take Socrates as an example. He would greet people in the street or adolescents in the gymnasium with the question: Are you caring for yourself? For he has been entrusted with this mission by a god and he will not abandon it even when threatened with death. He is the man who cares about the care of others; this is the particular position of the philosopher. But let me simply say that in the case of the free man, I think the postulate of this whole morality was that a person who took proper care of himself would, by the same token, be able to conduct himself properly in relation to others and for others. A city in which everybody took proper care of himself would be a city that functioned well and found in this the ethical principle of its permanence. But I don't think we can say that the Greek who cares for himself must first care for others. To my mind, this view only came later. Care for others should not be put before the care of oneself. The care of the self is ethically prior in that the relationship with oneself is ontologically prior.

Q. Can this care of the self, which possesses a positive ethical meaning, be understood as a sort of conversion of power?

M.F. A conversion, yes. In fact, it is a way of limiting and controlling power. For if it is true that slavery is the great risk that Greek freedom resists, there is also another danger that initially appears to be the opposite of slavery: the abuse of power. In the abuse of power, one exceeds the legitimate exercise of one's power and imposes one's fantasies, appetites, and desires on others. Here we have the image of the tyrant, or simply of the rich and powerful man who uses his wealth and power to abuse others, to impose an unwarranted power on them. But one can see—in any case, this is what the Greek philosophers say—that such a man is the slave of his appetites. And the good ruler is precisely the one who exercises his power as it ought to be exercised, that is, simultaneously exercising his power over himself. And it is the power over oneself that thus regulates one's power over others.

Q. Doesn't the care of the self, when separated from care for others, run the risk of becoming an absolute? And couldn't this "absolutization" of the care of the self become a way of exercising power over others, in the sense of dominating others?

M.F. No, because the risk of dominating others and exercising a tyrannical power over them arises precisely only when one has not taken care of the self and has become the slave of one's desires. But if you take proper care of yourself, that is, if you know ontologically what you are, if you know what you are capable of, if you know what it means for you to be a citizen of a city, to be the master of a household in an *oikos*, if you know what things you should and should not fear, if you know what you can reasonably hope for and, on the other hand, what things should not matter to you, if you know, finally, that you should not be afraid of death—if you know all this, you cannot abuse your power over others. Thus, there is no danger. That idea will appear much later, when love of self becomes suspect and comes to be perceived as one of the roots of various moral offenses. In this new context, renunciation of self will be the prime form of care of the self. All this is evident in Gregory of Nyssa's *Treatise on Virginity*, which defines the care of the self, the *epimeleia heautou*, as the renunciation of all earthly attachments. It is the renunciation of all that may be love of self, of attachment to an earthly self.[3] But I think that in Greek and Roman thought the care of the self cannot in itself tend toward so exaggerated a form of self-love as to neglect others or, worse still, to abuse one's power over them.

Q. Thus it is a care of the self that, in thinking of itself, thinks of others?

M.F. Yes, absolutely. He who takes care of himself to the point of knowing exactly what duties he has as master of a household and as a husband and father will find that he enjoys a proper relationship with his wife and children.

Q. But doesn't the human condition, in terms of its finitude, play a very important role here? You have talked about death: if you are not afraid of death, then you cannot abuse your power over others. It seems to me that this problem of finitude is very important; the fear of death, of finitude, of being hurt, is at the heart of the care of the self.

M.F. Of course. And this is where Christianity, by presenting salvation as occurring beyond life, in a way upsets or at least disturbs the balance of the care of the self. Although, let me say it again, to seek one's salvation definitely means to take care of oneself. But the condition required for attaining salvation is precisely renunciation. Among the Greeks and Romans, however, given that one takes care of oneself in one's own life, and that the reputation one leaves behind is the only afterlife one can expect, the care of the self can be centered entirely on oneself, on what one does, on the place one occupies among others. It can be centered totally on the acceptance of death—this will become quite evident in late Stoicism—and can even, up to a point, become almost a desire for death. At the same time, it can be, if not a care for others, at least a care of the self which will be beneficial to others. In Seneca, for example, it is interesting to note the importance of the theme, let us hurry and get old, let us hasten toward the end, so that we may thereby come back to ourselves. This type of moment before death, when nothing more can happen, is different from the desire for death one finds among the Christians, who expect salvation through death. It is like a movement to rush through life to the point where there is no longer anything ahead but the possibility of death.

Q. I would now like to turn to another topic. In your lectures at the Collège de France you spoke about the relationship between power and knowledge [*savoir*]. Now you are talking about the relationship between subject and truth. Are these pairs of concepts—power-knowledge and subject-truth—complementary in some way?

M.F. As I said when we started, I have always been interested in the problem of the relationship between subject and truth. I mean, how does the subject fit into a certain game of truth? The first problem I examined was why madness was problematized, starting at a certain time and following certain processes, as an illness falling under a certain model of medicine. How was the mad subject placed in this game of truth defined by a medical model or a knowledge? And it was while working on this analysis that I realized that, contrary to what was rather common practice at that time (around the early sixties), this phenomenon could not be properly accounted for simply by talking about ideology. In fact, there were practices—essentially the widespread use of incarceration which had been developed starting at the beginning of the seventeenth century, and had been the condition for the insertion of the mad subject in this type of truth game—that sent me back to the problem of institutions of power much more than to the problem of ideology. This is what led me to pose the problem of knowledge and power, which for me is not the fundamental problem but an instrument that makes it possible to analyze the problem of the relationship between subject and truth in what seems to me the most precise way.

Q. But you have always "forbidden" people to talk to you about the subject in general?

M.F. No, I have not "forbidden" them. Perhaps I did not explain myself adequately. What I rejected was the idea of starting out with a theory of the subject—as is done, for example, in phenomenology or existentialism—and, on the basis of this theory, asking how a given form of knowledge [*connaissance*] was possible. What I wanted to try to show was how the subject constituted itself, in one specific form or another, as a mad or a healthy subject, as a delinquent or nondelinquent subject, through certain practices that were also games of truth, practices of power, and so on. I had to reject a priori theories of the subject in order to analyze the relationships that may exist between the constitution of the subject or different forms of the subject and games of truth, practices of power, and so on.

Q. That means that the subject is not a substance.

M.F. It is not a substance. It is a form, and this form is not primarily or always identical to itself. You do not have the same type of relationship to yourself when you constitute yourself as a political subject who goes to vote or speaks at a meeting and when you are seeking to fulfill your desires in a sexual relationship. Undoubtedly there are relationships and interferences between these different forms of the subject; but we are not dealing with the same type of subject. In each case, one plays, one establishes a different type of relationship to oneself.

And it is precisely the historical constitution of these various forms of the subject in relation to the games of truth which interests me.

Q. But the mad, the ill, the delinquent subject—and perhaps even the sexual subject—was a subject that was the object of a theoretical discourse, let us say a "passive" subject, while the subject you have been speaking about over the past two years in your lectures at the Collège de France is an "active," a politically active subject. The care of the self concerns all the problems of political practice and government, and so on. It would seem, then, that there has been a change for you, a change not of perspective but of problematic.

M.F. If it is indeed true that the constitution of the mad subject may be considered the consequence of a system of coercion—this is the passive subject—you know very well that the mad subject is not an unfree subject, and that the mentally ill person is constituted as a mad subject precisely in relation to and over against the one who declares him mad. Hysteria, which was so important in the history of psychiatry and in the asylums of the nineteenth century, seems to me to be the very picture of how the subject is constituted as a mad subject. And it is certainly no accident that the major phenomena of hysteria were observed precisely in those situations where there was a maximum of coercion to force individuals to constitute themselves as mad. On the other hand, I would say that if I am now interested in how the subject constitutes itself in an active fashion through practices of the self, these practices are nevertheless not something invented by the individual himself. They are models that he finds in his culture and are proposed, suggested, imposed upon him by his culture, his society, and his social group.

Q. It would seem that there is something of a deficiency in your problematic, namely, in the notion of resistance against power. Which presupposes a very active subject, very concerned with the care of itself and of others and, therefore, competent politically and philosophically.

M.F. This brings us back to the problem of what I mean by power. I scarcely use the word *power*, and if I use it on occasion it is simply as shorthand for the expression I generally use: *relations of power*. But there are readymade models: when one speaks of *power*, people immediately think of a political structure, a government, a dominant social class, the master and the slave, and so on. I am not thinking of this at all when I speak of *relations of power*. I mean that in human relationships, whether they involve verbal communication such as we are engaged in at this moment, or amorous, institutional, or economic relationships, power is always present: I mean a relationship in which one person tries to control the conduct of the other. So I am speaking of relations that exist at different levels, in different forms; these power relations are mobile, they can be modified, they are not fixed once and for all. For example, the fact that I may be older than you, and that you may initially have been intimidated, may be turned around during the course of our conversation, and I may end up being intimidated before someone precisely because he is younger than I am. These power relations are thus mobile, reversible, and unstable. It should also be noted that power relations are possible only insofar as the subjects are free. If one of them were completely at the other's disposal and became his thing, an object on which he could wreak boundless and limitless violence, there wouldn't be any relations of power. Thus, in order for power relations to come into play, there must be at least a certain degree of freedom on both sides. Even when the power relation is completely out of balance, when it can truly be claimed that one side has "total power" over the other, a power can be exercised over the other only insofar as the other still has the option of killing himself, of leaping out the window, or of killing the other person. This means that in power relations there is necessarily the possibility of resistance because if there were no possibility of resistance (of violent resistance, flight, deception, strategies capable of reversing the situation), there would be no power relations at all. This being the general form, I refuse to reply to the question I am sometimes asked: "But if power is everywhere, there is no freedom." I answer that if there are relations of power in every social field, this is because there is freedom everywhere. Of course, states of domination do indeed exist. In a great many cases, power relations are fixed in such a way that they are perpetually asymmetrical and allow an extremely limited margin of freedom. To take what is undoubtedly a very simplified example, one cannot say that it was only men who wielded power in the conventional marital structure of the eighteenth and nineteenth centuries; women had quite a few options: they could deceive their husbands, pilfer money from them, refuse them sex. Yet they were still in a state of domination insofar as these options were ultimately only stratagems that never succeeded in reversing the situation. In such cases of domination, be they economic, social, institutional, or sexual, the problem is knowing where resistance will develop. For example, in a working class that will resist domination, will this be in unions or political parties; and what form will it take—a strike, a general strike, revolution, or parliamentary opposition? In such a situation of domination, all of these questions demand specific answers that take account of the kind and precise form of domination in question. But the claim that "you see power everywhere, thus there is no room for freedom" seems to me absolutely inadequate. The idea that power is a system of domination that controls everything and leaves no room for freedom cannot be attributed to me.

Q. You were talking before about the free man and the philosopher as two different modes of the care of the self. The care of the self of the philosopher would have a specificity that cannot be confused with that of the free man.

M.F. I would say that these figures represent two different places in the care of the self, rather than two forms of care of the self. I believe that the form of such care remains the same, but in terms of intensity, in the degree of zeal for the self, and, consequently, also for others, the place of the philosopher is not that of just any free man.

Q. Is there a fundamental link we can make at this point between philosophy and politics?

M.F. Yes, certainly. I believe that the relationship between philosophy and politics is permanent and fundamental. It is certain that if one takes the history of the care of the self in Greek philosophy, the relationship with politics is obvious. And it takes a very complex form: on the one hand, you have, for example, Socrates as well as Plato in the *Alcibiades*[4] and Xenophon in the *Memorabilia*[5]—greeting young men, saying to them: "You want to become a politician, to govern a city, to care for others, and you haven't even taken care of yourself. If you do not care for yourself you will make a poor ruler." From this perspective, the care of the self appears a pedagogical, ethical, and also ontological condition for the development of a good ruler. To constitute oneself as a governing subject implies that one has constituted oneself as a subject who cares for oneself. Yet, on the other hand, we have Socrates saying in the *Apology* that he approaches everyone because everyone has to take care of himself;[6] but he also adds, "In doing so, I am performing the highest service for the city, and instead of punishing me, you should reward me even more than you reward a winner in the Olympic Games."[7] Thus we see a very strong connection between philosophy and politics, which was to develop further when the philosopher would care not only for the soul of the citizen but for that of the prince. The philosopher becomes the prince's counselor, teacher, and spiritual adviser.

Q. Could the problematic of the care of the self be at the heart of a new way of thinking about politics, of a form of politics different from what we know today?

M.F. I admit that I have not got very far in this direction, and I would very much like to come back to more contemporary questions to try to see what can be made of all this in the context of the current political problematic. But I have the impression that in the political thought of the nineteenth century—and perhaps one should go back even farther, to Rousseau and Hobbes—the political subject was conceived of essentially as a subject of law, whether natural or positive. On the other hand, it seems to me that contemporary political thought allows very little room for the question of the ethical subject. I don't like to reply to questions I haven't studied. However, I would very much like to come back to the questions I examined through ancient culture.

Q. What is the relationship between the path of philosophy, which leads to knowledge of the self, and the path of spirituality?

M.F. By spirituality I mean—but I'm not sure this definition can hold for very long—the subject's attainment of a certain mode of being and the transformations that the subject must carry out on itself to attain this mode of being. I believe that spirituality and philosophy were identical or nearly identical in ancient spirituality. In any case, philosophy's most important preoccupation centered around the self, with knowledge [*connaissance*] of the world coming after and serving, most often, to support the care of the self. Reading Descartes, it is remarkable to find in the *Meditations* this same spiritual concern with the attainment of a mode of being where doubt was no longer possible, and where one could finally know [*connaît*].⁸ But by thus defining the mode of being to which philosophy gives access, one realizes that this mode of being is defined entirely in terms of knowledge, and that philosophy in turn is defined in terms of the development of the knowing [*connaissant*] subject, or of what qualifies the subject as such. From this perspective, it seems to me that philosophy superimposes the functions of spirituality upon the ideal of a grounding for scientificity.

Q. Should the concept of the care of the self in the classical sense be updated to confront this modern thought?

M.F. Absolutely, but I would certainly not do so just to say, "We have unfortunately forgotten about the care of the self; so here, here it is, the key to everything." Nothing is more foreign to me than the idea that, at a certain moment, philosophy went astray and forgot something, that somewhere in its history there is a principle, a foundation that must be rediscovered. I feel that all such forms of analysis, whether they take a radical form and claim that philosophy has from the outset been a forgetting, or whether they take a much more historical viewpoint and say, "Such and such a philosopher forgot something"— neither of these approaches is particularly interesting or useful. Which does not mean that contact with such and such a philosopher may not produce something, but it must be emphasized that it would be something new.

Q. This leads me to ask: Why should one have access to the truth today, to *truth* in the political sense, in other words, in the sense of a political strategy directed against the various "blockages" of power in the system of relations?

M.F. This is indeed a problem. After all, why truth? Why are we concerned with truth, and more so than with the care of the self? And why must the care of the self occur only through the concern for truth? I think we are touching on a fundamental question here, what I would call *the* question for the West: How did it come about that all of Western culture began to revolve around this obligation of truth which has taken a lot of different forms? Things being as they are, nothing so far has shown that it is possible to define a strategy outside of this concern. It is within the field of the obligation to truth that it is possible to move about in one way or another, sometimes against effects of domination which may be linked to structures of truth or institutions entrusted with truth. To greatly simplify matters, there are numerous examples: there has been a whole so-called ecological movement—a very ancient one, by the way, that did not just start in the twentieth century—that was often in opposition, as it were, to a science or, at least, to a technology underwritten by claims to truth. But this same ecology articulated its own discourse of truth: criticism was authorized in the name of a knowledge [*connaissance*] of nature, the balance of life processes, and so on. Thus, one escaped from a domination of truth not by playing a game that was totally different from the game of truth but by playing the same game differently, or playing another game, another hand, with other trump cards. I believe that the same holds true in the order of politics; here one can criticize on the basis, for example, of the consequences of the state of domination caused by an unjustified political situation, but one can only do so by playing a certain game of truth, by showing its consequences, by pointing out that there are other reasonable options, by teaching people what they don't know about their own situation, their working conditions, and their exploitation.

Q. With regard to the question of games of truth and games of power, don't you think that there can be found in history evidence of a particular kind of these games of truth, one that has a particular status in relation to all other possible games of truth and power, and is marked by its essential openness, its opposition to all blockages of power— power here meaning domination/subjugation?

M.F. Yes, absolutely. But when I talk about power relations and games of truth, I am absolutely not saying that games of truth are just concealed power relations—that would be a horrible exaggeration. My problem, as I have already said, is in understanding how truth games are set up and how they are connected with power relations. One can show, for example, that the medicalization of madness, in other words, the organization of medical knowledge [*savoir*] around individuals designated as mad, was connected with a whole series of social and economic processes at a given time, but also with institutions and practices of power. This fact in no way impugns the scientific validity or the therapeutic effectiveness of psychiatry: it does not endorse psychiatry, but neither does it invalidate it. It is also true that mathematics, for example, is linked, albeit in a completely different manner than psychiatry, to power structures, if only in the way it is taught, the way in which consensus among mathematicians is organized, functions in a closed circuit, has its values, determines what is good (true) or bad (false) in mathematics. This in no way means that mathematics is only a game of power, but that the game of truth of mathematics is linked in a certain way—without thereby being invalidated in any way—to games and institutions of power. It is clear that in some cases these connections are such that one could write the entire history of mathematics without taking them into account, although this problematic is always interesting and even historians of mathematics are now beginning to study the history of their institutions. Finally, it is clear that the connection that may exist between power relations and games of truth in mathematics is totally different from what it is in psychiatry; in any case, one simply cannot say that games of truth are nothing but games of power.

Q. This question takes us back to the problem of the subject because, with games of truth, it is a question of knowing *who* is speaking the truth, how he speaks it, and why he speaks it. For, in games of truth, one can play at speaking the truth: there is a game, one plays at truth or truth is a game.

M.F. The word "game" can lead you astray: when I say "game," I mean a set of rules by which truth is produced. It is not a game in the sense of an amusement; it is a set of procedures that lead to a certain result, which, on the basis of its principles and rules of procedure, may be considered valid or invalid, winning or losing.

Q. There remains the problem of "who": Is it a group, a body?

M.F. It may be a group or an individual. Indeed, there is a problem here. With regard to these multiple games of truth, one can see that ever since the age of the Greeks our society has been marked by the lack of a precise and imperative definition of the games of truth which are permitted to the exclusion of all others. In a given game of truth, it is always possible to discover something different and to more or less modify this or that rule, and sometimes even the entire game of truth. This has undoubtedly given the West possibilities for development not found in other societies. Who speaks the truth? Free individuals who establish a certain consensus, and who find themselves within a certain network of practices of power and constraining institutions.

Q. So truth is not a construction?

M.F. That depends. There are games of truth in which truth is a construction and others in which it is not. One can have, for example, a game of truth that consists of describing things in such and such a way: a person giving an anthropological description of a society supplies not a construction but a description, which itself has a certain number of historically changing rules, so that one can say that it is to a certain extent a construction with respect to another description. This does not mean that there's just a void, that everything is a figment of the imagination. On the basis of what can be said, for example, about this transformation of games of truth, some people conclude that I have said that nothing exists—I have been seen as saying that madness does not exist, whereas the problem is absolutely the converse: it was a question of knowing how madness, under the various definitions that have been given, was at a particular time integrated into an institutional field that constituted it as a mental illness occupying a specific place alongside other illnesses.

Q. At the heart of the problem of truth there is ultimately a problem of communication, of the transparency of the words of a discourse.

The person who has the capacity to formulate truths also has a power, the power of being able to speak the truth and to express it in the way he wants.

M.F. Yes, and yet this does not mean that what the person says is not true, which is what most people believe. When you tell people that there may be a relationship between truth and power, they say: "So it isn't truth after all!"

Q. This is tied up with the problem of communication because, in a society where communication has reached a high level of transparency, games of truth are perhaps more independent of structures of power.

M.F. This is indeed an important problem; I imagine you are thinking a little about Habermas when you say that. I am quite interested in his work, although I know he completely disagrees with my views. While I, for my part, tend to be a little more in agreement with what he says, I have always had a problem insofar as he gives communicative relations this place which is so important and, above all, a function that I would call "utopian." The idea that there could exist a state of communication that would allow games of truth to circulate freely, without any constraints or coercive effects, seems utopian to me. This is precisely a failure to see that power relations are not something that is bad in itself, that we have to break free of. I do not think that a society can exist without power relations, if by that one means the strategies by which individuals try to direct and control the conduct of others. The problem, then, is not to try to dissolve them in the utopia of completely transparent communication but to acquire the rules of law, the management techniques, and also the morality, the *ēthos*, the practice of the self, that will allow us to play these games of power with as little domination as possible.

Q. You are very far from Sartre, who told us power is evil.

M.F. Yes, and that idea, which is very far from my way of thinking, has often been attributed to me. Power is not evil. Power is games of strategy. We all know that power is not evil! For example, let us take sexual or amorous relationships: to wield power over the other in a sort of open-ended strategic game where the situation may be reversed is not evil; it's a part of love, of passion and sexual pleasure. And let us take, as another example, something that has often been rightly criticized—the pedagogical institution. I see nothing wrong in the practice of a person who, knowing more than others in a specific game of truth, tells those others what to do, teaches them, and transmits knowledge and techniques to them. The problem in such practices where power—which is not in itself a bad thing—must inevitably come into play is knowing how to avoid the kind of domination effects where a kid is subjected to the arbitrary and unnecessary authority of a teacher, or a student put under the thumb of a professor who abuses his authority. I believe that this problem must be framed in terms of rules of law, rational techniques of government and *ēthos*, practices of the self and of freedom.

Q. Are we to take what you have just said as the fundamental criteria of what you have called a new ethics? It is a question of playing with as little domination as possible...

M.F. I believe that this is, in fact, the hinge point of ethical concerns and the political struggle for respect of rights, of critical thought against abusive techniques of government and research in ethics that seeks to ground individual freedom.

Q. When Sartre speaks of power as the supreme evil, he seems to be alluding to the reality of power as domination. On this point you are probably in agreement with Sartre.

M.F. Yes, I believe that all these concepts have been ill defined, so that one hardly knows what one is talking about. I am not even sure if I made myself clear, or used the right words, when I first became interested in the problem of power. Now I have a clearer sense of the problem. It seems to me that we must distinguish between power relations understood as strategic games between liberties—in which some try to control the conduct of others, who in turn try to avoid allowing their conduct to be controlled or try to control the conduct of the others—and the states of domination that people ordinarily call "power." And between the two, between games of power and states of domination, you have technologies of government—understood, of course, in a very broad sense that includes not only the way institutions are governed but also the way one governs one's wife and children. The analysis of these techniques is necessary because it is very often through such techniques that states of domination are established and maintained. There are three levels to my analysis of power: strategic relations, techniques of government, and states of domination.

Q. In your lectures on the hermeneutics of the subject there is a passage in which you say that the first and only useful point of resistance to political power is in the relationship of the self to the self.

M.F. I do not believe that the only possible point of resistance to political power—understood, of course, as a state of domination—lies in the relationship of the self to the self. I am saying that "governmentality" implies the relationship of the self to itself, and I intend this concept of "governmentality" to cover the whole range of practices that constitute, define, organize, and instrumentalize the strategies that individuals in their freedom can use in dealing with each other. Those who try to control, determine, and limit the freedom of others are themselves free individuals who have at their disposal certain instruments they can use to govern others. Thus, the basis for all this is freedom, the relationship of the self to itself and the relationship to the other. Whereas, if you try to analyze power not on the basis of freedom, strategies, and governmentality, but on the basis of the political institution, you can only conceive of the subject as a subject of law. One then has a subject who has or does not have rights, who has had these rights either granted or removed by the institution of political society; and all this brings us back to a legal concept of the subject. On the other hand, I believe that the concept of governmentality makes it possible to bring out the freedom of the subject and its relationship to others— which constitutes the very stuff [*matière*] of ethics.

Q. Do you think that philosophy has anything to say about why there is this tendency to try to control the conduct of others?

M.F. The way the conduct of others is controlled takes very different forms and arouses desires and appetites that vary greatly in intensity depending on the society. I don't know anything about anthropology, but I can well imagine societies in which the control of the conduct of others is so well regulated in advance that, in a sense, the game is already over. On the other hand, in a society like our own, games can be very numerous, and the desire to control the conduct of others is all the greater—as we see in family relationships, for example, or emotional or sexual relationships. However, the freer people are with respect to each other, the more they want to control each other's conduct. The more open the game, the more appealing and fascinating it becomes.

Q. Do you think the role of philosophy is to warn of the dangers of power?

M.F. This has always been an important function of philosophy. In its critical aspect—and I mean critical in a broad sense—philosophy is that which calls into question domination at every level and in every form in which it exists, whether political, economic, sexual, institutional, or what have you. To a certain extent, this critical function of philosophy derives from the Socratic injunction "Take care of yourself," in other words, "Make freedom your foundation, through the mastery of yourself."

NOTES

1   Plato, *Alcibiade*, trans. M. Croiset (Paris: Belles Lettres, 1925), pp. 109–110 [*Alcibiades*, trans. W. R. M. Lamb, in *Plato* (Cambridge, Mass.: Harvard University, 1967), vol. 12, pp. 210–13].

2   Plutarch, *De la tranquillité de l'âme*, trans. J. Dumortier and J. Defradas, in *Oeuvres Morales* (Paris: Belles Lettres, 1975), vol. 3, pt. 1, 465c, p. 99 [*Tranquillity of Mind*, in *The Complete Works of Plutarch: Essays and Miscellanies*, ed. W. L. Bevan (New York: Thomas Y. Crowell, 1909), vol. 2, pp. 283–84]. The citation is an inexact paraphrase.

3   Gregory of Nyssa, *Traité de la virginité*, trans. M. Aubineau (Paris: Cerf, 1966), ch. 13, 303c–305c, pp. 411–17 [*Treatise on Virginity*, in *Saint Gregory of Nyssa: Ascetical Works*, trans. V. W. Callahan (Washington, D.C.: Catholic Universities of America Press, 1966), pp. 46–48].

4   Plato, *Alcibiade*, 124b, p. 92; 127d–e, p. 99 [*Alcibiades*, pp. 173–75; p. 189].

5   Xenophon, *Mémorables*, trans. E. Chambry (Paris: Garnier, 1935), bk. 3, ch. 7, §9, p. 412 [*Memorabilia*, trans. A. L. Bonnette (Ithaca: Cornell University, 1994), bk. 3, ch. 7, §9, p. 91].

6   Plato, *Apologie de Socrate*, trans. M. Croiset (Paris: Belles Lettres, 1925), 30b, p. 157 [*Socrates' Defense (Apology)*, trans. H. Tredennick, in *Plato: The Collected Dialogues*, eds. E. Hamilton and H. Cairns (Princeton: Princeton University Press, 1961), 30b, p. 16].

7   Plato, *Apologie de Socrate*, 36c–d, p. 166 [*Socrates' Defense (Apology)*, 36c–d, pp. 21–22].

8   R. Descartes, *Méditations sur la philosophie première*, in *Oeuvres* (Paris: Gallimard, 1952), pp. 253–334 [*Meditations on First Philosophy*, trans. and ed. J. Cottingham (Cambridge: Cambridge University Press, 1996)].

WHAT IS ENLIGHTENMENT?*

I

Today when a periodical asks its readers a question, it does so in order to collect opinions on some subject about which everyone has an opinion already; there is not much likelihood of learning anything new. In the eighteenth century, editors preferred to question the public on programs that did not yet have solutions. I do not know whether or not that practice was more effective; it was unquestionably more entertaining.

In any event, in line with this custom, in November 1784 a German periodical, *Berlinische Monatschrift*, published a response to the question: *Was ist Aufklärung?* And the respondent was Kant.

A minor text, perhaps. But it seems to me that it marks the discreet entrance into the history of thought of a question that modern philosophy has not been capable of answering but has never managed to get rid of either. And one that has been repeated in various forms for two centuries now. From Hegel through Nietzsche or Max Weber to Horkheimer or Habermas, hardly any philosophy has failed to confront this same question, directly or indirectly. What, then, is this event that is called the *Aufklärung* and that has determined, at least in part, what we are, what we think, and what we do today? Let us imagine that the *Berlinische Monatschrift* still exists and that it is asking its readers the question: What is modern philosophy? Perhaps we could respond with an echo: modern philosophy is the philosophy that is attempt-

---

*This translation, by Catherine Porter, has been amended.

ing to answer the question raised so imprudently two centuries ago: *Was ist Aufklärung?*

Let us linger a few moments over Kant's text. It merits attention for several reasons.

1. To this same question, Moses Mendelssohn had also replied in the same journal, just two months earlier. But Kant had not seen Mendelssohn's text when he wrote his. To be sure, the encounter of the German philosophical movement with the new development of Jewish culture does not date from this precise moment. Mendelssohn had been at that crossroads for thirty years or so, in company with Lessing. But up to this point it had been a matter of making a place for Jewish culture within German thought—which Lessing had tried to do in *Die Juden*—or else of identifying problems common to Jewish thought and to German philosophy; this is what Mendelssohn had done in his *Phädon; oder, über die Unsterblichkeit der Seele*. With the two texts published in the *Berlinische Monatschrift*, the German *Aufklärung* and the Jewish *Haskala* recognize that they belong to the same history; they are seeking to identify the common processes from which they stem. And it is perhaps a way of announcing the acceptance of a common destiny—we now know to what drama that was to lead.

2. But there is more. In itself and within the Christian tradition, Kant's text poses a new problem.

It was certainly not the first time that philosophical thought had sought to reflect on its own present. But, speaking schematically, we may say that this reflection had until then taken three main forms.

- The present may be represented as belonging to a certain era of the world, distinct from the others through some inherent characteristics, or separated from the others by some dramatic event. Thus, in Plato's *The Statesman* the interlocutors recognize that they belong to one of those revolutions of the world in which the world is turning backward, with all the negative consequences that may ensue.

- The present may be interrogated in an attempt to decipher in it the heralding signs of a forthcoming event. Here we have the principle of a kind of historical hermeneutics of which Augustine might provide an example.

• The present may also be analyzed as a point of transition toward the dawning of a new world. That is what Vico describes in the last chapter of *La Scienza nuova*; what he sees "today" is "a complete humanity... spread abroad through all nations, for a few great monarchs rule over this world of peoples"; it is also "Europe... radiant with such humanity that it abounds in all the good things that make for the happiness of human life."[1]

Now, the way Kant poses the question of *Aufklärung* is entirely different: it is neither a world era to which one belongs, nor an event whose signs are perceived, nor the dawning of an accomplishment. Kant defines *Aufklärung* in an almost entirely negative way, as an *Ausgang*, an "exit," a "way out." In his other texts on history, Kant occasionally raises questions of origin or defines the internal teleology of a historical process. In the text on *Aufklärung*, he deals with the question of contemporary reality alone. He is not seeking to understand the present on the basis of a totality or of a future achievement. He is looking for a difference: What difference does today introduce with respect to yesterday?

3. I shall not go into detail here concerning this text, which is not always very clear despite its brevity. I should simply like to point out three or four features that seem to me important if we are to understand how Kant raised the philosophical question of the present day [*du présent*].

Kant indicates right away that the "way out" which characterizes Enlightenment is a process that releases us from the status of "immaturity." And by "immaturity," he means a certain state of our will which makes us accept someone else's authority to lead us in areas where the use of reason is called for. Kant gives three examples: we are in a state of "immaturity" when a book takes the place of our understanding, when a spiritual director takes the place of our conscience, when a doctor decides for us what our diet is to be. (Let us note in passing that the register of these three critiques is easy to recognize, even though the text does not make it explicit.) In any case, Enlightenment is defined by a modification of the preexisting relation linking will, authority, and the use of reason.

We must also note that this way out is presented by Kant in a rather ambiguous manner. He characterizes it as a phenomenon, an ongoing process; but he also presents it as a task and an obligation. From the very first paragraph, he notes that man himself is responsible for his immature status. Thus, it has to be supposed that he will be able to escape from it only by a change that he himself will bring about in himself. Significantly, Kant says that this Enlightenment has a *Wahlspruch*: now, a *Wahlspruch* is a heraldic device, that is, a distinctive feature by which one can be recognized, and it is also a motto, an instruction that one gives oneself and proposes to others. What, then, is this instruction? *Aude sapere*: "dare to know," "have the courage, the audacity, to know." Thus, Enlightenment must be considered both as a process in which men participate collectively and as an act of courage to be accomplished personally. Men are at once elements and agents of a single process. They may be actors in the process to the extent that they participate in it; and the process occurs to the extent that men decide to be its voluntary actors.

A third difficulty appears here in Kant's text, in his use of the word "mankind," *Menschheit*. The importance of this word in the Kantian conception of history is well known. Are we to understand that the entire human race is caught up in the process of Enlightenment? In that case, we must imagine Enlightenment as a historical change that affects the political and social existence of all people on the face of the earth. Or are we to understand that it involves a change affecting what constitutes the humanity of human beings? But the question then arises of knowing what this change is. Here again, Kant's answer is not without a certain ambiguity. In any case, beneath its appearance of simplicity, it is rather complex.

Kant defines two essential conditions under which mankind can escape from its immaturity. And these two conditions are at once spiritual and institutional, ethical and political.

The first of these conditions is that the realm of obedience and the realm of the use of reason be clearly distinguished. Briefly characterizing the immature status, Kant invokes the familiar expression: "Don't think, just follow orders"; such is, according to him, the form in which military discipline, political power, and religious authority are usually exercised. Humanity will reach maturity when it is no longer required to obey, but when men are told: "Obey, and you will be able to reason as much as you like." We must note that the German word used here is *räsonieren*; this word, which is also used in the *Critiques*, refers not to just any use of reason but to a use of reason in which reason has no other end but itself: *räsonieren* is to reason for reasoning's sake. And

Kant gives examples, these too being perfectly trivial in appearance: paying one's taxes while being able to argue as much as one likes about the system of taxation, would be characteristic of the mature state; or again, taking responsibility for parish service, if one is a pastor, while reasoning freely about religious dogmas.

We might think that there is nothing very different here from what has been meant, since the sixteenth century, by freedom of conscience: the right to think as one pleases so long one obeys as one must. Yet it is here that Kant brings into play another distinction, and in a rather surprising way. The distinction he introduces is between the private and public uses of reason. Yet he adds at once that reason must be free in its public use and must be submissive in its private use. Which is, term for term, the opposite of what is ordinarily called freedom of conscience.

But we must be somewhat more precise. What constitutes, for Kant, this private use of reason? In what area is it exercised? Man, Kant says, makes a private use of reason when he is "a cog in a machine," that is, when he has a role to play in society and jobs to do: to be a soldier, to have taxes to pay, to be in charge of a parish, to be a civil servant, all this makes the human being a particular segment of society; he finds himself thereby placed in a circumscribed position, where he has to apply particular rules and pursue particular ends. Kant asks not that people practice a blind and foolish obedience but that they adapt the use they make of their reason to these determined circumstances; and reason must then be subjected to the particular ends in view. Thus, there cannot be, here, any free use of reason.

On the other hand, when one is reasoning only in order to use one's reason, when one is reasoning as a reasonable being (and not as a cog in a machine), when one is reasoning as a member of reasonable humanity, then the use of reason must be free and public. Enlightenment is thus not merely the process by which individuals would see their own personal freedom of thought guaranteed. There is Enlightenment when the universal, the free, and the public uses of reason are superimposed on one another.

Now this leads us to a fourth question that must be put to Kant's text. We can readily see how the universal use of reason (apart from any private end) is the business of the subject himself as an individual; we can readily see, too, how the freedom of this use may be assured in a purely negative manner through the absence of any challenge to it; but how is a public use of that reason to be assured? Enlightenment, as we see, must not be conceived simply as a general process affecting all humanity; it must not be conceived only as an obligation prescribed to individuals: it now appears as a political problem. The question, in any event, is that of knowing how the use of reason can take the public form that it requires, how the audacity to know can be exercised in broad daylight, while individuals are obeying as scrupulously as possible. And Kant, in conclusion, proposes to Frederick II, in scarcely veiled terms, a sort of contract—what might be called the contract of rational despotism with free reason: the public and free use of autonomous reason will be the best guarantee of obedience, on condition, however, that the political principle which must be obeyed itself be in conformity with universal reason.

Let us leave Kant's text here. I do not by any means propose to consider it as capable of constituting an adequate description of Enlightenment; and no historian, I think, could be satisfied with it for an analysis of the social, political, and cultural transformations that occurred at the end of the eighteenth century.

Nevertheless, notwithstanding its circumstantial nature, and without intending to give it an exaggerated place in Kant's work, I believe that it is necessary to stress the connection that exists between this brief article and the three *Critiques*. Kant, in fact, describes Enlightenment as the moment when humanity is going to put its own reason to use, without subjecting itself to any authority; now, it is precisely at this moment that the critique[a] is necessary, since its role is that of defining the conditions under which the use of reason is legitimate in order to determine what can be known [*connaître*], what must be done, and what may be hoped. Illegitimate uses of reason are what give rise to dogmatism and heteronomy, along with illusion; on the other hand, it is when the legitimate use of reason has been clearly defined in its principles that its autonomy can be assured. The critique is, in a sense, the handbook of reason that has grown up in Enlightenment; and, conversely, the Enlightenment is the age of the critique.

It is also necessary, I think, to underline the relation between this text of Kant's and the other texts he devoted to history. These latter, for the most part, seek to define the internal teleology of time and the point toward which history of humanity is moving. Now, the analysis of Enlightenment, defining this history as humanity's passage to its adult status, situates contemporary reality with respect to the overall movement and its basic directions. But at the same time, it shows how, at this very moment, each individual is responsible in a certain way for that overall process.

The hypothesis I should like to propose is that this little text is located, in a sense, at the crossroads of critical reflection and reflection on history. It is a reflection by Kant on the contemporary status of his own enterprise. No doubt, it is not the first time that a philosopher has given his reasons for undertaking his work at a particular moment. But it seems to me that it is the first time that a philosopher has connected in this way, closely and from the inside, the significance of his work with respect to knowledge [*connaissance*], a reflection on history and a particular analysis of the specific moment at which he is writing and because of which he is writing. It is in the reflection on "today" as difference in history and as motive for a particular philosophical task that the novelty of this text appears to me to lie.

And, by looking at it in this way, it seems to me we may recognize a point of departure: the outline of what one might call the attitude of modernity.

II

I know that modernity is often spoken of as an epoch, or at least as a set of features characteristic of an epoch; situated on a calendar, it would be preceded by a more or less naive or archaic premodernity, and followed by an enigmatic and troubling "postmodernity." And then we find ourselves asking whether modernity constitutes the sequel to the Enlightenment and its development, or whether we are to see it as a rupture or a deviation with respect to the basic principles of the eighteenth century.

Thinking back on Kant's text, I wonder whether we may not envisage modernity as an attitude rather than as a period of history. And by "attitude," I mean a mode of relating to contemporary reality; a voluntary choice made by certain people; in the end, a way of thinking and feeling; a way, too, of acting and behaving that at one and the same time marks a relation of belonging and presents itself as a task. No doubt, a bit like what the Greeks called an *ēthos*. And consequently, rather than seeking to distinguish the "modern era" from the "premodern" or "postmodern," I think it would be more useful to try to find out how the attitude of modernity, ever since its formation, has found itself struggling with attitudes of "countermodernity."

To characterize briefly this attitude of modernity, I shall take an almost-indispensable example, namely, Baudelaire; for his consciousness of modernity is widely recognized as one of the most acute in the nineteenth century.

1. Modernity is often characterized in terms of consciousness of the discontinuity of time: a break with tradition, a feeling of novelty, a vertigo in the face of the passing moment. And this is indeed what Baudelaire seems to be saying when he defines modernity as "the ephemeral, the fleeting, the contingent."[2] But, for him, being modern does not lie in recognizing and accepting this perpetual movement; on the contrary, it lies in adopting a certain attitude with respect to this movement; and this deliberate, difficult attitude consists in recapturing something eternal that is not beyond the present instant, nor behind it, but within it. Modernity is distinct from fashion, which does no more than call into question the course of time; modernity is the attitude that makes it possible to grasp the "heroic" aspect of the present moment. Modernity is not a phenomenon of sensitivity to the fleeting present; it is the will to "heroize" the present.

I shall restrict myself to what Baudelaire says about the painting of his contemporaries. Baudelaire makes fun of those painters who, finding nineteenth-century dress excessively ugly, want to depict nothing but ancient togas. But modernity in painting does not consist, for Baudelaire, in introducing black clothing onto the canvas. The modern painter is the one who can show the dark frock-coat as "the necessary costume of our time," the one who knows how to make manifest, in the fashion of the day, the essential, permanent, obsessive relation that our age entertains with death. "The dress-coat and frock-coat not only possess their political beauty, which is an expression of universal equality, but also their poetic beauty, which is an expression of the public soul—an immense cortège of undertaker's mutes (mutes in love, political mutes, bourgeois mutes...). We are each of us celebrating some funeral."[3] To designate this attitude of modernity, Baudelaire sometimes employs a litotes that is highly significant because it is presented in the form of a precept: "You have no right to despise the present."

2. This heroization is ironic, needless to say. The attitude of modernity does not treat the passing moment as sacred in order to try to maintain or perpetuate it. It certainly does not involve harvesting it as

a fleeting and interesting curiosity. That would be what Baudelaire would call the spectator's posture. The *flâneur*, the idle, strolling spectator, is satisfied to keep his eyes open, to pay attention and to build up a storehouse of memories. In opposition to the *flâneur*, Baudelaire describes the man of modernity: "Away he goes, hurrying, searching.... Be very sure that this man...this solitary, gifted with an active imagination, ceaselessly journeying across the great human desert—has an aim loftier than that of a mere *flâneur*, an aim more general, something other than the fugitive pleasure of circumstance. He is looking for that quality which you must allow me to call 'modernity.'... He makes it his business to extract from fashion whatever element it may contain of poetry, within history." As an example of modernity, Baudelaire cites the artist Constantin Guys. In appearance a spectator, a collector of curiosities, he remains "the last to linger wherever there can be a glow of light, an echo of poetry, a quiver of life or a chord of music; wherever a passion can *pose* before him, wherever natural man and conventional man display themselves in a strange beauty, wherever the sun lights up the swift joys of the *depraved animal*."[4]

But let us make no mistake. Constantin Guys is not a *flâneur*; what makes him the modern painter par excellence in Baudelaire's eyes is that, just when the whole world is falling asleep, he begins to work, and he transfigures that world. His transfiguration entails not an annulling of reality but a difficult interplay between the truth of what is real and the exercise of freedom; "natural" things become "more than natural," "beautiful" things become "more than beautiful," and individual objects appear "endowed with an impulsive life like the soul of [their] creator."[5] For the attitude of modernity, the high value of the present is indissociable from a desperate eagerness to imagine it, to imagine it otherwise than it is, and to transform it not by destroying it but by grasping it in what it is. Baudelairean modernity is an exercise in which extreme attention to what is real is confronted with the practice of a liberty that simultaneously respects this reality and violates it.

3. However, modernity for Baudelaire is not simply a form of relationship to the present; it is also a mode of relationship that must be established with oneself. The deliberate attitude of modernity is tied to an indispensable asceticism. To be modern is not to accept oneself as one is in the flux of the passing moments; it is to take oneself as object of a complex and difficult elaboration: what Baudelaire, in the vocabulary of his day, calls *dandysme*. Here I shall not recall in detail

the well-known passages on "vulgar, earthy, vile nature"; on man's indispensable revolt against himself; on the "doctrine of elegance" which imposes "upon its ambitious and humble disciples" a discipline more despotic than the most terrible religions; the pages, finally, on the asceticism of the dandy who makes of his body, his behavior, his feelings and passions, his very existence, a work of art. Modern man, for Baudelaire, is not the man who goes off to discover himself, his secrets and his hidden truth; he is the man who tries to invent himself. This modernity does not "liberate man in his own being"; it compels him to face the task of producing himself.

4. Let me add just one final word. This ironic heroization of the present, this transfiguring play of freedom with reality, this ascetic elaboration of the self—Baudelaire does not imagine that these have any place in society itself or in the body politic. They can only be produced in another, a different place, which Baudelaire calls art.

I do not pretend to be summarizing in these few lines either the complex historical event that was the Enlightenment, at the end of the eighteenth century, or the attitude of modernity in the various guises it may have taken on during the last two centuries.

I have been seeking, on the one hand, to emphasize the extent to which a type of philosophical interrogation—one that simultaneously problematizes man's relation to the present, man's historical mode of being, and the constitution of the self as an autonomous subject—is rooted in the Enlightenment. On the other hand, I have been seeking to stress that the thread which may connect us with the Enlightenment is not faithfulness to doctrinal elements but, rather, the permanent reactivation of an attitude—that is, of a philosophical ethos that could be described as a permanent critique of our historical era. I should like to characterize this ethos very briefly.

Negatively

1. This ethos implies, first, the refusal of what I like to call the "blackmail" of the Enlightenment. I think that the Enlightenment, as a set of political, economic, social, institutional, and cultural events on which we still depend in large part, constitutes a privileged domain for analysis. I also think that, as an enterprise for linking the progress of truth and the history of liberty in a bond of direct relation, it formulated a

philosophical question that remains for us to consider. I think, finally, as I have tried to show with reference to Kant's text, that it defined a certain manner of philosophizing.

Yet that does not mean that one has to be "for" or "against" the Enlightenment. It even means precisely that one must refuse everything that might present itself in the form of a simplistic and authoritarian alternative: you either accept the Enlightenment and remain within the tradition of its rationalism (this is considered a positive term by some and used by others, on the contrary, as a reproach), or else you criticize the Enlightenment and then try to escape from its principles of rationality (which may be seen once again as good or bad). And we do not break free of this blackmail by introducing "dialectical" nuances while seeking to determine what good and bad elements there may have been in the Enlightenment.

We must try to proceed with the analysis of ourselves as beings who are historically determined, to a certain extent, by the Enlightenment. Such an analysis implies a series of historical inquiries that are as precise as possible; and these inquiries will not be oriented retrospectively toward the "essential kernel of rationality" that can be found in the Enlightenment, which would have to be preserved in any event; they will be oriented toward the "contemporary limits of the necessary," that is, toward what is not or is no longer indispensable for the constitution of ourselves as autonomous subjects.

2. This permanent critique of ourselves must avoid the always too facile confusions between humanism and Enlightenment.

We must never forget that the Enlightenment is an event, or a set of events and complex historical processes, that is located at a certain point in the development of European societies. As such, it includes elements of social transformation, types of political institution, forms of knowledge, projects of rationalization of knowledge and practices, technological mutations that are very difficult to sum up in a word, even if many of these phenomena remain important today. The one I have pointed out, which seems to me to have been at the basis of an entire form of philosophical reflection, concerns only the mode of reflective relation to the present.

Humanism is something entirely different. It is a theme or, rather, a set of themes that have reappeared on several occasions, over time, in European societies; these themes, always tied to value judgments, have obviously varied greatly in their content as well as in the values they have preserved. Furthermore, they have served as a critical principle of differentiation. In the seventeenth century, there was a humanism that presented itself as a critique of Christianity or of religion in general; there was a Christian humanism opposed to an ascetic and much more theocentric humanism. In the nineteenth century, there was a suspicious humanism, hostile and critical toward science, and another that, to the contrary, placed its hope in that same science. Marxism has been a humanism; so have existentialism and personalism; there was a time when people supported the humanistic values represented by National Socialism, and when the Stalinists themselves said they were humanists.

From this, we must not conclude that everything which has ever been linked with humanism is to be rejected, but that the humanistic thematic is in itself too supple, too diverse, too inconsistent to serve as an axis for reflection. And it is a fact that, at least since the seventeenth century, what is called "humanism" has always been obliged to lean on certain conceptions of man borrowed from religion, science, or politics. Humanism serves to color and to justify the conceptions of man to which it is, after all, obliged to take recourse.

Now, in this connection, I believe that this thematic, which so often recurs, and always depends on humanism, can be opposed by the principle of a critique and a permanent creation of ourselves in our autonomy: that is, a principle at the heart of the historical consciousness that the Enlightenment has of itself. From this standpoint, I am inclined to see Enlightenment and humanism in a state of tension rather than identity.

In any case, it seems to me dangerous to confuse them; and further, it seems historically inaccurate. If the question of man, of the human species, of the humanist, was important throughout the eighteenth century, this is very rarely, I believe, because the Enlightenment considered itself a humanism. It is worthwhile, too, to note that throughout the nineteenth century, the historiography of sixteenth-century humanism, which was so important for people like Saint-Beuve or Burckhardt, was always distinct from, and sometimes explicitly opposed to, the Enlightenment and the eighteenth century. The nineteenth century had a tendency to oppose the two, at least as much as to confuse them.

In any case, I think that, just as we must free ourselves from the intellectual blackmail of "being for or against the Enlightenment," we must escape from the historical and moral confusionism that mixes the theme of humanism with the question of the Enlightenment. An analysis of their complex relations in the course of the last two centuries would be a worthwhile project, an important one if we are to bring some measure of clarity to the consciousness that we have of ourselves and of our past.

Positively

Yet while taking these precautions into account, we must obviously give a more positive content to what may be a philosophical ethos consisting in a critique of what we are saying, thinking, and doing, through a historical ontology of ourselves.

1. This philosophical ethos may be characterized as a *limit-attitude*. We are not talking about a gesture of rejection. We have to move beyond the outside–inside alternative; we have to be at the frontiers. Criticism indeed consists of analyzing and reflecting upon limits. But if the Kantian question was that of knowing [*savoir*] what limits knowledge [*connaissance*] must renounce exceeding, it seems to me that the critical question today must be turned back into a positive one: In what is given to us as universal, necessary, obligatory, what place is occupied by whatever is singular, contingent, and the product of arbitrary constraints? The point, in brief, is to transform the critique conducted in the form of necessary limitation into a practical critique that takes the form of a possible crossing-over [*franchissement*].

This entails an obvious consequence: that criticism is no longer going to be practiced in the search for formal structures with universal value but, rather, as a historical investigation into the events that have led us to constitute ourselves and to recognize ourselves as subjects of what we are doing, thinking, saying. In that sense, this criticism is not transcendental, and its goal is not that of making a metaphysics possible: it is genealogical in its design and archaeological in its method. Archaeological—and not transcendental—in the sense that it will not seek to identify the universal structures of all knowledge [*connaissance*] or of all possible moral action, but will seek to treat the instances of discourse that articulate what we think, say, and do as so many historical events. And this critique will be genealogical in the sense that it will not deduce from the form of what we are what it is impossible for us to do and to know; but it will separate out, from the contingency that has made us what we are, the possibility of no longer being, doing, or thinking what we are, do, or think. It is not seeking to make possible a metaphysics that has finally become a science; it is seeking to give new impetus, as far and wide as possible, to the undefined work of freedom.

2. Yet if we are not to settle for the affirmation or the empty dream of freedom, it seems to me that this historico-critical attitude must also be an experimental one. I mean that this work done at the limits of ourselves must, on the one hand, open up a realm of historical inquiry and, on the other, put itself to the test of reality, of contemporary reality, both to grasp the points where change is possible and desirable, and to determine the precise form this change should take. This means that the historical ontology of ourselves must turn away from all projects that claim to be global or radical. In fact, we know from experience that the claim to escape from the system of contemporary reality so as to produce the overall programs of another society, of another way of thinking, another culture, another vision of the world, has led only to the return of the most dangerous traditions.

I prefer the very specific transformations that have proved to be possible in the last twenty years in a certain number of areas which concern our ways of being and thinking, relations to authority, relations between the sexes, the way in which we perceive insanity or illness; I prefer even these partial transformations, which have been made in the correlation of historical analysis and the practical attitude, to the programs for a new man that the worst political systems have repeated throughout the twentieth century.

I shall thus characterize the philosophical ethos appropriate to the critical ontology of ourselves as a historico-practical test of the limits we may go beyond, and thus as work carried out by ourselves upon ourselves as free beings.

3. Still, the following objection would no doubt be entirely legitimate: If we limit ourselves to this type of always partial and local inquiry or test, do we not run the risk of letting ourselves be determined by more general structures of which we may well not be conscious and over which we may have no control?

To this, two responses. It is true that we have to give up hope of ever acceding to a point of view that could give us access to any complete and definitive knowledge [*connaissance*] of what may constitute our historical limits. And, from this point of view, the theoretical and practical experience we have of our limits, and of the possibility of moving beyond them, is always limited and determined; thus, we are always in the position of beginning again.

But that does not mean that no work can be done except in disorder and contingency. The work in question has its generality, its systematicity, its homogeneity, and its stakes.

ITS STAKES. These are indicated by what might be called "the paradox of the relations of capacity and power." We know that the great promise or the great hope of the eighteenth century, or a part of the eighteenth century, lay in the simultaneous and proportional growth of individuals with respect to one another. And, moreover, we can see that throughout the entire history of Western societies (it is perhaps here that the root of their singular historical destiny is located—such a peculiar destiny, so different from the others in its trajectory and so universalizing, so dominant with respect to the others), the acquisition of capabilities and the struggle for freedom have constituted permanent elements. Now, the relations between the growth of capabilities and the growth of autonomy are not as simple as the eighteenth century may have believed. And we have been able to see what forms of power relation were conveyed by various technologies (whether we are speaking of productions with economic aims, or institutions whose goal is social regulation, or of techniques of communication): disciplines, both collective and individual, procedures of normalization exercised in the name of the power of the state, demands of society or of population zones, are examples. What is at stake, then, is this: how can the growth of capabilities [*capacités*] be disconnected from the intensification of power relations?

HOMOGENEITY. This leads to the study of what could be called "practical systems." Here we are taking as a homogeneous domain of reference not the representations that men give of themselves, not the conditions that determine them without their knowledge, but rather what they do and the way they do it. That is, the forms of rationality that organize their ways of doing things (this might be called the technological aspect) and the freedom with which they act within these practical systems, reacting to what others do, modifying the rules of the game, up to a certain point (this might be called the strategic side of these practices). The homogeneity of these historico-critical analyses is thus ensured by this realm of practices, with their technological side and their strategic side.

SYSTEMATICITY. These practical systems stem from three broad areas: relations of control over things, relations of action upon others, relations with oneself. This does not mean that each of these three areas is completely foreign to the others. It is well known that control over things is mediated by relations with others; and relations with others in turn always entail relations with oneself, and vice versa. But we have three axes whose specificity and whose interconnections have to be analyzed: the axis of knowledge, the axis of power, the axis of ethics. In other words, the historical ontology of ourselves must answer an open series of questions; it must make an indefinite number of inquiries which may be multiplied and specified as much as we like, but which will all address the questions systematized as follows: How are we constituted as subjects of our own knowledge? How are we constituted as subjects who exercise or submit to power relations? How are we constituted as moral subjects of our own actions?

GENERALITY. Finally, these historico-critical investigations are quite specific in the sense that they always bear upon a material, an epoch, a body of determined practices and discourses. And yet, at least at the level of the Western societies from which we derive, they have their generality, in the sense that they have continued to recur up to our time: for example, the problem of the relationship between sanity and insanity, or sickness and health, or crime and the law; the problem of the role of sexual relations; and so on.

Yet by evoking this generality, I do not mean to suggest that it has to be retraced in its metahistorical continuity over time, nor that its variations have to be pursued. What must be grasped is the extent to which what we know of it, the forms of power that are exercised in it, and the experience that we have in it of ourselves constitute nothing but determined historical figures, through a certain form of problematization that defines objects, rules of action, modes of relation to oneself. The study of (modes of) problematization [*(modes de) problématizations*] (that is, of what is neither an anthropological constant nor a chronological variation) is thus the way to analyze questions of general import in their historically unique form.

A brief summary, to conclude and to come back to Kant.

I do not know whether we will ever reach mature adulthood. Many things in our experience convince us that the historical event of the Enlightenment did not make us mature adults, and we have not reached that stage yet. However, it seems to me that a meaning can be attributed to that critical interrogation on the present and on ourselves which Kant formulated by reflecting on the Enlightenment. It seems to me that Kant's reflection is even a way of philosophizing which has not been without its importance or effectiveness during the last two centuries. The critical ontology of ourselves must be considered not, certainly, as a theory, a doctrine, nor even as a permanent body of knowledge that is accumulating; it must be conceived as an attitude, an ethos, a philosophical life in which the critique of what we are is at one and the same time the historical analysis of the limits imposed on us and an experiment with the possibility of going beyond them [*de leur franchissement possible*].

This philosophical attitude must be translated into the labor of diverse inquiries. These inquiries have their methodological coherence in the at once archaeological and genealogical study of practices envisaged simultaneously as a technological type of rationality and as strategic games of liberties; they have their theoretical coherence in the definition of the historically unique forms in which the generalities of our relations to things, to others, to themselves, have been problematized. They have their practical coherence in the care brought to the process of putting historico-critical reflection to the test of concrete practices. I do not know whether it must be said today that the critical task still entails faith in Enlightenment; I continue to think that this task requires work on our limits, that is, a patient labor giving form to our impatience for liberty.

NOTES

1   Giambattista Vico, *The New Science of Giambattista Vico* (1744), abridged trans. T. G. Bergin and M. H. Fisch (Ithaca and London: Cornell University Press, 1970), pp. 370, 372.

a   In this paragraph, occurrences of the phrase "the critique" are glosses of "*la Critique*" (capitalized in the French); it should probably be understood as referring not to critique in general but, rather, to Kant's own works, or perhaps particularly to his "First Critique," *The Critique of Pure Reason.*

2   Charles Baudelaire, *The Painter of Modern Life and Other Essays*, trans. Jonathan Mayne (London: Phaidon, 1964), p. 13.

3   Charles Baudelaire, "On the Heroism of Modern Life," in *The Mirror of Art: Critical Studies by Charles Baudelaire*, trans. Jonathan Mayne (London: Phaidon, 1955), p. 127.

4   Baudelaire, *Painter*, pp. 12, 11.

5   Ibid., p. 12.

THE MASKED PHILOSOPHER*

C.D. Allow me to ask you first why you have chosen anonymity?

M.F. You know the story of the psychologists who went to make a little film test in a village in darkest Africa. They then asked the spectators to tell the story in their own words. Well, only one thing interested them in this story involving three characters: the movement of the light and shadow through the trees.

In our societies, characters dominate our perceptions. Our attention tends to be arrested by the activities of faces that come and go, emerge and disappear.

Why did I suggest that we use anonymity? Out of nostalgia for a time when, being quite unknown, what I said had some chance of being heard. With the potential reader, the surface of contact was unrippled. The effects of the book might land in unexpected places and form shapes that I had never thought of. A name makes reading too easy.

I shall propose a game: that of the "year without a name." For a year, books would be published without their authors' names. The critics would have to cope with a mass of entirely anonymous books. But,

---

*Between 1979 and 1984 the newspaper *Le Monde* published a weekly series of interviews with leading European intellectuals. On April 6-7, 1980, an interview between Christian Delacampagne and Michel Foucault was published in which the latter opted for the mask of anonymity—the philosopher declined to reveal his name—in order to demystify the power society ascribes to the "name" of the intellectual. Foucault set out to liberate the consumer of culture from a critical discourse that is overdetermined by the characters that dominate our perceptions. This interview was reprinted in *Entretiens avec Le Monde*, vol. 1: *Philosophies* (Paris: Découverte, 1984), pp. 21-30. The translation, by Alan Sheridan, has been amended.

now that I come to think of it, it's possible they would have nothing to do: all the authors would wait until the following year before publishing their books...

C.D. Do you think intellectuals today talk too much? That they encumber us with their discourses at every occasion, and more often than not independent of any occasion?

M.F. The word *intellectual* strikes me as odd. Personally, I've never met any intellectuals. I've met people who write novels, others who treat the sick; people who work in economics and others who compose electronic music. I've met people who teach, people who paint, and people of whom I have never really understood what they do. But intellectuals? Never.

On the other hand, I've met a lot of people who talk about "the intellectual." And, listening to them, I've got some idea of what such an animal could be. It's not difficult—he's quite personified. He's guilty of pretty well everything: of speaking out and of keeping silent, of doing nothing and of getting involved in everything.... In short, the intellectual is raw material for a verdict, a sentence, a condemnation, an exclusion...

I don't find that intellectuals talk too much, since for me they don't exist. But I do find that more and more is being said about intellectuals, and I don't find it very reassuring.

I have an unfortunate habit. When people speak about this or that, I try to imagine what the result would be if translated into reality. When they "criticize" someone, when they "denounce" his ideas, when they "condemn" what he writes, I imagine them in the ideal situation in which they would have complete power over him. I take the words they use—*demolish, destroy, reduce to silence, bury*—and see what the effect would be if they were taken literally. And I catch a glimpse of the radiant city in which the intellectual would be in prison or, if he were also a theoretician, hanged, of course. We don't, it's true, live under a regime in which intellectuals are sent to the ricefields. But have you heard of a certain Toni Negri?[1] Isn't he in prison simply for being an intellectual?

C.D. So what has led you to hide behind anonymity? Is it the way in which philosophers, nowadays, exploit the publicity surrounding their names?

M.F. That doesn't shock me in the least. In the corridors of my old *lycée* I used to see plaster busts of great men. And now at the bottom of the front pages of newspapers I see the photograph of some thinker or other. I don't know whether things have improved, from an aesthetic point of view. Economic rationality, certainly...

I'm very moved by a letter that Kant wrote when he was already very old: he was in a hurry, he says, against old age and declining sight, and confused ideas, to finish one of his books for the Leipzig Fair. I mention this to show that it isn't of the slightest importance. With or without publicity, with or without a fair, a book is something quite special. I shall never be convinced that a book is bad because its author has been seen on television. But, of course, it isn't good for that reason alone either.

If I have chosen anonymity, it is not, therefore, to criticize this or that individual, which I never do. It's a way of addressing the potential reader, the only individual here who is of interest to me, more directly: "Since you don't know who I am, you will be more inclined to find out why I say what you read; just allow yourself to say, quite simply, it's true, it's false. I like it or I don't like it. Period."

C.D. But doesn't the public expect the critic to provide him with precise assessments as to the value of a work?

M.F. I don't know whether the public does or does not expect the critic to judge works or authors. Judges were there, I think, before he was able to say what he wanted.

It seems that Courbet had a friend who used to wake up in the night yelling: "I want to judge, I want to judge." It's amazing how people like judging. Judgment is being passed everywhere, all the time. Perhaps it's one of the simplest things mankind has been given to do. And you know very well that the last man, when radiation has finally reduced his last enemy to ashes, will sit down behind some rickety table and begin the trial of the individual responsible.

I can't help but dream about a kind of criticism that would try not to judge but to bring an oeuvre, a book, a sentence, an idea to life; it would light fires, watch the grass grow, listen to the wind, and catch the sea foam in the breeze and scatter it. It would multiply not judgments but signs of existence; it would summon them, drag them from their sleep. Perhaps it would invent them sometimes—all the better. All the better. Criticism that hands down sentences sends me to sleep; I'd like a criticism of scintillating leaps of the imagination. It would not be sovereign or dressed in red. It would bear the lightning of possible storms.

C.D. So there are so many things to tell people about, so much inter-

esting work being done, that the mass media ought to talk about philosophy all the time...

M.F. It's true that there is a traditional discomfort between the "critics" and those who write books. The first feel misunderstood, and
the second think the first are trying to bring them to heel. But that's
the game.

It seems to me that today the situation is rather special. We have
institutions administering shortages, whereas we are in a situation
of superabundance.

Everybody has noticed the overexcitement that often accompanies
the publication (or reprinting) of some work that may in fact be quite
interesting. But it is never presented as being anything less than the
"subversion of all the codes," the "antithesis of contemporary culture,"
the "radical questioning of all our ways of thinking." One would be justified in thinking that its author must be some unknown fellow living
on the fringes of society.

On the other hand, others must be banished into total oblivion, from
which they must never be allowed to reemerge; they were only the
froth of "mere fashion," a mere product of the cultural institution, and
so forth.

A superficial, very Parisian phenomenon, it will be said. I see it,
rather, as the effect of a deep-seated anxiety. The feeling of "no room,"
"him or me," "it's my turn now." We have to walk in line because of
the extreme narrowness of the place where one can listen and make
oneself heard.

Hence a sort of anxiety that finds expression in innumerable symptoms, some funny, some less so. Hence, too, on the part of those who
write, a sense of impotence when confronted by the mass media, which
they criticize for running the world of books and creating or destroying
reputations at will. Hence, too, the feeling among the critics that they
will not be heard unless they shout louder and pull a rabbit out of the
hat each week. Hence, too, a pseudopoliticization that masks, beneath
the need to wage an "ideological struggle" or to root out "dangerous
thoughts," a deep-seated anxiety that one will not be heard or read.
Hence, too, the fantastic phobia for power: anybody who writes exerts
a disturbing power upon which one must try to place limitations, if not
actually to put an end to it. Hence, too, the declaration, repeated over
and over, that everything nowadays is empty, desolate, uninteresting,
unimportant: a declaration that obviously comes from those who, not

doing anything themselves, consider that there are too many others who are.

C.D. But don't you think that our period is really lacking in great writers and in minds capable of dealing with its problems?

M.F. No, I don't subscribe to the notion of a decadence, of a lack of writers, of the sterility of thought, of a gloomy future lacking in prospects.

On the contrary, I believe that there is a plethora. What we are suffering from is not a void but inadequate means for thinking about everything that is happening. There is an overabundance of things to be known: fundamental, terrible, wonderful, funny, insignificant, and crucial at the same time. And there is an enormous curiosity, a need, a desire to know. People are always complaining that the mass media stuff one's head with people. There is a certain misanthropy in this idea. On the contrary, I believe that people react; the more one convinces them, the more they question things. The mind isn't made of soft wax. It's a reactive substance. And the desire to know [*savoir*] more, and to know it more deeply and to know other things increases as one tries to stuff peoples' heads.

If you accept that, and if you add that there's a whole host of people being trained in the universities and elsewhere who could act as intermediaries between this mass of things and this thirst for knowledge, you will soon come to the conclusion that student unemployment is the most absurd thing imaginable. The problem is to multiply the channels, the bridges, the means of information, the radio and television networks, the newspapers.

Curiosity is a vice that has been stigmatized in turn by Christianity, by philosophy, and even by a certain conception of science. Curiosity is seen as futility. However, I like the word; it suggests something quite different to me. It evokes "care"; it evokes the care one takes of what exists and what might exist; a sharpened sense of reality, but one that is never immobilized before it; a readiness to find what surrounds us strange and odd; a certain determination to throw off familiar ways of thought and to look at the same things in a different way; a passion for seizing what is happening now and what is disappearing; a lack of respect for the traditional hierarchies of what is important and fundamental.

I dream of a new age of curiosity. We have the technical means; the desire is there; there is an infinity of things to know; the people capable of doing such work exist. So what is our problem? Too little: channels of communication that are too narrow, almost monopolistic, inadequate. We mustn't adopt a protectionist attitude, to stop "bad" information from invading and stifling the "good." Rather, we must increase the possibility for movement backward and forward. This would not lead, as people often fear, to uniformity and leveling-down, but, on the contrary, to the simultaneous existence and differentiation of these various networks.

c.d. I imagine that, at this level, the mass media and the universities, instead of continuing to oppose one another, might play complementary roles.

m.f. You remember Sylvain Lévi's wonderful saying: when you have one listener, it's teaching; when you have two, it's popularization. Books, universities, learned journals are also information media. One should refrain from calling every channel of information to which one cannot or does not wish to gain access a "mass medium." The problem is to know how to exploit the differences, whether we ought to set up a reserve, a "cultural park," for delicate species of scholars threatened by the rapacious inroads of mass information, while the rest of the space would be a huge market for shoddy products. Such a division does not seem to me to correspond to reality. What's more, it isn't at all desirable. If useful differentiations are to be brought into play, there must not be any such division.

c.d. Let's risk a few concrete propositions. If everything is going badly, where do we make a start?

m.f. But everything *isn't* going badly. In any case, I believe we shouldn't confuse useful criticism of things with repetitive jeremiads against people. As for concrete propositions, they can't just make an appearance like gadgets, unless certain general principles are accepted first. And the first of such general principles should be that the right to knowledge [*droit au savoir*] must not be reserved to a particular age group or to certain categories of people, but that one must be able to exercise it constantly and in many different ways.

c.d. Isn't this desire for knowledge [*envie de savoir*] somewhat ambiguous? What, in fact, are people to do with all that knowledge that they are going to acquire? What use will it be to them?

m.f. One of the main functions of teaching was that the training of the individual should be accompanied by his being situated in society. We should now see teaching in such a way that it allows the individual to change at will, which is possible only on condition that teaching is a possibility always being offered.

c.d. Are you in fact for a society of scholars [*société savante*]?

m.f. I'm saying that people must be constantly able to plug into culture and in as many ways as possible. There ought not to be, on the one hand, this education to which one is subjected and, on the other, this information one is fed.

c.d. What becomes of the eternal questions of philosophy in this learned society [*société savante*]?... Do we still need them, these unanswerable questions, these silences before the unknowable?

m.f. What is philosophy if not a way of reflecting, not so much on what is true and what is false, as on our relationship to truth? People sometimes complain that there is no dominant philosophy in France. So much the better for that! There is no sovereign philosophy, it's true, but a philosophy or rather philosophy in activity. The movement by which, not without effort and uncertainty, dreams and illusions, one detaches oneself from what is accepted as true and seeks other rules—that is philosophy. The displacement and transformation of frameworks of thinking, the changing of received values and all the work that has been done to think otherwise, to do something else, to become other than what one is—that, too, is philosophy. From this point of view, the last thirty years or so have been a period of intense philosophical activity. The interaction between analysis, research, "learned" or "theoretical" criticism, and changes in behavior, in people's real conduct, their way of being, their relation to themselves and to others has been constant and considerable.

I was saying just now that philosophy was a way of reflecting on our relationship to truth. It should also be added that it is a way of interrogating ourselves: If this is the relationship that we have with truth, how must we behave? I believe that a considerable and varied amount of work has been done and is still being done that alters both our relation to truth and our way of behaving. And this has taken place in a complex situation, between a whole series of investigations and a whole set of social movements. It's the very life of philosophy.

It is understandable that some people should weep over the present void and hanker instead, in the world of ideas, after a little monarchy. But those who, for once in their lives, have found a new tone, a new way of looking, a new way of doing, those people, I believe, will never feel the need to lament that the world is error, that history is filled with people of no consequence, and that it is time for others to keep quiet so that at last the sound of their disapproval may be heard...

NOTE

1 Italian philosopher, ex-professor at the University of Padua; a leading intellectual influence in the extreme-left movement Workers' Autonomy, he underwent four years and three months pre-ventative detention for armed insurrection against the state, subversive association, and the formation of armed gangs. He was freed on July 8, 1983, after being elected a Radical deputy during his imprisonment. His parliamentary immunity was lifted by the Chamber of Deputies, new warrants for his arrest were issued, and he took refuge in France.

INDEX